CAMBRIDGE LIBRARY COLLECTION

Books of enduring scholarly value

Music

The systematic academic study of music gave rise to works of description, analysis and criticism, by composers and performers, philosophers and anthropologists, historians and teachers, and by a new kind of scholar - the musicologist. This series makes available a range of significant works encompassing all aspects of the developing discipline.

General Musical Instruction

Adolf Bernhard Marx (1795–1866) was an influential music theorist, critic, composer and pedagogue. He believed that music should be part of everyone's general education and lobbied the Prussian government for a comprehensive national music-education scheme. This English translation by George Macirone of Marx's 1839 *Allgemeine Musiklehre* was published in 1854 as the first work in the series Novello's Library for the Diffusion of Musical Knowledge. The series, described by the publisher as 'a collection of standard treatises on the art of music written by the most esteemed English and foreign masters', was devised in response to a growing demand for training books and manuals to support domestic music-making. It also included Berlioz's famous treatise on instrumentation (also reissued in this series). Marx's work covers the basic elements of music theory, musical instruments, compositional techniques, forms of music, performance advice, and the importance of musical education in general.

Cambridge University Press has long been a pioneer in the reissuing of out-of-print titles from its own backlist, producing digital reprints of books that are still sought after by scholars and students but could not be reprinted economically using traditional technology. The Cambridge Library Collection extends this activity to a wider range of books which are still of importance to researchers and professionals, either for the source material they contain, or as landmarks in the history of their academic discipline.

Drawing from the world-renowned collections in the Cambridge University Library and other partner libraries, and guided by the advice of experts in each subject area, Cambridge University Press is using state-of-the-art scanning machines in its own Printing House to capture the content of each book selected for inclusion. The files are processed to give a consistently clear, crisp image, and the books finished to the high quality standard for which the Press is recognised around the world. The latest print-on-demand technology ensures that the books will remain available indefinitely, and that orders for single or multiple copies can quickly be supplied.

The Cambridge Library Collection brings back to life books of enduring scholarly value (including out-of-copyright works originally issued by other publishers) across a wide range of disciplines in the humanities and social sciences and in science and technology.

General Musical Instruction

Adolf Bernhard Marx
Translated by George Macirone

CAMBRIDGE UNIVERSITY PRESS

Cambridge, New York, Melbourne, Madrid, Cape Town,
Singapore, São Paolo, Delhi, Mexico City

Published in the United States of America by Cambridge University Press, New York

www.cambridge.org
Information on this title: www.cambridge.org/9781108051750

© in this compilation Cambridge University Press 2012

This edition first published 1854
This digitally printed version 2012

ISBN 978-1-108-05175-0 Paperback

This book reproduces the text of the original edition. The content and language reflect
the beliefs, practices and terminology of their time, and have not been updated.

Cambridge University Press wishes to make clear that the book, unless originally published
by Cambridge, is not being republished by, in association or collaboration with, or
with the endorsement or approval of, the original publisher or its successors in title.

NOVELLO'S LIBRARY for the DIFFUSION of MUSICAL KNOWLEDGE.

"Studies serve for delight, for ornament, and ability. * * * There is no stond or impediment in the wit, but may be wrought out by fit studies."—*Lord Bacon.*

GENERAL MUSICAL INSTRUCTION.

(ALLGEMEINE MUSIKLEHRE.)

AN AID TO TEACHERS AND LEARNERS IN EVERY BRANCH OF MUSICAL KNOWLEDGE.

BY

DR. ADOLF BERNHARD MARX,

PROFESSOR OF MUSIC IN BERLIN.

Translated, by GEORGE MACIRONE, from the original German, expressly for NOVELLO'S LIBRARY for the diffusion of MUSICAL KNOWLEDGE. The musical portion has been revised by Mr. JOSIAH PITTMAN, Organist of Lincoln's Inn.

LONDON:
J. ALFRED NOVELLO, 69, DEAN STREET, SOHO, AND 24, POULTRY:
ALSO IN NEW YORK, AT 389, BROADWAY.
1854.

To Parents, conscientious Teachers, and others concerned in Education,

By whom it is considered a matter of Duty to see that the Musical Education of Youth be real, refreshing to the heart and senses, and elevating to the mind; who are anxious and watchful that Art be not perverted and debased into a source of enervating dissipation and vanity,

This book is dedicated,
In faithful sympathy,
By
THE AUTHOR.

GENERAL TABLE OF CONTENTS.

	PAGE
INTRODUCTION.—Review of the province of Music, and of the object of General Musical Instruction	5

FIRST DIVISION.—Of the Doctrine of *Tones*.

			PAGE
1st SECTION.—The Tonal System			7
2nd "	The System of Notation		8
3rd "	Auxiliary Forms and Signs in Notation		12
4th "	Of Raising and Depressing		14
A. Raising—B. Depressing—C. The sign Natural			14
D. Double Raising and Depression			15
5th SECTION.—Measurement of Relation of *Tones*			15
6th "	Modes, Scales, and Keys		18
7th "	Major and Minor Keys		19
8th "	Combination of all the Scales		20
A. The Major Scales			20
B. The Minor Scales			22
9th SECTION.—Nearer view of the Scales			22
A. The Signature			22
1, Major Scales			22
2, Minor Scales			23
B. Chief Points of the Scale—C. Relationship of the Scales			24
1, Relationship of the Major Scales			24
2, Relationship of the Relative Keys			25
3, Relationship of the Minor Scales, with their Major, and among themselves			25
APPENDIX.—Of Ecclesiastical Modes			25

SECOND DIVISION.—Of Rhythm.

			PAGE
1st SECTION.—Of the value of *Tones*			26
A. Value by division by two			26
B. Value by division by three—C. Groups of mixed value			28
D. More numerous groups			29
2nd SECTION.—Of Rests			29
3rd "	Indefinite signs of duration		30
1, Staccato—2, Legato			30
4th SECTION.—Of absolute time			31
1, Of the slowest motion—2, Moderately slow motion—3, Moderately quick motion—4, Quick motion—5, The quickest motion			31
APPENDIX.—Of the Metronome and Chronometer			32
5th SECTION.—The nature and regulation of bars			33
6th "	The kinds of bars		34
7th "	The management and division of bars		36
8th "	Exceptional forms		40
1, Initial imperfect bar—2, Irregular bars—3, Mixed measures and values			41
9th SECTION.—Chromatic signs within the bar			42
10th "	Of Accentuation		42
1, Accentuation of the parts of a bar			42
2, Accentuation of the members of a bar			43
Concluding Remarks			44

THIRD DIVISION.—Instruments.

			PAGE
1st SECTION.—Review of Instruments			44
2nd "	Vocal Music		46
A. The human voice			46
B. Speech			47
3rd SECTION.—Stringed instruments			47
4th "	Bowed instruments		48
5th "	Reed or tubular instruments		50
6th "	Brass instruments		51
7th "	The Organ		63
8th "	Percussive instruments		54
9th "	Instruments of friction		54
10th "	Of Score		55

FOURTH DIVISION.—Of Elementary Forms of Composition.

			PAGE
1st SECTION.—The foundations of melody			58
A. The succession of *tones*			58
B. Of Rhythm			59
2nd SECTION.—Fundamental forms			60
1, The Passage—2, The Phrase			60
3, The Subject			61
3rd SECTION.—Greater rhythmic arrangements			61
4th "	Melodic graces		64
5th "	Introduction to Harmony		66
6th "	The most important Chords, major and minor		67
7th SECTION.—The employment of the Chords			69
1, Duplication—2, Omission—3, Transposition—4, Inversion			69
5, Close or dispersed position			70
6, Combination			71
A. Connexion—B. Certain progressions—C. Determinate resolution			71
7, The Close			71
8, The Prelude			72
8th SECTION.—Of Modulation			73
A. The law of Modulation—B. Means of Modulation			73
9th SECTION.—Of the movement of the parts in Chords			75
1, Motion within a Chord—2, Equal movement in the Chords—3, Unequal movement in the Chords			75
A. Suspension or retardation—B. Anticipation			75
C. Organ point			76
4, Motion between the Chords			76
10th SECTION.—Figuring of Basses			78

FIFTH DIVISION.—Artistic Forms of Composition.

			PAGE
1st SECTION.—General considerations on artistic forms			80
2nd "	Differences of forms in the construction of the parts		81
3rd "	Polyphonic forms		83
1, Figuration			83
2, Fugue			84
3, Double and manifold Fugue			86
4, Canon			87
4th SECTION.—Homophonic and mixed forms			88
1, Song form			88
2, Rondo form—3, Sonata form			89
5th SECTION.—Peculiar forms of Instrumental Music			90
1, The Sonata			90
2, The Overture—3, The Symphony—4, The Concerto—5, The Fantasia—6, The Capriccio, Toccata, and Study			91
6th SECTION.—Peculiar forms of Vocal Music			91
1, The Recitative—2, The Aria			91
3, The Chorus—4, The Cantata—Finale			92
7th SECTION.—Music in combination with other objects			92
1, The Ballet—2, The Melodrama			92
3, The Play with music—4, The Opera			93

SIXTH DIVISION.—Artistic Performance.

			PAGE
1st SECTION.—General ideas of performance			94
2nd "	The meaning of artistic configurations		99
A. Rhythm			99
1, Motion			99
2, Accent—3, Larger rhythmic members			100
A. On *Tones*			101
1, Kinds of tonic movement			101
2, Intervals—3, Chords			102
4, The Major and Minor modes—5, Various scales—Observations			103
3rd SECTION.—The meaning of artistic forms			103
4th "	The comprehension and performance of particular works		104
5th "	Concerted or Orchestral performance		106
APPENDIX.—On Score Playing			108

SEVENTH DIVISION.—On Musical Education and Instruction.

			PAGE
1st SECTION.—Remarks on the present state of Music			110
2nd "	The right object and the right means		113
3rd "	Disposition or vocation for Music		115
4th "	Development of the musical faculties		118
The time previous to learning			118
The time for instruction			119
Development of the feeling of measure—Development of the feeling of tone			120
5th SECTION.—Objects of musical education, and their time			122
Song			122
Playing on the Piano			123
Composition			125
6th SECTION.—Teachers and methods of teaching			126

APPENDIX.

	PAGE
A. Rhythmic Divisions	129
B. On the form of Fugues—C. On the form of Rondos	130
D. On the form of Sonatas	131

DR. MARX'S
GENERAL MUSICAL INSTRUCTION.

INTRODUCTION.

REVIEW OF THE PROVINCE OF MUSIC, AND OF THE OBJECT OF GENERAL MUSICAL INSTRUCTION.

General musical instruction is essential to every person who in any manner, whether as Singer or Player, as Composer or Teacher, desires to employ himself in music on a solid foundation,—in order that with full preparation and foreknowledge he himself may be enabled to pursue, or may be capable of communicating to others, the special branch which may be the peculiar object of attainment. This treatise is therefore the elementary school for the musical world in general; and by its assistance, instruction may be obtained in vocal and instrumental performance and in composition, while, so far as music is concerned, its materials can be wholly dispensed with by no one. As moreover, our work bears a character of universality, in necessary information on our subject, we will not scruple to communicate some peculiar methods (for example, of score reading and playing) which are indeed not indispensable to every musician, but are nevertheless desired by many, and can be nowhere better given than in this book.

General musical instruction is not desired to be merely a grade of scientific distinction, but is intended for all who take any interest in music, that they may have a full comprehension and just appreciation of the art in all its aspects. In order, therefore, the better and more extensively to accomplish our object, we will assume no previous instruction. We will take nothing for granted—but what is universally known by common intercourse, or what is self-evident. By this it will be seen at once that our instruction will be eminently practical. Its rational foundation is demonstrated by the science of Music, whereof in this book, we can only here and there throw in a ray of enlightenment, and then, simply to develop and fix irremovably some important and fundamental ideas, which would not be sufficiently understood and impressed without the deeper illustrations of Science.

If we wish, then, to collect the universal elements of musical knowledge, we must first learn what are those elements upon the nature of which we desire to obtain information. In our conception they are everything that belongs or relates to music. Let us therefore contemplate this art as we everywhere find it.

We know that music works first upon our hearing. Everything that we hear is known by the general name of

SOUND,

in what manner soever that sensation may affect us; whether it be loud or soft, pleasant or repulsive, and so forth.

In the application of the human voice to music, words are in general combined with it; and in this operation, not only the meaning of the words is manifested, but also their manner of utterance and the single sounds of which the words are composed. The single sounds are called

VOCAL SOUNDS (Laut*).

We see, further, that music is produced either by the human voice or by instruments of various kinds; as flutes, violins, trumpets, and so forth. Everyone knows, that these different instruments are distinguished by their respective kinds of sound. The flute gives a gentle, soft, flowing sound—the trumpet resounds with vehemence, forcing and crashing, and so forth. This distinguishing quality we will call

TIMBRE, OR CHARACTER OF SOUND.

We ought to have said, therefore, just now, the character of the sound of the flute is soft; that of the trumpet is crashing, and so forth.

We observe, lastly, that in one and the same instrument the sounds produced have another special difference between themselves. That, for example, the four strings of a violin, or the strings of a harp, sound on each instrument quite differently among themselves. In common parlance, some coarser, some finer; that is, the longer strings of the harp and the thicker strings of the violin sound coarser (lower), and the shorter strings of the harp and thinner strings of the violin sound finer (higher). Considering sound in this relationship, we call it

Tone.†

---

* The expression *Laut* is indeed understood to be synonymous with *Schall* (Sound): it seems, however, advisable to use it in the above sense exclusively, as the prescribed name for a determined and really distinct object. The distinction of *Laute* into *Selbstlaute* (Vowels), *Doppellaute* (Diphthongs), and *Mitlaute* or *Beilaute* (Consonants), is familiar.

† This word is in italics to distinguish it from tone meaning distance or interval, and this practice will be observed throughout the book. Thus the middle C on the piano (called in this book the one-lined <u>c</u>), which is represented in notation by the note on the first ledger line under the staff in the G clef, and on the first ledger line above the staff in the F clef, is called the *tone* C—the fixed and determined sound C, or one-lined <u>c</u>, of an absolutely fixed and invariable pitch or height in the scale. In like manner we might say the *tone* C♯, or the *tone* D, or D♭, or D♯, or any other *tone* whose height or depth is determined. But on the other hand we should say, the *tone* C is one tone below D, two tones below E, &c., speaking of the tones D and E next higher than C.—TRANSLATOR.

We therefore have several and very different *tones*. The *tones* of the longer and thicker strings we call *deeper tones*—those of the shorter or thinner strings, *higher tones*. In general, the *tones* of men's voices are deeper than those of boys or women's voices. The *tones* of flutes, violins, or trumpets, are higher than those of the bassoon, bass, or French horn. We say the *tones* in general, because as each voice and instrument is capable of producing many *tones*, it may well happen, that the highest *tones* of a deep voice, be higher than the lowest *tones* of a high voice.

The clearest idea of the difference of height and depth of *tone* will be obtained by the inspection of a pianoforte or other keyed instrument. Here every key—be it a black or a white key*—gives a particular *tone*. We have in this sketch before us:

twelve or thirteen keys, for just that number of different *tones*. The *tones* towards the left, are the deep—those towards the right, the high *tones*. The extreme left therefore gives the lowest *tone*, the next a higher, and the keys 12 and 13 the highest *tone*.†

Let us now proceed to other matters.

Every *tone* or sound produced, must begin at a certain time and occupy a certain time, longer or shorter, determinately measured, or indeterminate. The prescribed time for a *tone* or sound we call its

VALUE.

We therefore say of a *tone*, it has no determined value, or it has a value of such and such a length, or it has a definite value longer or shorter than, or equal to, that of another *tone*.

* See page 8.

† Timbre or character of sound and *tone*, therefore, are not, as it were, in themselves substantive appearances; but merely *qualities* which we distinguish in sound or in that which is audible. If we consider a sound (of an instrument or of a bell, for example) in regard to its height or depth, we call it *tone*; but if we contemplate a sound (irrespective of its height or depth) as distinguished from other sounds (as for example, all the *tones*, or the same *tone* of the flute as distinguished from the same or from all the *tones* of the trumpet), we call it timbre or character of sound.

There are sounds, indeed, which have neither any distinct appreciable timbre or character, nor any determined *tone*. These we call by various names: noise (*Geräusch*), clashing, or clattering (*Getöse*), whistling, roaring (*Sausen*), chirping, warbling (*Schwirren*), and many others, imitative of various kinds of noise. Other sounds have a definite character, but no determined height or depth; for example, drums, bells, and others. One can indeed perceive, approximatively, that such and such drums or bells are higher or lower than others; but their difference cannot be measured with exactness. All this, however, may be set aside for the present · we do not as yet want it, and have only introduced it here to prevent misapprehension.

We must here mention that the term *Klang* (timbre or character) in musical instruction, has been hitherto used in a different sense. A. Gottfr. Weber, in the Introduction to his Theory of Music, has characterized Klang as being a sound of *determinable* height; *Ton* (*tone*), a sound of *determined* height. For the musician, this distinction seems unimportant; while a sure and precise designation of what we call *Klang* (timbre or character) appears to be indispensable, and therefore justifies our manner of appropriating it. In the absence of any such correctly distinctive term, various expressions have been used, such as, *the inherent stamp of the tone, timbre, colour of the tone, colour of the Klang, quality of the Klang*, and several others. This wavering and uncertainty shewed of itself that none of the terms completely satisfied the feeling: indeed, they are partly circumlocutions, partly comparisons, and partly quite incorrect. A more particular explanation belongs to the Science of Music.

In fine, let it be further observed, that in common conversation, also, the word tone is often incorrectly used for Klang. We hear—"This instrument, this voice has a good tone," whereas the expression should properly be,—"They have a good *Klang*" (timbre or character of sounds).

Now, if we produce a succession of *tones*, or sounds of any determined value according to any law, in any order of succession in time, this order of succession in time is called

RHYTHM.

If such an order do not exist—if the *tones* have either no determined value, or follow each other in no determined order of duration—the succession of *tones* is called unrhythmic. A succession of *tones* without rhythm, and also without any determined value, is certainly imaginable; as for example, in most of the singing of birds. On the other hand, rhythm may be easily produced without determined *tones*, by means of sound only, as for example, by drums.

A rhythmically arranged succession of *tones* (whether it be pleasing, expressive, &c., or not) is called

MELODY.

A piece of music may consist of one single line of successive *tones*, which is then described as

IN ONE PART,

or of two, three, four, or more simultaneous lines of single successive *tones*; this is said to be

IN TWO, THREE, FOUR, OR MORE PARTS;

but every line of successive *tones*, whether sung or produced by an instrument, is called, in technical language,

A PART.

Also, if various simultaneous lines of successive *tones* are produced on one and the same instrument —for instance, on a pianoforte—they are considered as so many *separate parts*.

The simultaneously uniting *tones* of different parts must have some rational relationship among themselves, in conformity with the rules of art; they must in some manner agree with or be adapted to each other. This relationship is called

HARMONY.

In ordinary intercourse we apply this name to the agreement or compatibility of different things: thus we say of two colours suitable to each other, or of two persons agreeing together, that they *harmonize* with each other.

Out of all these essential parts—*tones* and characteristic sounds, successions of *tones* and rhythm, melodies and harmonies—is produced

MUSICAL COMPOSITION.

Whoever has heard various musical compositions, and compared them together, must have remarked, superficially at least, that many of them differ considerably in extent and management; while others are more or less of a similar arrangement with each other. So we soon become aware that Marches differ from Dances—Secular Songs from Chorales—even in outward appearance; while on the other hand, all Marches, among themselves, Chorales, &c., in their general appearance, more or less resemble each other. These arrangements—these outward distinguishing appearances of works of art—we will call

FORMS OF COMPOSITION.

From the above examples we can now specify the form of the March, of the Dance, and of the Chorale, as different artistic forms. There are, however, many others.

Now let us return to the beginning of our considerations. We have already observed that Music may be produced both by the human voice and by instruments. Musical instruments, and the human voice in its application to music, we will distinguish collectively by the name of

MUSICAL APPARATUS.

According to the different species of apparatus brought into action, so is the music divided and classed into different species. If instruments alone are used, the music is called

INSTRUMENTAL MUSIC:

if the human voice be used, the music is called

SONG, OR VOCAL MUSIC.

Vocal music and instrumental music may each be used separately, as

PURE VOCAL AND PURE INSTRUMENTAL MUSIC;

or united, as

ACCOMPANIED VOCAL MUSIC.

Finally, music may have simply itself for its object, or it may be dedicated to other specific purposes; to the social dance, for instance, as

DANCE MUSIC:

to artistic representations in Ballets and Pantomime, as

BALLET MUSIC:

to the Drama, as

DRAMATIC MUSIC:

to religious objects in public devotion and edification, as

ECCLESIASTICAL MUSIC.

So far, then, we have given a general sketch of the fundamental elements, forms, and objects of music.

According to, or in, all these directions, music may be employed

PRACTICALLY,

as by a Singer, Player, Director, Conductor, or Composer; and

THEORETICALLY,

as by a Teacher or Learner. Every branch, however, of practical employment presupposes more or less theoretical education.

Instruction in the nature and properties of tones is called

THE SCIENCE OF *Tones* (Tonlehre).

It comprehends instruction in

MELODY and HARMONY,

and in the uniting of several parts in one score; or

INSTRUCTION IN COUNTERPOINT.

The instruction for producing pieces of music according to the rules of art, is called

COMPOSITION,

which embraces, besides the science of *tones* and rhythm, the setting or arrangement of vocal and instrumental subjects, or the realization of musical ideas, through the organ of the voice, in union with the text or words and the accompanying musical instruments.

The scientific foundation of all musical knowledge we will call, in fine,

THE SCIENCE OF MUSIC.

To this may be added the art of

MUSICAL NOTATION,

and instruction in Playing and Singing.

This latter instruction we leave to the singing and instrumental schools, and to the able Professors of these various arts. Composition and the Science of Music require separate treatises. The other branches of our subject we shall either unfold completely, or explain in their elemental principles or general ideas, so far as they may be universally necessary.

These, then, are the indispensable contents of General Musical Instruction. We shall conclude with a few general observations (as an Appendix) on musical education and instruction—on the vocation to music as a profession—and on the manner of learning, as the most important of our additional matter, promised in the beginning of our Introduction.

The History of Music and the building or construction of instruments, do not come within the compass of our present treatise. They must be the objects of separate works.

FIRST DIVISION.

OF THE DOCTRINE OF *Tones*.

FIRST SECTION—OF THE TONAL SYSTEM

A *Tone* is a sound of a determined height or pitch.

We have already seen in the Introduction, that there are many *tones*, many sounds of different height and depth: the number indeed of the different possible gradations of *tones* must be infinite. In music, however, all possible gradations of *tones* are not employed, but only a certain number in a determined arrangement.*—The totality of these *tones* is called the

TONAL SYSTEM.

This system of *tones* contains, therefore, all the *tones* employed in music.

These *tones* are above a hundred. Now, it would manifestly cause difficulty if we assigned a different name to each of these. It has therefore been judged expedient to comprise them all in *seven* groups and names, which are called the seven

DEGREES.

These degrees are named† after the letters of the alphabet:

C—D—E—F—G—A—B.

---

* The gradations of *tones* really used in the production of music, are not selected arbitrarily nor indeterminately, but according to fixed principles, evolved from the laws of Acoustics. We wish to say a few words here, merely to fix the idea of *tone* more distinctly.

Acoustics show that sound is produced by the vibration of an elastic body. Elasticity is the property of a body, whereby its parts return to rest after being set in motion by an external force.—So we see, with a sword-blade, that if we bend it out of the straight line, and suddenly set it free, it will vibrate until it recover its original state of rest; and so with the low strings of a pianoforte, when we strike them forcibly and hold up the dampers, the vibration goes on visibly before us, while the sound gradually subsides and at length dies away, as the strings resume their former position of rest.

Such an audible vibration may be irregular, as to the continuance of each vibration, as in the drum for instance, and then we hear simply a noise; or it may be regular, each single vibration occupying the same space of time, so that the vibrations can be counted or numbered, and then a *tone* is produced.

In our system, we place those gradations together, which, while they are perfectly and clearly distinguishable, are still in near, easy, and therefore agreeable relationship to each other: other gradations which are difficult to distinguish, and are moreover repulsive to each other, we reject.

The determination of the relationship of *tones*, as applicable to the wants of our art (in which, for reasons which cannot be now detailed, we are not allowed to use the *tones* in their original most simple and natural relationships) is called Temperament, and the practical operation of preparing an instrument (namely, a pianoforte, violin, organ, &c.) so as to render it capable of producing those *tones*, is called tuning. Should the instrument not give the true relationship of *tone*, it is said to be *out of tune*, but the incorrect *tones* themselves we call false.

† In France, Italy, and the Southern Nations, the syllables,

ut, re, mi, fa, sol, la, si

are used for the names of the *tones*, instead of our *c d*, &c. The first six

All *tones* bear the name of one of these letters, or a name derived from them.*

We easily understand this system of names if we look at the keys of a pianoforte, or the fig. at page 6. We there see longer and wider keys, generally white, and between them, shorter and thinner keys, usually black. Of these black keys, first two, and then three, lie nearer to each other—for instance—in our fig. page 6, those marked 2 and 4, and further on, those marked 7, 9, 11, lie nearer to each other than the black keys, 4 and 7, or 11 and 14. These divisions, easily perceived, will serve us for landmarks.

The nearest white key placed immediately before two black keys (we proceed always from Left to Right), gives us

THE DEGREE—*c*;

the following white key, *d*—the next, *e*; the white key lying on the left, before three black keys, gives *f*, and so on. In our figure, all the names of the degrees are written on the white keys.

We see on the pianoforte many more keys than we have represented, but the same arrangement of *tones* and of keys, and therefore of names, constantly returns. The next white key after *b* (marked 13 on the figure) gives consequently again *c*; then follows again, *d*, *e*, &c., always in the same relationship of *tone*, but always higher.

We observe, therefore, that every degree in our system of *tones*, that the whole scale of degrees appears several times; that we have more than one *c*, *d*, &c. How shall we distinguish them from each other?

We range the seven degrees together until we return to the first, and, since this would be the eighth, we call it the

OCTAVE.

An octave is therefore a group of all the seven degrees up to the return of the first, which is considered as it were an eighth degree.

These octaves again are distinguished from each other by particular names. The deepest *tones* on the pianoforte, beginning at *c*, up to the next *c*, are called the

COUNTERTONES;

the next octave is called the

GREAT OCTAVE;

then follows the

SMALL OCTAVE;

are the initial syllables of a verse in a hymn to St. John, and were employed by a music master, the Monk Guido d'Arezzo, in the eleventh century, in order to enable his scholars to pitch their voices more easily. The producing of these *tones* according to these six syllables, is called solfaing, and was long the torment of students of music. Much later, the thought occurred, to give a seventh name (*si*) to the seventh degree; and it was taken from the initial letters of the last line of that verse, Sancte Johannes.

* Why exactly these, and not the first seven letters of our alphabet in its original order? This arrangement arose as follows: Originally, the alphabetical names were, in fact, used in their common order, *A*, *B*, *c*, *d*, *e*, *f*, *g*, and *B* denoted the *tone* now called by us *H*, (*B* in English): but the *tones* produced by our black keys were then defective; and that key which lies under our *H*, (*B* English), was introduced, and was also called B. There were, therefore, two different *tones*, both having the same name, *B*. They were at first distinguished by the names of *B quadratum*, our *H*, (*B* English), and *B rotundum*; and later, the *B quadratum* received the name of the following letter (after *G*), *H*. Still later, the succession of *tones* beginning with *C*, [therefore *c*, *d*, *e*, *f*, *g*, *a*, *h*, (*B* English),] was recognised as the most important; as the true foundation of all the others; and so, in substance, the matter became correct, although the succession of names remained irregular.

after which follow the

ONE-LINE OCTAVE, TWO, THREE, FOUR-LINE OCTAVE, &c.

Higher octaves would require additional lines.

The deepest string on the violoncello gives *c* in the great octave, or the *great C*. The deepest string on the tenor is the *c* in the small octave, or the *small c*; and the deepest string on the violin, the small *g*, and so forth.

In writing, great roman characters are used for the great octave, and small for the small octave—small with one line above or below for the one-lined octave—small with two lines above or below for the two-lined octave, and so forth. The whole succession of names of *tones*, from the Counter-*B*, is therefore as follows:—

Counter-*B*,—*C*, *D*, *E*, *F*, *G*, *A*, *B*,—*c*, *d*, *e*, *f*, *g*, *a*, *b*,—*c*, *d*, *e*, *f*, *g*, *a*, *b*,—*c*, *d*, *e*,—and so forth.

Such a succession of *tones*, in which we proceed constantly from degree to degree, higher or lower, as on a ladder, is called the

SCALE,

or also, in a Latin or Italian word, *Scala*. The scale is complete whether it contain the seven degrees only, or also the eighth; for all beyond is indeed mere repetition in a higher or lower octave.

The countertones, the great and small octaves, and at all events a part of the one-lined octave, are comprehended under the name of the

BASS,

or bass *tones*. The higher octaves, with the whole of the one-lined octave and the higher *tones* of the small octave, are included under the name of the

TREBLE,

or treble *tones*. The exact boundary would therefore be the one-lined *c*, but it is allowable not to adhere rigidly to that limitation. The whole distribution is but superficial, for the sake of dispatch when no precise object is in question.*

SECOND SECTION—THE SYSTEM OF NOTATION.

For the representation or indication of *tones* we use a particular kind of writing, called

NOTATION.

This invention is suggested by the idea of the scale (*note ladder*), which has indicated the steps (*Stufen*) or degrees whereon the notes in the form of round, blackened or empty spots, are placed.†

It would seem necessary to make as many degrees as there were tones; for example, seven or eight degrees for an octave:—

* Is now, our system of *tones*, such and so far as we here know it, the only one that has been employed—the only one that can be used? By no means. History informs us that in ancient times, instead of *seven* degrees, five only were employed, and in the following order:—

c—*d*—*e*—*g*—*a*—

to which, after a while, the octave of the first *tone* was added. This five *tone* system remained in use even after the intervening *tones* were known. The Greeks (see the Author's Article on Greek Music, in the Universal Lexicon of Music), first adopted the seven *tone* system, which they arranged in this order,—

g—*a*—*b*—*c*—*d*—*e*—*f*.

Their *tone* system was (in part) employed by the Christian Church; and now first appeared by degrees the semitones. The temperament which we now use, has not been thoroughly and firmly established in theory and practice much more than a hundred years.

† Formerly, square notes were in use; of which we shall have to say something hereafter.

1.

that the undermost of these lines or degrees should have been the place of the lowest or deepest *tone*; for example, *c*—that the next line should have been the place of *d*, the third, of *e*, and so on. But upon that plan, so many lines would have been necessary, that it would have been scarcely possible to identify the notes upon them.

Therefore the number of *lines* for places of notes, has been limited to *five*,* together with the *spaces* between, above and below them. This combination of five lines is called the

STAFF,

which furnishes, together with the spaces and the places immediately above and below it, positions for eleven notes, as we here see—

2.

Here, also, the note of the deepest *tone* is the undermost, and under the first line; the following *tone* is on the first line—the third *tone* between the first and second lines, therefore in the *first space*, &c. The highest *tone* is over the last or fifth line.

Now we have many more than eleven *tones*. How do we represent higher *tones* than the above eleven?

The twelfth *tone* would require another line. But as we wish to avoid a superabundance of lines, so, instead of a complete line, we place a small supernumerary line, called a Ledger line, near the staff which still strikes the eye as the principal object. Now we can

3.

place the twelfth *tone* on the ledger line, and the thirteenth over the ledger line. A second ledger line would give us places

4.

for a fourteenth and fifteenth *tone*, and so forth.

Let us apply the same expedient to the lower *tones*. Let us place (for example) the one-lined *c* on the first line: then we should have to write the little *b*, under the first line. If we wish to note deeper *tones*, we must have for *a*, the first ledger line (that is, under the staff); *g* would be under the first ledger line; *f* on the second ledger line; and so on, as is here shewn,—

5.

Now, we should be in a condition to write and

* Why exactly limited to five lines? In the first place, because an odd number of lines has a middle line, which divides the staff into halves, and so makes it easier of inspection. Secondly, three lines with their spaces, do not give room, even for an octave, and therefore do not suffice for our system: whereas, five lines, from the undermost to the uppermost, gives ample room for the octave. It follows that a greater number of lines—seven, for example—are not wanted.

read all the notes, if we only knew which particular *tone* should be on any particular line. If we agreed, for example, as in No. 5, that the one-lined *c* should be on the first line, then we should know that the one-lined *d* would be immediately over that first line —the one-lined *e*, on the second line—the small *b* under the said first line, &c., since the notes follow each other in the same order as on the scale. But instead of the one-lined *c*, we might place any other *tone* on the first line; and then all the other *tones* would take their places thereby. Suppose, for instance, that *e* stood on the first line, instead of *c*; then would *d* be under it, *f* over it, *g* on the second line, and so forth. It must be settled, therefore, where any particular *tone* shall be fixed, whereby the places of all the rest shall be determined.

For this object, there are certain signs, called

CLEFS;

which indicate that the line on which they are placed, is appropriated to a certain determined *tone*. There are three of these Clefs:

The *G* or Violin Clef, *C* Clef, and *F* or Bass Clef.

1. THE *G* CLEF,

has this form,— 𝄞 or 𝄞

and shews that the *one-lined g* is to be placed on the line encompassed by its lower curve. It is at present constantly put on the second line. Formerly (especially in French notation) it was placed also on the first line, so that on that line the one-lined *g* was written. In this application it was called the *French Violin Clef*.

We present here a succession of notes in the violin clef now in use:—

6.

If it were desired to write the small *f* in this clef, it should be placed on the third ledger line under the staff. The three-lined *a* would be placed above the fourth leger line over the staff, and so forth.

2. THE *C* CLEF

intimates that the one-lined *C* is to be placed on the line on which it is marked. It has this form:

𝄢 or 𝄡 or ‖: or ‖⊣

and is used in three ways, viz: as soprano, alto, and tenor clef.

a, THE SOPRANO CLEF,

shews the place of the one-lined *C* to be on the first line, viz:—

7.

This succession of notes might be extended upwards or downwards, according to the foregoing instructions.

b, THE ALTO CLEF

indicates the third line as the position of the one-lined *C*, and therefore produces the following succession of notes.

c, THE TENOR CLEF

places the one-lined *c* on the fourth line, and has the following succession of notes.

These are the three usual applications of the *c* clef. In old writings, it is also found occasionally on the second line. We come now to the third clef.

3. THE *F* CLEF.

It has this form,— or

and shews us that the line it encompasses is the place for the small *f*. With us it is invariably put on the fourth line, and has the following succession of notes:—

If we wish to extend this line of notes, the double *G* must be placed under the third ledger line, double *F* on a fourth ledger line, double *E* under it; and in like manner the one-lined *f* over the staff must be placed *over* the second ledger line, the one-lined *g* on a third ledger line, and so forth. In old notation, the *F* clef is sometimes found on the third, and sometimes on the fifth line.

What is the use of so many clefs? Would not one have been sufficient? We shall soon be persuaded of the contrary. If we used any one clef only, we should want too many ledger lines, either above or below. With the *F* clef, for instance, we should want two ledger lines for the one-lined *e*; the two-lined *e* would require five, and the three-lined *e* nine ledger lines. If with the *G* clef we wanted to write the great and double G, we must use six and nine ledger lines. How inconvenient such a method as this would be to write and to read.

Manifestly, the violin clef is the most appropriate for the higher octaves (for instance, for violins, flutes, &c.), and the bass clef for the deep octaves, such as those of the double bass, low voices, the bass, &c., while the first is unsuitable for low and the last for high successions of sounds. Accordingly, we soon perceive why even two clefs, for instance, the G and F clefs, are not sufficiently accommodating for all successions of sounds and voices. For a voice, such as the Tenor, or Alto, or the Tenor Violin, which reaches from about the small to the two-lined *c*, the F clef would be too low and the G clef too high—the first would require more than four ledger lines above and the other as many below. How much more ease is obtained from the alto clef,—

or even from the tenor clef. It seems, therefore, that we require intermediate clefs for intermediate successions of sounds, and that want is fulfilled by the three C clefs: for the soprano clef is two degrees lower than the violin (G) clef; the alto clef is four degrees lower than the soprano clef; the tenor clef two degrees lower than the alto clef; and, in fine, the bass clef four degrees lower than the tenor; so that every division of sounds has its appropriate clef.*

We must mention another expedient used to express successions of sounds, widely different in pitch. If, namely, a succession of sounds should stretch so far apart, that no clef can conveniently include them, we change the clefs. A succession of sounds, for instance, from the great to the two-lined *g*, would not suit the violin clef, nor the bass, nor any one of the intermediate clefs, as we here shew:—

We introduce, therefore, another clef at the appropriate situation,—

and thus, without a single ledger line, all the *tones* of these three octaves can be clearly expressed by the change of clef.

When several voices are united in a musical composition, they are noted on several staves running simultaneously together, and to every staff is given the proper clef for the voice to be written on it; that is, for instance, the G clef for the high, and the F clef for the low voices.† Under this arrangement

---

* It is true on the other hand, that by superabundance, the clefs may become perplexing and burthensome. So, formerly, the violin clef was found on the first line (as before-mentioned) and also the *C* clef, on the second line, as *Mezzo* soprano clef; the *F* clef was used on the third line, as baritone clef, and on the fifth line as deep bass clef. These supernumerary clefs, however, are now very properly abandoned.

† A case, of rare occurrence however, must here be stated. Occasionally, in works of many voices, space is deficient for the introduction of each particular succession of sounds, or for the admission of separate staves, for successions of sounds, widely differing from each other. In this case, the two voices are compressed into one staff, with the clef most appropriate for both; and, if needful, a second clef is added for such notes as could not be written conveniently under the clef first chosen, while this first chosen clef remains in operation for all the other voices. Thus in the richly scored Mass of Beethoven, S. 48, space is wanting to give

each clef is considered as operative for the whole length of the staff at the beginning of which it is placed, until the introduction of another clef. If the intrusive clef is to continue its effect in the following line of staff, it is customary to place first on that staff the original clef, and then the clef newly introduced: for instance, if the violin clef is to avail from the beginning of a staff of bass-notes, it should be written thus:—*

Method of learning to read the Notation.

Those who proceed no further in music than singing or playing some instrument, will not, in general, separate staves for the high and low bassoons, and therefore their parts were thus written:—

The upper succession of notes here is throughout in the tenor clef; the under, from the second to the last bar but one (what we have so far said does not exemplify this case) is in the F clef. Let it be remarked, that the F clef, merely to strike the eye, is falsely placed; which seems to show that this manner of writing was solely employed as an expedient of necessity. It ought, indeed, to be avoided if possible, and is only justifiable, as in this instance, by its object and its success.

* It is very desirable that every one who takes an interest in music, should thoroughly comprehend the advantages of our system of notation (which will be still more manifest when we shew in the first section of the second division, its singular aptitude for the exemplification of rythmical proportions) since from time to time, up to the present moment, schemes for new systems, often of the most extraordinary description, have been made public. Such propositions, to abandon a system whose origin recedes unknown, into tens of centuries, coeval with all art, and improved and illustrated by all art-loving nations; such propositions can be entertained only where the reasonableness, necessity, and power of historical development are forgotten. These undertakings can indeed have no influence on the steadfastness and prosperity of art; but they may disturb and mislead the inexperienced, and the perhaps numerous bodies of students for a time, and even detach them from high musical education. Of this kind is the *Cypher System*, which is not as yet altogether laid aside. This was introduced many years ago by some well-intentioned schoolmasters, who were, however, not over well informed in music, for the purpose of facilitating the progress of their scholars. The Cyphers were in three compartments, (representing three octaves) whereby the elevation of the octave and the degree of sound could be expressed, viz:—

That the vivid self-descriptiveness of our notation is entirely absent from this cypher system, and that it can only recite a number of notes without exhibiting their rhythmic proportions, is abundantly manifest. Moreover, the supporters of this system do not attribute to it an equal rank with our notation. It is to be used *for a time only*, to spare the learning of the notation until further advancement: but the notation must be learned at last, and therefore two systems instead of one only.

In other respects, there is scarcely a way or a bye-way that has not been searched for improvements or alterations in musical notation. The Greeks and their followers employed their variously placed and transformed alphabet, as signs of sounds. Then, out of, and with these, was formed a notation of separate signs, called *Neumen*, which were in use until the twelfth century. In order to assist their inspection, and make their height and depth more perceptible, the Neumen were placed higher or lower. Then, in the ninth or tenth century, *one single line* was drawn, as it were a foundation line. Afterwards *two lines* were used, the under one red, and the upper yellow. To these Guido Aretino added a black line over each, so that in all there were *four lines*, and at the beginning of these, the names of the notes were placed in letters of the alphabet, from which, in after time, arose our clefs. It was not until the tenth century, that some attempts at *notes* appeared, on seven, eight, ten, and even twelve lines and more. By about the twelfth century, the use of notes had become more general; still, however, the *neumen* signs, and various other forms of expressing sounds, particularly for different instruments (the lute for instance) called *Tablatures*, maintained a partial dominion during another century. See the article, *Notensystem*, &c., in the *Universal Lexicon der Tonkunst*.

require the knowledge of more than two clefs. It must, however, be desirable to every such student, to read the notes easily and with certainty; and moreover, to learn them in such a manner as to render the acquirement of an instant command of the other clefs, a matter of equal facility.

This is not to be obtained by learning by rote, nor by the note-table introduced by some Professors;† but by a clear insight into the notation, and its agreement or coincidence with the tonal system. It must be felt, that the *scale of notes is a true image of the scale of sounds*, this latter being the scale, properly so called—that the notes ascend and descend by degrees on the lines and spaces, in like manner as do the *tones* in the scale. Now, the first exercise, is to fix upon any *tone* or clef—for example, the *G* clef (the one-lined *g* on the second line)—and from that point, to *write* and *name*, upwards and downwards, the following gradation of notes; viz.:—

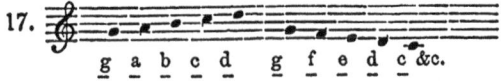

Now, let it be observed, that from line to line and space to space, a third *tone* is noted; and let this succession of notes be *written* upwards and downwards, as follows:—

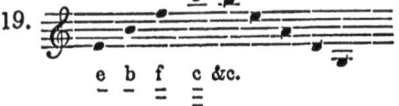

It will be observed also, that upon every third line and every third space, a fifth *tone* is noted, viz.—

Then make a combination of all these enumerations, first one and then the other, thus:—

Lastly, take a good musical composition, and read out aloud all the notes from it; and if a note should not be immediately recognised, its name can be soon discovered by ascending or descending, degree by degree, to its next neighbouring note. It is indeed possible, that this method may take more time in the beginning than learning by rote; but it impresses the knowledge more firmly, and has the effect besides, that if one or two clefs have been studied in this manner, the other clefs become known as it were of themselves, while the eye has already acquired much

† This is, as we are informed, an invention of Mr. J. B. Logier, and manifests equal ingenuity with the other inventions of this brilliant and highly talented instructor, but it is too mechanical; as, indeed, the whole system of this professor could not avoid being, with the particular objects he had in view. The Note-table is a board placed between the keys and the reading-desk. Upon it all the keys of the instrument are represented, as so many equal divisions, and upon each division are marked the clef (F or G) the name of the note of the key immediately under it. In this manner the student has constantly before his eyes four objects in combination,—the key, the clef, the name, and the note, which thus imperceptibly fix themselves by degrees in his memory. It is, therefore, a facilitated learning by rote.

facility in the swift reading of notation. Furthermore, it secures a promptitude, which in all cases *must* be obtained, in finding and naming the *tones* of the tonal system, upwards and downwards, and in any order, with rapidity and decision.

THIRD SECTION—AUXILIARY FORMS AND SIGNS IN NOTATION.

We have no higher clef than the *G* clef, and no lower than the *F* clef. Nevertheless, we require in the former many ledger lines for the higher *tones*, and in the latter many also for the lower *tones*. *Tones* of the three and four-lined octaves are written for the former thus,—

21.

and for the counter *tones* thus,—

22.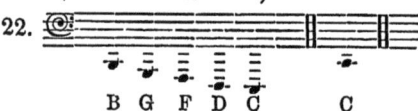

and are inconvenient to read.

With such *tones*, therefore, an auxiliary kind of writing is used: that is, the higher *tones* are written an octave *lower*, and over the notes is placed the cypher,

8, or 8*va*,

(ottava), in order to point out that they are to be played or sung an octave higher than written. If a succession of such *tones* should be written lower, the sign of the octave is elongated by a line so far as it is intended to act, thus,—

8⁓⁓⁓, or 8*va*⁓⁓⁓,

and the place where the notation is to have its regular meaning again, is marked with

l, or *loco*,

signifying, "at the right place." This succession of notes, for instance,—

23.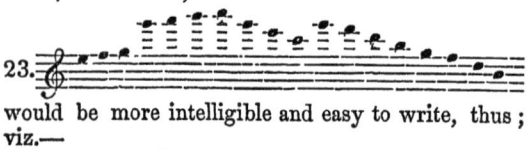

would be more intelligible and easy to write, thus; viz.—

24.

On the other hand, if very low notes are to be written, they are placed an octave higher, and the sign of the octave (8, 8*va*) is placed *under them*, viz.—

25.

Here the second note is to be read as counter *C*, the eighth to the tenth as counter *G*, *E*, *C*, but the eleventh as great *C*.

This manner of writing is of course applicable to every clef. It is well, however, not to use it too frequently, lest this method become rather an impediment than a facilitation. Nobody, for example, would think it reasonable to write this passage,—

26.

in this manner,—

27.

It would clearly be better, either to mark the whole passage with an 8*va*, thus,—

28.

or, if for any reason this would not suit, it would be preferable to use ledger lines, as in No. 26.

Another similar abbreviation is used when a succession of *tones* is accompanied by another succession either higher or lower. If the succession proceeds thus,—

29.

by octaves, then, instead of the outward line of notes (the lowest in the bass and highest in the treble), we may write under or over the inner line of notes,

all' 8va, or *all' ottava*

(to be played with the octave), as in No. 28, thus,—

30.

The sign, ⁓⁓⁓⁓⁓⁓

prolongs the effect of the 8*va* sign here, so far as it extends, as before in No. 24.

Sometimes we find in musical writings, instead of *all' ottava*, simply *ottava* (8*va*), which is an inexact, or rather an erroneous manner of writing. When this occurs, we are obliged to guess from circumstances, what was the real intention of the composer. If a passage began with a succession of octaves, and it were followed by a simple 8 or 8*va*, as in this instance,—

31.

we might imagine that the succession of octaves was to continue; not, that perhaps, the lower notes from *c* upwards, were to be played in their higher octaves alone.

More rarely we meet with the sign—

alla 3*za* (*terza*).

and

alla 6*ta* (*sesta*).

meaning that with each of the *tones* indicated by the succession of notes,—

32.

a higher *tone* (or lower, if the signs were under the staff), at the distance of a third or sixth, is to be played also; thus—

33.

In passages of several voices, for example, in choral and orchestral compositions, it is usual also to refer from one voice to another: to write, for instance, in the tenor voice, instead of the notes, simply,—

col Basso.

(*with the bass*) or in the second violin,

col 1mo. (violino.)

to indicate, that the former is to play the notes of the bass, and the latter, those of the first violin.

Moreover, there are certain signs and intimations whereby, in part, the notes are omitted.

If a passage is to be repeated, or played, two, three, or four times, the notes are written once only, with these marks over them; viz.—

bis,—ter,—quater.

For better intelligence, the whole passage is included under a bow, or dotted lines, thus:—

34.

If a long passage or a large part of a composition is to be repeated, we use the—

Sign of repetition or Repeat.

Two bars across the lines, with dots between the lines, on the left of the bars. Here the following distinctions must be observed.

If a part or passage of the composition is to be repeated from the beginning, it is only necessary to place the repeat as above, at the point from which the performer is to return to the beginning; but if the repetition is not to be from the beginning, the opposite sign of repetition must be placed at the point where the repetition is to commence, thus:—

So that the whole passage to be repeated is enclosed between the two signs: viz.—

35.

This passage is performed until the last note but one (*g*), then, repeated from the third note (*e*), now for the first time, to *a*, and then, the movement proceeds.*

If after the repetition of one passage or part, another is to be repeated immediately following it, the dots are placed on both sides of the bars thus:—

in order to intimate beforehand that the passage beginning at that point is also to be repeated.

If a longer passage is to be repeated, but, after the repetition, a small change is to be made in the termination, the end to be changed is to be marked with a bow or a parenthesis, and the words,—

1*ma* (*prima volta*).

and the substituted passage which is placed after the sign of repetition, is marked,—

2*da* (*seconda*).

in order to express, that on the *first time* of playing the passage, the place marked 1*ma* is to be played; but on the *repetition* of the passage, that place is to be omitted and the place marked 2*da* is to be played in lieu of it.

The foregoing passage written so,—

36.

would be repeated as before; but the repetition would only go as far as the twelfth note (*f*), then the four following (*e—g—c—g*), would be passed over, and in lieu of them, those after the sign of repetition (*e—g—f—e*), would be played.

The following words or signs have the same meaning,—

Da capo (*D. C.*, or *D. c.*, or *d. c.*)

from the beginning; that is, to repeat from the beginning. If the repetition is to reach only to a certain point, and the piece of music there close, that point is indicated by—

F. or *Fine* (*end*).

It is well also to add to this sign, in order to make it more striking to the eye, this mark, over the last note,—

(which we shall find further on, employed for another object), and to write, instead of simply *da capo*,—

D. C. al fine.

that is, from the beginning to the (indicated) end.

If the part is not to be repeated quite from the beginning, but only from a certain point, that point is indicated by the sign—

and instead of *da capo*

d. s. (*dal segno.*)

which means, *from the sign*, is written.

This passage for example,—

37.

would be played through from beginning to end, and then be repeated from the sign at the third note *c*, to the note where *Fine* and the sign are placed, which is the lower *c*, as the end of the passage.†

Other abbreviations and facilitations we shall learn hereafter.

Finally, we will mention one other sign which is used at the end of a side or of an incomplete pas-

---

* Instead of the few notes enclosed in this example, the reader is requested to represent to himself a whole subject, or part, of considerable length. Such a short passage as we have here given for the sake of brevity, would only require the word *bis*.

† Here also it is necessary to imagine a piece of music of some extent, instead of the trifle above. One would rather write those few notes over again, than employ the abbreviations.

sage, to shew what follows on the next side, or note the next continuation of the passage: it is this,— and may be called

A Direct.

Here for example:—

it means that the next notes will be the two-lined *f*, and the one-lined *a*.

FOURTH SECTION—RAISING AND DEPRESSING.*

If we compare our systems of notation and *tones*, so far as we have hitherto considered them, with the row of keys of a pianoforte, or with our representation at page 6, we shall perceive that we have not as yet learned to know and to write all the *tones*, and, therefore, that we are not in possession of the whole system. We know nothing of the *tones* given by the black keys, which are distinguished in the figure above quoted by the numbers 2, 4, 7, 9, and 11. We have allowed ourselves this postponement, in order to secure a good foundation, and shall now proceed to the elucidation of the omitted *tones*, in doing which we crave reference to our said representation of the key-board at page 6.

(*A.*) RAISING.

If we place before any note this sign,

called a *sharp*, or sign of raising, the key and *tone* originally indicated by that note, are no longer meant, but the key and *tone* next above it, whether this latter be a black or a white key. If, for example, we place a ♯ before the note *c*—

it is not the key *c* (fig. page 6, No. 1), but the next higher—a black key, No. 2—which is intended. If a sharp were before *d*, the black key 4 would be understood. If it were before *e*, the key 6, which we see is a white key, would be meant.

The *tone* so raised must now also change its name, which is done by simply adding the word *sharp* after it. Thus *c* so raised, is called *c* sharp, and so of the rest.

There would seem to be 14 of these *tones* in the octave—

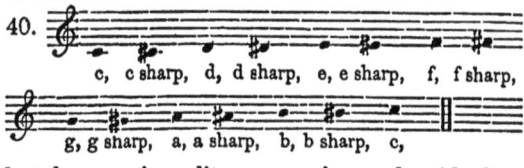

but there are in reality no more in use than 12, since practically *e*♯ and *b*♯ are the same as *f* and *c*.

The same process may now be gone through in an opposite direction.

(*B.*) DEPRESSING.

If we place before any note the sign,

called a *flat*, instead of the original key and *tone*

* The instruction beginning here cannot be completed until the ninth section of the second division.

being meant, the note is understood to indicate the key and *tone* next lower, or deeper, whether that be a black or a white key. If, for example, a ♭ be placed before *c*, the key *c* (in the fig. No. 13) is not meant, but the next deeper, No. 12, and, as we see, a white key. If a ♭ be before *b*, the key No. 12 is not understood, but the next lower, No. 11, which is a black key. Such a lowered *tone* changes its name in a similar manner as the raised *tones*, by adding the word *flat* to the name of the tone.

Here we see the *tones* of an octave,—

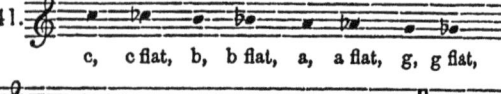

Such *tones* as differ in name only, but are in reality the same in pitch, we call enharmonic. Thus *b* and *c*♭, *e* and *f* ♭, *e*♯ and *f*, *b*♯ and *c*, *c*♯ and *d*♭, *a*♮ and *g*♯, *b*♭ and *a*♯, and so forth, are enharmonic *tones*.

It may seem surprising that we should have double names for the *tones*. Why don't we name the black keys *c*♯, *d*♯, &c., only, or *d*♭, *e*♭, &c., only? Why should *e* be sometimes *f*♭, and *f* sometimes *e*♯? These apparently superfluous double names, have been adopted for very sufficient reasons. They are quite indispensable to clearness and facility of notation. This will in part be shewn in this work; but it can be done conclusively only in the treatise on composition and the science of music.

The scale in which all the raised and depressed *tones* are introduced, which we have not already described above, under the name of enharmonic, we call the

CHROMATIC SCALE.

Here we see it,—

with the ascending progression marked A, and the descending, B.

On the other hand the succession of all the degrees (shewn at page 7), in which each degree appears but once, is called the

DIATONIC SCALE,

which going through the *tones* omits no degree, but in one form and one scale only.

If we have employed a sharp or a flat, and wish the effect of either to cease, we use a sign called a

(*C.*) NATURAL.

which is of this shape,—

and replaces the *tone* which had been either raised or depressed, on its original pitch. So, for example, *c*♯ would become again *c*, and *e*♭ again *e*.

The sharp had raised *c* to *c*♯, but the natural reduces it again to *c*. In like manner the *e* had been depressed to *e♭*, but by the natural it again becomes *e*.

We will not refrain from a remark in this place; simple as it may appear, it will be found of use hereafter. It is this: that the effect of the natural is two-fold, viz., if it remove a sharp, it depresses the *tone*: if it remove a flat, it sharpens the *tone*.

(D.) DOUBLE RAISING AND DOUBLE DEPRESSION.

There are circumstances, which will be explained hereafter, in which it is necessary to raise or depress a *tone* doubly; so that instead of its own key, the second key from it, either above or below, must be used.

The double raising is signified by a double sharp, which is thus formed:—

If a double sharp is placed, for example, before *c*, neither *c* nor *c♯* is meant, but the key next above that of *c♯* (which we have hitherto called *d*, and is numbered 3 in the Fig. page 6). The name of a *tone* thus circumstanced is now formed by adding "double sharp" after it; as *c* double sharp, *d* double sharp &c.

The *double depression* is signified thus,—♭♭
If this sign be placed before a note, it will mean the *second* next lower key. If it were, for example, before *d*, neither *d* nor *d♭* is to be struck, but *c* No. 1, in the above Fig. p. 6. The name is now formed by adding "double flat" to the name of the *tone* so qualified.

Here is an example of double raising and double depressing.—

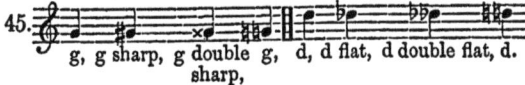

44. g, g sharp, g double sharp, d, d flat, d double flat.

How is a double sharp or double flat to be removed? By a *double natural*; for instance,—

45. g, g sharp, g double g, d, d flat, d double flat, d.
                          sharp,

But how, if we want to remove half only of the raising or depressing, and so reduce them to one sharp or one flat? Then we might employ one natural only, which in strictness ought to be sufficient; but in order that no oversight may occur, whereby the natural might be considered as a total removal of the double sign, one of these latter signs is allowed to remain with the natural; thus,—

46. g, g sharp, g double g sharp, d, d flat, d double d flat,
                sharp,   flat,

We perceive, moreover, that by the double sharps and flats, more names are introduced for one and the same *tone* than we have hitherto had (page 14), for now, every *tone* may be called by three names; viz.—

c may also be called *b* sharp or *d* double flat,
c♯   "   "   *d* flat or *b* double sharp,
d   "   "   *e* double flat or *c* double sharp,

which faculty applies equally to all in the same relative positions. Why these several names are necessary and what object they serve, must be explained elsewhere. We will merely take notice of the names and again impress upon our minds, that *tones* possessed of several names, but of the same pitch in our system (produced by the same keys), are called enharmonic *tones*. Therefore, *c*, *b♯* and *d♭♭*, and also *c♯*, *d♭*, and *b♯♯*, &c. are enharmonic *tones*.

We must confess that the object of the mark ♮, natural, cannot be clearly perceived, until we know how long the effect of the sharps and flats generally lasts; but the whole of this instruction on signs hangs so easily together that it has not been thought expedient to omit it here.

Now let us return to the
SEVEN DEGREES,
in order to understand them completely.

When we introduced them at page 7, we said that all *tones* bore their names, or names derived from them. We see now that each degree is susceptible of appearing in *five forms*, viz., its own original, sharp, double sharp, flat, and double flat; and that it is therefore appropriate for five *tones* and five names. We therefore will reckon all *tones* named from one degree as belonging to it. Therefore to the degree belong the *tones*,

c, *c* sharp, *c* double sharp, *c* flat, and *c* double flat,
to *d*, *d* " *d* " *d* " *d* "
and so forth; although these *tones under another name* may be reckoned as belonging to another degree; for instance, the *tone c* sharp, as *d* flat towards *d*, and as *b* double sharp towards the degree *b*.

Finally, we now only, know all the contents of our tonal system, of which, in the first section, we were acquainted with only the unaltered degrees. We know that every octave, besides the seven degrees (*c, d, e, f, g, a, b*), contains five raised or depressed intervening *tones* (*c♯, d♯, f♯, g♯, a♯*, or *d♭, e♭, g♭, a♭, b♭*), and therefore all together twelve different *tones*, and we can now under the tonal system understand the *contents of all the seven degrees*, with their elevations and depressions, through all octaves.

FIFTH SECTION—MEASUREMENT OF THE RELATION OF TONES.

Since in Music, *tones* must be combined together, their reciprocal relationships must be estimated.

With the most superficial observation, we perceive that one *tone* is higher than another: that *g* or *a* for example, is higher than *c*, in the same octave. But as there are several *tones* higher and lower, that difference of height requires to be more precisely determined. The enumeration of the degrees is more exact. We begin at one which we call the *first*, the next, proceeding upwards, is the *second*, the following is the *third*, and so on.

The *tones* are named in the order of the degrees, first, second, third, &c. up to the octave, which is the same in both successions. Above the octave, however, the *tones* are called ninth, tenth, eleventh, &c.

It is easy to perceive that the eighth degree is no other than the first, in a higher octave; the ninth nothing but the second in a higher octave, and so forth.

For most persons, it will be sufficient to observe the names of the degrees up to the octave and ninth.

The others do not come into use until late in the study of composition, that is, in double counterpoint.

Thus, if C be taken as first, D becomes the second, E the third, F the fourth, and so forth. If F be taken as first, G is the second, A the third, and so forth. Hereby we can give the relationship of the *tones* more exactly; we can say for example of G, not only *that it is higher* than C (in the same octave), but also, that it is *four degrees higher*; that it is the fifth degree, the fifth of C.*

If we compare two *tones* in respect of their height, we establish them in a relationship towards each other. The general name of that relationship is

INTERVAL.

We say, therefore, that C and D form with each other an *interval of a second*, G and D the *interval of a fifth*, C with C (figuratively), the interval of a first.

But also, these determinations are not completely sufficient: for we already know that each of our degrees includes five different *tones*. Which of them is now meant? If for instance, we want the fifth of C, do we mean g, or $g\sharp$, or $g\times$, or $g\flat$, or $g\flat\flat$? They are all on the fifth degree from C, and are therefore all fifths of this *tone*. Here the enumerations of the degrees and the mere name of the interval, leave us in uncertainty.

We require, therefore, a more exact

TONE MEASUREMENT,

and for that end the smallest intervals of our system are taken.

We want two such measures, which we call

THE TONE AND THE SEMITONE.†

A tone is the interval between any immediately adjacent degrees, having in our system some other *tone* between them. Therefore c and d form the interval of a tone; for they are degrees lying next to each other, and between them there is the *tone* $c\sharp$ or $d\flat$. In like manner $c\sharp$ and $d\sharp$, e and $f\sharp$, $b\flat$ and c are intervals of a tone, since they are on degrees next to each other ($c\sharp$ and $d\sharp$ on the C and D degrees, $f\sharp$ on the F degree, $b\flat$ on the B degree, and therefore in these cases the degrees C and D, E and F, B and C, are next to each other), and between them lies a *tone*; namely, d between $c\sharp$ and $d\sharp$, f between e and $f\sharp$, and b between $b\flat$ and c.‡

---

* According to custom, we count from the lower to the upper. If, on the contrary, we count from above to below, from an upper *tone* downwards, we put the word *inverted* before the name of the number. Therefore F is from G the *inverted second*, from A, the inverted third, and so forth.

† The doctrine hitherto has been, and it is inculcated also in the former editions of this work, that it is necessary to employ *three measures*, derived from Acoustics—the tone, the *greater semitone*, and the *lesser semitone*. The greater semitone was the interval between two *tones*, named *from adjoining* degrees, and without an intervening *tone*, as for example, between b and c, c and $d\flat$, and $f\sharp$ and g. The lesser semitone, the interval between two *tones*, named *from the same* degree, without an intervening *tone*, as for instance, between b and $b\sharp$, c and $c\sharp$, $f\sharp$ and $f\times$, and so forth. As a *foundation* for these three measures, the least perceptible gradation of sound was assumed and called a *comma*, of which a *tone* is said to consist of nine, a greater semitone of five, and a lesser of four.

But *the whole of these distinctions can be dispensed with in practice*, and therefore need not be discussed in this work.

‡ Here we perceive the influence of the double names, which we mentioned at pages 14 and 15; $c\sharp$ and $d\sharp$ form between them a tone, e and $f\sharp$ also; but $d\flat$ and $d\sharp$, or e and $g\flat$ do not do so: for $d\flat$ and $d\sharp$ belong to the same degree; while e and $g\flat$ are not degrees next adjoining to each other, although of the same height as e and $f\sharp$. We must wait till a later period of our instruction, to comprehend why a difference, apparently in name only, should be necessary.

It is therefore apparent, moreover, that in this matter, it is of no consequence whether any of the *tones* belong to black or to white keys.

A semitone is formed between two *tones* belonging to the same degree, or belonging to next adjoining degrees, between which, in our system, no *tone* intervenes. Therefore, b and $b\sharp$, c and $c\sharp$, $f\sharp$ and $f\times$, $d\flat$ and $d\flat\flat$, form semitones; for they belong to the same degree, and there is not in our system any intervening *tone* between them: and moreover, no key on our key-board. In like manner, b and c, c and $d\flat$, $f\sharp$ and g, form semitones; for they belong to adjoining degrees, and have no intervening *tone*.§

With these measures, all the relationships‖ in our tonal system can be given with precision: that is, we can count how many tones and semitones they contain.

If we examine first the tone, for example, c—d, we find that it contains two semitones; viz., c—$c\sharp$, and $c\sharp$—d, or, what is the same, c—$d\flat$ and $d\flat$—d.

If we examine the third, c—e, we find that it contains two tones: c—d and d—e.

If we examine the seventh, c—b, we find in it
2 Tones, c—d and d—e;
1 Semitone, e—f;
and moreover
3 Tones, f—g, g—a, and a—b.

We should have the same result from any kind of measurement; for example thus,—
2 Tones, c—d, d—e;
1 Tone, e—$f\sharp$;
1 Tone, $f\sharp$—$g\sharp$;
1 Semitone, $g\sharp$—a; or 1 Tone, $g\sharp$—$a\sharp$,
1 Tone, a—b; or 1 Semitone, $a\sharp$—b.

We measure therefore as we please, or as it is most convenient.

Now only can we give the relationships of *tones* with precision. If starting from c we require that seventh which lies five tones and one semitone higher, b alone can have been intended, for $b\flat$ would have been only four tones (c—d, d—e, f—g, g—a), and two semitones (e—f, a—$b\flat$¶) distant; and therefore a semitone too near, while $b\sharp$ would have been six tones distant, viz., c—d, d—e, e—$f\sharp$, $f\sharp$—$g\sharp$, $g\sharp$—$a\sharp$, $a\sharp$—$b\sharp$, and therefore a semitone too distant. $B\flat\flat$ would be still nearer than $b\flat$, and $b\times$ still further than $b\sharp$.

But it would be tediously minute were we to introduce the measure, whenever we have to speak of the quantity of an interval; therefore we adopt

FOUR CLASSES OF INTERVALS,

and can now with one single adjective for each, give its exact quantity. Every interval may be

---

§ Here also, the enharmonic equality (*gleichheit*) of b—$b\sharp$, c—$c\sharp$, &c., to b—c, c—$d\flat$, &c., strikes the eye.

‖ Not every relationship of tone in general can be given. For the mathematics teach us, that all quantity and consequently the interval or distance between two *tones* is endlessly divisible, and therefore numberless relationships of *tones* are possible. Further, it is not the fact that always and everywhere the relationships of *tones* admitted and familiar with us, have been and are alone used. On the contrary, many quite different relationships have been employed or attempted: as we learn from the history of music. (See the author's article on Greek music, in the Universal Lexicon of Music.)

¶ Cannot we say five tones, or reckon one tone for two half tones? We should then be obliged to reckon so, viz., c—d, d—e, e—$f\sharp$, $f\sharp$—$g\sharp$; but $a\sharp$ is not the seventh from c, although enharmonically equal to it; and $g\sharp$—$b\flat$ is not a tone, because the (degrees) g and b do not lie next to each other.

MUSICAL INSTRUCTION.

Major,
Minor,
Diminished, and
Extreme or Augmented.

Every minor interval is produced by reducing a major one by a semitone, or is a semitone *less* than the major interval of the same original name. Thus a minor fifth or sixth is a semitone less than a major fifth or sixth.

Every diminished interval is a semitone less than a minor interval, or two semitones *less* than the major interval.

Every extreme interval is a semitone greater than a major interval. We will observe that—

Diminished means *less than minor*,
Extreme   „   *greater than major*.

So soon, therefore, as we know the quantities of the major intervals, we can easily make from them, minor, diminished, and extreme, by lessening by one or two semitones, or by adding one. For the representation of the major intervals we here present a figure not easily forgotten—

The Succession of Degrees.

In this succession every *tone* forms a major interval with the first *tone*;

c   d   e   f   g   a   b   c   d

So then, c—d forms a major second
c—e   „   „   third
c—f   „   „   fourth
c—g   „   „   fifth*
c—a   „   „   sixth
c—b   „   „   seventh
c—c   „   „   octave
c—d   „   „   ninth

and so forth.† We cannot easily forget this so long as we remember the names of the degrees, and that the rule for the major intervals lies in them.

We see, therefore, that the—

major second contains 1 tone
  „   third   „   2 tones
  „   fourth   „   2 „   and 1 semitone
  „   fifth   „   3 „   1   „
  „   sixth   „   4 „   1   „
  „   seventh   „   5 „   1   „
  „   octave   „   5 „   2   „
  „   ninth   „   6 „   2   „

* There does not reign among musicians and authors the desirable unanimity in the naming of these intervals. The major and minor third are also called *hard* and *soft*, *greater* and *lesser*: the major fifth is also called the *perfect* fifth, as if any interval could be anything else but *perfect*. The major fifth is even called the *false* fifth, as if it in its proper place, were not, by nature, as true and right as any other interval. The most remarkable is the naming of the fourth (of two tones and a semitone) *c—f* as a *minor fourth*, and the fourth *f—b* or *c—f♯* (of three tones) as a *major fourth*. These appellations, however, have not only the authority of earlier writers, but also the support of parallel cases; for the *major second* and *third* give inverted the *minor seventh* and *sixth*, whence it seemed to follow, that the inversion of the *major fifth* should be called a *minor fourth*. But these inverted intervals have no practical importance, and it seems more appropriate to consider all the relations of the original degrees in like manner towards or with the first, and all, as *major*. This gives us the advantage of the above easy method of estimating the intervals.

† Let us remember that the distance only of the higher *tone* from the first (*c*) gives the true intervals. The names of the degrees among themselves produce all kinds of intervals: for example, *d—f* and *e—g*

If we should forget any of these quantities, we have only to extract the interval from the names of the degrees, and measure it.‡

If we desire to find out a major interval from any given *tone*, we first fix upon the proper degree, then measure the distance, and add or deduct, if it be too great or too little. If for example, we want to know which *tone* is a major fourth from *f*; we see, first of all, that the fourth degree from *f* is *b*; but *f—b* contains three tones, and our normal fourth *c—f* has only two tones and a semitone; consequently we must lessen *f—b* by changing *b* into *b♭*, and we have then the tones *f—g*, *g—a*, and the semitone *a—b♭*. Or if from *b* we sought a major fifth, we must in the first place fix upon the fifth degree *f*, and then measure against the normal fifth *c—g*. This latter contains three tones (*c—d*, *d—e*, *f—g*), and a semitone (*e—f*), but our fifth contains only two tones (*c—d*, *d—e*), and two semitones (*b—c* and *e—f*), and therefore is too small. We therefore raise *f* to *f♯*, convert thereby the semitone *e—f* into a tone, and have acquired our major fifth *b—f♯*.

When we have once determined a major interval, it is easy to make therefrom, a minor, diminished,

are not major thirds; *neither* is *f—b* a major fourth, as the above measures will shew.

‡ We think proper to notice here a particular distinction of intervals, which is most ancient in the theory of music; and which, though unimportant as to our main object, ought not to be unknown to the musician or to the lover of art.

In order to understand it, we must remember that in acoustics (page 7) a sound is called higher, the greater the number is of vibrations made by the sounding body in a given time. That if a given *tone* requires *one* vibration, *its higher octave* will require *two* vibrations in the same time (consequently of double velocity); the *higher fifth* three vibrations, the *second* higher octave *four* vibrations, the next *major third* over this latter octave *five* vibrations, the next *minor third* over the major third, *six* vibrations. It being granted that a sounding body making one vibration in a second produced the great C, a sounding body which made two vibrations in a second would produce the small c. The sounds would stand in this relation—

as $C : c : g : c : e : g$
so $1 : 2 : 3 : \overline{4} : \overline{5} : \overline{6}$

The next relation would be 6 : 7. It would produce a sound which we should call *b♭*, the minor seventh from *c*.

Now we may understand the distinctions in the ancient theory of sounds. They distinguished *two kinds* of intervals—

Consonances—sounding well or agreeably together, and
Dissonances—sounding ill or disagreeably together, or less agreeably.

The consonances were said to be, the unison, octave, fifth, fourth, major and minor third and sixth; all the rest were dissonances.

This distinction is of all things the least essential to mention, since music is in no way simply or chiefly concerned with the diversion or excitement of the senses by pleasant or repulsive sounds. It is much rather the province of music, through the senses, to act on the mind and soul: so that this distinction is merely superficial. An interval, and the sense of perception of it, do not comprehend by far all the requisites wherefrom we should call it beneficial, that is, more simple and easier to be understood. Even in this work, (in the second section of the sixth division,) when better grounded in the science of music, we shall have far different ideas to give. The superficial character of such distinctions is manifest when we see that intervals so different as the fourth, third, and octave, or all the diminished and extreme intervals without exception, are to be all comprehended in one class. In fine, the distinction is quite *arbitrary* at least in any way in which it might have been made available; for in the perfectly regular progression, 1 : 2 : 3 : 4 : 5 : 6 : 7, there is no more reason to draw a line of separation at 6 : 7 than at 5 : 6 or 7 : 8. And, in fact, some theorists did not stop at that line. Now, they divided the consonances into *perfect* (the octave and fifth) and *imperfect*, (the fourth, major and minor thirds and sixth); then, again, the dissonances, into essential and accidental, which last comprised all foreign sounds that entered into a mode or scale. Some, again, on the other hand, have declared the fourth to be a dissonance altogether; while others have considered it to be so only occasionally. Thus they have taken wondrous pains to torment themselves and their scholars, and abandon the essential object of pursuit.

This point and many others of much importance in music are fundamentally discussed in the author's publication, "Die alte Musiklehre im Streit mit unsrer Zeit," at Messrs. Breitkopf and Härtel, in Leipzig.

For the convenience of inspection, we have assumed that a sound could be produced by one or two vibrations in a second. This assumption is far from being the fact. The smallest number of vibrations in a second capable of producing a sound, is ascertained to be about 32, and the sound produced is the octave under double C.

B

and extreme interval. We have merely to add or deduct, by raising or lowering, so many semitones as the difference may require (page 17,). If the major fifth $c—g$ is to become a minor fifth, we must take off a semitone, and therefore lower g to $g♭$: $c—g♭$ is a minor fifth. The minor intervals from c, are therefore—

$c—d♭$	the minor	second
$c—e♭$	„	third
$c—f♭$	„	fourth
$c—g♭$	„	fifth
$c—a♭$	„	sixth
$c—b♭$	„	seventh

If $c—g$ is to become an *extreme fifth*, g must be raised a semitone. Do we wish to convert $c♯—b♯$, (a major seventh) into a minor seventh? $b♯$ must be depressed a semitone to become b. If the minor seventh $c♯—b$ is to become a diminished seventh, b must be again depressed to $b♭$: $c♯—b♭$ is a diminished seventh. In this manner, it is easy to produce minor, diminished, or extreme intervals.

To the beginner, we recommend two practices. *First, in writing.* Let him sketch out the major intervals from every *tone* (as we have done at page 17), then all the minor (as we have above). Then let him take first one, then the other major interval, (for example, $g—d$, $g♭—d♭$, a major fifth), and convert it into a minor ($g—d♭$, $g♭—d♭♭$), diminished ($g—d♭♭$, $g♭—d♭♭♭$),* extreme ($g—d♯$, $g♭—d$). *Secondly,* let him use his faculties in recognising the intervals, particularly the major and minor. Let him seek by the ear the different intervals (for example, major fifths, major and minor thirds and sixths, minor sevenths), from any degree at pleasure. If he think he has hit on them, let him name the *tone* and measure the quantity of the interval; this will shew him whether he has been successful or not.

It is clear, that with the assistance of the double elevations and depressions, many more intervals might be contrived. The diminished seventh, $c♯—b♭$, might by a further depression of the $b♭$, and by the further raising of the $c♯$, be converted into a doubly and trebly diminished seventh ($c♯—b♭♭$ and $c×—b♭♭$). The extreme fifth, $c—g♯$, in like manner, might be twice or three times extended. If it were desirable, indeed, to increase the double sharps and flats, there is no limit to their extension. Fortunately, however, we cannot (as we mentioned in our last note) employ all these easy fabrications in practical art, therefore we will at once lay them aside.

In the previous section we became acquainted with enharmonic *tones*. We now perceive intervals, which, while both of the same height, are named quite differently, according to the tones on either side of them. They must therefore be called—

ENHARMONIC INTERVALS.

They are easily found, if, in any given interval, one or other of the *tones* be changed enharmonically. If, for example, in the minor third, $c—e♭$, we change the $e♭$ enharmonically into $d♯$, we produce the extreme second, $c—d♯$, whose *tones* have the same height in our system as the third, $c—e♭$. If in the extreme fifth, $c—g♯$, we change the name of the upper *tone*, we produce the minor sixth, $c—a♭$. In like manner, from the diminished seventh, $c♯—b♭$, a major sixth, $c♯—a♯$ or $d♭—b♭$, would be produced, or also from the fifth, $c♯—g♯$, by changing the names of both *tones*, another fifth, $d♭—a♭$, would be produced; and other similar changes might be exemplified.

SIXTH SECTION—OF MODES, SCALES, OR SYSTEMS OF DEGREES, USUALLY CALLED KEYS.

We have learned that Music has seven degrees, each containing many *tones* and relations at command. By possibility all the *tones* and their relations may be brought forward in every piece of music. But as every production of art has a limited sphere of action, and in some sense a determined object, to express a particular and circumscribed range of thoughts and feelings, it is natural, that all *tones* and their relations should not constantly be used, at least not in the same amplitude and force. On the contrary, every piece of music requires an appropriate selection of *tones* and their combinations, in which exclusively, or at least principally, the artist should work out his conceptions.

This circumstance also reduces the labour of conducting the student in the wide region of musical forms, and prevents his being perplexed and dismayed by their numberless and diversified images.

For every composition

SEVEN DEGREES

present themselves as a foundation. But each one has five forms, and thus furnishes the means of endless varieties of combination. We might begin with $c—d—e—f$, or $c♯—d—e—f$, or $c♭—d—e—f$, or $c—d♯—e—f$, $c♯—d♯—e—f$, &c. But from all these possibilities our system has selected two only, as essentially serviceable. We call them

THE MODES, SCALES,† OR KEYS, MAJOR AND MINOR.

They both agree, in containing the seven degrees. Wherein then do they differ? In the relation which the degrees bear to each other: in the quantities of the intervals formed by each degree, with the first,—

THE SCALES OF THE MAJOR KEYS

have major intervals only, between all the other degrees and the first. Therefore the first is followed by a major second, major third, fourth, fifth, sixth

---

* Here we meet with a threefold depression, of which we said nothing at page 15. The reason of our silence was, that such depressions or elevations are *not* in use, or at least, most rare. Such intervals, never scarcely appearing in practice, and displayed only by pedantry, have acquired the inglorious name of paper intervals. They exist, indeed, only on the patient paper, already overburdened enough, even in our days, with useless matter, to the grief of many a weary student. Even our exceptional $d♭♭♭$ above, has been introduced merely to give us the opportunity of cautioning both teachers and scholars against its use, since it is neither necessary nor of any value.

† The succession of *tones* in which each degree enters only once (or which proceeds in tones or semitones), is called the *Diatonic* scale. The succession of *tones* proceding by semitones only, is called the Chromatic scale (page 14). Lastly, that, in which all the *tones* (at least the chromatic) with their enharmonic double names are introduced ($c—c♯—d♭—d—d♯$ —$e♭—e$, and so forth), is called the enharmonic scale.
But these two last modes are not calculated to be a foundation for musical composition. It seems even to have been a misunderstanding, to imagine that the ancient Greek musicians made any use of these successions of sounds, or anything resembling them, as modes or grounds of musical construction; although the assertions of the Greek theorists sustain that opinion (see the author's article on Gr. Music, in the Universal *Lexikon der Tonkunst*). From those theorists the idea has descended to us. There remains, however, but one thing to say of these three pretended Modes, which is, that the whole arrangement in this view is utterly worthless.

and seventh. Consequently, we see in the original succession of degrees (page 7),—
c—d—e—f—g—a—b
the type of the major scale.

If we are desirous of not always calculating the relation from the first *tone*, we may reckon the distance between each degree to its next following. So doing we should find that the first was a tone distant from the second; this latter again a tone from the third, this again a semitone from the fourth, and so forth. Here—

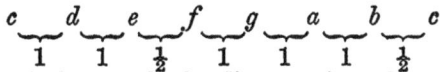

we see before us all the distances from degree to degree. There follow two tones and a semitone; and then three tones and a semitone.

THE MINOR SCALE

in like manner has major intervals only, excepting the third and sixth, which are minor. As we know how major intervals are changed into minor, we can easily convert major scales into minor. We need only depress the third and sixth. For example,—

C major, c—d—e—f—g—a—b—c
into C minor, c—d—e♭—f—g—a♭—b—c

Here we find that the succession of *tones* makes the following steps:—

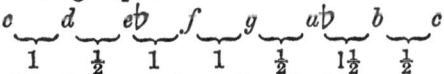

The step of a tone and semitone in this progression is very striking, from a♭ to b. There is no such interval in the major. It affects our sensations very forcibly (as indeed do all extreme intervals), in the progress of the scale.

But this does not exist in every succession of *tones*: not in this, for instance,—

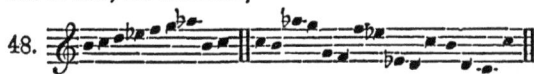

where the extreme second is avoided; but in the formation of a scale, the object is not the most sweet or gentle succession of *tones*,* but the most strictly appropriate succession as a foundation for composition.

---

* This entirely foreign consideration has misled many teachers in the construction of the minor scale, which they have therefore formed in various ways. In ascending they give it merely a minor third—
c—d—e♭—f—g—a—b—c
but in descending they give it a minor third, sixth, and seventh—
c—b♭—a♭—g—f—e♭—d—c
No doubt these successions of *tones* are softer than that with the extreme second; but the idea of *one* mode is entirely destroyed—the sixth is as well a♭ as a, the seventh b♭ as b, therefore the pretended scale should be declared to be a double foundation or two scales; or again, both successions of *tones* should be mixed together, thus:—
c—d—e♭—f—g—a♭—a—b♭—b—c
which would form a scale, half diatonic, half chromatic, but which would disagree too much with itself to answer the object. This will be shewn more distinctly in the Theory of Harmony, and also in the first part of the Author's Instructions in Composition.

It is quite another question, whether the composer may not in particular cases (in order to make the succession more soft and flowing) deviate from the systematic progression, No. 47, and so arrange his *tones* as in No. 48, or other different ways. The rules of composition allow him this liberty, and moreover shew him how and on what grounds he should use it. The teacher may therefore permit his pupil (in order to acquire ease and readiness in playing and singing) to use the flowing forms in conjunction with the fundamental scale, nay, even to use them preferably for technical practice, in order that the harsh effect of the systematic scale may not have a torporific and annoying influence on the pupil by too frequent repetition. But this concession to particular cases in composition and to kind feeling towards the pupil, must not be construed into a departure from the true and indispensable system.

Why have we formed our two scales in this manner and no other? why has the major, major intervals only? and why in the minor are the third and sixth alone minor? These questions will all be answered hereafter: for the present it is sufficient to know the real construction of each, and to learn their succession of sounds.

SEVENTH SECTION—THE MAJOR AND MINOR SCALES OR KEYS.

We have already remarked, that the intervals may be made to proceed from any degree, whether from d or e, or d♯ as well as from c. Therefore we can form from any degree at will, all the major and minor intervals, as we have done at page 17, merely as an example.

Consequently we can construct our scales on every *tone*, as well as upon c♯, d or e♭, &c.

The representation of a major or minor key or scale on determined degrees, we call

THE SCALE.

There are, therefore major scales and minor scales, that is, one of each for every *tone* of our system.

How many *tones* are there in our system?

First—the *seven* root *tones*—
c—d—e—f—g—a—b.

Secondly—the *five tones* lying between them,—
c♯—d♯—f♯—g♯—a♯

therefore all together *twelve*. There must therefore be

TWELVE MAJOR SCALES, AND TWELVE MINOR SCALES.

All our enharmonic *tones* need not now be mentioned. The *tones* between c—d, &c., which we have called above c♯, d♯, &c., might also have been called

d♭—e♭—g♭—a♭—b♭

in short, every *tone* might have been called by three different names. But by so doing, we should not have acquired new *tones*, but only additional names.

How can we now construct the different scales? We fix upon all the degrees from that one with which we have chosen to begin, and compare the succession of tones and semitones with the model successions as above, whether the intervals be for the major, 1, 1, ½, 1, 1, 1, ½ tones, and for the minor, 1, ½, 1, 1, ½, 1½, ½ tones.

Where the step is too small, we must raise, and where too large, we must depress the upper *tones* to the right measure.

If it be desired, for example, to write down the major scale of a, or

A, MAJOR.

We put down first of all, the degrees from *a*, thus,—
a—b—c—d—e—f—g—a

Now, we examine the intervals step by step, a—b is right, a tone; b—c is only a semitone, but should be a whole tone; therefore we raise c to c♯, and so get the tone b—c♯. The distance between c♯—d and d—e is correct. Now a whole tone must come again, but e—f is only a semitone; we must therefore change f into $f\sharp$. In like manner, g must be changed into $g\sharp$, in order to obtain the last whole tone, $f\sharp$—$g\sharp$, instead of the semitone, $f\sharp$—g.

The scale, then, of A major, is therefore—

$$a—b—c\sharp—d—e—f\sharp—g\sharp—a$$

If we wish to erect a major scale upon $a\flat$, we first write out the degrees from $a\flat$—

$$a\flat—b—c—d—e—f—g—a$$

and then measure the steps. Here we find $a\flat$—b too large for a tone, and must therefore lower it to $b\flat$; so we must proceed and shall finally get the scale—

$$a\flat—b\flat—c—d\flat—e\flat—f—g—a\flat$$

In like manner, we can now form any minor scale. We get it, however, much more easily when we know the major scale of the same *tone*; for in that case, without any more measuring, we have only to depress the third and sixth. In order to change* A major, for example, into A minor,—

$$a—b—c\sharp—d—e—f\sharp—g\sharp—a$$
$$cf$$
$$a—b—c—d—e—f—g\sharp—a$$

or $a\flat$ major into $a\flat$ minor,—

$$a\flat—b\flat—c—d\flat—e\flat—f—g—a\flat$$
$$c\flatf\flat$$
$$a\flat—b\flat—c\flat—d\flat—e\flat—f\flat—g—a\flat$$

Now only, have we a fully established foundation for any musical composition. We can now say whether it is altogether or chiefly in the major or minor key, and to what particular major or minor scale it belongs; that the composition is in A major, or A minor, in the usual technical expression.

Commonly (not without exceptions) a composition proceeds in one key, and if it abandon that key, for a time, to move into another, it returns to the original key, for its close. It will facilitate our comprehension and performance of a composition, if we know in what key it is written.

EIGHTH SECTION—COMBINATION OF ALL THE SCALES.

We cannot deny that the mode of constructing the scales, as set forth in the preceding section, is minute and circuitous: particularly if the operation is to be often repeated. We require, therefore, a more convenient process, by which we may in a moment, produce in our imagination at pleasure, any one, or all such similar arrangements.

What is the meaning of imagining or conceiving a scale?

Perceiving which degrees in it are to be raised or depressed; for the seven degrees belong in common to all the scales.

Here then is a more expeditious procedure:—

(A)   MAJOR SCALES.

C major is the normal major scale which requires neither elevation nor depression, since it contains nothing but the seven original *tones*,—

$$C—D—E—F—G—A—B$$

We begin, therefore, with C, place it as the beginning, and put a nought over it, as a sign that in it, nothing is to be either raised or depressed. Then we write after C, the fifth degree from it, in ascending, G, and each succeeding fifth degree upwards, until we come again to C. Lastly, we mark out of the line, the fifth degree before C, thus:—

F. 0
C G D A E B F C

Now, we find that in each successive scale afterwards, one *tone* becomes raised and remains so, for the rest, which follow. In G major, therefore, *one tone* is raised, and remains so throughout; in D major the one elevation continues, and another is added; in A major two remain, and a third is added, &c. Here for example:—

F. 0 1 2 3 4 5 6 7$\sharp$
C G D A E B F C

we have marked over each scale how many degrees are raised in it.

But hitherto we do not know which degree is raised. Each time the second preceding is raised; therefore, in G major, the F degree from F becomes F$\sharp$.

We will mark this by the following sign:—

F. 0 1
C G D A E, and so forth,

therefore in D major the C degree from C becomes C$\sharp$.

F. 0 1 2
C G D A, &c.

But at the same time, the former elevation remains, consequently there are in D major, f and c, raised into $f\sharp$ and $c\sharp$.

Now, we must follow our succession of *tones*, in order to see what raisings we want for every tone. G major had F$\sharp$; D major, F$\sharp$ and C$\sharp$; consequently

A major will have F$\sharp$, C$\sharp$ and G$\sharp$
E major   „   „   „ and D$\sharp$
B major   „   „   „   „ and A$\sharp$, &c.

But we will go beyond C$\sharp$, and get to G$\sharp$ with eight,† D$\sharp$ with nine, A$\sharp$ with ten, E$\sharp$ with eleven, and B$\sharp$

† Here we must wonder whither we are to go with our eight elevations, since we have only seven degrees, all of which have been raised in C$\sharp$ major.

49.

Which degree did we raise last? B. Which must be now raised? According to the order F.—But that is already become F$\sharp$, it has already been raised once—consequently it must be raised *again*,—it must have two sharps instead of one only:—

50.

D$\sharp$ major will therefore have two double sharps (besides the continuing five single sharps) before F and C; A$\sharp$ three double sharps (besides the continuing four single sharps) F, C and G, &c.; but we shall soon see that we do not want these scales.

---

* This operation must become familiar to every person who wishes to be, in any degree, fundamentally instructed. But we urgently recommend to the beginner *for the first cultivation of the ear and the imagination*, to play diligently C major, and then the other major scales—and lastly to seek out the minor scales, *by the ear only*, with a pianoforte. If he thinks he has found a scale correctly, let him name the *tones*, taking the names from the next following degrees—thus, for example, not calling the second tone in A$\flat$ major from a, $a\sharp$, but $b\flat$, since the degree of a is already occupied. Then let him measure the distance of his steps and prove the correctness of his discovery. He may begin this exercise with the more convenient tones G, D, A, E, F, B$\flat$, E$\flat$, A$\flat$, but he must work with diligence. The time dedicated to this object will greatly profit musical conception; more by far than simple intellectual comprehension of what we have said above, or mere learning by rote, with which alone many teachers content themselves.

with twelve raisings. But b♯ is enharmonically the same as C.

We are now, therefore, returned through all the twelve major scales, to the first C again; and by steps of fifths only. This representation of the scales, is called the

CIRCLE OF FIFTHS.

But we know that scales may be also produced by depressed degrees. We formed in that manner A♭ major, page 20. What are the contents of these scales? Depressing is the opposite of raising. Consequently the *contrary operation* will give us the scales with depressed degrees. We write, therefore, the circle of fifths towards the left hand, in contrary order, C—F—B, &c. and know that in C major there is no depression; in F major, *one* degree will be depressed; in the next scale, two degrees, and so forth. We remember also, that (as formerly in the raising) every depression will be continued for the following scale. Here is our new plan,—

```
       ♭
F  7 6 5 4 3 2 1 0
   C G D A E B F C
```

But how do we find which degree is to be each time lowered? Each time that which is to the left in the plan.* Therefore, in F major, b is lowered to b♭. Now, we see immediately, that the next scale cannot be B, but B♭ major. In B♭ major, in the first place, b♭ is retained, and e depressed to e♭; consequently, the following scale is not E major but E♭ major. While we proceed in this manner, our former plan assumes this form—

```
                ♭
F  7  6  5  4  3  2  1  0
   C  G  D  A  E  B  F  C
   C♭ G♭ D♭ A♭ E♭ B♭
```

We see, therefore, that in E♭ major there appear *three* depressed degrees, b♭, e♭ and a♭; in D♭, *five*, b♭, e♭, a♭, d♭, g♭; in C♭, *seven*, b♭, e♭, a♭, d♭, g♭, c♭ and f♭.

If we would proceed further, we should find after C♭ major, F♭ major with *eight*; B♭♭ major with *nine*; E♭♭ with *ten*; A♭♭ with *eleven*; and D♭♭ with *twelve* depressions. But D♭♭ is enharmonically the same as C major, consequently we have here also completed the circuit of the chain of fifths, and returned to its beginning. By these plans, by the circle of fifths with elevations, and that with depres-

* This seems arbitrary and not in agreement with the supposition that in the depression the contrary effect occurs to what takes place in the elevation. But this *seems* only; because for the sake of brevity, we did not pursue the circle of fifths to the end: if we were to continue it from page 20, we should find

```
   5  6   7   8   9   10  11  12
   b  f♯  c♯  g♯  d♯  a♯  e♯  b♯
```

that (according to the first sign) the raisings for E♯ would reach to D×, (that is to say, d became d♯ already in E major, and is now raised again in E♯ major) and the succession of tones for E♯ is—

```
   e♯, f×, g×, a♯, b♯, c×, d×, e♯.
```

In B♯ major, the twelfth raising appears and points according to the second sign) to a♯ which therefore becomes a×.

If it be desired to change back B♯ major to E♯ major, the last elevation a× must revert to a♯ and therefore a× be lowered; then we have again the above succession E♯. The depression has therefore fallen on the *tone* to the left before E♯, the scale which we sought.

Now, B♯ major is nothing but C major, E♯ major nothing but F major; a× is enharmonically the same as b, and a♯ as b♭. As, in order to form E♯ major from B♯, we were obliged to depress a × into a♯, so in order to form F major from C major, we must depress b into b♭; and that is what we did above.

sions, we are in a condition to point out immediately and surely, any major scale, at pleasure. It is very easy to form the scales, which have few elevations or depressions,—more tedious naturally to arrange those which have many.† But here we meet, most joyfully, the reflection that the scales with so many changes are quite superfluous.

Let us place here for example:—

```
 0    1    2    3    4    5    6    7    8    9   10   11   12
 C    G    D    A    E    B    F♯   C♯   G♯   D♯   A♯   E♯   B♯
 D♭♭  A♭♭  E♭♭  B♭♭  F♭   C♭   G♭   D♭   A♭   E♭   B♭   F    C
 12   11   10   9    8    7    6    5    4    3    2    1    0
```

Comparing the above scales, with sharps, together with those with flats, we find—

D♭♭ with 12 depressions is the same as C major without change
A♭♭ ,, 11 ,, ,, ,, G ,, with 1 raising
E♭♭ ,, 10 ,, ,, ,, D ,, ,, 2 ,,
B♭♭ ,,   9 ,, ,, ,, A ,, ,, 3 ,,
F♭   ,,   8 ,, ,, ,, E ,, ,, 4 ,,
C♭   ,,   7 ,, ,, ,, B ,, ,, 5 ,,

that in like manner :—

B♯ with 12 sharps is the same as C major without change
E♯ ,, 11 ,, ,, ,, F ,, with 1 flat
A♯ ,, 10 ,, ,, ,, B♭ ,, ,, 2 ,,
D♯ ,,   9 ,, ,, ,, E♭ ,, ,, 3 ,,
G♯ ,,   8 ,, ,, ,, A♭ ,, ,, 4 ,,
C♯ ,,   7 ,, ,, ,, D♭ ,, ,, 5 ,,

for all the scales, here placed against each other, are only enharmonic changes of name; which are, therefore, also called

ENHARMONIC SCALES.

Who would trouble himself with twelve, or ten, or seven changes in D♭♭ or B♯, E♭♭ or A♯, C♭ or C♯, when he finds the same scales, without any change, or with only two or five changes.‡ We shall therefore, *in general*, make no use of those scales which have seven or more changes. The greatest indispensable number of changes is *six*; that is, six sharps in F♯ major, and as many flats in G♭ major; which scales are also enharmonically

† Mr. Logier's method of exemplifying to and impressing on a number of pupils the collective scales, is very ingenious. He turns towards them his left hand, open; calls the arm (the trunk of the hand) C, and this, the trunk scale; the thumb G, the first finger D, the second A, the third E, and the fourth B.—The index finger of the right hand F. The Trunk exhibits no sign. The next *tone* G receives a sharp. Here the right index finger is raised and therefore indicates F. The following *tone* D receives a second sharp, C. Here the Trunk (the arm) is referred to. The next following *tone*, A, receives a third sharp, G. Here the left thumb is pointed out, and so forth. On the other hand, F receives its flat from the foresaid little finger, which represents B, and so forth.

The name, circle of fifths, may indeed be considered more appropriate to a method which conveys us round through all the scales back again to the point whence we started. I will not omit that some have preferred the scales to be represented in the form of a circle, somewhat in this way—

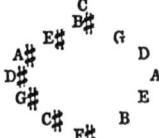

and to exemplify with this figure what we have detailed in the text.

‡ In order to fix deeper the recollection of the number of changes required in any scale, let it be remarked that the changes of two enharmonic scales amount constantly, when added together, *to twelve*. For example, B♯ or D♭♭ has each twelve changes, while C has none; E♭♭ has ten and D two; D♯ has nine and E♭ three. If, therefore, the number of changes in one scale be known, the number for the other is manifest.—Deduct the known from 12. Thus G Major has one, consequently A♭♭ must have eleven.

the same. Only in particular and rare cases, will there be reasonable occasion for a step beyond; excepting perhaps, to C♯ major, with seven sharps, or C♭ major, with as many flats. This latter procedure is especially advisable, if we have been beforehand in a scale with many sharps or flats, and desire to pass to another with the same kind of changes. If we had been, for example, in B or in F♯ major, and wished to pass to C♯ or D♭ major, it would be manifestly more eligible to add two or one to the five or six sharps already present, than to remove these latter by so many naturals, and then replace them with five flats. In the first manner one or two signs would be wanted; in the latter ten or eleven. This will become more clearly seen in the following section.

(B)   THE MINOR SCALES.

No further instruction is necessary for the formation of the minor scales. Every minor scale is formed from its major (beginning on the same *tone*), by lowering its third and sixth, as we have already shewn (page 19) in the example C minor from C major.

NINTH SECTION—NEARER VIEW OF THE SCALES.

(A)   THE SIGNATURE.

1. THE MAJOR SCALES.

We have seen in the last section, that in all major scales, with the exception of C major, more or less sharps or flats occur: these are signified by their sign and number at the beginning of every piece of music, or more properly of every line, immediately after the clef, and are called the *signature*. Here we see—

all the signatures of the most usual scales. Let it be remarked that the sharps and flats make their appearance in the same succession, as we found them in the circle of fifths (page 21): first, F♯ and then C♯; or first, B♭ then E♭, &c.

The signature influences not only the octave where it may chance to be written, but all the degrees which it concerns, in whatever octave they may be. In G major, for example, not only the two-lined *f,* but every *f* wherever it may be, is converted into *f♯*.

If, however, the effect of the signature is to be suspended for a time,—if, for example, in G major, *f♯* be desired not to be used, but *f* instead of it, a natural is placed before the note; and here we see this sign (♮), for the first time practically applied.

51.

In this passage, for example, the three first *f*'s are considered as *f♯*, by virtue of the signature; but the fourth is considered really as *f*, by virtue of the natural which is placed before it, and not as *f♯*. So also, if a piece of music is to leave its scale, the signature of that scale must be contradicted, and the signature of the new scale inserted. This may be done in the course of the music and in the middle of the line of notes. Here for example—

52.

we see the signature of D major, and some notes which seem to be the close of a passage in D major. Now, the movement is to proceed in B♭ major; the sharps then of D major are contradicted, and the two flats of B♭ major are inserted.

Sometimes a partial contradiction alone is required: that is, if from a scale with many sharps we pass to one with fewer sharps, or from a scale with many flats to one with less. In this case, contradicting the superfluous signs is sufficient; as for example at (*a*), where a transition is made from B major—

53.

to D major. But for the sake of clearness, we add, as in (*b*), those signs whose effect is to continue; in order that the player may not imagine, at the appearance of so many naturals, that the whole signature is contradicted.

A similar proceeding is adopted if it be required to pass from a scale with few flats or sharps to one which has many: from D major or B♭ major, with two sharps or flats, to E or A♭ major, with four changes each. In this case, it would be sufficient, strictly speaking, to inscribe the two new signs, for example:—

54.

But it is more clear, and therefore customary, to insert the whole signature, thus:—

55.

Such a change of signature is, however, only used when it is intended that the new scale shall last a considerable time. But on a merely momentary occasion, the original signature is allowed to continue, and any note that requires alteration, is changed by the immediate application to it, of a sharp, flat, or natural, as may be necessary. Let us imagine this passage,—

56.

to be part of a longer movement in D major. Now, we see at (*a*) the *tone* C, which in D major does not exist. But at (*b*) we meet C♯ again. We have not left D major for a long period, and therefore do not change the signature: we only give the C note a natural, and the next time it appears, a sharp again. Such is the case also at (*c*) and (*d*,) where we make B♭ from B, and again turn B♭ into B.

2. The Minor Scales or Keys.

One peculiar law determines the signature of the minor scales. They are not signatured as their *place in the succession of* TONES *would require, but*

Every minor scale has the signature of the major scale, which is situated a minor third above it.*

Therefore, A minor is not, as one might expect (consisting of *a—b—c—d—e—f—g♯*), signatured with a sharp before *g*, neither is D minor (*d—e—f—g—a—b♭—c♯*), signatured with a *c♯* or a *b♭*: but A minor has the signature of C, that is, none at all, and D minor that of F major: for C lies a minor third over A, and F a minor third above D. Here we see—

the signatures of the most useful minor scales. The signature of E minor is the same as that of G major, D minor as that of F major, B minor as that of D major, and so forth.

Two scales (one major and the other minor), which have the same signature, are called—

Relative Scales.

The relative major of a minor key lies, as we have seen, *a minor third higher*: therefore the relative minor of every major scale lies a minor third lower than its relative major. The relative minor of A♭ major, for example, was F minor; the relative minor of B major must be G♯ minor—of D♭ major, B♭ minor—and so forth. Thus we know how to find all the relative scales, and how to mark their signatures.

It is only now that we can recognise fully the object of the signature. First, that of shewing us which degrees in the composition are to be raised or depressed, and of sparing us a number of flats and sharps which otherwise would have to be inserted on the degrees in the course of the notation. Secondly, to serve as a

Sign of the Scale or Key

in which the composition is written. But we know already that each signature belongs in common to two scales (the relative keys), and does not distinguish which is meant. Here we can only refer to the instruction in Harmony and Modulation, in which we should find the proper indications to determine this point. In the interim, let it be observed, that *usually*

The Last Tone

of a piece of music, and, if it close with a harmony, *usually*

The Lowest Tone

of this harmony, in conjunction with the signature, determines the key distinctly. If, for example, the signature were two sharps, the key must be either D major or B minor. If, therefore, the last *tone*, or the lowest *tone* of the last harmony, were B, we should consider that, according to custom, the key to which the movement belonged was B minor.

But what is to be done for the degrees in compositions in a minor key, which degrees the signature does not affect? They each receive individually their proper sharp or flat in the course of the composition. So, for example, in D minor, the signature only makes B♭; but it contains also C♯. So often, then, as this latter note occurs, it is marked with a sharp.

Why this extraordinary manner of giving signatures to the minor scales which call them out of their proper names? We are certainly obliged to conform to it, because it is the general custom; but we cannot do so contentedly, unless we perceive a reasonable ground for the custom. At present, we shall allege only what follows.

In the first place, an exact signature for the minor scales would occasion many inconveniences. Two minor scales would require both flats and sharps; for example,—

D—*e—f—g—a—b♭—c♯—d*, . . . *c♯* and *b♭*,
G—*a—b♭—c—d—e♭—f♯—g*, . . *f♯, b♭*, and *e♭*,

whereby the accustomed and natural development visible in the signatures of the major mode, is abandoned. The others, for example,—

A—*b—c—d—e—f—g♯—a*, . . . *g♯*,
E—*f♯—g—a—b—c—d♯—e*, . . *f♯* and *d♯*,
C—*d—e♭—f—g—a♭—b—c*, . . . *e♭* and *a♭*,
F—*g—a♭—b♭—c—d♭—e—f*, . . *b♭, a♭*, and *d♭*,

would receive one, two, or more sharps and flats for signatures, as if they were quite unknown major keys. How many errors would creep in—how often would the signature of A minor be mistaken for that of G major, and that of F minor for that of E♭ major,—

A minor.   G major.   F minor.   E♭ major.

since in the major, the number alone, of the flats or sharps, decides of itself.† It would be necessary, therefore, to inspect and observe much more closely. This would, at the same time, be much more troublesome than in the major scales; for in these latter, the sharps and flats follow each other constantly in fifths,—after the sharp of F, those of C and G *must* follow, &c. Of the flats, that of B *must* be the first, and those of E and A *must* follow. This regular progression vastly facilitates the apprehension; and nothing of the kind is exhibited in the signatures of the minor scales.

---

* Let the learner distinguish well that each minor scale is *formed* from its major scale; that is, from the major scale which begins on the same tone as itself: but it takes its *signature not from its own said major scale*, but from the major scale which lies at the distance of a minor third higher in the scale than itself.

† Therefore it has been proposed to change in the minor signature those degrees, by naturals, which had been raised or depressed in the same tonic major, or the relative minor; for example, A minor and C minor to be marked thus:—

But setting aside that this principle would not apply throughout (D minor and G minor could not be so represented), it is contrary to good sense to apply a natural when previously no elevation nor depression has taken place.

In the second place, most compositions (especially those of considerable length, to which the signature is of most importance) do not remain in one key, but pass to others, and generally, indeed, to those most convenient to them—that is, which do not stray too far from the original key. A signature, therefore, which is favorable for the development of the nearest related scale, must have evidently the preference. Which scale, then, lies nearest to a minor scale,—its own major, or its relative key? The latter, since from this, the minor varies in only one degree, while from its own major it differs in two · thus, C minor, for example,

Major $C—d—e—f—g—a—b—c—d—e$,
Minor $C—d—e\flat—f—g—a\flat—b—c—d—e\flat$,
Major $E\flat—f—g—a\flat—b\flat—c—d—e\flat$,

differs from C major in two *tones* ($e\flat$ and $a\flat$), but from $E\flat$ major in only one.*

(*B*)   Chief Points of the Scale.

We have seen that a scale may be formed on every *tone*. This *tone* is the first, the foundation of all the *tones* in the scale which is grounded on and named after it. In this sense it is called peculiarly
The Tonic.
The fifth degree in each scale (the major fifth of the scale) is called
The Dominant,
the governing degree. We shall not understand fully, why it enjoys this name, until we have entered into the study of Harmony. We will merely point out now, that the dominant is the *tone* by which and to which we proceed step by step in the circle of fifths. From C, for example, to G, from G to D, G and D are the dominants. In the circle of fifths we go from C to G and from G to D.

But there is also a circle of fifths proceeding from depressions, which leads us step by step by a descending series; thus, from C to F, from F to B$\flat$. And in scales with sharps, this reverse method can be practised also; thus, from D to G and from G to C. Referring then again to the scale, we shall observe the *major* fifth *under* the tonic, and call it
The Subdominant.
In contradistinction to which, the dominant is sometimes called the
Superdominant.
We will further note two denominations, which, however, are of less importance. The third degree in each scale (the third of the tonic), is called the
Mediant.
We will for the moment say only, that it lies between the tonic and the dominant, and is the means of binding, as it were, or combining both these together. The manner of action in this union, and of what importance it is, will not be manifest until we come to the study of Harmony. In like manner, the third *under* the tonic, the medium of combination between it and the subdominant, is therefore called the
Submediant,
and in contradistinction to this, the mediant is called the
Supermediant.
Therefore, in C major, e is the mediant, and a the submediant; e is the medium between c and g, and a between f and c. In C minor, $e\flat$ is the mediant, and $a\flat$ the submediant: the first is the medium between c and g, the second between f and c.†

(*C*)   Relationship of the Scales.

If we return to the preceding section, in which we formed all the scales, after and with each other, we find indeed that every scale differs from the other, but some more and some less. If we compare, for example, C major with G major,—

$$c—d—e—f—g—a—b—c—d—e—f—g$$
$$g—a—b—c—d—e—f\sharp—g$$

we see they differ from each other in one *tone* only: C major has f, and G major $f\sharp$: all the other degrees they have in common. Let us compare on the other hand C major, suppose with E major,—

$$c—d—e—f—g—a—b—c—d—e$$
$$e—f\sharp—g\sharp—a—b—c\sharp—d\sharp—e$$

and we see that the two scales differ from each other in four degrees: C major has f, c, g, d, while E major has $f\sharp, c\sharp, g\sharp$ and $d\sharp$. Two scales which have several *tones* in common, are called
Related.
Now, we have just seen that this relationship may be nearer or more distant, according to the number of *tones* which the scales may have in common. There are, therefore, several
Degrees of Relationship.
In fine, we have ourselves found out *several ways* in which scales are mutually connected. We found the major scales linked together in the form of the circle of fifths, the minor scales with their relative keys and with their own major scales. There must be, therefore, *three kinds* of relationship:—

1. Relationship of the Major Scales.

Here the circle of fifths shews us the relationships, with their grades. The scales, lying immediately next adjoining to each other in the circle of fifths, differ from each other only in one *tone*; therefore they are in the *first degree* of relationship towards each other. We see here,—

$\flat$ $\sharp$
6 5 4 3 2 1 0 1 2 3 4 5 6
$G\flat$ $D\flat$ $A\flat$ $E\flat$ $B\flat$ F C G D A E B .$F\sharp$

the united circle of fifths of the sharp and flat scales (so far as we found them indispensable), and we perceive that each scale has its neighbour right and left, as its nearest relative next to itself. C major, for example, has for relative of the first degree, G major and F major: in like manner, E major has

---

* A third and more important reason, which determines a minor key to pass rather to its relative major than to its own (A minor rather to C major than to A major), belongs to the study of composition. It is, that its own major would be less effective in operation, because, whether in major or minor, the most important degrees (the tonic and dominant) and that busy harmony, (the chord of the dominant,) are common to both, while the relative key gives quite a new set.

† It is scarcely worth mentioning that all these names belong to each *tone, in one determined scale only;* and that one and the same *tone*, in *different scales*, bears quite a different character. For example, we called a, above, the *submediant*, that is, of C major: in F major it would be the *mediant;* in D the dominant; in E the subdominant; in A major or minor it would be the tonic.

for relatives of the first degree, B major and A major next to it. Which are the nearest relatives of G♭ major? On one side D♭ major, on the other C♭ major, in lieu of which we can set down B major;* and in the same way F♯ major is related on the one side to B major, and on the other to C♯ major (for which we can place D♮ major,) in the first degree.

Relatives of the second degree, are those, one step more distant from each other; for example, from D major on one side of C major to B♭ major on the other. In this manner we may when necessary ascertain all degrees of relationship.

2. RELATIONSHIP OF THE RELATIVE KEYS.

The relative scales are in the *first degree* of relationship, for they differ from each other only in one *tone*. So, therefore, C major and A minor, C minor and E♭ major, &c., are relatives in the first degree.

If we combine this manner of relationship with the previous one, a new species of relative connexion becomes manifest among the scales. We have found in the first place, that every major scale is related to both its neighbouring major keys in the first degree, and moreover with its relative scale in the same degree; for example, C major with G major, F major, and A minor. Now the major scales, G major and F major, are again related to *their* relative scales (E minor and D minor) in the first degree; consequently we may consider these minor scales as *relatives* in the *second degree* of the first major scale, C major. This figure shews it :—

C major.

F major. A minor. G major.   Relatives of the 1st degree.

D minor.   E minor.   „   „   2nd degree.

But we can extend this line of affinities, thus :—

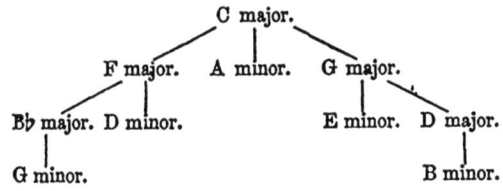

Here we have a table of affinities of the *first* degree, as G major, F major, and A minor ; of the *second* degree, as D major, E minor, B♭ major and D minor ; of the *third* degree, as B minor and G minor. But it is not necessary for us to follow these affinities so far, still less, farther.

3. RELATIONSHIP OF THE MINOR SCALES WITH THEIR MAJOR SCALES, AND AMONG THEMSELVES.

We have already learned (page 24) that every minor scale differs from its own scale in *two degrees*, the third and sixth. Hence we should consider them as related in the *second degree*.

But a particular circumstance intervenes, to draw the bonds of union closer. This is, that major and minor have in common, the most important part of every scale; the

TONIC, DOMINANT, AND SUBDOMINANT,

and this (as we shall see in the study of Harmony) is so influential, that we are obliged to consider them as related in the first degree.

And so we do consider the minor scales among themselves, which stand towards each other in the relationship of tonic and dominant or subdominant, as nearest related, by virtue of the internal affinity of the tonic, dominant, and subdominant. So A minor avails us as next related to E minor and D minor, although it differs from them not in one point only, but even in three ; as we here shew :—

D—e—f—g—a—b♭—c♯—d—e—f—g—a
a—b—c—d—e—f—g♯—a—b—c—d—e
e—f♯—g—a—b—c—d♯—e

If these relationships be combined with the two underneath, a table may be made for minor relationships of the first and second degree, as before shewn, for the major, thus :—

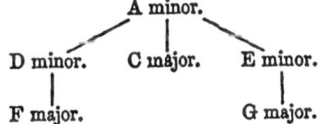

APPENDIX—OF ECCLESIASTICAL MODES.

In the preceding sections we have represented the modes and scales as they are now used in our system of music.

But this system has not long been the most general. In the sixteenth and seventeenth centuries, a system entirely different was universally prevalent, which we call the

SYSTEM OF ECCLESIASTICAL MODES,

or Church Scales. According to the fashion of those days, it was assumed to be (and by preference), the system of Greek scales. The scales were *Greek* and were called by the names of the ancient Greek scales, although they had nothing else in common with, nor other resemblance to, them, than their names.

This system has five or six different scales :—

   The Ionic .... c—d—e—f—g—a—b—c
   Doric .... d—e—f—g—a—b—c—d
   Phrygian .. e—f—g a—b—c—d—e
   Lydian (which, however, was never firmly established) .. f—g—a—b—c—d—e—f
   Mixolydian. g—a—b—c—d—e—f—g
   Æolian ... a.- b—c—d—e—f—g—a

of which only one, as may be seen, is exactly similar to our major scale, and (we may say in passing) to our succession of degrees. Two others, the Mixolydian and Lydian, resemble our major, but differ in having, the former a minor seventh and the latter an extreme fourth, while our major scales have major

---

* While the student is mastering the above open and broad relationships, we must not omit remarking for the benefit of those more deeply versed in music, that in the region of the scales, there lie many quite different, we might almost say *sympathetic* interweavings. They exist, for example, in the scales now under consideration, whose tonics lie at the distance of a third from each other, such as C major with A minor, and A♭ major, with E minor, and E♭ major, &c. Simply from the outward point of view it is certain that B major (instead of C♭) and C♯ (instead of D♭) must be called the nearest relatives to G♭ major. This point of view suffices for early tuition. A precocious knowledge of deeper matters would remain fruitless, or only create a fantastic juggle of ideas.

sevenths and fourths. The other three scales are somewhat similar to our minor; but the Doric has a major sixth and a minor seventh, the Æolian a minor sixth and seventh, and the Phrygian a minor second.

From these scales the ancients were enabled to form collateral scales a fifth higher or a fourth lower, arranged exactly in conformity with the originals, and named after them, with the prefix of "*Hypo.*" Thus the collateral scale of the Ionic was called the *Hypoionic* scale,—

g—a—b—c—d—e—f♯—g

the collateral scale of the Doric was called *Hypodoric*,

a—b—c—d—e—f♯—g—a

and so of the rest.

These scales could also be formed on other degrees; for example, the Æolic on G,—

g—a—b♭—c—d—e♭—f—g

and in fine, it was allowed to employ foreign scales also under certain relationships. Besides the *tones* c, d, e, f, g, a and b, there were also present b♭ and e♭, f♯, c♯ and g♯. The tuning, however, of the whole system of *tones* was different from ours and in such a manner, that f♯, c♯ and g♯, could not be used as g♭, d♭ or a♭, nor could b♭ and e♭ be employed as a♯ or d♯.* This old system, differing from ours, more especially in its principles of modulation, is not merely a matter of historical record; but in its application in our days, particularly to Church music, it is become a matter of peculiar interest. For we possess abundance of Church chants (and they are our best), which were composed under the dominion of the old system, and cannot be well and surely performed without a knowledge of it. But intimate acquaintance with this branch, belongs to the study of composition,† where it enters into immediate operation. Here we must limit the (we confess) very superficial account we have given of this matter. We will merely add, as perhaps a slight insight, the most eligible kind of closing cadence for each of the Ecclesiastical Modes, which may in some measure serve to give a feeble conception of them,—

57.

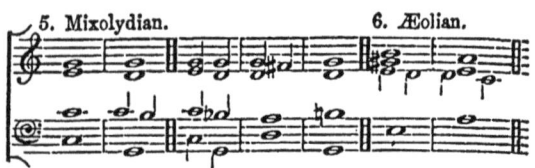

and which can be compared with the modern cadence given at No. 7 in the 7th Section of the 4th Division.

SECOND DIVISION.

FIRST SECTION—THE VALUE OF TONES.

We have already said in the introduction, that every *tone* must have some duration, longer or shorter; and that the time given or ascribed to any *tone* is called its value.

The value of a *tone* is that duration of time allowed to it, relatively to the amount or quantity of time allowed to other *tones*, It is not absolute time, that is attributed to any *tone* (so that *this tone* is to last so many seconds, while *that* is to last such another number of seconds), but a certain proportion of time when compared with other *tones*: that is, one *tone* shall last twice, thrice, or more times as long as another, or *vice versa*, shall last one half, one third or a still smaller portion of the duration of another.

The most simple division is by the number two. With that, we will begin.

(*A*)   Value.

By division by two.

We begin with a duration which we call a
SEMIBREVE.
The semibreve shall last as long as two others together, which we will call
MINIMS.
The minim is divided into two
CROTCHETS.
The crotchet into two
QUAVERS.
The quaver into two
SEMIQUAVERS.
The semiquaver into two
DEMISEMIQUAVERS.
The demisemiquaver into two
SEMIDEMISEMIQUAVERS.
The semidemisemiquaver into two
DEMISEMIDEMISEMIQUAVERS.

We have here divided a unit of duration, successively by two into smaller durations.

It follows thence,—

that a semibreve has four crotchets, eight quavers, &c.
that a minim has four quavers, eight semiquavers.
that a crotchet has four semiquavers, eight demisemiquavers.

How do we mark the duration in notes? By the shape of the note itself.

---

* No temperament was then admitted in the tuning (Obs: page 7) as with us—b♭ and e♭ were too deep for a♯ and d♯; and f♯, c♯, and g♯ were too high for g♭, d♭, and a♭. The difference between greater and lesser semitones was, with them, real (Note, page 16).

† The necessary instruction on this subject is in Part I. of Instructions for Composition.

A semibreve is signified by an *empty* circle (or oval) 𝅗𝅥
A minim   „   „   with a line (tail) 𝅗𝅥
A crotchet   „   a *filled* circle and line (tail) ♩
A quaver   „   „   and additional } ♪
                                          short line }
A semiquaver   „   „   two   „   ♬
A demisemiquaver „   „   three „
A semidemisemiquaver „   „   four   „
A demisemidemisemiquaver „   „   five   „

𝅝 has two minims or four crotchets.

𝅗𝅥 has two crotchets.

If many notes with the small lines occur together, they may be written in groups, thus:—

58.

with what are called

LINES OF DURATION (*Geltungstriche.*)*

Whether the two lines be upwards or downwards, on the right or left of the note, is immaterial. It is usual, however, to write the longer line of the deep notes upwards and opposite the right hand, and that of the higher notes downwards and opposite the left hand; and to draw the lines of duration from the left towards the right. Here,—

we see once again all the values produced by the division by two. Only one crotchet, however, is completely carried out. We see here, that

1 Semidemisemiquaver has 2 Demisemidemisemiquavers,
1 Demisemiquaver . . . 2 Semidemisemiquavers,
                       4 Demisemidemisemiquavers,
1 Semiquaver . . . . . 2 Demisemiquavers,
                       4 Semidemisemiquavers,
                       8 Demisemidemisemiquavers,
                       and so forth.

But what if we have *tones* to note of longer duration than a semibreve? For this object we have three expedients.

In the *first place* we find that formerly, notes of longer duration were used. In the period of *measurable music*,† when value and division into bars were first reduced to order, notes of the following form were in use:—

▬▬ Maxima or duplex longa,
▬ Longa,
▭ Brevis,
◊ Semibrevis,
𝆹 Minima,

From the Minima is derived our minim, as may be guessed at once; from the Semibrevis our semibreve. Therefore we may use the

Brevis, ▭

which has with us the value of

TWO SEMIBREVES.

The longer notes are not used in modern music.

Secondly, when we want to lengthen a note in a manner not feasible by the preceding system, we use the

BIND.

This is done by repeating the note until we make up the amount of value which we desire, and then binding them together by a sign in the curve of a bow, which indicates that the notes are not to be considered as separate, but as one note, whose value is equal to the sum of the values of all the notes so bound. If we wished, for example, a sound to continue during the value of four semibreves, we should write thus:—

𝅝‿𝅝‿𝅝‿𝅝

if it should last the time of seven or five crotchets,

---

* I have attempted here—and elsewhere—to give a descriptive English name for a German compound word; there being, as I believe, no exact equivalent single word in English for the German. The liberty allowed to every one in Germany of composing what words they please or may judge convenient, renders literal translation from the German, at times, very difficult, if not impossible, without |circumlocution or descriptive invention. It must, however, be conceded to Dr. Marx, that his explanations are so strikingly plain and minutely exact, that it matters not what name you put at the head of a section or paragraph: you see the object before you, call it what you will. A rare talent, this; far beyond the choice of a name. If I am not so perspicuous in English, the fault is mine—the Doctor is broad daylight.—TRANSLATOR.

† A nearer insight into this matter is given in the *Universal Lexicon, der Tonkunst*. We have said sufficient for this place. The name, *measurable music* (*musica mensurabilis* or *mensurata*) signifies music brought into measurable condition, which originated from the *longs* and *shorts* of the words in church music. The first teacher of this method, whose name has descended to us, was Frank, of Cologne, until the sixteenth and seventeenth centuries, when the old system of notation or measurable method, was superseded by the present system of bars. The music contradistinguished from the *musica mensurata*, was the *musica plana*, or the *cantus planus*, the church song, which proceeded chiefly by one or two notes. The *measured* theory was, however, extremely intricate and unpractical.

it should be written so,—

consequently, the following should last the time of—

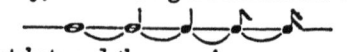

seven crotchets and three semiquavers.

It is manifest that in this manner any desired value of notes may be expressed.

Thirdly, by means of

Dots

after the notes, we express that the proper value of a note is increased by its half. For example, a semibreve is equal to two minims; with a dot—

it would be of the value of three minims. A quaver is equal to two semiquavers; with a dot—

it is equal to three semiquavers.

If to such a dot we add another, and make it, as it is called, a

Double Dot,

the second dot is equal to half the first, and lengthens to that extent, the value of the *tone*. A crotchet, with two dots—

is equal to a crotchet, a quaver and a semiquaver; a minim—to seven quavers.

We might also employ a third dot, as for example here at *a*:—

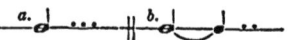

in order to produce a value of three crotchets and three semiquavers; but this accumulation of small signs would, occasion mistakes, and be difficult to recognise: it would be better to write another note (as at *b*), and two dots only. But in some cases the first manner of writing may seem preferable.

(B) Value.

By division by three.

After the representation of division by two, we are led to expect from the division by three, that a semibreve would be divided into three thirds, a third into three ninths, and so forth: and that for these thirds and ninths a peculiarly formed note would be introduced. This, however, is not the case, as it would have encumbered our measurement with a perplexing mass of names and signs. The division by three, however, has not been left unaccomplished.

If it be desired to signify a third of a unit, we use the same names and signs as in the division by two; but with the understanding that, not two, but three of the parts. shall be valued as one.

A group of the three notes which are to have the value of two, is called a

Triplet,

and the three notes are marked with a bow and a 3 under it.* Here,—

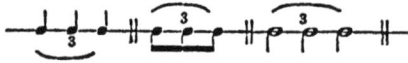

* This sign is often underneath, and then the proper value must be estimated from the circumstances—of which more hereafter.

we see triplets of crotchets, of quavers, and of minims; three crotchets in the triplet are equal to two crotchets or one minim; three quavers are equal to one crotchet; three minims to one semibreve. Two of the parts of a triplet may be united by a bind,—

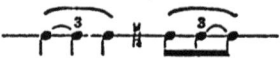

or a note equal to them may be used instead. Here a triplet of crotchets is the equivalent of a minim, and a triplet of quavers is the equivalent of a crotchet. This is equally represented thus:—

where instead of the two triplet-crotchets and two triplet-quavers, we use a triplet-minim and a triplet-crotchet.

Now we have acquired a knowledge of quite a different order of divisions. We can now divide a semibreve into three minims, a minim into three crotchets, a crotchet into three quavers, and so forth.

and so forth.

Hence arises a derivative form of notes.

If we draw together *two triplets*, for example, two triplets of crotchets equal to two minims, or two triplets of quavers equal to two crotchets,—

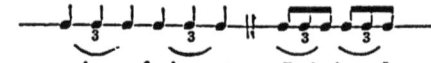

a group arises of six notes. It is in value a semibreve divided into six crotchets, and a minim divided into six quavers. Such a group is called a

Sextriplet.

As we shall find further on, a similar although internally different group of notes, under the same name, it might be desirable to call the sextriplet formed from two triplets, by some other name; suppose

Double Triplet,

and give it a different representation, say—

and to give the name of sextuplet to the following arrangement,—

Custom, however, has in the meantime decided otherwise. The name of sextriplet is used for both the representations, and most frequently for that which we wished to call double triplet, as the other form in reality much more rarely appears.

Accordingly, we can now use the division by two and three, in

(C) Groups of Mixed Value.

We may begin in the division by two, and proceed

in that by three. Here for example:—

We have a crotchet divided into *two* quavers, but each quaver divided into three semiquavers (triplet-semiquavers). The result is a couple of triplets, a double triplet, or according to the above method of naming, a sextriplet. Here,—

we have a crotchet solved into a triplet of quavers, but then, each triplet-quaver into two semiquavers. We have, therefore, again a group of six notes, a sextriplet (and this is the forementioned second kind of sextuplet), but differently derived. Further on (in the 10th section of this division), we shall see, that the derivation has an influence on its nature, and distinguishes the last from the first.

Hitherto we have been occupied with the dual and triform values; and moreover with the development of groups of crotchets and quavers (for instance, four quavers to a minim, and eight quavers to a semibreve), and in the explanation of the other groups of six notes, that is the so-called sextriplet or double triplet, and both kinds mingled together. Now, let us proceed to—

(*D*) MORE NUMEROUS GROUPS.

We divide a note into *five* instead of *four* parts: for example, a minim into five quavers, a crotchet into five semiquavers; whereby the notes, quavers and semiquavers, again lose their proper or legitimate values. Thus these,—

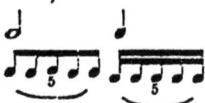

taken collectively have only the original value of four.
Such a group is called
A QUINTUPLET.
In like manner is formed
A SEPTUPLET.

In which there are *seven* parts instead of *four*—or also instead of *six*.* Or the
NONUPLET,

* If it were desired to place seven quavers instead of six in a six-eight bar $\frac{6}{8}$ (what to understand by this will be explained further on) this would be a septuplet, in which seven would not be instead of four, but of six.

which has nine parts instead of eight—or six. And the
DECUPLET,

in which ten parts appear in lieu of eight or four; and so any value may be divided at pleasure into eleven, thirteen, &c. For example, here,—

59.

is a crotchet in *fifteen* parts instead of *four* or *eight*, and the cypher placed over it is sufficient for universal intelligence, without any rigorous† inquiry into the number of the lines of duration: everywhere the same value is attributed to the notes alone, without regard to their derivation.

A more distinct recognition of similar groups, which are, however, not of frequent occurrence, will be obtained from the study of the formation of bars, and its distributive arrangements.

SECOND SECTION.—OF RESTS.

We have now determined the duration of the *tones*, and also how to regulate the succession of time for whole ranges of *tones*. For the latter case we have presupposed that one *tone* immediately follows another without any intervention of time. But the contrary is possible; that between the end of one *tone* and the beginning of another, some time may intervene, may pass without sound. These moments of silence, called
RESTS,
are determined in the same manner as the values of the *tones*, by particular signs, which are likewise called rests.

Here is a specification of the Rests:—

1. ═ The semibreve rest, (corresponding with the semibreve; therefore equal to two minims, or four crotchets,)—a line *under* one of the lines of the staff.
2. ═ Minim rest, equal to two crotchets, a line lying *on* one of the lines of the staff.‡
3. ⌐ the rest of a crotchet,
4. ⌐ „ „ quaver,
5. ⌐ „ „ semiquaver,
6. ⌐ „ „ demisemiquaver,
7. ⌐ „ „ semidemisemiquaver,
8. ⌐ „ „ demisemidemisemiquaver

† It is usual to write from the next preceding subdivision—for example, nonuplets, from the next preceding subdivision of *eight* notes: therefore a nonuplet of a minim with semiquavers, a nonuplet of a crotchet with demisemiquavers. Others content themselves with dashing the group together with a single or double line of duration. J. Haydn wrote so in the introduction to the *Creation* (page 5 of the score) that genial volley of clarinets of 15 notes on a minim, with quavers:—

60.

‡ It is of no consequence on which line these rests are placed. Indeed, if two or more successions of tones are written upon one staff, and a rest be necessary in one of the successions in a position where there is not

The forms of the five last are distinguished as the notes by the number of the little additional lines.

All these rests may be increased in value or duration by dots and double dots, in the same manner as the notes.

For longer rests, which are more particularly required for single parts in compositions in parts, we have the following signs:—

1. ━━ A rest of two semibreves.
2. ━━ „ four „
3. ━━ „ six „
4. ━━ „ eight „

With a combination of these rests it is clear, that any given quantity of relatively determined time may be expressed. Here, for example,—

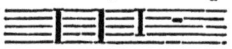

we see rests of 8, 8, 6, and 1; therefore, all together twenty-three semibreve rests. It is customary, also, to mark long pauses by a still easier method. Instead of using the above measure, cross dashes are made on the staff, and the required number of bars rest written in ciphers over them, thus,—

for the above rest.

If a note be divided into smaller portions, it is clear that some of these portions may be occupied by rests, others by other notes. Here, for example,—

are three crotchets, of which the
1st is solved into a quaver and a quaver rest
2nd „ „ triplet quaver, a quaver rest, and a quaver
3rd „ „ crotchet rest and triplet quaver
similar solutions and combinations of notes and rests, any one may unravel or construct.

THIRD SECTION.—INDEFINITE SIGNS OF DURATION.

In the preceding sections we have become acquainted with notes and rests of determinate value and relationship in time, towards each other. There remain now, some cases to mention, in which the exact measure is more or less, either abbreviated or extended.

1. STACCATO.

When single *tones* or successions of *tones* are to last a shorter time than would be their due, according to the value of the notation, they are marked *staccato* (detached), or with little thin lines, thus;—

62.

or, if they are not to be made so short, with dots against or over the notes, thus :—

63.

How much shorter notes so marked should be, is not determined. The foregoing, with dots, may be, perhaps, as quavers equal to *three* demisemiquavers instead of *four*, those with little lines, still shorter, perhaps equal to only one semiquaver, thus :—

Written,
64.
Played,

while the remainder of the value is occupied in momentary rests after each note. If a still shorter duration is desired for each note, the staccato and rests may be used in conjunction, thus :—

65.

or *staccatissimo* may be written over the passage.

2. LEGATO.

If in any passage, every sound is to be held on, or continued until the immediate commencement of the following sound, or longer if possible, so that the two sounds may melt as it were into each other, *Legato* (bound) is placed over the notes, or *Legato assai* (very bound), or *Legatissimo* (bound in the utmost degree); or in lieu of these, a bind is placed over them with the same effect, thus :—

66.

Here, therefore, the value of each separate *tone* is secured against any diminution, or even extended into the time of the next *tone*.

If any particular *tone* is to endure quite its full time, or rather more, it is marked

Tenuto (ten.) or *Ben tenuto*—held on, sustained fully. Of late it has become customary, particularly when several notes after each other are to be played *tenuto*, to place a little dash over every such note. So here,—

67.

the three last crotchets must be allowed their full time, and perhaps a little more.

When the time or value is unappreciably taken from or added to the notes, such a passage is marked

Tempo rubato (stolen time), or also, *a piacere, ad libitum*, at the will of the performer. If in any principal part (such, for example, as the voice in a song), an *ad libitum*, or *a piacere*, should occur, the accompanying parts must govern themselves by it;

convenient room for it, a little ledger line is drawn, simply to put the rest on or under it. Here, for example, we see a semibreve rest for the lower part, then a crotchet and a minim rest for the upper part:—

61.

and that is indicated to them on the staves of their respective notations by the words—

Colla parte (*c. p.*) (meaning) with the principal part. If the value is to be entirely voluntary, the words—

Senza tempo, or *Senza ritmo*—without determined measure—are written.

All these optional directions are withdrawn by the words—

A tempo, al rigore del tempo—according to determined or strict time.

If, in fine, the value of a note or of a rest is to be considerably, but indefinitely, prolonged, a bow with a dot is written over it, thus:—

68.

and is called a pause.

It has been proposed, that this sign should have the effect of doubling the value of whatever may be under it—but this estimation is not admissible: it must in each individual case be regulated by the nature of the passage.

We will add in conclusion, that a rest which runs through all the parts of a composition, a general rest, together with a pause occurring at the same moment in all the parts, is called

A CLOSE.

FOURTH SECTION.—OF TIME. ABSOLUTE.

All the foregoing varieties of duration gave the notes and rests merely a relative value. They determined that a crotchet should be equal to two quavers, or half as much as a minim; and this, again, half as much as a semibreve. But how long any one of them—that is, how many seconds for example, or what part of a second, a semibreve should last, *that* the valuation does not determine.

Now it is clear, that in some compositions a lively quick motion would be appropriate; while in others, the sentiment would require the time to be slow, lingering, and solemn. Joyful, excited sensations, animate and hasten all our motions, and, therefore, our voices: sad and dejected feelings, on the other hand, render us in all respects slothful and torpid. Different degrees and kinds of motion have been adopted, therefore, with suitable designations, as expressive of various states of the mind, whereby an attempt is made to give an approximate idea of absolute time.

Motion may be considered as divided into five chief gradations, each of which may again be subdivided into smaller variations. They are all indicated by the following list of words, which are generally written at the beginning of the composition over the notes.

1. THE SLOWEST MOTION.

Largo—slow; *Largo assai*—*assai* means *very*; or *Larghissimo*—extremely slow.
Adagio—slow; *Adagiosissimo*—very slow.
Lento—lingering, dragging.
Grave—heavy.
Largo and its augmentatives generally mean the slowest motion; *Adagio* and *Grave* are often taken as less slow than *Lento*.

2. MODERATELY SLOW MOTION.

Larghetto—rather slow.
Andante—going, but *walking*, not running.
Andantino—somewhat slower than *Andante*.
Sostenuto—sustained, maintained without change.
Commodo—leisurely.

Here also the names are arranged in the gradation of increasing swiftness. There is, however, no unanimity among composers and teachers in these fine distinctions; there are many, for instance, who consider *Andantino* as *quicker* than *Andante*.

3. MODERATELY QUICK MOTION

has the following signs :—

Allegretto—rather lively.
Moderato—moderate.
Allegramente—approaching to *Allegro*, nearly as lively.
Allegro Moderato—moderately lively.
Allegro, ma non troppo—lively, but restrained.

4. QUICK MOTION.

Allegro—merry, cheerful.
Animato—animated, lively.
Allegro con brio (or *brioso*)—joyful and bold.
Allegro con moto—lively, with increased motion.
Allegro con fuoco (or *fuocoso*)—very animated.
Allegro agitato—strongly excited with joy.
Allegro appassionato—vehemently joyful.

5. THE QUICKEST MOTION.

Allegro assai—very cheerful or joyful.
Allegro vivace, or *Allegrissimo*—most lively.
Vivace, Vivacissimo—most animated or lively.
Presto—quick; *Presto assai, Prestissimo*—as quick as possible.

That with these expressions, and any definite number more, all possible gradations of musical motion would not be exhausted, must be abundantly evident. We seek for assistance, therefore, from augmentatives and diminutives. Such are—

Più—more.
Meno—less.

So, for instance,—

Più allegro means more lively (than before).
Meno allegro means less lively (than before).
Più moto, and *mosso*, means with more motion.
Più vivo means more animated.

And after all, the most apt, minute, and vivid directions must be intrusted to the comprehension of the performer and the taste of the moment.

All these expressions serve to give a sufficiently definite style and character to the whole course of a musical composition. But it may be desirable that some portions of the composition be played faster or slower than the general time of the piece. On such occasions we use—

Vivo, più vivo—lively, more lively.
Veloce—rapid.
Ritenuto (*riten., rit.,* and *ritardando*)—slower.

And afterwards—
A tempo—return to the original time.
Or, it may be the object to proceed by imperceptible gradations from one kind of motion to another. For this, there are many technical expressions, and moreover, the general direction—
Tempo assimilando al movimento seguente—assimilating in time to the following movement.

If the time is to become gradually slower, the words used are—
Rilasciando—relaxing, slackening.
Ritardando—retarding, keeping back.
Rallentando or *rallent.* or *rall.*, also *allentand.* and *lentando*—becoming slower.

The last expression is generally used as the strongest for indicating a diminution or cessation of motion; also the word—
Calando—sinking, declining, falling away,
has the intention of producing a slower motion.

If a slower motion is to be quickened into swiftness, the following expressions are employed:—
Accelerando—accelerating.
Precipitando—urging onwards.
Stringendo—pressing forwards.

If the increase or diminution of speed is desired to be by very small degrees, the foregoing expressions are accompanied by—
Poco a poco—little by little; thus
Poco a poco rallentando—becoming slower little by little.
Poco a poco più moto—faster and faster by small degrees.

If a considerable movement throughout, or towards the conclusion, is to be urged constantly faster, the words—
Più stretto—more strained or urged,
are written over the movement. The movement so marked is also called the
STRETTA.
So concludes, for example, the first finale in *Don Giovanni*, with a stretta.

When the state of changing from one condition of motion to another ceases, the new or required condition is indicated; thus, for example,—
Allegro | *Accelerando* | *Presto*
starting from *Allegro*, we meet on our way with *Accelerando*, which we put into practice until we fall in with *Presto*, which we then continue. Or, if after a change in time we are to revert to the original prescription, this intention is indicated by
Tempo primo (t. p.)
meaning the original time.

*When it is desired that the time marked should be rigidly adhered to, without either acceleration or retardation, we use the words
Tempo giusto (exact time).

---

* This paragraph is my own, in lieu of the original, in which the Author gives to the Italian words "Tempo giusto" a meaning of which they may indeed be in some cases susceptible, but which they certainly do not mean in this instance.
The paragraph of Marx would run thus, in English:—"An extraordinary indication of time must be noticed in conclusion. The direction is sometimes found 'Tempo giusto,' that is to say 'the right time.'—The motion is to be as fast or as slow as we please or think proper.—A very innocent determination, for it determines just nothing."
—TRANSLATOR.

APPENDIX.—THE CHRONOMETER.

Neither the descriptions of time in the last section, nor the fixed relative durations in the first (both of this division), have furnished us with a measure for *absolute* time. They merely determine that the motion in one passage, according to the determined value of the notes, shall be quicker or slower than in another passage; or again, that a crotchet, for example, in an *Andante* movement, should be of longer duration than in an *Allegro*, and shorter duration than in a *Largo* movement. There still remains the question, how long should they be in any one of these designations of time?

This can be determined only by our absolute astronomical divisions of time into minutes, seconds, &c. If we could obtain, therefore, the means of measuring motion with precision, we might establish, that a crotchet or a minim should have the duration of any certain fraction of a minute or of a second.

Many expedients have been thought of for this object. The most generally known, however, is Mälzel's

METRONOME.

An instrument consisting of a pendulum with movable weight and wheelwork. Behind the pendulum there is a table divided into 110 degrees, No. 50 to 160. If the weight be applied to the pendulum at one of these degrees, the pendulum vibrates so many times in a minute as is the number itself of the degree. It vibrates, therefore, in the minute from 50 to 160 times, according to its being placed on the uppermost or the undermost degree. By this instrument a quantity of absolute duration can be measured for any note. We determine, for instance, that any value, as that of a crotchet, for example, shall be the sixtieth or hundred-and-twentieth of a minute. We place the weight at 60 or 120, accordingly, and the vibration of the pendulum will give the desired absolute measure. The measure of the crotchet being known, those of the minim and semibreve follow of course. In this manner the time may be signified in the most definite and absolute sense. The above cases would be indicated in the following manner:—

M.M. (Mälzel's Metronome) ♩ = 60
M.M. ♩ = 120.

If the motion be too slow to measure (according to the degree table) one kind of note, a smaller note must be measured. Thus, for example, if it were desired to show a motion in which the crotchet would require only 30 vibrations in a minute (and would therefore last two seconds), it might be represented thus:—

M.M. ♪ = 60,

the vibrations of the metronome would then be quavers, from which the crotchets would become known.

If on the other hand we wished to express so quick a motion, that it could not be shown for any value on the degree table, we must then have the assistance of larger denominations. If, for example, we want to express three crotchets as lasting a second (or 180 in the minute), we may do it so:—

M.M. 𝅗𝅥 = 90; or rather—
M.M. 𝅗𝅥. = 60.*

We can understand in this way, how one and the same degree of motion, may have various ways of expression.

More simple, cheaper, and liable to no derangement (as with the wheelwork of Mälzel), is the

CHRONOMETER (OR STRING PENDULUM)

of Gottfried Weber, which with any weight, for instance a ball of clay and a string marked into lengths, any how, by knots for example, is at once complete. The shorter such a string is, the quicker are its vibrations; the longer, of course the slower are the vibrations. So, therefore, the degree of motion can be determined by the length of the string. A string, for example, of 55 Rhenish inches vibrates 50 times, and of five such inches, 160 times in a minute. The first of these measures applied to a crotchet would be thus expressed:—

♩ = 55″ Rh., (56⅝ English.)

the latter, applied also to a crotchet, thus:—

♩ = 5″ Rh., (5⅛ English.)

Here follows a comparative table of the measures of Weber and Mälzel [and the approximate English measures are added]:—

Metron.		Rh. inches		Eng.	Metron.		Rh. inches.		Eng.
50	=	55	...	56⅝	92	=	16	...	16½
52	=	50	...	51½	96	=	15	...	15½
54	=	47	...	48⅜	100	=	14	...	14⅜
56	=	44	...	45⅜	104	=	13	...	13⅜
58	=	41	...	42¼	108	=	12	...	12⅜
60	=	38	...	39⅛	112	=	11	...	11⅜
63	=	34	...	35	116	=	10	...	10¼
66	=	31	...	31⅞	120	=	9	...	9¼
69	=	29	...	29⅞	126	=	8	...	8¼
72	=	26	...	26¾	132	=	7½	...	7¾
76	=	24	...	24¾	138	=	7	...	7¼
80	=	21	...	21⅝	144	=	6½	...	6⅝
84	=	19	...	19⅝	152	=	6	...	6⅛
88	=	18	...	18½	160	=	5	...	5⅛

whereby we may be enabled to use both or either. If the string be fastened by the extreme end, it makes fifty vibrations in a minute; if it be fastened so that thirty-eight inches remain free, it will vibrate seconds, that is sixty vibrations in a minute, as the metronome when at sixty. If only nine inches of the string be allowed to be free, each vibration lasts only half a second, as the metronome indicates at 120.

Now, it may be asked what quantity of absolute time is occupied by each of our signs or prescriptions for time? It has been suggested that the crotchet in the movement *Andante*, of our *second* gradation (page 31), should be considered as a second of absolute time.

M. M. ♩ = 60.

Web. Chron. ♩ = 38″ Rh., (39⅛ English.)

and as a standard for all other measurements. From this we might assume the lowest degree for the *first* gradation, to be about

M. M. ♩ = 50
𝅗𝅥 = 60, &c.

* We have chosen this example merely on account of the simplicity of its relationship in time. For in the following Table of the Metronome, each separate degree is not given (to have done so would have overburthened the Table), but only every second, third, fourth, sixth, and eighth degree. And this is sufficient; for the difference of one, or in quicker motion of two or three degrees, is of no characteristic importance.

for the third gradation, about the motion of

M. M. ♩ = 90
for the fourth, *M. M.* ♩ = 120 to 130
for the fifth, *M. M.* ♩ = 140 to 160

In truth, however, music is little concerned with the mathematically-exact division of quantities. Her object is to excite and to manifest the emotions of the heart and of the soul; and in that view, the *approximative directions* of the composer are more appropriate for her and true to nature, than *metronomic exactitude*.† The leader or conductor of a great performance, is bound most assuredly to comprehend perfectly, and endeavour to produce as faithfully as possible, the conceptions and feelings of the composer; and it therefore is incumbent upon him, to acquaint himself intimately with the composer's intentions as to time. But after all, everything depends upon his having formed a correct apprehension of his subject, and his having made the work a living thing in his own heart and mind; for from his own inward emotion alone can it issue forth with life and effect. Produced from outward mechanical tradition or prescription, without inward appropriation in feeling, it is dead—it neither has nor can give vitality. Moreover, there are other circumstances, which in the metronomic system of time cannot be provided for. In great compositions, for example, and large places, the time, particularly in florid passages, must be taken slower, because the sound spreads more slowly, and therefore in rapid motion, the sounds become confused, notwithstanding the most correct execution. It is necessary, therefore, to have a strong impression of the *approximate time* which is commonly attributed to the various expressions used in its indication, consistently always with the usual meaning of the words. Further *minutiæ* should and must be left to the artistic judgment and inspiration of the executants.

We shall have a more intimate comprehension of these matters when we get to the instructions on Performance.

FIFTH SECTION.—THE NATURE AND REGULATION OF BARS.

We can now produce whole successions of sounds of equal or various value. But such a range, if it be of considerable extent, would not be appreciable by the eye: it would not have the advantage of *order*, even though it proceeded regularly in single notes of the same value.

How then are we to make any mass of notes intelligible? By dividing them into smaller and more comprehensible totals. So we distribute, for example, a heap of coin into small rows of four or five each, and we then easily reckon the whole quantity.

Let us apply this to our string of notes. We take in the first instance, notes of the same value, crotchets for example, and we will call the notes separately. *parts* of the string.

A long line of such notes or parts

♩♩♩♩♩♩♩♩♩♩♩♩♩♩♩♩♩♩♩ and so forth.

† On this point, see the Author's Article *Metronom*, in the *Universal Lexikon der Tonkunst*.

taken in its whole length would be nearly inappreciable (as to number) to the eye. But let us cut the line into smaller portions, and then we can inspect and count it. Each portion must be of equal size, and then the whole will not only be divided, but also assume the appearance of order.

The smallest number of which these portions must consist, to have the desired effect, is *two*.

The division and arrangement of a line of notes into twos, thus for example,—

♩ ♩ | ♩ ♩ | ♩ ♩ | ♩ ♩ — and so forth.

we call

COMMON TIMES,

or two-part order.

The next division is by threes, thus :—

♩ ♩ ♩ | ♩ ♩ ♩ | ♩ ♩ ♩ — and so forth.

which we call

TRIPLE TIMES,

or three-part order.

If now we come to very long ranges of notes, we encounter so many divisions of twos and threes, that we again fall into the original difficulty of distinguishing so many unities, namely, the single divisions. If we had such a long row as this, for example,—

♩ ♩ | ♩ ♩ | ♩ ♩ | ♩ ♩ | ♩ ♩ | ♩ ♩ | ♩ ♩ | ♩ ♩ | ♩ ♩ — and so forth.

we should be obliged to avail ourselves again of our former facilitation. Thus, we should add together every two or three divisions, and the groups thus formed we should call

COMBINED ORDER.

So from the Common times arises the

FOUR-PART ORDER,

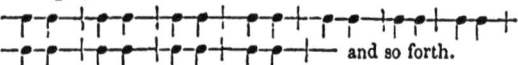

in which four portions, or two dual divisions, make another larger and four-part section. Out of the four-part we can form an

EIGHT-PART ORDER,

by the combination of every two four-part sections.

In the same manner, from the three-part arises the

SIX-PART ORDER,

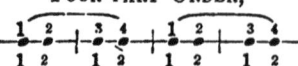

in which each section contains six parts, or two three-part divisions. From a second combination of two sections, is formed, from the six-part order, the

TWELVE-PART ORDER.

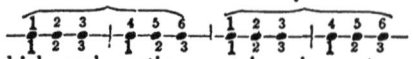

which therefore contains two six-part, or four three-part divisions, or twelve parts united into one section. If we combine three three-part divisions, there arises a

NINE-PART ORDER,

in which every section has nine parts: and in like manner other combinations might be made.

We will call every part which begins a section, the

CHIEF PART.

It is distinguished in the preceding examples by a larger figure. Every part in the combined arrangements which had been a chief part in the simple original divisions, we shall call an

EX-CHIEF PART,

and all others

SECONDARY PARTS.

Therefore, in the four-part order, the part numbered 3 is an ex-chief part; in the six-part order, that numbered 4; in the nine-part, those numbered 4 and 7; and in the twelve-part, those numbered 4, 7, and 10, are ex-chief parts. In the twelve-part order, a preferential rank is attributed to the part numbered 7 over those numbered 4 and 10; for that number was the chief part in the preceding six-part order.

It is easy to perceive, that besides the two simple orders of bars (the two and three-part) which we have been just now elucidating, other simple arrangements are imaginable; as for example, of five and seven parts, and from these, the combinations of ten and fourteen, and so forth: but we must pass them over; for on the one hand, they are never, or scarcely ever used;* and on the other, the division into two and three parts, affords, with their derivatives, ample facilities for all the arrangements which can be required and understood.

SIXTH SECTION.—OF THE KINDS OF BARS.

In the sketch of the orders of bars, we have left the value of the parts undetermined. We merely settled that they were all equal, and for the sake of convenience only, used crotchets in the examples.

If we give a determined value to the parts of bars, we shall institute the several

KINDS OF BARS,

which are therefore different arrangements of bars, with parts of a determined value, in any order, and any value at pleasure, from those enumerated at page 26; therefore there must be as many kinds of bars as there are arrangements and values in which the *tones* can be combined. Here we give a list of the most usual kinds of bars, and add thereunto the

TIME SIGNATURE,

which is placed on the staff at the beginning of every composition, or at the place where a new kind of bar is required by the composition. It consists in general, of two figures, in the form of a fraction, one over the other; the upper of which (the numerator) indicates the order of the bar, and the under (the denominator) shows the size of the parts of the bar.

---

* And for this reason, that these divisions, with one chief part against four, six and more secondary parts, have no such well measured or equipoised relationship as to fit them for the groundwork of a whole composition, extraordinary cases excepted. Nevertheless, that they are unnatural or incapable of being used (as some theorists have asserted) is undeniably contradicted by the popular song, *Prince Eugen der edle Ritter*, which goes very naturally in $\frac{5}{4}$ time, and cannot, without injury, be set in any other measure.—*M.S.*, Erk & Irmer, *German Popular Songs*, Part I. The same will apply to the well-known English instance of "Come stain your cheeks with nut or berry," from the Glee, "Oh, who has seen the miller's wife!"

The two-part order produces—

1. The two crotchet bar. $\frac{2}{4}$
2. (*rare*) the two quaver bar $\frac{2}{8}$
3. (*so called*) little alla breve or two minim bar, which is marked $\frac{2}{2}$, or also with 2 or ₵

4. The (proper or great) alla breve bar, in which each bar contains two semibreves (brevis, page 27), and which is marked $\frac{2}{1}$ or ₵ or also ₵ (in this last case, the same as the four crotchet bar). It seems more correct to consider it as a kind of four-part bar, as which it is again introduced into this list at No. 3.

The four-part order gives—

1. The four crotchet bar (called also whole bar), and marked C, instead of $\frac{4}{4}$.
2. The four quaver bar, $\frac{4}{8}$.
3. The (rare) four minim bar, $\frac{4}{2}$, which is also exchanged with the two semibreve bar, and is marked in the same way.

The three-part order gives—

1. The three crotchet bar, $\frac{3}{4}$.
2. The three quaver bar, $\frac{3}{8}$.
3. The (rare) three minim bar, $\frac{3}{2}$.

The six-part order gives

1. The six quaver bar, $\frac{6}{8}$.
2. The (rare) six crotchet bar, $\frac{6}{4}$.
3. The (rare) six semiquaver bar, $\frac{6}{16}$.

The nine-part order gives—

1. The nine quaver bar, $\frac{9}{8}$.
2. The (rare) nine crotchet bar, $\frac{9}{4}$.
3. The (rare) nine semiquaver bar, $\frac{9}{16}$.

Of the twelve-part order, we will mention only the Twelve Quaver bar, $\frac{12}{8}$, as the most used of this order, although the twelve semiquaver bar is sometimes met with, and even the twelve demisemiquaver bar. Occasionally composers have tried a

Five crotchet bar, $\frac{5}{4}$

and forms still more extraordinary, upon which we have remarked already, at page 34.*

The spaces between the sections in the ordering are called

BARS.

The perpendicular lines which we have used (page 34 and forward) in making the sections, are called

BAR-LINES.

The bar-lines are therefore boundary lines of the bars.

Greater portions of a piece of music, or the conclusion of a movement or of a composition, are marked with double bar-lines, called the

SIGN OF CONCLUSION, OR CLOSE,

* However true our observations at that place may be, on the inappropriateness of such bars, and however small the pretensions of such unusual forms to be tolerated, when employed solely, perhaps, for the sake of a little cheap originality, still the composer must not be forbidden to use them when they appear natural and required. Such an occasion presents itself in the Oratorio *Mosé*, (in the Author's *Klavierauszug*, page 105,) where the five crotchet bar was neither sought nor arbitrarily adopted, but—at least in the conscience and apprehension of the composer—sprang, as it were, of necessity, out of the text and feeling.

and are made in this manner:—

We have already used them at page 22 and elsewhere.

The sign of conclusion is often strengthened by additions at pleasure, thus:—

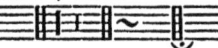

If after the close of a movement, another movement is to begin and proceed immediately, without any delay between the two, the words

ATTACCA SUBITO,

meaning, *join immediately*,† are added to the sign of conclusion of the first.

All the bars in a succession of bars are equal, as indeed follows from the idea of an order of bars; that is to say—

1. They have an equal number of parts,
2. Those parts are equal.

In a composition in two crotchet time, every bar has the value of two crotchets; in a composition in three quaver time, every bar has the value of three quavers.

But these contents of a bar may be composed of any number of notes within the value of the bar. Each part of the bar may therefore be a single note, thus:—

69.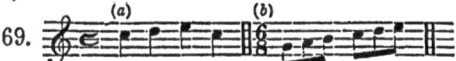

or two, three, or more parts, may be comprehended in larger notes, thus:—

70.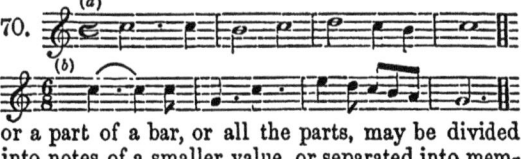

or a part of a bar, or all the parts, may be divided into notes of a smaller value, or separated into members, which then are called

MEMBERS OF A BAR,

as here for example:—

71.

In the first bar, each part is divided into two quavers (members); in the third bar, each part into four semiquavers (smaller members); in the last, the second part has remained whole, but the first part is separated into one quaver and two semiquavers.

Moreover, every part and member of a bar can be represented by rests as well as by notes. Thus we see here—

72.

in the first bar, the second and third parts,—and in the second, the fourth part—are occupied by rests. At (*b*) in the first bar, the fourth and fifth parts—and

† Here we will mention another customary sign. At the end of a side of quick music the words *Volti subito (v. s.)* are often seen; they direct the performer to turn over quickly.

in the second, the third part—are rests. The sixth part of the first bar is subdivided, and the first member is a rest. The three last parts of the second bar are in like manner subdivided into semiquavers and rests.

Whole bars may also be filled with rests, as for example, here at (a)—

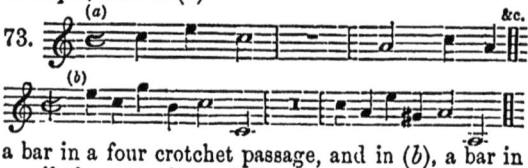

a bar in a four crotchet passage, and in (b), a bar in an alla breve or four minim passage. Here we must remark, that in all kinds of bars of less than four crotchets, a semibreve rest and a bar rest are equivalent; such a rest is therefore called a

BAR REST.

The rests, therefore, at page 30

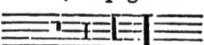

signify respectively two, four, six, and eight bars rest. Therefore in a passage in three crotchets, for example at (a),

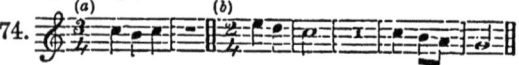

the rest in the second bar means a bar rest of three crotchets, although otherwise, as a rest in general, equivalent to four crotchets. In the two crotchets passage marked (b), the rest in the third bar, equal in general to two semibreves or eight crotchets, is here the equivalent of only two bars or four crotchets. Half bars, however, are always written with rests of their exact value. Thus in a six quaver bar, a half-bar rest would not be indicated by a minim rest, but by three quaver rests, or one crotchet and one quaver rests.

In long rests, comprehending many bars, it is usual to write the number of bars in figures over the rests; for example:—

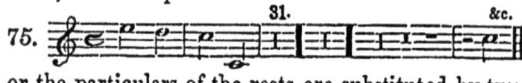

or the particulars of the rests are substituted by two cross bars, as at page 30, thus:—

with the figures over them.

Here we may mention some abbreviations which are connected with the subject of bars.

If a semibreve or larger note, or a minim, three crotchets (minim with a dot) or also a crotchet or quaver, be required to be divided into quavers or smaller members, the sign of the quaver or semiquaver, &c., is added to it; thus, for example, these

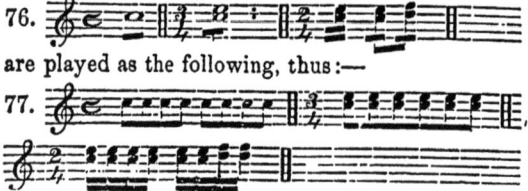

are played as the following, thus:—

The same is the case with these characters,

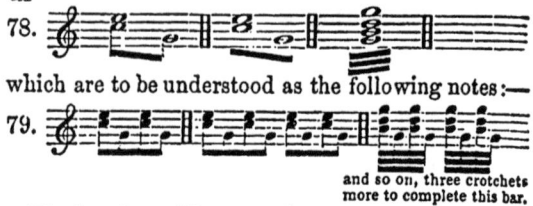

which are to be understood as the following notes:—

and so on, three crotchets more to complete this bar.

The last bar will serve also as an explanation of the words

Trem. (*tremando*) or *tremolo*,

meaning *trembling*, or tremulous, when the notes are to be played with the greatest possible velocity.

If a group of notes forming a part, or half of a bar, or a whole bar, is to be repeated, the cross signs may be written in lieu of the notes, and also in continuation of them, with the word

Segue,

(meaning) *it follows or goes on so,* or

Simile. (sim.)

(meaning) *the same, in the same manner.* So here for example:—

Here, first, the group of four quavers is to be repeated once, then the group of semiquavers, three times, and then in the third bar, the second bar is to be repeated altogether. This abreviation is used also in the following form—

signifying, that the groups of notes placed over each other, are to be played in the same manner as the first group; thus:—

82.

In strictness, the word *sim.* or *simile* ought not to be absent; for this abreviation, No. 81, might also be played so—

83.

or rather, it ought to have been so understood, according to the rule above-mentioned.

SEVENTH SECTION.—MANAGEMENT AND DIVISION OF BARS.

All compositions (at least with few exceptions) are written in a determined measure (fixed bar), which is signified at the beginning.

But one and the same kind of bar is not continued throughout. Now and then

CHANGES OF MEASURE,

as they are technically called, intervene. Such changes may even occur several times in the same composition. For instance, a piece of music may begin in three-part order, from that pass to the two-part, and then return to the three-part.*

The change of measure occurs, in general, only

---

* Such a change (among others) occurs in the *Scherzo* in Beethoven's Pastoral Symphony; wherein three and four-part measure exchange twice—and the close is in three-part.

after the close of considerable portions of the composition. Sometimes, however, it is introduced in the mid-course of a movement; and then the appropriate mark of the new measure is written on the staff, as for example, in this passage:—

84.

which, without any conclusion, passes at once from the six-quaver bar to the four-crotchet.

If with this change of bar, a change of absolute time is to take place, it must be signified. If such indication should be wanting, it must be assumed* that the same parts of bars must have equal length in the new measure; for example here—

every crotchet in the two-fourths bar is to last as long as before in the three-fourths bar. For greater clearness also,

L'istesso tempo, or *medesimo tempo*.

(meaning) the same absolute time, is sometimes added.

Sometimes the measure is changed, without any change of sign, the arrangement only of the bar being altered.

85.

Here we have a passage out of the Andante of Mozart's Symphony in C major.† The movement is in $\frac{3}{4}$ measure, as the passage itself is noted; nevertheless the $\frac{2}{4}$ measure reigns in it, in a manner not to be mistaken. Mozart formed the melody in four groups of two crotchets, and has indicated their connexion by binds. The bass in four groups of every four quavers, the horns sounding four notes in $\frac{2}{4}$ measure, the marking of the *f* and *p* (of which we shall speak in the tenth section)—everything convinces us of the change of measure, without any

* The composer, however, has good reason occasionally for departing from this assumption; which, nevertheless, must certainly be considered as the rule. Thus in a change of $\frac{6}{8}$ to $\frac{4}{4}$ measure, in the oratorio of *Moses, Klavierauszug*, page 28, the composer wished here, at the introduction of the $\frac{4}{4}$ measure, that *two* quavers should have the same value as *three* in the former ($\frac{6}{8}$) measure—therefore, rigidly speaking, he ought to have employed the $\frac{2}{4}$ measure instead of the $\frac{4}{4}$. But he preferred this latter measure in order to secure the smooth flow of the quavers

(see the 10th section of this book). In the score, page 49, every kind of doubt ceases: for therein, the same $\frac{6}{8}$ figure (as double triplet) which existed also in the $\frac{6}{8}$ measure, appears in $\frac{4}{4}$ measure.

† The extract is imperfect, it contains merely what concerned the bar.

sign or alteration of mark. After the four two-fourths measures, there comes even a $\frac{4}{4}$ measure (combined $\frac{2}{4}$ measure) and then only recurs the regular $\frac{3}{4}$ measure. A similar change of measure appears soon after, although not so important nor so easy of recognition.

86.

The under-current of $\frac{2}{4}$ measure is made observable here merely by the sameness of the proceeding in melody and harmony, by crotchets two by two. The figures placed underneath will make the measure of both passages perceptible.

We have already learned that all the bars of one determined measure, contain the same number of parts; and as these are all equal, those bars must be of equal size or quantity, although this quantity may be represented by notes and rests of different values: thus, for example, a bar in a passage in four crotchets must contain either four crotchets, or one semibreve, or two minims, or eight quavers, or equivalent rests, &c., or two crotchet or four quaver triplets, and so forth; or mixtures of all these quantities to the amount of four crotchets. Of course in performance every part must be produced with its duly allotted measure or value.

But how is this to be done? If every note were to be measured by itself, a variety of notation would occasion the greatest confusion. In this passage, for example—

87.

there are minims, quaver triplets, semiquavers, &c., to be measured. The minims would furnish no measure for the quaver triplet, these, none for the semiquavers, and so one would confound the other.

This difficulty ceases when a fundamental measure for the estimation of the value or quantity of each single note is established, and for such a fundamental measure we employ again the

PARTS OF THE BAR.

We reckon to what notes the first, second, &c. parts of the bar will amount. We see then, at least in the gross, the quantity of duration fixed. So in the preceding passage, for example, each note of the first bar contains two parts, and these latter are crotchets; each triplet of quavers in the following bar, one part; and so forth. We know so far, at least, that the three first notes of the second bar are to have the length of a crotchet only, and that the second crotchet must begin with the *tone D*; that the notes, *d, e, c,* are not to have more nor less, duration than the first triplet, &c.*

Now, after this procedure in the gross, there remain only groups of much smaller notes to measure and reckon. These are naturally much easier to divide, and moreover a small failure in them is not so injurious in effect. If, for example, the notes of the first triplet were not measured and performed in perfect equality with respect to each other, but erroneously in some degree, as if they had been written thus—

90. [musical notation] &c.

nevertheless, if the performance of *d* corresponded exactly with the occurrence of the second part of the bar, the chief object of the bar would be correct again.

It is expected, however, that the measure be observed with the utmost presicion in the smallest matters; and if we cannot appreciate the lesser notes and rests by the feeling only, we must contrive a smaller fundamental measure from the

MEMBERS OF THE BAR.

We separate, for instance, in No. 87, the third bar into its eight quavers, and we see now the first quaver *a*, the second quaver represented by the two semiquavers, *b* and *c*♯, and so forth; we have now then at the utmost, only two notes (semiquavers) to measure. Moreover, if this should not suffice, we should be obliged to take still smaller members.

All this operation is called

DIVIDING THE BAR.

We acquire a perception and feeling of it by practice in beating with the foot or hand, &c., for every single part of a bar, or by calling out the numbers of the parts, &c.—

One! Two! &c.

If the time be very quick, instead of counting by parts of the bar, we may count by halves or thirds of it, thus :—

If the time be very slow, the members of the bar

* This kind of measurement is not practicable in an arrangement of bars wherein the parts of the bar do not exist; thus we see here—

88.

a passage in ¾ measure, in which, however, the 4th bar has a crotchet triplet instead of the two last crotchets; then come three bars of nothing but triplets. That neither these triplets, nor three nor six notes, can be conveniently measured by two or four, is manifest. In this case we must seek a larger measure therefore, which will suit equally the two regular crotchets and the triplets. We must divide by half bars.

But even this measure is sometimes not long enough. Here—

89. [musical notation]

we see in a passage in ¾ measure, in the 5th and 7th bars, triplets of minims. These can neither be measured by four crotchets nor by two minims; we must therefore use the whole bar as a measure.

must be counted: for example, instead of four crotchets, eight quavers; or in difficult cases, still smaller subdivisions.

After these explanations, the dividing of the bars can have no peculiar difficulty.

If the passage, No. 71, for example, were to be divided, it strikes the eye at once that two and again two quavers in the first bar, and four and again four semiquavers in the third bar, make each a crotchet, that is, altogether four crotchets. In the second bar *g* is a crotchet, therefore it is the first part, and consequently the dot and quaver must be the second part. In the last bar the last note is a crotchet, and consequently the second part of the bar, therefore the preceding notes must together form a part. If one were to divide into members of the bar, the quaver *c* would be the first member, consequently the following notes, *g* and *e*, must form together the second member.

This process is facilitated in difficult cases, by first separating and estimating the easiest groups. Thus here,—

91.

in the first place, the fourth crotchet is immediately recognized as contained in the last three notes. The two quavers in the middle of the bar make also a crotchet; so we suppose at once that the preceding notes form the first crotchet. Then there remain only the groups of notes between the second and fourth parts, and upon these groups depends the most important point, that they should contain exactly the third part, as they must necessarily end in time for the beginning of the fourth part, which is unquestionably at *g*.

The mode of notation affords great facilities to the dividing of the bars. All the notes, excepting semibreves, minims, and crotchets, may be so grouped together,† that from the binding only, the halves or

† Sometimes this grouping is partially avoided, in order to shew that the members of a bar are not connected together solely, but are some of them, to a certain degree, engaged with other members. Here, for example,—

92. [musical notation]

we see, in the upper succession of notes, the first of four semiquavers constantly separated until the last group, where it assumes the regular form. In the 2nd bar this semiquaver remains alone, while the others are grouped. In the 3rd and 4th bars the first separated semiquaver is united with the three last of the preceding bars. This method of notation has been carried to excess, particularly in modern compositions called Chamber music, in order to ensure as far as possible its faultless and passionate execution. This form,—

92A.

in which the notes are bound by a quaver *line of duration* (even through and beyond two bar lines) and are broken up again by the interruptions of the semiquaver *lines of duration*, is still intelligible, although the same passage might have been written, with the aid of staccato dots ad libitum, in this manner,—

92B.

the parts of bars, are often recognized at once; but generally, it is not usual so to group less than three, nor more than eight notes, unless in the case of nonuplets, decuplets, and other combinations of that species. Hence, in 2/4 measure, it is usual to unite four quavers, or four and four semiquavers, or a quaver with two semiquavers.

93.

In 3/4 measure, all the six quavers, or two of them, or every four semiquavers, thus:—

94.

In 6/8 measure, all the six quavers, or by three and three (for the 6/8 measure, is a combination of two 3/8 measures) or in six semiquavers:—

95.

In 6/4 measure, every six followed by two or four quavers; in 12/8 every three or six quavers, six semiquavers, &c. Of demisemiquavers and all shorter notes, it is not customary to group more than four, or at the utmost, eight. The notes forming any special measurable combinations, such as quintuplets, sextuplets, &c., are always grouped together.

So much for dividing the bars when it is a matter of one succession of notes only. We know already, from the Introduction, that in a composition, two and more simultaneous successions of *tones* can exist, that there is music of more than one part.

These combinations require particular consideration in respect of the division of the bar.

In the first place, as to the manner of writing this description of music, it is two fold. The successions of sounds may be written on one staff, as here for example—

96.

where we see three successions of *tones*—

1st. . . . *c, d, e, f, e, d, c,*
2nd. . . *g, a, b, c, b, a, g,*
3rd. . . *e, f, g, a, g, f, e,*

united on one staff. Or we use (when the notes are too numerous, or the successions too far apart to be comprehended on one staff or in one clef) two or more staves, as mentioned already at page 10, and exhibited at No. 85. These staves are joined together at the beginning by a

BRACE

Thus, here are two,—

97.

and here three staves,—

98.

bound together. In the first passage, the two staves are connected by the closing double bar, as well as by the brace. In the last, besides the brace, there are moreover cross bars passing through all the staves, although this assistance is not generally given.

If we wish to divide the bars in a composition in several parts, we must consider each part by itself, and so divide it. Now, as they must all begin at the same time, the first, second, third, &c., crotchet, quaver, &c., of all the parts must fall together. So in No. 97 above, the united three successions of crotchets proceed together, while the succession on the lower staff begins with the first combination of crotchets above it, and continues until their termination. In No. 98, the first *tones* in the upper staff continue during the time of two crotchets. In union with these *tones* there appear on the second staff, eight semiquavers, the first of which begins with the said *tones* on the upper staff, while the lowest part begins with a quaver rest, and is followed by quavers. The first quaver, therefore, coincides with the third semiquaver of the succession next above it, the fourth quaver (or the fifth quaver including the rest) with the ninth semiquaver, and with the crotchets, the third part of the upper succession.

There is an exception from the regular division of several combined parts. This occurs when several notes of the same length are placed over each other on the staff, and are accompanied by the word *Arpeggio*, (meaning) *in the manner of harp playing,*

or with this sign ≬ before the notes.

In this case, the notes are not to be played literally, all together at the same instant, but a mere trifle after each other, the lowest generally first. If their succession should be as swift as possible, a line is drawn across the notes. Thus for example—

99. written, ..
played, ..

we here see at (*a*) the slower, and at (*b*) the quicker *arpeggio*, with an approach to the manner of its performance.

In order to facilitate the reckoning of one succession of notes against another, it is customary to write those parts under each other, which occur at the same moment. In this passage, for example—

100.

the upper succession of notes is variegated enough to give us a little trouble in the division: but in the simple lower line, we see at once the six parts of the bar, and thereby the notes corresponding to each in the upper line. However, we must not rely blindly on this favourable position of the notes, as above. They ought indeed to be exactly so arranged, but often, from the neglect of the writer or of the engraver, they are not so.

We will notice two manners of writing, not very uncommon, but which are deficient in perspicuity. The first is, placing notes of a whole bar's duration, not at the beginning of a bar, as here—

101.

but in the middle of the bar, thus:—

102.

The other, which is more frequently found in music somewhat old, is to express the continuation of notes from one bar into another, not by binds, thus,—

103.

but by a note placed on the dividing line between the bars, thus:—

104.

Here we return to the singular change of measure in No. 85 and 86, particularly to the first. It is not to be denied that such configurations have peculiar difficulties in division and performance, which lie in the contradiction between the manner of writing and the contents.

The accompanying parts give some assistance, since they make the real measure clearly perceptible. It is therefore only the upper part that presents some obscurity. Now, let us change it into its proper $\frac{3}{4}$ measure:—

105.

or imagine it to be so changed, and the difficulty vanishes.

But this passage (No. 105) still leaves a little uneasiness. Neither the parts of the bar, nor the members, strike the eye: the second, third and fourth quavers are in like manner split asunder:—

106.
1 2   3   4

and the halves drawn to the following note, until the last half (the last semiquaver), remains by itself. Such notes are called
SYNCOPATED,
and such a rhythmic form, a
SYNCOPATION.

We can here clear up the ambiguity concerning the sextulet, which we mentioned at page 28, by the division of another succession of *tones* of equivalent time. In this passage—

107.

we see that for every three notes in the upper succession there occurs one quaver in the under.

Here, on the other hand,—

108.

triplets are opposite the sextulets. There are, therefore, two sextulet notes to one triplet quaver: consequently the upper succession consists of real sextulets.

Furthermore, we facilitate the division of compositions in many parts, by beginning with the easiest (as at page 39), that is, by that part in which the parts of the bars are most intelligibly written. So in No. 100, we have begun by the lower part, where the six parts of the bar instantly strike the eye. In No. 103, for the same reason, we should begin with the upper part. In No 98 it would be most advisable to follow the part with the semiquavers; for this is the most regular, and enables us by its groups of notes to discern and recognise the parts of the bar. Also, it would not be difficult for the beginner to divide the other parts. The minims of the upper part would receive two groups of four semiquavers, and each quaver of the lower part would have two semiquavers.

EIGHTH SECTION.—EXCEPTIONAL FORMS.

Of these we can notice only the most important, in order not to enter too much into detail, in a work of elementary instruction. Such minutiæ were better left to the private instructor, and the occasions that may prompt them.

MUSICAL INSTRUCTION.

1. THE INITIAL IMPERFECT BAR (*Auftakt*).

By this expression we understand the few notes at the beginning of a piece of music, which do not form a perfect bar, or in other words, which form a bar deficient in quantity:—

109. [musical example with labels (a), (b), (c), (d)]

Here we see some beginnings with such imperfect bars. At (*a*) the first crotchet is wanting; (*b*) begins with the fourth part; (*c*) with the eighth quaver; (*d*) with the second quaver.

What such a bar is deficient in quantity, must appear at the end of the composition; so that the first imperfect bar and last bar added together, must make a perfect bar.* Therefore, in the above examples, the last bar of (*a*) must contain a crotchet, of (*b*) three crotchets, of (*c*) seven quavers, and of (*d*) one quaver. In very extended compositions, for greater convenience, or in order to make a more important close, we may release ourselves from this obligation, and write a conclusion in full.

Compositions beginning with a complete bar, are said to be (in contradistinction to those with initial imperfect bars)—

WITH INITIAL PERFECT BARS (*ein Niederschlage*).

2. IRREGULAR BARS.

As we have found in page 36, that the governing measure may be departed from without any previous mark or sign, so single bars are sometimes introduced, which differ from the general measure, without any notice or warning. This is more especially done in combinations of measures, by allowing a simple half bar to slip in, for the sake of the rhythmic correctness of the whole. For example:—

110.

(Let it be understood that the whole composition is in simple measure). It is sometimes also done to make particular notes more impressive; as for instance, in that well known passage in Graun's *Tod Jesu*:—

111.
Und was er zu - sa - get, hält er ge - wiss

The double bar could have been made clearer, in two ways, thus:—

112.

3. MIXED MEASURES AND VALUES.

It sometimes happens, though rarely, that two successions are made to proceed simultaneously together, but in different measures. This is done when one succession could not conveniently be represented in the measure of the other. Here for example—

113. [musical example]

triplets and sextulets of ambiguous form would have been necessary, if it had been essential to write the upper part in $\frac{6}{8}$ measure.†

---

* But how is the form of this imperfect bar to be explained? It flows of itself from the idea of the arrangement of bars, and we only postponed it from the beginning in order to have more leisure for its elucidation. Our only object in the development of the orders of bars was to obtain smaller visible sections of equal size, and naturally we measured from the principal part. Might we not, however, begin with any other part, so long as the equality of the sections were adhered to? Here, for example,

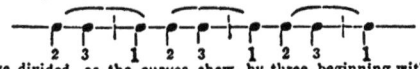

we have divided, as the curves shew, by three, beginning with No. 2. But the section No. 2 3 1 is a three part section, just as well as No. 1 2 3. This then is the initial imperfect bar.

† The most remarkable and ingenious application of mixed measures is in the first finale of *Don Juan*. When the minuet begins a second time (in G major, see the Score, Part I, page 259, published by Breitkopf and Härtel), Mozart places three different orchestras on the theatre. The first plays the minuet. On the repetition, the second begins to tune and prelude a little, in the measure of the minuet. But now, on the repetition from the beginning, it joins the minuet with an *Anglaise* (country dance), in ⅔ measure. On attaining the second part of the minuet, the *Anglaise* continues, and the third orchestra begins to tune and prelude, as was previously done by the second. In fine, on the second recommencement of the minuet, the second orchestra begins again its *Anglaise* and the third falls in with a jovial Schleifer.‡ So at last the three orchestras are playing three different dances, in three different measures:—

114.

and the dance swarms with the most enchanting variety of figures, apparently full of disorder, but intertwined with measure and grace, while the choristers, now in this group, now in that, pour forth their bright and perspicuous melodies throughout the threefold dance. The suitableness and pictorial effect of the situation, and the cordial geniality with which Mozart created and combined it, are indeed wonderful. Having said thus much, and turning to the technical construction of this composition, it is not difficult of inspection. For every crotchet in the minuet there comes a bar of the waltz (like a triplet of quavers); for every two bars of the minuet there are three bars of the *Anglaise*; and for each crotchet of the *Anglaise*, a bar of the waltz.

In Beethoven, in his second quintet (in C major), Op. 29, in the *finale* (page 30 of the score), we find a masterly and extended combination of two measures, of which the following is the beginning,—

115.

with the themes which progress together. Mozart was inspired by a dramatic intention, as Beethoven was by a feeling purely musical.

‡ The name of an ancient German dance.—TRANSLATOR.

Fourthly, we may mention here the frequent case of two concurrent successions of *tones*, in the one of which, groups of two or four notes are placed against groups of three or five notes in the other. For instance:—

These and similar momentary infractions are not generally treated with scrupulous rigidity, but are left to be overcome by routine and practice. We must let the simplest succession pursue its course as it were mechanically and unconsciously, while we attend more especially to the deviating line. Until we can do this, the lesser evil is to play the first note of the triplet with the first member of the bar, and the two last triplet notes with the second member, as at (*a*):—

on the contrary, the way indicated at (*b*) would be the worst.

NINTH SECTION.—CHROMATIC SIGNS WITHIN THE BAR.

This is at last the place, where we shall give the final elucidation of the value of chromatic signs.

Every sharp or flat in the signature at the beginning of a composition continues effective during the whole progress thereof, unless contradicted as we have already stated at page 22.

Every chromatic sign before a single note is effective only in the bar where it occurs, and not beyond. In this passage, for instance—

the notes *c* and *g* in the first bar are rendered *c♯* and *g♯*, by the introduction of the sharp before them at Nos. 1 and 2; but they are no longer sharp in the next bar, where at Nos. 3 and 4 they are restored to their original names. Moreover, as a chromatic sign operates upon all the octaves of the degree upon which it is placed, so it must, of course, operate upon all such degrees within the bar; for example here,—

the notes at Nos. 1 and 2 must be read *b♭*, until the recall at No. 3. The same is the case with concurrent successions of *tones*. Here for example:—

the fifth and eighth notes in the lower succession are also *f♯*, unless the contrary be expressly indicated by a natural, as here:—

Notwithstanding that these rules are generally established, it is not customary, particularly in extensive and many-part compositions, to limit the signs to those which are described above as strictly necessary. It is considered preferable to add a few signs, not absolutely required, indeed, but possibly useful, rather than expose the performer to failure from doubt or inadvertence. For this reason, therefore, and moreover for symmetrical appearance, the needful signs are usually placed as in the following example—

through all the octaves; and they are even repeated in the same bar, when, from the multiplicity of notes, they might possibly be forgotten. Thus here—

a sharp is placed a second time before the last note but one, *c*, although the first had not been recalled, and therefore the second was, in principle, unnecessary. It would also have been advisable to repeat the flat at *b*, under the cross .+ Moreover, for the sake of uniformity, a repetition of the signature would be desirable, whenever by the course of the harmony the earlier signature might be supposed to be removed. This very easy base—

has been played erroneously in many rehearsals of a large work in various places; at NB. 1, the base has been played *e♭* instead of *e*; and at NB. 2, *a♭* instead of *a*, because the chord immediately preceding inclines to *e♭—g—b♭* and *a♭—c—e♭*.

However, we must be careful not to carry this precaution too far, whereby the notation might become overcharged; and moreover, the performer might be left in doubt, whether the superfluous signs were meant as elucidations, or were not perhaps errors of the pen.

TENTH SECTION.—ON ACCENTS.

1. ACCENTUATION OF THE PARTS OF A BAR.

We have now learned the fundamental lines of musical rhythm in the dividing of a bar. We know which are the Chief Parts, Secondary Parts, &c. and how to divide the bar in conformity with them. But what signification, what value, have these parts in the performance?

The chief part is distinguished before all others. We give it

AN ACCENT,

whereby it is produced with greater force, and is made impressive on the ear, as it has hitherto been conspicuous to the eye. Its recurrence, therefore, must always be perceptible. In this passage in ¾ measure,—

125.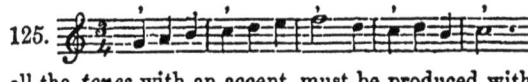

all the *tones* with an accent must be produced with greater loudness than the others. The ex-chief parts are preferable to the secondary parts, and are therefore made to sound louder than these latter, but not so loud as the present chief parts. Here,—

126.

we have repeated the foregoing passage in combined measure. The notes to be produced the loudest, the chief parts, are marked with two accents; the ex-chief parts, less loud, with one accent; and the secondary parts, least sounding, with no accent at all.

In doubly combined measure, for example the $1\frac{2}{8}$,—

127.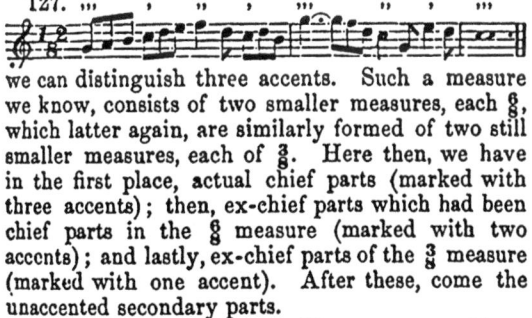

we can distinguish three accents. Such a measure we know, consists of two smaller measures, each ⁶⁄₈, which latter again, are similarly formed of two still smaller measures, each of ¾. Here then, we have in the first place, actual chief parts (marked with three accents); then, ex-chief parts which had been chief parts in the ⁶⁄₈ measure (marked with two accents); and lastly, ex-chief parts of the ¾ measure (marked with one accent). After these, come the unaccented secondary parts.

2. ACCENTUATION OF THE MEMBERS OF A BAR.

Let us now begin to dissect parts of a bar. For example, crotchets into quavers, or triplets of quavers,—

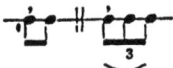

so begins the play of accents. The first member of a part appears as a chief member; the second or following ones, as secondary members: the first is accented, the others are not.

If we dissect further, for instance, a quaver into semiquavers—

the first will be the chief member of a part: the first member of a preceding member (here, the third semiquaver) will be an ex-member—therefore the first must sound loudest, the second less loud, and the secondary members still more gently, as the double and single accentuation is intended to show.

If we now exhibit all these gradations of loudness in a passage in appropriate measure, we shall find numerous varieties of sound. We have chief parts, ex-chief parts, chief members, ex-chief members, secondary members, &c.

128. *Adagio.*

Here we have had to mark (not quite exactly nor fully), about five gradations of accent. It is of course understood, that the law of accentuation is not supposed to be carried out to this extremity of fine gradations and petty differences. For flowing performance, and especially in lively movements, it is sufficient that, passing over small differences, the most important accents be observed. In an *Andante* or *Larghetto*, the foregoing passage might be played nearly in this manner:—

129.

In quicker movements, in *Allegro* for instance, the following accentuation alone might be necessary,—

130.

and thereby the running passages marked by curves would gain in fluency. This freedom from the severity of rules will be more carefully weighed in the instructions for performance. But the rules with all their consequences must be known in order to observe them so far as may seem appropriate.

We now return to a form of double derivation or interpretation, that is, the sextulet. If we consider it as a double triplet, the first and fourth *tones* become chief parts (or the latter an ex-chief part), and must be accentuated as follows:—

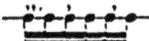

But if we consider it as a two-part dissection of a triplet, the first, third and fifth must be accented, the two last as ex-parts:—

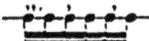

The external uniformity is therefore internally well distinguished. So is distinguished a ⁶⁄₈ measure from a ¾ measure, dissected into quavers. The first has the accent on the first and fourth, and the latter on the first, third and fifth tones:—

131.

If an accent is to be produced expressly, or a note to be played with greater force than it ought to have according to rule, this sign is used,—

> ∧

or the words—

Sforzato, sforzando (*sf.*), *Rinforzato* (*rinf.*) which are placed over or under the note, and indicate that it is to be produced with greater strength.

A higher degree of that strength is indicated by—
Sforzato assai (sff.)
or by both the sign and the words in conjunction, thus:—

sfz

The composer may, however, require an increase of sound to several successive *tones*, or even to whole passages. In the first case the notes are marked with dots, over which a curve is drawn, as here:—

132. (a)... *(b) ... (c) ...

or with signs at (*b*), when the expression is meant to be very strong and overwhelming; or the signs at (*c*), when at the same time the notes are desired to be protracted beyond their full time. The following directions are also usual, for some varieties of the same object:—

Ben pronunziato—meaning well, firmly expressed,
Accentuato—distinctly and strongly accented,
Marcato—clearly and forcibly expressed,
Pesante—heavily, impressively,
Martellato—(hammered), with suddenness and force,

and are placed over the notes.

For the lesser or greater loudness of considerably extended passages, the same terms are used, and also the following, again, in about five gradations:—

1 *Pianissimo, piano assai, pp*, and also *ppp*—meaning very gently or softly.
2 *Piano, p*—softly.
3 *Poco forte, pf, mezzo forte*—a little loud, rather loud.
  Meno forte—less loud, when *forte* has occurred previously,
  Meno piano—less soft, when *piano* has occurred previously.
4 *Forte, f*—loud.
5 *Fortissimo, ff,* and *fff; forte possibile; con tutta la forza*—very loud, as loud as possible.

We may further note, that, as in the descriptions of time, the minor gradations between *forte* and *fortissimo* are also indicated by the qualifying words—
Più forte—louder,
Poco più forte—a little louder,
Meno forte—less loud.

Each of these expressions refers to whole passages in a composition, and its effect endures until it be contradicted, or another gradation of sound be enjoined.

The above five gradations give us distinct conditions or states of sound: but we may wish to pass imperceptibly, from one to the other.

The imperceptible passage from *piano* to *forte* is thus represented:—

or (particularly in cases of great extension), by—
Crescendo, cresc.—increasing,
Poco a poco cresc.—increasing gradually,
Cres. al forte, or *al fortissimo*—increasing to loud, or to very loud,

The imperceptible transition from *loud* to *soft* is signified thus—

or by the words—
Decrescendo, decresc, decr., or *Diminuendo dim.*—decreasing,

with the addition of *poco a poco—al piano* or *al pianissimo*. For the last, the following words are used also:—
Diluendo†—diluting,
Mancando—failing, subsiding,
Perdendosi—dying away,
Smorzando—extinguishing,
Morendo—dying,

and other similar expressions.

Concluding Remark.

This division, which has been entirely devoted to rhythm, has shewn us only one side of it, namely, the formation of bars, the fundamental forms of measures of sound, together with motion and accentuation.

So far, the doctrine of musical rhythm is by no means exhausted. We shall enter much more fully into this branch in the first to the third sections of the fourth division. This separation is indispensable; For without a knowledge of the principles of bars, instruction in melody cannot be represented; and without melody, the doctrine of more elevated rhythm must remain an empty word, without living application.

THIRD DIVISION.

FIRST SECTION.—INSTRUMENTS.

Music requires a medium—an instrument whereby it may be made perceptible. The human voice, and a variety of artistic contrivances serve for effecting this object. These we have named collectively

Musical Instruments.

Every musician ought to take a general survey, and acquire some knowledge of the most useful of these instruments, in order that he may be aware of their peculiarities, and that an increased familiarity with them may be more easy of attainment. Only so far, will our present instructions go. The more intimate knowledge which belongs to the real use of an instrument, must be left to particular study, from the third and fourth parts of the author's instructions for composition.

The instrument given to us by nature is the human voice; and its musical application is called

Song.

Song is usually combined with

Speech,

and this also, from its position, demands the due consideration of the musician.

The artistic mechanical contrivances known under the general name of

Musical Instruments,

are of many kinds and species.

---

* The signs at (*b*) are not usual in England.—Translator.

† Diluendo is very little, if at all, used in England.—Translator.

MUSICAL INSTRUCTION.

We will first divide them into
FOUR CLASSES:—
1. Stringed instruments,
2. Wind ditto,
3. Instruments whose sound is produced by percussion or beating,
4. Ditto, by friction or rubbing.

Each of these classes contains many individuals, of which we shall mention the most usual only.

Stringed instruments are of two species, viz:—those whose sound is produced by striking or drawing the string out of its position of rest, and those whose sound is produced by rubbing the string with a bow.

Wind instruments are of three species, viz:—those whose body is made of wood, ivory, &c., which we comprise under the name of
REED INSTRUMENTS;
such as are made of metal, called
BRASS INSTRUMENTS.
A third species consists alone of
THE ORGAN,
in which by pipes, a bellows and keyboard, the sounds are created and displayed.
PERCUSSIVE INSTRUMENTS
are reduced here to such as produce their sound by the blow of a stick or hammer on a distended skin. We will only mention in passing, such as are made of disks, or rods of metal. Others, such as bells &c., we omit, as not belonging to music. Of
INSTRUMENTS BY FRICTION
we shall not have many observations to make.

The combination of all or many of the instruments of friction for the production of music, is called a
STRINGED ORCHESTRA.
A similar combination of wind instruments is called a
WIND ORCHESTRA,
A general combination of both the preceding, (more or less perfect) is called a
FULL ORCHESTRA.
If the instruments of friction, reed instruments, and brass instruments, with their proportion of percussive instruments act, in concert, they are called a
GREAT ORCHESTRA.
The combination of several singing voices is called a
CHOIR.
Music is divided into different species, according to the organs brought into action in its production. Compositions for singing are called
VOCAL MUSIC.
For instruments,
INSTRUMENTAL MUSIC.
Vocal music may be alone, or united with instrumental music; in the former case it is called
PURE VOCAL MUSIC.
Choral music (particularly of devotional subjects and in appropriate form) without accompaniment, is marked with the words
A CAPELLA;
it is said to be set *a capella*.

Compositions for several voices or instruments are usually so written that each single voice or instrument, or at least each kind thereof, has a separate staff or notation for itself, and all these staves are placed, bar corresponding to bar, over each other. Such a piece of written music is called a
SCORE.
Many scores, indeed, have been made also for few instruments, or for one only—the pianoforte, and have been called arrangements; but the best of these combinations can no more represent the score, than an engraving can irradiate the living colours of a painting. It must therefore be desirable to every friend of art, to make himself somewhat at home in scores. To the composer, conductor, or teacher, this knowledge is absolutely indispensable.

A peculiar relationship between the pitch of certain instruments and their notation, requires here a few explanations. There are some instruments whose *tones* are an octave lower than they are written. In such, therefore, these *tones*—

133. [musical notation]

would not be produced as such, but as the following:

134. [musical notation]

in the lower octave. It is said of them, that they are
OF SIXTEEN FEET *tone*.
Secondly, there are *tones* in the organ, which sound two octaves lower than they are written, and consequently they are called
OF THIRTY-TWO FEET *tone*.
Thirdly, there are *tones* also in the organ, an octave higher than they are written, and which would make the example above, No. 133, sound as if it were written thus:—

135. [musical notation]

They are called
OF FOUR FEET *tone*.
Other mechanisms produce *tones* two or three octaves higher.*

On the other hand, all instruments, registers, and voices, which produce their *tones* as written, are called of
EIGHT FEET *tone*.†
Further on, we shall become acquainted with other deviations in the notation, and with instruments whose *tone* appears to be one, two, three, and more degrees higher than it is written.

Now we come to a musical element, particularly suggested in this division, which is
TIMBRE OR CHARACTER OF SOUND.
All musical mechanisms (with the exception of

---
* These are also in the organ.

† A pipe in any simple wind instrument (or in an open flute stop of an organ), of about eight feet in length, gives the great C; the deepest and therefore in this respect, the normal *tone* on the key board of the organ. A similar organ pipe, twice as long, that is, of sixteen feet, gives the deeper octave (the double C). Again doubled in length (thirty-two feet), the pipe produces an octave still lower. Half the normal length (four feet), gives the higher octave, that is, the little c, and so forth.

According to this proportion in measurement, the increasing or diminishing pipes of the organ are called of eight feet, of sixteen feet, or of four feet, &c.; and hence this manner of naming has passed generally to all other musical instruments. Thus much in explanation of the singularity of the expression.

some percussive instruments) have the property in common of producing some part of our system of *tones*. Their difference in this respect consists merely in the number of *tones* which each can produce, some producing many, others only a few. The *tone*, however, is alike in all, and it is of no importance that any particular instrument should, or should not, be able to produce any given *tone*. The difference now material to us in this place is, the Timbre or Character of Sound. The same *tone*, in consequence of the *difference of character*, is quite another thing when heard from the flute or the trumpet, from the violin or the human voice, &c.

On this matter, however, we cannot in this book* do more than make some passing remarks, and this chiefly to excite and direct the observation of beginners and other attentive students, so that they may acquire at least a general conception of musical effects in this regard.

SECOND SECTION.—VOCAL MUSIC.

The human voice is the material with which vocal music is formed, generally combined with speech, but sometimes not.

(A) THE HUMAN VOICE.

Everyone knows this, and the manner of producing it, at least superficially. We will therefore make some observations only upon the two most important kinds of character which are especially distinguished in the voice.

The sounds which proceed directly and with strength from the generative mechanism of voice, are called

CHEST SOUNDS,

or chest voice. It is the voice in which we speak, which the organs of voice produce most easily, and in which we speak most aptly and effectively to each other. From this voice we can distinguish at once, what is called the

HEAD VOICE,

or *falsetto*. The sounds of the head voice are produced by a more or less forcible constriction of the cavity whence the voice proceeds.† Through this, to a certain degree unnatural contraction, the voice assumes a fife-like character, gentle but weak, and far inferior to the full and bold, but cordial and expressive voice of the chest.

The *falsetto* is used only in the higher *tones*. The lower, and by far the greater part of the *tones*, are given in the chest voice. Some *tones* on the adjoining borders of the registers may be given in either.

A particular way of producing the voice is called

MEZZA VOCE.

(meaning) half voice. This is a kind of *piano*, in which the voice is very gentle and tender, but perfectly distinct in its character.‡

The voice is divided into two classes, the male and the female; in the latter of which, boys' voices may be included.

The female voice lies an octave higher than the male. If, for example, a female or boy's voice intends to produce the *tone* which in a male voice would be the little *c*, it would in reality sound the one-lined *c*. And in like manner, if a male voice were to follow a female voice in singing this passage—

136.

he would intonate it an octave lower, and, therefore, thus:—

137.

The male and female voices are each divided into two chief species.

The chief species of the male voice are

THE BASE, the deep; and TENOR,§ the high.

The chief species of the female class are

COUNTER-TENOR, or CONTRALTO,‖ the deep; TREBLE or SOPRANO, the high.

Besides the principal species, secondary divisions likewise occur, such as the

BARYTONE,

a higher bass, between the bass proper and the tenor;

MEZZO SOPRANO,

a deeper treble, between the treble proper and the contralto. Or they are distinguished simply as

FIRST, SECOND, THIRD, &c.

Bass, tenor, contralto, soprano, &c., the highest voice counting as the first.

Apart from these secondary divisions,

THE BASS (*basso*)

comprises the *tones* (about) from great *F*, up to the one-lined *d* or *e*. It is almost entirely chest voice, and has the firmest, most massive, but also roughest character. Its tones are almost without exception, written in the F or bass clef.

THE TENOR (*tenore*)

extends from about the little *c d* to the one-lined *g* or *a*. Its three or four upper *tones* belong mostly to head voice. Its character is more gentle, yielding, but giving an impression of youthful strength. It is also more capable in general of fiery inward passion than the bass character. Its *tones* are usually written in the tenor clef. It may be observed that this clef comprises most conveniently, all its *tones*; that is, with the fewest ledger lines—

138.

---

* More minute information upon this point will be found in the Author's Treatise on Composition, Parts 3 and 4.

† The *tone* of the voice is formed in the Larynx, a mechanism consisting of cartilage, ligaments, and muscles, at the upper end of the Trachea, or more properly it is the highest part thereof, which, especially in men, can be seen and felt exteriorly, under the throat. The *Cordæ vocales*, with the muscles attached to them, together with the mucous membrane, form an opening termed *rima glottidis*, which leads upwards from the trachea into the cavity of the mouth. On the greater or less tension of the *cordæ vocales* and contraction of the *rima glottidis*, depends the height or depth of the voice. The more forcible the tension, the higher is the *tone*.

‡ Mezza-voce singing has been latterly much admired in Lind, and earlier in Sontag. It might have been considered still more wonderful in the great Catalani, who, though but rarely, interwove it with matchless grace in her otherwise colossal and magnificent song. Inimitable was she in a passage peculiar to herself, in which she ran up the scale in mezza voce, repeating each *tone* three or four times with the utmost rapidity, while panting in the tenderest emotion.

§ The Tenor has had its name *Tenor* (contents, chief contents), from the ecclesiastical music of the middle ages, it being the function of this voice, in preference, to sing the plain chant (cantus firmus), which as the principal part, was therefore the chief thing or contents to be done.

‖ (In German) "*All*" from *Altus, alta vox*—properly the *high* voice, in respect of the tenor, then considered the chief voice.

and we have here also another proof of the fit adaptation of the clefs.

Besides this proper clef, the tenor is also set in the G clef, but then its *tones* sound an octave lower than they are written.* This passage, for example—

139. [musical notation]

will sound like this—

140. [musical notation]

The Contralto

has an extent from about the little g or a, up to the two-lined c or d. Its *tones* are mostly chest voice. Its character is full, but femininely benign. It is best noted in the alto clef, or at any rate, in the soprano, but for the sake of facility, it may perhaps be allowed in the G clef.

The Treble or Soprano

comprises the *tones* from about the one-lined c to the two-lined g or a, or also b.† Its upper *tones* belong chiefly to the head voice. Its character is gentle, but more lightsome and youthful than the contralto, and more appropriate for the expression of lively, joyous, or passionate emotions. It is noted either in the soprano or in the G clef.

(B)   SPEECH.

Since song is usually combined with speech, we must consider this latter as an organ of music, without inquiring into the meaning of the words or the purport of the discourse. Here we may remark, in brief, that speech also, has its own longs and shorts, emphatic and unemphatic syllables, arising and falling (although not in clearly appreciable intervals), and therefore contains in itself elements of music. It has also a variety of characteristic sounds, the elements of its

Articulation

being indeed the several vowel sounds. We will place first the vowels themselves, as pure vowel or vocal sounds, and arrange them in the order of their aptitude for height and depth, beginning with the former :—

$$I—E—A—O—U.‡$$

The dipthongs are mixtures or combinations of the vowels. The consonants are accompanying characteristic sounds, added to the vowel sounds. Of the consonants, we shall only give the following sibilants, as an example :—

s, sch, sz, c, z, ts, tz, &c.

With all these materials, speech, musically considered, exhibits a large variety of forms and broadly marked differences of expression. It seems clear and full in the Latin, lofty and ingenious in the Greek, picturesque and sublime in the Hebrew, passionate in the Italian or Spanish, mixed and cloudy in the French, and especially in the English. The German has not the advantage of pleasing the ear, but in deep significance of characteristic expression, it stands preeminent.

These assertions, however, must be considered as merely superficial notices, upon a subject very interesting for many reasons to a musician. Least of all, can the character of a language be given or estimated from its characteristic sound only. French has been elevated by its poets and by Gluck, in union with music, to the highest dignity and most appropriate expression: and who can ever forget that Shakspeare and Byron have spoken to us in English.

We have yet an observation to make respecting the notation of songs, with regard to the placing of the syllables under the notes.

We have before stated that two, four, and more quavers, semiquavers, &c., may be joined together by a common line of duration, thus :—

[musical notation]

This takes place in singing notes, solely when they are all to be sung to one syllable, for example :—

141. [musical notation]
    A - - - men.

But notes belonging to different syllables, are always written separately, for instance :—

142. [musical notation]
    A - men.   Hal-le-lu-jah.

On the other hand, notes written separately on account of the notation, are bound together by a curve, if they are to be sung on one syllable, thus—

143. [musical notation]
    A - - - - men.

THIRD SECTION.—STRINGED INSTRUMENTS.

According to our intimation at page 45, we shall consider under this head (the bowed instruments being excluded) only the stringed instruments most in use, and shall therefore limit ourselves to the keyed instruments, the harp, and guitar.

KEYED INSTRUMENTS. §

Such are in general, all instruments whose sound is

---

* They would therefore be of sixteen feet tone, as explained at page 45.

† The extent attributed in the text to the several voices, is what is usually required of good choristers. Some voices, however, exceed greatly the limits so prescribed. Old Fischer, the singer, sustained the great D against trumpets and drums for four bars. Mozart heard a bravura when in Italy, for a female voice, which reached up to the four-lined e.

The author, and many persons still living in Berlin, have several times heard the sister (then twelve years old), of a female singer of that place, produce five E's (the little, 1, 2, 3 and 4 lined),

and moreover, with the greatest clearness and purity of intonation.

An amateur friend of ours of St. Petersburg, used to find the deep bass parts *too high* for him. He sang with a full beautiful voice, the double AA, but could not reach higher than the one-lined c.

‡	I	E	A	O	U
			To be pronounced as—		
			first as—		
	e—in me	a—in may	a—in mar	a—in all	ou—in you
	she	say	tar	call	o „ who
	ee „ eel	day	far	fall	oo „ moon
				then as—	
				o—in so	
				low	
				show	

TRANSLATOR.

§ However superfluous it may appear to enter into any particulars concerning the nature of these universally familiar instruments, a few words touching their *principal feature* will not perhaps be useless. That, is the *sounding board*, which in the pianoforte is under the strings; it is the body (as it is called) of the harp, and the body of the guitar, and of bowed instruments, whose strings are stretched upon it.

The strings of all these instruments have by themselves alone, but a feeble sound, which to be musically serviceable must be increased in volume. Now, it has been observed that when any sonorous body, such as a pipe or string, is made to sound, all sonorous bodies sufficiently near and at liberty to vibrate, produce of themselves, either the same sound, produced by pressure or percussion by means of a finger-board. Of all this class,

THE PIANOFORTE

alone, has established itself in full artistic citizenship.

It is well known that in the pianoforte, the sound is produced by striking each string with a hammer moved by the keys: that the compass of the instrument extends from double F, double E, or double C, up to the four-lined octave, to f, or still higher,

and that as many *tones* may be played together as the hands can grasp. Its characteristic sound also, slighter and less enduring than that of most other instruments, is known to everyone, as well as, that compositions for this instrument are usually written on two combined staves in the G and F clefs.

144.

or also (in older works) in the soprano and F clefs.

The importance of this instrument arises from its being capable of producing harmony as well as melody; and indeed (to a certain degree) compositions of numerous parts.

We will call such instruments

SELF-SUFFICING,

since they can produce a complete work of art, not merely a single succession of sounds. Considering, then, the comparative mechanical easiness of the pianoforte, and the great advantage of its remaining so long in tune, beyond other stringed instruments, it is no wonder that it has been so generally patronized, nor that so much music, and of such an important character, should have been written for it.

2.—THE HARP *(arpa).*

This instrument also, is so well known, that we need but say few words about it.

The harp, as is well known, has many strings, freely exposed to the impact or seizure of the fingers on both sides, and is therefore capable of producing harmony as well as melody. It is inferior, however, in this respect, to the pianoforte, from the short duration of its sounds, whereby (in its present construction at least) the effect of the combination of long and short sounds cannot be produced. But, for pure musical sounds, of silvery, bell-like character, the harp is most admirable: these, particularly in *pianissimo,* it can evolve in really delicious and aërial harmonies.

A still greater disadvantage of the harp, as compared to the pianoforte, is the impossibility of its possessing simultaneously, all the semitones.

The harp, in its quiescent state, is limited to one major scale; and if a *tone* be required, which is not contained in that scale, a string must be altered to produce it. There are two ways of effecting this object, and therefore two kinds of harps.

The Hook, or Irish harp, is of the earlier kind. In the neck of this, there is near the peg for each string, a little metal hook, by the turning of which, the strings are drawn tighter, and are thereby raised a semitone. But this process requires a pause in the playing, since it must be applied to each string separately.

The Pedal Harp has in a great degree overcome this imperfection. By this invention, the strings required are raised a semitone throughout all their octaves. The pedal harp is tuned to E♭ major. By the pedals, d may be converted into $d\sharp$, c into $c\sharp$, $b\flat$ into b, $e\flat$ into e, f into $f\sharp$, g into $g\sharp$, and $a\flat$ into a.

The harp extends to five octaves. Its notation is in all respects similar to that of the pianoforte, on two staves, in the clefs of G and F.

Finally, we must mention the universally familiar

GUITAR,*

a small and very imperfect variety of the harp species. It has six strings tuned to these *tones—*

145.

By means of pressure with the fingers at the divisions, called *frets*, on the finger-board, this instrument may be made to produce all the semitones from the great E up to the two-lined e. The notation is written in the violin clef, an *octave higher*. The open strings would therefore be written so—

146.

but they are heard to sound an octave deeper. The instrument is therefore said to be of sixteen feet *tone,* as we have explained at page 45.

FOURTH SECTION.—BOWED INSTRUMENTS.

Bowed instruments are those whose strings, mostly four, are stretched over a sounding and finger-board, and whose sound is produced, as the name imports, by the friction of a bow. By this manner of production, the character of their sound is sometimes highly attractive, at others most harshly repulsive;

---

or a sound nearly related to it, and thus strengthen the original sound. So, on the pianoforte, (the dampers being raised,) if a deep *tone* be produced with force, the nearest related *tones* will be heard with it. Thus, the deep *tone,* being for example C, the sounds produced of themselves would be the octave c, then the fifth g, then again, c, e, g and $b\flat$, (see note at page 17). This sympathetic vibration can not only be heard, but seen also. This may be effected by placing little saddles of light paper on several of the strings of a pianoforte. On the deep key being struck, the little saddles will be thrown off the related strings, by their vibrations, but will remain quiescent on the unrelated strings, although these may lie nearer to the deep *tone.* Now, the air under the sounding board, and these several contrivances themselves, are the accompanying vibrators for all the sounds, and by their means alone the required power is given to the strings. A violinist can produce a similar effect by placing an open vessel on his violin, whereby the air in the vessel is found to vibrate. From this same source proceeds the resonance, sometimes favourable, sometimes the contrary, in a musical sense, of vaulted roofs and hollow floors.

* The Mandolin and Cithern are inferior specimens of this class of instruments, which has been well known from the earliest antiquity in Greece, India, and China. The first is common in Italy. The second, set with wires and struck by a bit of quill, is still occasionally met with in the Alpine regions. Formerly the beautiful and comparatively powerful lute was much admired. This instrument had supernumerary strings, which resounded with those played upon: owing, however, to the difficulty of keeping it in tune, it fell out of use. The Theorbo was a more important instrument: it was of the nature of a large guitar, but had strings on two or three sides, and was principally used in orchestras for the thorough bass, or in *obligato* accompaniments.

The Æolian harp might also be mentioned here, were it not rather a natural than an artistic instrument. Its strings are distended over a sounding board and tuned to unison. When properly exposed to a current of air, whereby the strings may be set in motion, fairy-like and enchanting harmonies are wafted from its coincident vibrations.

and in the gradations of *piano* and *forte*, they are illimitably comprehensive, so that their application is almost universal. Very high *tones* of a peculiar character are obtained from these instruments, by a manner of fingering, which allows only certain proportions* of the string to vibrate, preventing at the same time, its vibration in its entire length. These tones are called

HARMONICS,

and are of a dulcet, flute-like character.

Stringed instruments undergo an extraordinary change by placing a mute on the bridge. The sound not only becomes diminished, but it acquires also a gloomy timidity of character, which properly introduced, has a powerful effect. The application of the mute is signified by—

C. S., Con sordino;

the detachment by—

S. S., Senza sordino,

placed over the notes.

Bowed instruments may also be played on by nipping or twitching the strings with the fingers, in which case they assume a harp or guitar-like character of sound, but harder and of less duration. This manner of playing is indicated by—

pizz., pizzicato;

and on the other hand—

C. A., col arco

signifies that the bow is to be used.

There are at present four kinds of bowed instruments in use :—

1.—THE VIOLIN.

It has four strings, tuned thus :—

147.

But by stopping or pressing the strings with the fingers on the finger board, it is capable of producing all the semitones up to the four-lined c, and still higher.

Two strings may be made to sound simultaneously; and even three may be taken with such rapidity in one bow, that the ear imagines the sounds to be simultaneous. The violin is therefore like all other bowed instruments capable of producing harmony; but only in a very limited degree: it cannot perform part-compositions, properly so called. It is also, like all bowed instruments, peculiarly appropriate for melody, and therefore, in general,‡ should be used only in conjunction with other instruments.

---

* Under ordinary circumstances of tension, a string vibrates in its whole length, between its two fixed ends. It may be imagined thus:—

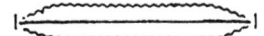

The *tone* is the result of the vibration of the whole length of the string. But the harmonics are the result of the vibrations of sections of the string, and their *tone* corresponds with the quantity of each section in proportion to the length of the whole string. This figure may be understood to represent vibration in sections :—

More intimate knowledge in this matter belongs to Acoustics.

† The above supposed vibration in sections would be heard, I apprehend, as the double octave of the whole string.—TRANSLATOR.

‡ It is quite possible, no doubt, for a violin alone to perform a complete composition. Seb. Bach even wrote a fugue in four parts for a violin—but such feats are extraordinary—they are exceptions, depending upon artistic combinations.

But this, its destiny, it is in the highest degree capable of accomplishing, far, very far beyond the reach of any other instrument. Its compass is almost beyond limitation; its power, from the nearly imperceptible *piano*, to the most piercing *forte;* its continuity at will in slow, and velocity in quick passages; its endless variety of kinds and degrees of *staccato* and *legato* all combined, give it a high pre-eminence among musical instruments.

Its notation is written in the G clef.

2.—THE TENOR (*Viola*).§

This is a large violin, and it is thus tuned :—

148.

Its compass extends up to the two-lined *g*, and still higher. Its notation is written in the alto clef.

3.—THE VIOLONCELLO∥

has four strings, thus tuned :—

149.

Its compass reaches to the one-lined *a*, and, with the assistance of the harmonics, one or two octaves higher. Generally its notation is in the F clef, but for higher *tones* the tenor and G clefs are used.

Our additional remarks on the violin may be applied equally to the tenor and violoncello.

4.—THE DOUBLE BASS

has commonly four (sometimes three or five) strings, which are usually tuned from *E* upwards in fourths. Its notation is in the F clef, but being a sixteen feet instrument, its great *E* sounds the double *E*, &c. It is seldom or never double stopped, and is as rarely used with a mute. It can be made to produce its *tones* up to the one-lined *e*, and higher, but as it is of sixteen feet, that would be the sound of the small *e*.

Bowed instruments are used either for solos or for

DUOS,

generally two violins, or a violin and violoncello; or for

TRIOS,

usually the violin, tenor, and violoncello; or for

QUATUORS,

generally two violins, tenor, and violoncello; or for Quintuors, Double Quatuors, or also in conjunction with a pianoforte, or some wind instruments; or, in fine, to form an

ORCHESTRA.

In this event they are increased in number. Generally there are two (sometimes more) separate parts for the violin, violoncello, and double bass; for the two latter united into *one* part,¶ (proceeding

---

§ The name in full is *viola di braccio,* (arm violin), in contradistinction to the *violoncello* (which is held between the legs or knees), or rather more properly, to the predecessor of this latter, the *viol di gamba* (leg viola). From *braccio* is derived the German *bratsche*, meaning a tenor violin.

∥ The root name of the double bass is *violono* the largest or deepest bass. The next smaller or higher is the *violoncello*. The next in the diminishing gradation is the *viola*, and the smallest is the *violino* or small *viola*. The violoncello was formerly called in Germany the *Bassatel* or little bass. It is also called in that country, for shortness, the *Cello*.

¶ It is very rarely that two separate parts are used for the double bass. It may happen, indeed, where two orchestras are formed to play at the same time: as for example, in the *matthäischen Passionsmusik* of Seb. Bach. Mozart introduced three orchestras at once, as we have shewn at page 41, together with three different double basses.

usually in octaves) so that a bow orchestra consists usually of the following parts:—

  Violino Primo (1mo.)
  Violino Secondo (2do.)
  Viola,
  Violoncello and Double Bass.

If a passage is to be played by the violoncello alone, it is marked

  VC., Violoncello.

If the double bass is to accompany, it is marked

  CB., Contrabasso.

If a part is to be divided or separated for a certain time into two, three, or four, it is signified by

  div. (divise),

or by

  a due, a tre, &c. (by two, or by three, &c.)

The mass of the bowed instruments is to be considered as the chief support in a grand orchestra; both in itself from its peculiar attributions, and, moreover, from its singular adaptation to the most diversified of all parts, namely, the human voice.

FIFTH SECTION.—REED OR TUBULAR INSTRUMENTS.

We have already said, that we shall include in this class all wind instruments whose tube is usually made of wood.

All these instruments have more or less, a gentle, soft, and smooth character of sound, resembling in some degree the human voice. They are capable of producing a considerable extent of *tones*, but of these they can only bring forth one at a time. They are superseded, however, by the bowed instruments, in fine gradation of *piano* and *forte*, in progressive *diminuendo* and *crescendo*, and in the length of continuous sound.

We shall mention the following kinds and their derivatives.

1.—The Flute, (*Flauto*)

This has the most smooth and soft character of sound, and usually comprises an extent of *tones* from the one-lined *d* (sometimes *c*), up to the three-lined *a*, and still higher. Its notation is in the G clef, and in sound it is of eight feet tone.

A derivative hereof is the

  Flauto Piccolo,

or octave flute. It has a more piercing, tingling sound than the common flute, and its *tones* are heard an octave higher than they are written. It is consequently a four-feet tone instrument, and on it, the two-lined *d* sounds as the three-lined *d* on the common flute or pianoforte.

In character of sound,

2.—The Clarinet

approaches nearest to the flute. It has, however, a fuller and more powerful expression, which it acquires by means of a strip of reed in the mouthpiece. Its compass extends from the small *e*, up to the three-lined *e* or *f*, and still higher. It is also noted in the G clef.

As all successions of *tones* cannot be produced upon this instrument with equal facility, and as those farther removed from its own natural succession present considerable imperfections, clarinets of different pitch have been introduced, in order to accommodate the most usual successions. Three kinds are usual in our orchestra:—

  The C Clarinet,

whose *tones* sound as they are written;

  The B♭ Clarinet,

whose *tones* sound a whole tone deeper than they are written;

  The A Clarinet,

which is a minor third deeper than the C clarinet.

This passage, therefore—

150.

would be played as it is written, on the C clarinet: a tone deeper on the B♭ clarinet, so:—

151.

and on the A clarinet, a tone and semitone deeper still, so:—

152.

or *C, G, D* major, become on the B♭ clarinet as *B♭, F, C* major, and on the A clarinet the sound as *A, E, B* major.

Of these three kinds, the highest, the C clarinet, has the clearest and sharpest character of sound; the B♭ clarinet combines fulness with geniality; the A clarinet is the softest, but at the same time the most feeble.

Higher clarinets, such as in D, E♭, and F, (in which *c* sounds as the higher *d, e♭,* or *f*) are confined almost exclusively to military music, and are still shriller than the C clarinet.

  The Basset Horn (*corno di bassetto*),

is a derivative of the clarinet, and sounds a fifth deeper than it is written. Therefore the one-lined *c* as the small *f*. This passage—

153.

sounds as:—

154.

It is a clarinet bent at a blunt angle, for facility of use, with a metallic bell. By means of particular keys it can produce two *tones* (the little *c* and *d*, that is, therefore, *F* and *G*) which other clarinets cannot. Its compass, written in the G clef, goes from the small *c*, up to the three-lined *d*; therefore from the great *F* to the two-lined *g*. This gentle, elegiac, or more properly, funereal instrument, is comparatively speaking, very little in use; the more powerful clarinets have not allowed it. Mozart was the first to recognize the peculiar attributes of this instrument, which no other species of clarinet could satisfactorily replace; and availed himself thereof in the *Titus*, and quite specially in the *Requiem*, in which two basset horns and two bassoons form the whole choir of tubular instruments. These, indeed, spread a most appropriate pall of grief and mourning over the solemn service for the dead, which the introduction of clarinets, oboes, or flutes, however these might be managed, would only disturb.

A much inferior derivative of the clarinet has appeared of late, under the name of

ALT (tenor) CLARINET,

introduced by Ivan Müller. This is only a large clarinet, curved near the mouth-piece, and is also a fifth deeper than the ordinary clarinet, (therefore the small *e* is as the great *A*). In this, however, not only the two deep tones of the basset horn are wanting, but also the peculiar and characteristic sounds of the latter instrument are absent. The management of the Alt clarinet in the massive military bands and orchestras of wind instruments now in vogue, has become more feasible; and here and there a conductor may be found, willing to employ the Alt clarinet in lieu of the basset horn,* perhaps, in some degree, from want of players on the latter instrument.

3. THE HAUTBOY (*oboe*)

is an instrument similar to the clarinet, but which has a mouth-piece formed of two flat bits of reed laid together, and is also smaller and thinner in the body than the clarinet.

In compass, the hautboy resembles more the flute than the clarinet. It has usually the *tones* from the small *b*, up to the three-lined *d̳*, or *e̳* and *f̳*, and is noted in the G clef. Its character, however, is broadly distinguished from that of the flute. From its construction, greater narrowness of tube, and form of embouchure, its character of sound is more shrill and cutting, whereby it is possibly less removed from the violin than from the flute. It is susceptible, nevertheless, of great delicacy, and sometimes exhibits power.

A species of the hautboy is the

ENGLISH HORN (*corno Inglese*),

which is called also the Oboe di caccia, (hunting hautboy). This has the same notation as the hautboy; but its *tones* are a fifth deeper; therefore, the one-lined *c* is as the small *f*. This passage—

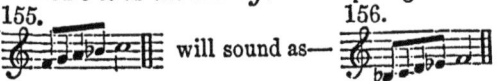

This instrument also, is at present but rarely used. Among the moderns, Spontini employed it occasionally. In Seb. Bach's scores, it appears constantly.

4.—THE BASSOON (*fagotto*).

The bassoon is a wind instrument with a long and sufficiently thick tube, and is played by means of a double reed (larger than in the hautboy) fixed in a thin metallic tube, called the S. Its sound is soft and full, but in consequence of the reed (as in the hautboy) it is rather nasal, so that it approaches somewhat to the character of the violoncello. The compass of this instrument reaches from the double B♭, up to the one-lined *g*, and a few degrees higher Its notation is in the F clef, the higher *tones* are sometimes in the tenor.

THE DOUBLE BASSOON

has a compass from the great *D* up to the one-lined *d̲*. Its *tones*, however, sound an octave lower than they are written, it being of sixteen-feet tone.†

With the bassoon and double bassoon, particularly in wind orchestras to strengthen the bass, are combined the

BASS HORN (*corno basso*) and the OPHICLEIDE.

This last is a metallic tube, and therefore an exception from our rule touching tubular instruments. It has the great compass from double *B* to the two-lined *c̲*, and is of sixteen-feet tone, but is difficult of intonation. To these may be added the

SERPENT (*serpente*).

All these three instruments, particularly the last, differ materially in their construction from the bassoon, and they are here aggregated to it, merely because from their character and employment they associate better with the bassoon than with any other class of instruments. The most important among them is the serpent, which has a compass from double B♭, up to the one-lined *g*, or, indeed, to the two-lined *c̲*, and in character of sound is about midway between the bassoon and trombone, from the latter of which it has taken its mouth-piece.

In grand orchestras there are generally *two* separate flutes, hautboys, clarinets, bassoons,—also, if wanted, two basset horns and as many piccolo flutes, or of the latter, only one; but of the derivatives of the bassoon, only the double bassoon, or a serpent; and unless the setting of the bowed orchestra be uncommonly numerous, each part is played singly.

SIXTH SECTION.—BRASS INSTRUMENTS.

Under this head we comprehend wind instruments whose body is made of metal, with the exception of some (the ophicleide for instance) whose employment and character associate them rather with the tubular instruments. We are peculiarly concerned with three descriptions.

1.—THE HORN (*corno*).

The body of this instrument is long and wide, and is wound in a circular form. By means of a mouth-piece, it produces a soft and gentle, but full and powerful sound. Its natural serviceable *tones* are the following:—

which can be lowered a half or whole tone, by more or less closing the bell with the inserted hand. But the sounds then assume a dead, hollow character, and are not so much at command as the natural *tones*. In order to make the horn serviceable in several successions of tones, many kinds, of dif-

---

* A bass clarinet (an octave deeper than the C or B♭ clarinet) has also lately come into use through Meyerbeer.

† The quart bassoon and the fagottino are rare and useless derivations from the bassoon. The quart was a fourth lower, and the fagottino a fourth higher.

ferent height in *tone* have been invented. The most useful are

THE DEEP B♭ HORN,

in which every *tone* sounds a degree lower: and therefore *c* sounds as the *b♭* next below it.

THE C HORN,
THE D HORN,

the sound of each of which is a tone higher; therefore, for example, *c* is as *d*.

THE E♭ HORN,
THE E HORN,
THE F HORN,
THE G HORN,
THE A HORN,
THE HIGH B♭ HORN.

It will be guessed at once that on the E♭ horn, *c* sounds as *e♭* (each note a minor third higher); on the E horn *c* sounds like *e*; and so forth.

All these different kinds of horns, however, are in sixteen-feet tone, and therefore, in conformity with the general rule, give their *tones* an octave lower than written. This passage, therefore,—

158.

produces upon the various horns the *tones* noted respectively under them, as follows:—

Deep Horn in B♭.   Horn in C.   Horn in D.
159.
Horn in E♭.   Horn in E.   Horn in F.

Horn in G.   Horn in A.   High Horn in B♭.

All horn notation is in the G clef; and in conformity with the foregoing elucidation, the notes must be first placed on the correct degrees, and then transferred to the deeper octave. The lowest octave, *C—c*, is, however, generally noted in the F clef:—

160.

and these, exceptionally, are not considered of sixteen-feet tone, but of eight-feet tone.

2.—THE TRUMPET (*Clarino or Tromba*).

This instrument has the same natural *tones* as the horn, and is employed in the same manner, in many successions of *tones*. It is not, however, of sixteen-feet tone, but of eight-feet tone. The most usual kinds are—

THE B♭ TRUMPET,

which sounds one tone deeper, that is, *c* like *b♭*.

THE C TRUMPET,

which sounds as it is written.

THE D TRUMPET,
THE E♭ TRUMPET,
THE E TRUMPET,
THE F TRUMPET,

in which *c* sounds as *d*, *e♭*, *e* and *f*.

The characteristic sound of the trumpet is clear and powerful—in the lower tones, vibrant.*

3. THE TROMBONE

is a large trumpet, which is however so constructed, that the two tubes of which it consists may be lengthened at pleasure by two other inserted tubes. The length of the whole tube may thus be varied at will by the player, whereby various successions of tones may be produced, including all the semitones within the compass of the instrument.

The character of the sound of the trombone is similar to that of the trumpet, but more powerful. Three kinds of trombones are in use of different ranges:—

(*A*) THE ALTO TROMBONE (*Trombone alto*) has a compass from the small *c* or *e* to the one-lined *a*, or two-lined *c*, and is noted in the alto clef.

(*B*) THE TENOR TROMBONE (*Trombone tenore*) has a compass from the small *c*, to the one-lined *g*, but has more power and character, particularly in the lower tones, than the alto trombone. Its notation is in the tenor clef.

(*C*) THE BASS TROMBONE (*Trombone basso*) has a compass from the great *C* to the one-lined *e*, and is noted in the F clef.

There are generally in an orchestra, two, or it may be, four horns, two trumpets, and three trombones.

Besides the instruments mentioned, another class has been recently introduced, partly old instruments improved, and partly inventions originally introduced into military music, and subsequently into orchestras, which we shall comprise under the name of

4. TUBES.

Of these we shall say a word concerning the principal kinds.

(*A*)   THE HIGH B♭ CORNET.

This is a tube bearing some resemblance to a trumpet, but is wider, and spreads out more suddenly. By means of additional crooks and three valves, it produces the succession of tones noted as at (*a*), but which sound as at (*b*):—

161.

(*B*)   THE E♭ CORNET

has a compass from the one-lined *c*, to three-lined *c*, and is noted in the G clef, but sounds a *minor* sixth deeper.

---

* In order to facilitate the use of the trumpet and horn, valve-trumpets and valve-horns have recently been invented. In these instruments a portion of the tube is opened or shut, and thus a higher or a lower pitch may be given to them; and indeed, very easily. But by this arrangement, and the compressed curvature of the tube connected with it, the instruments lose much of their original freshness and power, which was so essential to their peculiar character. Moreover, a complete scale of their characteristic sounds, so precious to a composer, is not necessary: and that their natural tones have been employed because they were the most characteristic, can be shewn from the works of the greatest instrumentalists, namely, Haydn and Beethoven. Only in military music, subject to the fashion or caprice of the moment and heedless of musical reputation, are these instruments become a necessary evil. It is to be lamented, that under the influence of the French-Italian Opera, the most natural instruments, full of health and character, are constantly decreasing in our orchestras.

(*C*) The Tenor Horn (*corno cromatico di tenore*), also called the chromatic tenor horn, is noted in the tenor clef, and has a compass from great $A\flat$, to the two-lined c.

(*D*) The Tenor Bass is noted in the *F* clef, and has a compass from the great F, to the one-lined $b\flat$.

(*E*) The Bass Tube, which, with five valves, has the great compass from double *D* to the two-lined $e\flat$ and g.

Of these instruments, the high $B\flat$ cornet may be considered as the treble (treble tube), the $E\flat$ cornet as the alto (alto tube), the tenor horn as the tenor (tenor tube), the tenor bass as bass, and the bass tube as the double bass.

Other instruments, such as the bass trumpet, klappen horn (kent horn) post horn, and so forth, we must pass over.

The foregoing instruments have a medium character between the horn and the trombone, and form by their capabilities, sufficient scales of metallic sound to establish an intervening class between the reed instruments—which they threaten to banish or to overwhelm—and the brass instruments, whose pure and decided characteristics they do not possess, but much rather injure by being too copiously employed.

SEVENTH SECTION.—THE ORGAN.

The organ is, in its essence, nothing more than an assemblage of many wind instruments; not blown, however, by mouth, but by a magazine of wind, and brought into operation so soon as the communication between the air and the instruments or pipes are opened by the player.

The organ is incomparably rich in such pipes, which it possesses in the greatest diversity of pitch and character of sound.

The player commands the instrument through one or several key-boards, of which some, generally two, and rarely more than three, are played with the hands (manuals)—and one, with the feet, (pedals) unless the organ be too small to admit of a pedal.

The manuals are precisely similar to the finger-board of a pianoforte, and generally extend from the great *C* to the three-lined d.

The pedals are correspondingly arranged, with this variation, that being for the use of the feet, they are larger and further apart than the keys in the manual. They extend from the great *C* to the one-lined d.

To each claviature, or key-board, several ranges of pipes belong, of which either a single range, or any number in conjunction, or altogether in one massive sound, may be set in operation. The admittance of wind to the various ranges of pipes is effected by handles, called stops or registers. The range only, whose stop is drawn out, is capable of producing sound.

The manuals and pedals may be joined together by attaching wires, and then all the drawn-out stops may produce sound at once.

Every sound continues with equable force, so long as the key be pressed down.

The sounds vary both in pitch and in character.

The deepest sounds are in thirty-two feet *tone*, and therefore intonate *two octaves* deeper than written: thus, the one-lined *c*, as the great *c*.

Then come those of sixteen-feet *tone*, which are one octave deeper; the one-lined *c*, as the small *c*.

Of eight-feet *tone*, the standard number.

Of four-feet *tone*, which are an octave higher, the one-lined *c*, as the two-lined *c*.

Of two and one-feet *tone*, which sound two and three octaves higher, respectively.

Other stops sound a third and fifth higher or lower; others, again, called mixtures, produce to each key several pipes, tuned relatively to each other in octaves, thirds, and fifths, &c., sounding of necessity, simultaneously: so that when any key on the key-board is pressed down, its own *tone*, and its octave, or itself, octave and fifth, or these intervals in several octaves, with the addition in some cases of the major third, are all heard together.*

Many of the registers are intended to imitate or

---

* We are under a twofold obligation to enter into a more minute explanation here. In the first place, the employment of mixtures for harmonic effect, may appear to those unacquainted with the organ, inconceivable, nay, contrary to common sense. If every key besides its own *tone*, produces its octave, third, and fifth, the most simple chord (see Sect. 5 of 4th Division), for instance, $c-e-g$, would produce the following chaos of harmonically contradictory *tones*:—

$$c-e-g-c-e-g-b-c-d-e-g-g\sharp-b$$

and the chord, second in importance in music, $c-e-g-b\flat$, would have the following:—

$$c-e-g-b\flat-c-e-g-b\flat-b-c-d-e-f-g-g\sharp-b\flat-b-d$$

produced and sounding in confusion all together. Here it must serve as an explanation, that mixtures are to be employed only with judgment, taking care that the principal melody and harmony be enforced by sufficiently numerous and powerful registers, so that out of the above storms of vibrations, nothing but the chords $c-e-g$ and $c-e-g-b\flat$, shall come clearly and prominently forth.

In the second place, we must not omit to mention on the other hand, the condemnation of these mixtures by the important voices of Gottfried Weber and the celebrated Chladny, so famed in the science of sound. These and others have declared the mixtures to be at variance with all our ideas of harmony and music, a pernicious error derived from mediæval barbarism. Of many well-informed and able defenders of the ancient system, we will name but one, the highly respected music-director, Wilke, justly esteemed for his knowledge of organ building, and his dissertations in the *Leipziger allg. mus. zeitg.*

We will only remark briefly, that as it appears to us, the opposition to mixtures arises from our too confined apprehension of musical truth. The theory hitherto has proceeded on the mere presumption that music is an art producing melody and harmony *by means of tones*. Everything else—sound, character of sound, even rhythm—has been considered but of secondary importance, and fundamentally unessential. Weber indeed, and almost alone, has entered into the examination of rhythm in the arrangement of music; but even he, most unsatisfactorily. Regarding sound and its qualities in relation to music, we have nothing at all worth naming.

Now, the mixtures are exactly appropriate (as must have been remarked), for the production of masses of sound, for the accumulation of that all-powerful element in the organ, independently of the melodious or harmonious effect. We find many types in nature and in sounding materials, that a *mighty manifestation* forms at the same time *its own proper atmosphere*—so light is accompanied by either sparkling or faint radiations; thunder is enveloped in hollow reverberations; bells, besides their deep and powerful sound, evolve repeated secondary sounds; even strings give supplementary vibrations (as *C* gives $c-g-c-e-g$, and one like $b\flat$,) more or less perceptible. This atmosphere may be considered as the fulness of effects and combinations. which in the mere sound or ray, are presented to us in an abstract, dry, and unconnected form. So in the vast cathedral, the powerful organ evolves its atmosphere of secondary sounds, which convert the whole space into a resounding medium, most appropriate for influential effect upon the hearer. The same effect is aimed at in the orchestra, when in the masses of *forte* the middle parts are crowded with various forms of composition, not for the sake of melody, but for the production of a mass of sound, which, involving and involved, shall work out its own proper object. An attentive and educated ear can perceive secondary sounds proceeding from the whole mass of an orchestra; not from one instrument or the other, but waves of sounds, the result of, or springing from, countless and inappreciable vibrations.

So much for this point of contention. Every one indeed should stand up for this view; for if, on the contrary, the mixtures were to be abolished or expelled, permanent injury would be done to many works properly adapted to the real character of the organ.

represent the sounds of other instruments;—some ancient and gone out of use, and others forming still, part of our orchestras. To these belong the double bass, 16 and 8 feet; flute or reed flute, 8 and 4 feet; hautboy, 8 feet; bassoon, 16 and 8 feet; trumpet, 8 feet; and so forth. There is a register, also, called the *vox humana*, intended to imitate the human voice. Other ranges of pipes are proper to the organ itself, such as the principal and many others.

The various orders of pipes are divided into labial stops, whose pipes have a mouth narrowed from the inside, and to which order the principal belongs; two reed stops, in which the sound is produced or modified by a tongue, which vibrates in the interior of the pipe; and lastly, the *stopped pipes*, which are covered or closed at the top, and sound, in consequence thereof, an octave deeper than they otherwise would in proportion to their length.

When we reflect that a superior organ has forty, sixty, and more registers at command, whose diversity of character may be endlessly increased by combinations of the individual ranges, some more delicate than any orchestral instrument, others of vibrating power, and that the full organ in its whole power is sufficient to overwhelm any orchestra,—we cannot but acknowledge its vast superiority over every other instrument, and the propriety of its name from *organum* (Instrument, engine), it being assuredly and supereminently the instrument; since none other can be compared with or stand against it. The proper use, combination, and change of the stops or registers, is of itself an object of much study and ingenuity. The notation for the organ is the same as that of the pianoforte, generally in two staves in the G and F clefs; but in old compositions, the soprano, alto, and tenor clefs are occasionally found.

The pedal notes are marked
PED. (*pedale*),
and the manual notes,
MAN. (*manuale, manualmente*),
or *S. P., Senza pedale*.

If the pedal is rich and belongs to a full manual, it may be proper to write it on a third staff, under the first and second, which would then be reserved for the manual alone.

The combination of the registers is seldom indicated by composers; neither indeed can it be determined with exactness and for general application. Organs differ very much from each other in the number, choice, and composition of their registers; and therefore a combination, perfectly suitable on one, might be unfavourable, or impossible on another. In case particular feet tone, different key-boards, the full organ, or soft combinations of stops, be required, these circumstances are usually expressed in general terms at the beginning of the composition.

EIGHTH SECTION.—PERCUSSIVE INSTRUMENTS.

Here we are concerned with the most usual only. The chief is the
KETTLE-DRUM (*timpano*),
of a hollow, echoing sound. This instrument gives out one serviceable *tone*; but it can be tuned to any *tone* between the great and small *F*. Two kettle-drums are therefore generally used, and they are tuned to a fourth, consisting of the dominant and tonic.*

If the kettle-drums are muffled, which is indicated by
TIMP. (*timpani*) COPERTI,
their sound becomes dull and suppressed.

They are noted in the F clef. The above tuning is observed; thus, for example:—

162. Timp. in d, A.

and the notation is written in C, or also (which strictly speaking is incorrect, and in contradiction to the notation of the trumpets and horns, usually associated with the drums) in the *tones* which must sound according to the tuning indicated; thus, for example:—

163. Timp. in d, A.

Here it might be thought, according to the usage of speech mentioned under wind instruments, that the *tones e—B* would be produced; but those at the beginning of the staff are to be understood, and as the drums give only one *tone*, a misunderstanding is impossible.

2. BANDA.

We comprehend under this head—
THE GREAT DRUM (*gran tamburo*),
THE CYMBALS (*piatti, cinelli*),
THE TRIANGLE (*triangulo*),

Instruments of no determined tone, but of mere sound, and too well known to require further notice here.

In military music there are still more instruments of mere sound, such as the Turkish crescent (bell-work), the wooden roll drum (*tamburo rulante*), and the military drum. In the orchestra, also, we sometimes find the Chinese gong—a bason or bowl of very powerful sound.†

NINTH SECTION.—INSTRUMENTS OF FRICTION.

The chief of this class is the
1. HARMONICA,
whose tones are produced from hollow vessels of glass, put into vibration by the application of the fingers. The sounds of this instrument are indescribably sweet and delicate, and it is susceptible of the most perfect *crescendo* and *diminuendo*, from the gentlest breathing, to harassing power. It is even dangerous, in its extreme intensity, to persons of weak nerves, in whom it has been known to produce fainting and other inconveniences. Nevertheless, this instrument, invented in 1762, by Benjamin Franklin, has not been able to maintain its position in practical art, owing to its difficulty of performance and limited powers. It is adapted merely to slow and simple successions of harmony; and truly, the charms of its characteristic sounds are not a sufficient compensation for its inability to follow the composer.

* A late invention makes the tuning of kettle-drums so easy, that it can be done during the time of playing.

† We may mention also here, the Moorish drum, or hand drum (*tamburino*), and the Spanish castagnets, which have become familiar in our ballets.

2. THE CLAVICYLINDER

is principally indebted to the fame and travels of its inventor, the celebrated Chladni, for becoming known to the world. Since his time it has been no more noticed. Its tones, similar to those of the clarinet, were produced by means of a key-board, from glass rods under the friction of a glass cylinder.

We must pass over all further information upon this and other instruments which have never got into lasting or extensive use, such as the euphon, the terpodion, the uranion, &c.

TENTH SECTION.—OF SCORE.

We have been aware since page 45, that compositions to be performed by several instruments or voices, are usually set in score; that is to say, a separate staff is assigned to each instrument and to each voice, and all the staves are arranged exactly bar for bar over each other. If there be a deficiency of staves for so many parts, or if any of the parts have so little to do, that it is not worth while to assign them a separate staff, parts related to, or connected with each other, may be set on the same staff together; thus, the two flutes, clarinets, &c., the three trombones, &c., may be written on one staff.

In one way or other, the score is the true and faithful impression of each individual trait, and of all the combinations and joint workings of a great composition. No selection of parts for the piano, however skilfully or completely elaborated, no arrangement, can be an equivalent for the score of a full-parted composition. There are no means of enjoying and studying such a composition to be compared, in faithfulness and ease to the score. For composers, conductors, readers, and generally for all well-educated musicians and amateurs, emulous of a deep enjoyment of and insight into music, the capability of reading and playing score with confidence and facility, is an inestimable, not to say an indispensable faculty.

Perfection cannot be obtained in this power without a fundamental study of composition; at least, of harmony. In the meanwhile, every step in advance is rich in knowledge and satisfaction; and, in reality, the trouble it costs is absolutely as nothing, compared to the reward. It is therefore hoped that a method to understand score, together with an elucidation of its arrangement, and some assistance towards becoming familiar with it, will be welcome to most musicians and lovers of musical art.

Another ground for entering more at large into this matter at present, is, that many customs and failings have crept into the arrangement of score, which can by no means be approved of, and concerning which, the want of unanimity of opinion is much to be regretted. It is therefore desirable that composers and authors should bring this subject into public consideration.

The score, for its essential object, must contain *all the parts* in staves, one over the other, in order that the totality of the composition may be seen at once. Only in cases of extreme necessity, when there is absolute want of room to place all the parts on one side, can it be allowed to divide the score, and write some of the parts elsewhere. In this event, however, the parts separated should be the least important, which might therefore be best dispensed with.

All the parts must be placed according to their elevation in sound, exactly bar under bar, and part of a bar under part of a bar, &c., as the following examples will show. The staves in connexion with each other are visibly pointed out by the brace at the beginning of each line; by the closing lines at the end, or at the close of any considerable portion; and also, in the course of the composition, by the bar lines drawn through the whole.

Every staff has its clef and signature, suitable to the notation of the part. The name of each part is placed at the beginning of its staff. If the score should begin with some of the parts only, in order to save room, while for a time, other parts rest, and appear only later; these latter must be marked in the list of the parts—

CONT. (*contano*),

(they count, or rest). Similar marks ought not to be omitted in the course of the composition, whenever some of the parts should have considerable rests, and the score should be, in like manner, reduced in extent.

The directions for performance, such as *piano*, *forte*, and so forth, should be placed at every part, or at least at every chorus. If this be not done, these directions affect the whole of the parts, excepting those where other directions contradict them. The directions for absolute time (*tempo*, quickness or slowness) are usually given only over the score.

Each part should be written out completely. It is allowable, indeed, when two parts are exactly alike, or when one part follows another in octaves, to refer from one part to the other, thus :—

COL. (*colla*)—*all' 8va. col.*

for example, to refer the hautboy part to the flutes, by inserting *col flauti*; the second violin to the first, by *col primo*; signifying that the same notes are to serve for both: but this should be done only in case of necessity, from want of time, or to avoid too great a crowding of notes.

We sometimes find, when a passage is repeated, that only the highest and lowest parts are written again; and as a substitution for the intervening parts, the words—

COME SOPRA, (*as above*),

are written across the space where the omitted notes would have been, to indicate that the other parts are to proceed as before. This occasions, however, a very inconvenient and considerable effort of memory to the reader, and still more to the conductor, and is a practice not to be recommended.

Thus much upon the composition of scores in general. A more important point is their *arrangement*, that is, the order of distributing the parts. Here two rules are generally to be observed :—

1st. All the parts belonging to a chorus are usually placed together.

2nd. The highest parts are usually placed uppermost, the nearest lower comes next, and they descend as they deepen, until the undermost is the lowest.

These rules certainly leave much open to selection, and it is plain at once, that more than one arrangement is possible and eligible. We will go through the most important points.

The most simple and the easiest, is the arrangement of a score, in which there is only one vocal chorus; in this case the second of the above rules is sufficient, and requires scarcely any exception.

A vocal score of three, four, or five voices, is arranged according to the height of the voices. Each voice has its staff—unless, perhaps, the soprano and alto, the tenor and bass, or two soprani, two tenors, &c., should be noted on one staff. This, however, should be done only when the voices run near each other, or if there be not sufficient space for separate staves; and the tails of the notes of the upper part should be drawn upwards, and of the lower part downwards. Here we have before us—

the opening chorus (omitting the orchestra) of Seb. Bach's wonderfully beautiful mass in A major. Here is a repetition of the same:—

in compressed arrangement, wherein the soprano and tenor have exchanged melodies: the alto is placed with the soprano, and the tenor with the bass.

A quartet for bowed instruments is arranged in a manner equally free and easy of inspection, from the first violin down to the violoncello, as this beginning of one of Haydn's quartets satisfactorily shews:—

If the double bass were added, it would be placed on the staff of the violoncello, as we have already said at page 49. It is only when these instruments deviate often and considerably from each other, that a separate staff is given, and then of course the lowest to the double bass. Single deviations are indicated by giving a different direction to the tails of the notes, thus:—

and then, the downward tails belong to the double bass.

In a chorus of tubular instruments (named so by us at page 50) the same instruments, for example, the two flutes, the two clarinets, and so forth, have generally but one staff in common, excepting in case one part, for example the first flute, should be so abundant in notes, as not to have room for the other part; otherwise, the second rule must be followed. Instead of one score on an extensive scale, we here offer two plans for compositions of a greater or less number of parts:—

	Flauto piccolo
Flauti	*Flauti*
Oboi	*Oboi*
	Clarinetto in E♭
Clarinetti in B♭ .	*Clarinetti in B♮*
	Corni di bassetto
Fagotti	*Fagotti*
	Contra fagotto.

If space is deficient for the full setting, the double bassoon and its associates (see page 51) must be written on the bassoon staff, where it will sometimes go with the second—

COL SECONDO,

and sometimes separately. In this latter case, the tails of its notes must be drawn downwards, while those of the notes of the bassoon must be drawn upwards. Thus, for example:—

The following is to be observed with regard to the brass instruments:—

The trumpets in general are considered as the highest instruments, over the horns. If different horns are employed, the highest will be placed uppermost, unless it be judged more advantageous to place those horns which are in tune with the trumpets, next to them.

To horns and trumpets, kettle-drums are associated as their bass. They belong, however, more nearly to the trumpets. If, therefore, in a composition the horns are peculiarly combined with the tubular instruments, it may be advisable, contrary to the second rule, to place the trumpets under the horns, and immediately next to the kettle-drums, as if they made a chorus with these alone. Here are two plans for brass chorusses:—

Clarini (Trombe) in D
Corni in D

Timpani in d, A

Trombe in C
Corni in E♭
Corni in C
Timpani in c, G

The first is intended for the key of D major, the second for perhaps C minor. If in the latter, the C trumpets and C horns should be much occupied together, it might be more suitable (again, contrary to the second rule) to set the E♭ horns under the C horns. We exemplify the third of the above cases by the following passage out of Handel's *Alexander's Feast*:—

from which we place it here, whether or not it be faithful to the original score, or the most suitable arrangement of the parts for the composition. If it were agreed to write in this manner, it would certainly be the most appropriate, that is to say, the easiest of inspection.

Of course the trombones (page 52) also belong to the brass chorus. They form, however, a division by themselves, which associates itself most appropriately (as it were, as lower part) to the so-called band, when they are to be brought into use. The trombones also are arranged according to their height. At times, the alto and tenor trombones are placed on one staff, and then, generally in the tenor clef; and again, when space is deficient, all the three are set on the same staff, and are then most conveniently written in the tenor clef.

If several vocal chorusses are combined, the first rule comes into action. If each vocal chorus is kept to itself, then the second rule applies. In every vocal chorus the highest voice must be set first. But how shall we place the chorusses with respect to each other? Here it seems to be most advisable to place that chorus undermost, which has the most continuous bass voice; and for the reason, that (as the doctrine of harmony will show) the bass is the surest guide and indicator of what are the contents of the other voices.

If reed and brass instruments be united together, the first would be most properly placed lowest, according to this list:—

{ *Trombe*
  Corni,
  Timpani,
  Trombone,
{ *Flauti,*
  Oboi,
  Clarinetti,
  Fagotti,
  Contrafagotto.

If bowed instruments are combined with wind instruments, the former are placed lowest. Here it seems most proper to set the reed instruments uppermost, and the brass instruments in the middle, thus:—

1 { *Flauti, &c.*
    Fagotti.
2 { *Trombe, &c.*
    Timpani.
3 { *Violino,* 1°. *&c.*
    Violoncello e contrabasso.

Then at least, the second rule is observed among the wind instruments. The first flute in the upper line has space for its high passages, and the other instruments which have little to do, and consequently, frequent rests, make a convenient separation between the bowed, quartet, and the tubular instruments. Moreover, the first violin being set under the kettle-drums, will have plenty of room for its high notation. But we meet with scores (particularly those containing the newly invented instruments) in which this order is altered; the brass instruments are placed above, and the tubular instruments beneath.

In vocal compositions for double or more extensive chorusses, each chorus is to be arranged according to the first rule. If solo voices should occur with the chorus, for which there is not space among the staves of the voices of the chorus, they must be placed over the chorus.

If, in fine, song parts are combined with the orchestra, it is desirable that the staves of the former should be next to the violoncello and contrabasso, the most important parts of the orchestra, see above. Here also the first rule is abandoned, and the chorus of song parts is admitted into the chorus of bowed instruments, immediately over the violoncello and contrabasso. Such an arrangement we see here:—

{ { *Flauti, &c.*
    Fagotti,
  { *Clarini, &c.*
    Timpani,
  { *Trombone alto, &c.*
    Gran tamburo,
  Violino 1,
  Violino 2,
  Viola,
  { *Canto,*
    Alto,
    Tenore,
    Basso,
  Violoncello e contrabasso,

Formerly, scores differed often from this arrangement, in placing the violin and tenor parts above all the wind instruments, in order to make the first violin conspicuous, as the most important orchestral part next to the bass; but the injury of disuniting the most essential division or band in the orchestra, seems to us to outweigh the advantage.

We pass over the scores of military music, as in that branch, no real works of art have hitherto appeared.

For reading score, the first thing necessary after

the knowledge of its general arrangement, is the capacity of reading all the parts in their respective clefs, and of transposing those which are written in other feet *tone*, that is of imagining how they really sound: for instance, that the B♭ clarinets, sound a tone deeper than they are noted. To those who, at least, can read with fluency the different clefs enumerated at page 9, we can offer some facilitations. We assume however, for granted, that the transposing into higher or lower octaves can present no difficulty.

1. Let the notes of the A clarinet and of the A horn be read as if they were in the soprano clef, with three signs of raising (♯). Thus, this passage—

read as if written so :—

If such a clarinet part should have a signature of one or two signs of raising, four or five raisings (that is, the three imagined and the one or two visibly present) must be imagined, in the transposition into the soprano clef; therefore this passage—

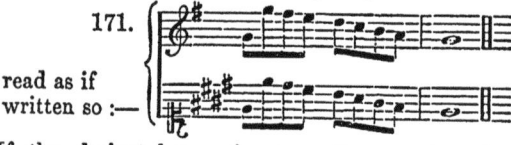

read as if written so :—

If the clarinet has a signature of one or two depressions (♭), one or two sharps less must be imagined in the transposition; thus—

should be read thus :—

The rest is easily understood if the imagination can hold fast (see page 14) that

a sharp raises, a flat lowers,
the recall (♮) of a sharp lowers,
the recall (♮) of a flat raises,

whatever name the tones may have through these transpositions.

2. Let the notation of the deep B♭ horn be imagined as written in the tenor clef with two flats. Thus, this passage—

must be read as :—

3. High B♭ horns, B♭ trumpets, and B♭ clarinets, are to be read in the same manner, but must be imagined an octave higher. With B♭ clarinets, which may be signatured with one sharp, one flat only must be imagined in the transposition; and of course three or four flats must be imagined, should the clarinets have a signature of one or two flats, in the same manner as we have detailed at No. 1.

4. Let the D horns be imagined to be written in the alto clef, with the signature of two raisings, thus :—

D trumpets and D clarinets in the same manner, but an octave higher, if it should not be easier to read them at once a tone higher.

5. Let the E♭ horns and E horns be imagined as in the F clef, the former with three flats, and the latter with four sharps :—

but then they must be placed an octave higher.

Clarinets in E♭, and trumpets in E♭ and E, may be read in the same manner; but then, two octaves higher, if the simple transposition by a minor or major third should not be found more easy.

Different imaginary representations suit different individuals, while to some, immediate transposition appears more easy. All however, with a little industry, speedily find the seeming difficulties vanish before them.

The knowledge of harmony, thorough bass, and composition in general, and acquaintance with the manner of the composer, whose score we wish to read and study, are of vast importance in aiding and fructifying our researches.

FOURTH DIVISION.

ELEMENTARY FORMS OF COMPOSITION.

SECTION THE FIRST.—THE FOUNDATIONS OF MELODY.

By melody, we understand a succession of single *tones*, appropriate in itself, and rhythmically arranged for the expression of a determined musical thought.* We have first to consider, then, the succession of *tones* and afterwards their rhythm.

(A)   THE SUCCESSION OF *Tones*.

Where shall we find our succession of *tones?* and when can we call it arranged? There are three materials or foundations for successions of *tones*. The first is the

DIATONIC SCALE,

upwards or downwards, or both, the one after the other. In this scale we perceive the degrees of the *tones*, following each other in regulated order from below upwards, and from above downwards. We know that we have at least two diatonic scales, the

---

* Such a thought, like any other, must have its limits. Since it expresses something specific, it must at some time or other have expressed or finished expressing it, and there close. This close of the thought or of the melody may be at the same time the end of the composition, or it may proceed to new thoughts or melodies. The melodies collectively of a voice or part produced in the course of a composition, are called its tune or air (*Cantilena*).

major and the minor, and that we can form both upon every tonic.

A second foundation for regulated successions of *tones* is the so-called

CHROMATIC SCALE,

proceeding upwards or downwards, or both in succession. But a melody will rarely be formed entirely from this scale only; since its progression, by semitones only, is too uniform and minute. The chromatic scale indeed, as we have shewn (page 18, in note), cannot be the foundation of any scale; it is no fundamental form in our tonic system.

A third foundation for a regulated succession of *tones*, is

THE SUCCESSION OF *Tones* IN A CHORD,

or several chords, which combinations we shall understand better in the course of the following sections; for example:—

176.

but such a succession is visibly too confined, and at too large intervals, to be a foundation for any considerable time.

Out of these materials are constructed all possible successions of *tones*; seldom from one source alone, but mostly from two, or indeed, from the contributions of all three. In the above example, two foundations are mixed. The tones of the first bar and those of the second, each by themselves, belong to a chord foundation; but from the first to the second, and from the second to the third bar (*c—b* and *d—c*), the passage is diatonic. Such an interchange of foundations may proceed with greater variety, as for example in this passage:—

177.

Here at No. 1, is a chromatic foundation—at No. 2, a diatonic—at No. 3, a derivation from a chord, and so forth.

But however rich a succession of *tones* may be in variety, if it aspire to become a melody and attain artistic meaning, it must observe in the interchange and selection, a certain order; a succession with an intention; in fine, an artistic plan. So, for example, the foregoing passage begins chromatically, proceeds diatonically to a harmonical succession, and then repeats and strengthens this order in the second and third bars. But it must not be expected that the order will always be so simple and transparent as in this instance. Here, for example,—

178.

we see a much more variegated arrangement. After the chromatic (1) and diatonic (2) portions, two harmonic successions (3 and 4) follow; and only then again, a diatonic and chromatic sequence; so that the harmonic successions are made prominently important. But that superiority is claimed again by the third preferably harmonic bar (7 and 8), so that two similar halves are formed, both of which begin diatonically and chromatically, and then proceed harmonically.

Every group of two, three, or more *tones*, which serves as material for a succession of *tones*, we will call a

MOTIVE OF THE SUCCESSION OF TONES.

Thus, Nos. 1, 2, 3, &c., in the preceding passage, were motives of that succession. In these two successions—

179.

the motives are the sequences of the two *tones* next to each other. Out of the repetition, transposition, alteration, mixture and combination of motives, long successions of *tones* are formed; and it is manifest from the foregoing, that with the same motive, passages quite different may be constructed. Moreover, two motives may be combined to form a larger one. The preceding succession might have been formed of groups of four *tones*, thus:—

180.

Again, the motives Nos. 2 and 3, from the passage No. 178, might be combined thus,—

181.

and new successions be discovered.

After the foundation and motive, in fine, the

DIRECTION

of the succession comes into consideration. This may be altogether rising or falling, or an alternation of both (as in No. 181), or chiefly rising or chiefly falling; with contrary secondary movements: that is, for example, continuing to fall in the whole, but partially rising occasionally—or the contrary; or again, rambling up and down without any decided direction in any way; as here for example:—

182.

(B)   OF RHYTHM.

The rhythmic arrangement of a melody ought also to be regulated so as to express some idea or intention.

After our elucidations on the successions of *tones*, we need not occupy much time upon this point.

The rhythmic arrangement is founded on value, and on the nature and laws of bars; and, like the arrangement of *tones*, has for its object the formation of a consistent whole, combined with judgment to produce an intended effect. It proceeds in its constructions from one or more fundamental conceptions, which we may call

RHYTHMIC MOTIVES,

and forms by equal or similar repetitions, continuations, and alternations—always according to the laws of proportion and of agreeableness, and with a view to the object of each particular work—a more or less extensive rhythmic combination. In this manner, rhythm is the governing attendant in the management of *tones*, from the smallest melodic conception, up to the greatest and most comprehensive forms of art.

Here we give an example of a rhythmical motive. In the passages immediately preceding, the successions have been in *tones* of equal and short duration. We give now a succession of a quaver and two semiquavers, which is the rhythmic motive:—

Rhythmic motives may also be enlarged or diminished, separated or united, as is here shewn:—

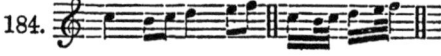

SECOND SECTION.—FUNDAMENTAL FORMS.

All melodies can be traced to three fundamental forms, which we call passage, phrase, and subject.

1. A PASSAGE.

Every melodiously organised succession of sounds, without a satisfactory close, is called a passage. Here—

and so forth.

and at No. 177, we have passages before us. Such a passage may consist of determined and different groups; as is seen at No. 178, in groups of four, and in No. 181, in groups of six *tones*, and in this following passage, in groups of seven *tones*,—

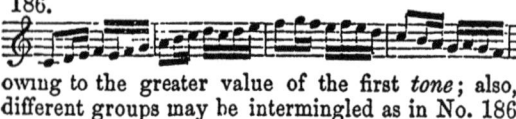

owing to the greater value of the first *tone*; also, different groups may be intermingled as in No. 186 and here,—

All freedom in the construction of melodies is here admitted.

A flight of rapid and mostly similar notes is also called

A PASSAGE,

particularly when of considerable extent. A passage formed of diatonic or chromatic intervals is called

A RUN,

more especially if of great length (running at least through an octave), and is chiefly confined to diatonic successions in one direction. If its performance should be accompanied with extraordinary technical difficulty, if it be calculated to produce a brilliant display of the skill and boldness of the executant, it is called

A BRAVURA PASSAGE.

2. THE PHRASE.

A melody which is constituted into a whole, by having a determined beginning and end, is called a phrase.

By what means is that conclusion effected?

In respect of *tone*, by the melody's beginning with a *tone* which becomes important throughout, and closing with the same. In respect of rhythm, by its beginning on a chief part (of a bar) or an ex-chief part, and closing exclusively on a similar part. For these reasons the foregoing successions of *tones*, Nos. 185 to 187, and others, are only passages, and not phrases, because they are deficient of that decisive rhythmic-tonic conclusion.

Which are tonically important *tones?*

We can, in the first place, name only one—the *tonic*. We shall learn hereafter, from instruction in harmony and modulation, that other *tones* belonging to tonic harmony (the third and fifth of the tonic), when they act as constituent parts of this harmony, must be considered as effective for a close. That, moreover, a phrase may close in a *tone* different from that in which it began; in which case the tonic of the new scale and its harmonies are available as closing *tones*. Finally, that also, the dominant and its harmonies may become the closing *tones* of a phrase.

In order to return to the important closing *tone*—the tonic, we shew here—

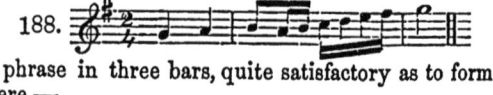

a phrase in three bars, quite satisfactory as to form; here,—

189.

another equally so, of four bars. But does not the latter close unsatisfactorily as to rhythm? No: for its last *tone* is an ex-chief part; and moreover, only the echo of the really closing *tone* in its octave. Here—

190.

we have a phrase indeterminate in the initial bar, and also tonically, but still closing satisfactorily. Here—

191.

is a phrase closing unsatisfactorily even in rhythm. It is only by the *tone* that we guess at the close. Such an indecision is not perhaps to be considered an absolute fault. It may be for some ideas or objects the most appropriate form.

Every phrase, as every melody, consists of regulated motives, which are connected together either uninterruptedly, or are formed into separate divisions. Thus here,—

we have a phrase of four bars, which in its second bar makes a well-marked rhythmic separation. We call such divisions

SECTIONS.

A section, again, may be divided into smaller parts, which we call

MEMBERS.

Here, for example,—

we have a phrase in two sections (1 and 2, and 3 and 4 bars), and each separates into members of different dimensions; first, into two members, each of two crotchets (the *rest* included), then into a member of four crotchets.

3. A SUBJECT.

This consists of a phrase and counter-phrase, or of several united phrases, forming together a great

MUSICAL SUBJECT.

The subject comprises, therefore, two or more small unities more or less closed, under one larger unity. This can take place according to rule, only when the second and following phrases are similar in contents to the first, or at least, are of the same derivation. In the following sections of this work we shall find new methods for combining phrases into subjects.

In the first place, we have only one chief means of distinction, viz., *the direction of the succession of tones.* If the first phrase rises, the second falls. Here we recognise that the essential form of a subject, the union of two phrases, is the phrase and counter-phrase, as we say above. Thus here,—

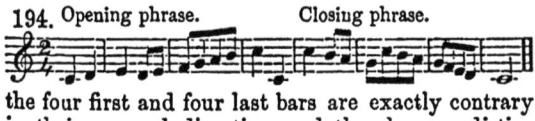

the four first and four last bars are exactly contrary in their general direction, and thereby are distinguished. On the other hand, if the first falls, the second rises; for example :—

We call the first phrase (as we have done over the notes)

OPENING PHRASE;

and the second or counter-phrase,

CLOSING PHRASE.

How does the construction of subjects proceed beyond these limits, beyond the compass of two phrases? It can combine

THREE OR FOUR PHRASES,

and more. But it is manifest that the relation of opening phrase and closing phrase, of phrase and counter-phrase, can no longer remain so conspicuous. The three or four phrases, however long they may be, will always appear rather as long sections of an extended phrase. Thus here :—

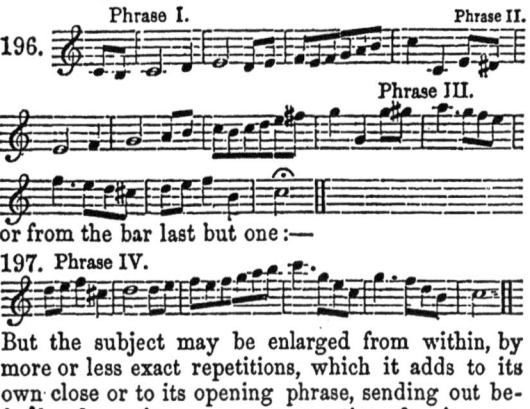

or from the bar last but one :—

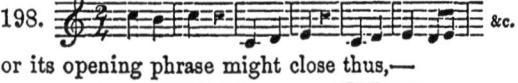

But the subject may be enlarged from within, by more or less exact repetitions, which it adds to its own close or to its opening phrase, sending out beforehand, as it were, a preparation, for its own beginning. Thus the subject, No. 194, might begin so—with two little phrases or members, each of two bars, as forerunners,—

or its opening phrase might close thus,—

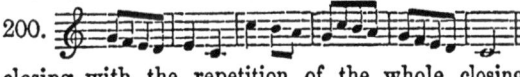

with a repetition of the last *tones*; or the whole might proceed from the seventh bar, thus :—

200.

closing with the repetition of the whole closing phrase.

In all such

APPENDAGES AND INTERMIXINGS

it is generally advisable, and therefore customary, to preserve the symmetry or proportion between the fore and after phrase, by using nearly similar sections of similar length. Where this, however, on deeper grounds, is not done, we shall soon learn by a little practice, after the foregoing intimations, to distinguish the different forms in any composition before us. Only thus far is it fitting that we should proceed upon this point in our General Musical Instruction. More intimate acquaintance herewith, will be furnished in the doctrine of composition, and in the Science of Music.

THIRD SECTION.—GREATER RHYTHMIC ARRANGEMENTS.

We have already remarked (page 33), and we will repeat the observation, that it is rhythm chiefly, which gives order, comprehensibility, and signification to our compositions; and renders them capable of producing an unfailing and determined effect. It was rhythm which singled out and reduced to order an unintelligible mass of notes, which brought equal and unequal notes into parts of bars and into whole bars, and thence into passages, phrases and subjects; in fine, into appreciable and effective combination.

Now, we know from daily experience (and the fifth division of this book will instruct us further) that there are much larger compositions than movements—compositions which consist of many passages, phrases, and subjects, combined together. What preserves order among them? In the first place again—rhythm. Then, or next in authority or governing influence (as we shall learn later in the description of artistic forms), the arrangements of modulation and the several chief subjects of the composition.

For the study and performance of a composition, it is highly profitable to understand clearly its entire construction and arrangement. We must not therefore remain satisfied with our development so far, but must pursue these rhythmic combinations into their most comprehensive formations. This we can do nowhere better than here.

What was the first object of rhythm? *Equal measure*—and then? *variety* combined with symmetry—*Equilibrium*. So rhythmical order began by notes of equal value, and proceeded thence to notes of the most diversified description but which are easily arranged (being minims, crotchets, &c.*) in proportionate relation to each other. It began with two-fold order, but thence unfolded many and various kinds of measure. The bars of a musical theme were equal, but they could contain notes and rests of the most varied nature, all of which could be comprised in parts of a bar of equal length and measure.

So now, rhythm continues to labour in its double capacity for a single object.

Equal members combined together throughout a whole movement, constitute

EQUAL RHYTHM.

For example, of two and two bars:—†

201.

as here for an opening phrase of eight bars in $\frac{2}{4}$ time, or of four and four bars:—

202.

or, which is rare, of three and three bars, as in this Swiss popular song:—‡

203.

Gang mer nit ü-ber mis Mät-te-li, gang mer nit

geng dur mis Gras, gang mer nit geng zue mim Schätze-li,

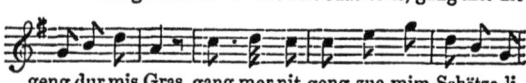

o - der i prügle di ab.

That rhythms also of six and six, and even of five and five bars, are possible—nay, even of seven and seven, can be easily perceived; but the wider the single rhythms become, the more both they and the whole composition lose in apprehension and mobility.

Now, however, the four-part, six-part, &c. rhythmic combinations, are known to be nothing more than annexations or groupings of the simple two and three-part unities. We can therefore change the $\frac{4}{4}$ phrase, No. 202, into a $\frac{2}{4}$ phrase of sixteen bars, by merely halving the bars, or at least with very slight alteration; for example:—

204.

or *vice versa*, we might revert this $\frac{2}{4}$ phrase into a $\frac{4}{4}$ phrase, or group the above $\frac{3}{4}$ phrase into a $\frac{9}{8}$ phrase.

Hence it is clear, that we can place not only equal or similar rhythms together, but also

RHYTHMS OF THE SAME KIND.

Thus, for example, a section of four bars may follow two sections of two bars each, and *vice versa*; and this may be taken advantage of in every variety of manner. As examples from extensive compositions occupy too much room, we give one, in few notes, of our own construction.—

205.

---

* Here the point of the Author's observation is lost, by translating the German names of the notes, namely (literally), halves, fourths, eighths, &c., into the English names, minims, crotchets, &c., which have no self-evident relation to each other.—TRANSLATOR.

† This and most of the other examples are set too high and too meagrely, for the sake of brevity and space, to produce their attainable effect when carried out at length.

‡ In the second number (*Hefte*) of the extremely rich and attractive collection of German popular songs, with their manner of singing, by L. Erk and W. Irmer. Berlin, at Plahn's.

MUSICAL INSTRUCTION.

This represents to us the following rhythmic quantities:—

    1, 1 Bar—2, 2 Bars—1, 1 Bar—2 Bars
             1, 1 Bar—1, 1 Bar.

If we add together the members of each single bar, we shall have nothing but equal sections—

    2—2, 2—2—2—2—2 Bars*

which are as comprehensible and easy of inspection as bars with parts and members of a bar. Many similar combinations can be found. An attentive observer will perceive them easily in extensive and richly elaborated compositions. Numeration by two, as the most simple partitive number, is predominant most assuredly; as for example, rhythms of 1, 1 and 2—or 2, 2 and 4—or 4, 4 and 8 bars. Rarely do we find *numeration by three*, during a whole composition: as for example, 3, 3 and 6.† Still less frequently by five, as we have already found among the like-formed rhythms. But we find in large compositions, after a series of two or four bar rhythms, two or more sections of *three*, *six*, or *five* bars each in such an arrangement as this, for example,—

    4, 4,—4, 4,—3, 3,—6,—4, 4—and so forth,
            5,—5

which appear conformable to order, merely because two or three of them present themselves occasionally, and may be compared together. We would call these rhythms

SYMMETRICAL RHYTHMS.

In fine, in large compositions, particularly when descriptive of passionate, vehement feelings, single sections may very well be introduced, larger or smaller than those preceding or following them; for example, a five bar section, amid sections of two and four bars only. Such a construction should be called

IRREGULAR RHYTHM.

No blame, however, should be attached to such an expression. On the contrary, it should be considered as a case of exemption from the governing rule. In the proper place, that is, for the expression of passion, the irregular rhythm may probably be the only right one.

As we have formed sections by the union of single bars, so by combining sections, two and two, three and three, and so forth, we may produce larger divisions. If we divide, for instance, No. 193 into bars of $\frac{2}{4}$, the following fundamental rhythmic sections would appear:—

    1, 1, 2 Bars, 1, 1, 2 Bars.

Then, we should become perceptive of greater combinations, out of the twice one-bar sections of two bars, and out of the four and four bars: so that the whole phrase has the following rhythm:—

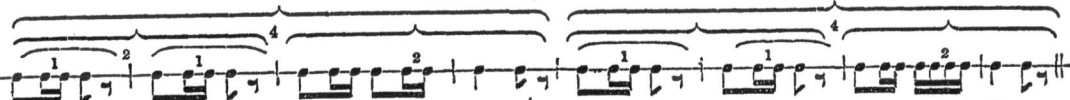

The phrases hitherto considered, have shown us very easily distinguishable sections. The borders or limits of the sections (called intersections) were shown at one time by rests, as in No. 203 and 205; at another, by chief parts of greater value in quantity or length, which made the intersection perceptible. But the point of limitation has not been always so striking to the eye.

Sometimes the single sections and phrases were combined by passages or phrases of transition, or passing notes and small intermediate phrases. Such an one is seen in the last bar of No. 204. The phrase itself closes with the first crotchet of this bar, but the under part leads by an intervening phrase to the following one, whose beginning is to be seen in No. 202. The transition might have been made more effective, in this way, for instance—

206.

with under and upper parts, or all the parts together.

At times the entrance of the phrase is concealed by its beginning too late or too early. Here for example,—

207.

we see two phrases, each of two bars, united by one part; but in everything else, manifestly separated. We recognize the entrance of the second by its similarity to the first. Here we have the same phrase, a trifle varied in the harmony—

208.

but the second section enters later—too late, according to the model of the first, and with a retrenched beginning. Here, in fine, we have again the same phrase—

209.

but its second section appears half a bar too soon, with a longer and repeated beginning. Nevertheless, its beginning. and the order which presides in the groundwork of the whole (No. 207), remain perceptible in all the deviations.

Finally, the close of a section or of a phrase may be effected by the beginning of another, or by the recommencement of the first; in such a manner, that the closing tone of the one becomes the first tone of the other. We give as an example, a phrase contracted as much as possible:—

---

* Therefore this is again a subject of several phrases, only not formed so regularly, nor so easily to be recognized as the former No. 196.

† In Beethoven's ninth symphony, the triform enumeration appears in a whole part of the *Scherzo*.

210.

The close of the fourth bar would be *c* in a value of three quavers; but *c* becomes immediately, the beginning of the repetition, which (in respect of rhythmical arrangement) must be considered as a second phrase; and moreover, in virtue of the sign of repetition, the same *c* serves as a close for the said second phrase (that is, the repetition); and for the beginning of a third one, quite new, of which only two bars are written above.

There are no exterior marks, none at least which are satisfactory, for these greater rhythmical sections. Sometimes large sections, large divisions of the whole, are marked with closing lines (with or without the sign of repetition), or with the intervening words *al fine*.

Sometimes, if the closing and recommencement is in tailed notes (quavers, semiquavers, &c.) the beginning of the second section is made perceptible, by writing separately the closing and beginning notes, which would otherwise be bound by a line of duration. For example, as at (*a*), not as at (*b*):—

211.

But these intimations are not always given, and are never sufficient for the rhythmic direction of a whole composition.

After the knowledge of rhythm, at least so far as it is here communicated,* and of harmony and construction, of which we have something more to say, although complete satisfaction is to be had only in the doctrine of composition, the observant student is committed to his own judgment and attentive consideration, which will in most cases lead him aright.

FOURTH SECTION.—MELODIC GRACES.

We have now to speak concerning a few figures in melody, and to show the usual mode of marking them. We limit ourselves to essential and practical observations, casting aside those subtle distinctions, and that long list of names, with which it was the fashion during many years for professors to torment their scholars and themselves.

1. THE APPOGGIATURA.

By appoggiatura is understood a note written in a small character, and placed before a note of a melody, as it were by accident or unnecessarily.

There are two kinds of appoggiaturas, which must be distinguished, the long and the short

THE LONG APPOGGIATURA
is written, according to the value of the note before which it is placed, in a note of the same or half its

* And in the Appendix A.

value. Before a crotchet it therefore becomes a crotchet or a quaver; before a quaver it is either a quaver or a semiquaver.

Such an appoggiatura in either case, is of the value of half the note it precedes, so that this latter retains only half of its nominal value. These notes therefore with appoggiaturas at (*a*)—

212.

are to be played as at (*b*).

If a dotted note should be preceded by an appoggiatura, this latter assumes the whole value of the note; while to the chief note the value of the dot is alone assigned. Thus, in these appoggiaturas—

213.

the first would have the value of two crotchets and the note of one, and the second of two quavers and the note of one quaver.

THE SHORT APPOGGIATURA (*accacciatura*) is written shorter than the long; for instance, as a semiquaver before a crotchet, and as a demisemiquaver before a semiquaver; or it is written without any attention to the value of the note which it precedes, as a quaver or semiquaver with a dash across its hook.

214.

It has no determined value; but is merely played quite short before the chief *tone*; its value must therefore depend upon the note it precedes.

Generally the next note either above or below the chief *tone* is used for an appoggiatura; but sometimes a more distant note, as for example:—

215.

the last chiefly for short appoggiaturas.

2. THE DOUBLE APPOGGIATURA
is the union of two short appoggiatura notes before a chief note:—

216.

This, in like manner, has no determined value, but must be appreciated from its chief note.

3. THE TURN
is a double appoggiatura, formed out of the chief *tone* and the *tones* next above and next below it. It is sometimes written in notes, thus:—

217.

or it is indicated by this sign, ∽

If this sign be placed after the chief note, as at (*a*), the turn is played before the rhythmic time of playing the next *tone*, and therefore during the value of the chief note; nearly, perhaps, as at (*b*):—

218.

In any such case, as here at (*a*), if any other note but itself should follow the chief note, the said chief note is added to the turn, so that it now consists of four *tones* (*b*) as is here shown:—

219.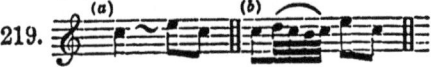

But if the sign be found over or under the chief note, the turn takes the position and time of the note so marked, nearly as indicated in (*b*), but in undetermined value relatively to the rhythm of the bar, thus:—

220.

In the execution of a turn, the upper and under *tones* are taken as intimated by the signature; thus, in the foregoing cases, Nos. 218 and 220, not *f* but *f*♯, because the latter is so signatured. If one or the other, or both the *tones* of the turn are to be raised or lowered, the requisite sign is placed over or under the sign of the turn, in the relative position in notation of the *tone* to be altered.

These turns (the signature of F♯ being always understood), for example—

221.

are performed thus:—

222

We have seen cursorily in No. 217, that turns may begin by the upper or by the under *tone*; that there are *turns from above and from below*. This distinction is not shown by the sign of the turn alone. The choice, therefore, of either is left to the executants, if the composer do not point out which he intends to be played.

If several notes are placed over each other on the staff, the sign for a turn is placed either over the upper note or under the lowest. Here for example—

223.

at (*a*) there is to be a turn on *e*, at (*b*) a turn on *f*, therefore these notes—

224.

are to be played.

If there is to be a turn on both the upper and under note, the sign must be placed both above and below, thus:—

225.

If a turn were required on an inner note, but not on the two exterior, it would be advisable to write it in notes—

226.

The sign placed between the notes is unintelligible and confusing.—

227.

4. THE SHAKE.

The shake consists of numerous, rapid, and equidistant repetitions of an appoggiatura from above, with the chief *tone*, and beginning according to custom with the chief tone. Its sign is—

tr. or *tr* ⸺⸺⸺

over or under the note, and its execution is at (*b*):—

228.

The value of the single *tones* of a shake is undetermined, but the whole shake must be of equal length with the note to which it was indicated.

If it be desired to have some other note than the degree above for the auxiliary note,—the under degree for example, or the under degree for the first time, but the upper one afterwards, or *vice versa*, this may all be indicated as follows:—

229.

In order to finish the shake more ornamentally, it is usually ended by a turn. The foregoing shake ought therefore to have closed thus:—

230.

A very short shake without any finishing turn (or simply the striking of the chief *tone*, appoggiatura and chief tone again) is called

A TRILL,

and in its quickest operation

A BEAT,

and is signified by this sign, under or over the note:—

♦♦ or ♦♦, or in England ∾

Shakes upon two notes at once, thus—

231.

are called

DOUBLE SHAKES.

A series of shakes upon several tones, thus—

232.

is called

A CHAIN OF SHAKES.

All these and similar melodic forms are comprised under the term of

GRACES,

because they are in general merely an arbitrary

addition of the composer or performer, to the essential matter of the composition.

In order to preserve beginners from a possible mistake, we think fit to advert to what indeed might be deemed self-evident, that all graces affect solely that succession of *tones* for which they are indicated. The other successions of *tones* or parts continue their course in complete independence. Here, for example, the appoggiatura and turn—

233.

alter the value of the crotchet in the upper parts only, not in the under parts. These notes must therefore *not* be played so:—

234.

but thus :—

235.

FIFTH SECTION.—INTRODUCTION TO HARMONY.

We know that in musical compositions, two, three, four, and more successions of *tones*, called *parts*, are combined together for simultaneous performance, and that hence, such compositions are said to be in two, three, four, or more parts. The highest of such parts is called the

UPPER PART,

the deepest, the

LOWER PART;

all the intervening parts are called the

MIDDLE PARTS.

We are to distinguish principally, four classes.—

SOPRANO (the highest part),
ALTO,
TENOR,
BASS (the lowest part),

which first became known to us (page 46) as the chief kinds of singing parts.

When two or more successions of *tones* are to be heard simultaneously, they must be in some compatible relation towards each other, according to the rules of art.

This relation of different *tones* is called harmony. We must seek how two, three, or more *tones* become thus harmoniously related.

All harmonic combinations *originate from thirds*. Why this is so, and all its consequences, cannot be demonstrated here, but must be referred to the science of music and art of composition.*

---

* We will, however, say thus much. Our conviction that we derive all our harmonic constructions from a combination of thirds, is not the result of arbitrary, accidental, or unenlightened observation, because it is founded on scientific demonstration. It has been proved that the *tones* nearest related to each other (as mentioned at page 17), are the octave, the fifth above it, the next octave, the third above—this latter, the octave of the previous fifth, and finally, a *tone* which we in our system must consider as the nearest flat seventh. Therefore, from C there are first the *tones*—

C, c, g, c, e, g,

and then, one step further,—

C, c, g, c, e, g, b♭

which *tones* (as before said) are in the relation towards each other of

The ternary combination consists in adding to any given *tone* a second *tone* which is a third higher; a third *tone*, which is a second third higher; and in like manner a fourth, and a fifth *tone*.

A ternary combination of three, four, or five *tones*, is called a

CHORD.

The *tone* from or on which a chord is constructed, is called its

FUNDAMENTAL *Tone*,

and reciprocally, a chord is named from its fundamental *tone*; thus we say the chord of *C*, of *D*, &c. All the other *tones* in the chord are numbered from the fundamental *tone*; the second nearest the fundamental *tone* is therefore called

THE THIRD;

The third (a third higher than the third, and on the fifth degree of the scale from the fundamental *tone*) is called

THE FIFTH;

the fourth, a third higher than the fifth, and on the seventh degree,

THE SEVENTH;

the fifth, a third higher than the seventh, and on the ninth degree,

THE NINTH

of the chord, or of the fundamental *tone*.

A chord of three tones is called

A TRIAD.

A chord of four tones is called,—from the fourth tone, which it is in reality from the fundamental *tone*, and by which it is distinguished from a triad,—

THE CHORD OF THE SEVENTH.

A chord of five tones, is called from the accruing fifth *tone*, by which it is distinguished from the chord of the seventh,—

THE CHORD OF THE NINTH.†

1:2:3:4:5:6:7 (estimating the relation by the number of vibrations in a given time.)

Let us now omit the three first supernumerary *tones* (1:2:3) and assemble the following which lie nearest to each other, and we shall then have a structure in thirds, which comprises both the two principal chords:—

c, e, g.
and . . . c, e, g, b♭

(the great triad and the chord of the dominant), out of and according to which, all other chords are formed. All harmony is to be deduced from this one, or it may be said, these two root-chords, as the author thinks he has proved in his doctrine of composition, with full evidence of reason existing in the art itself, but not to be found in the books of instruction.

Gott. Weber, among others, places a row of chords *mechanically* together, as they are found near each other in the scale: and of necessity, having lost the natural and scientific foundation, he is betrayed into numberless deviations and perplexing doubts, while—if what is essential alone were held in view—ONE SINGLE FUNDAMENTAL PRINCIPLE FOR ALL HARMONY is sufficient. And moreover, this principle is so simple and comprehensible, that a boy can understand and retain it. A new teacher of harmony has even ventured on the extraordinary idea of considering the *minor triad*, as the second fundamental chord. It is no wonder that such modes of teaching should drag the students along through years—whereas, a system founded on reason gives more, and safer, and better grounded knowledge in three months, nay, in twenty or thirty lessons.

† Are there not chords of more than five tones? Some theorists have formed such. They say there are chords of two tones, thus :—

236.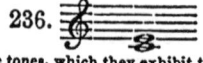

of three, four, and five tones, which they exhibit thus :—

237.

and further chords of six tones—chords of the eleventh :—

238.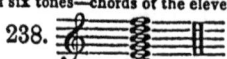

If therefore we ask again, how two or more *tones* can become harmonically related to each other, we are answered—

First, by their forming a chord together.

Which *tones* are susceptible of this combination, and how they are to retain their functions as parts of the union, we are now to examine more minutely. We know well so far, that to a fundamental *tone*, a third, fifth, &c. may be combined; but not what kind of a third, fifth, &c., since, as we are aware, the names of the intervals do not determine their quantities nor values.

After we have considered the subject of chords, other forms of harmonic combination will come under review. This will be more conveniently done in separate sections.

Otherwise, it is not the function of general musical instruction to elucidate completely all these forms (if that indeed were possible), but to introduce and exemplify the fundamental forms and their chief application. Beyond this, belongs to composition.*

SIXTH SECTION.—THE MOST IMPORTANT CHORDS, MAJOR AND MINOR.

We seek now for the most important and nearest chords in major and minor, beginning with the triads as the most simple chords, in order to proceed from them to the more numerous and complex chords of the seventh and of the ninth. As the major and minor modes are each respectively similar among themselves, what we say with regard to one major mode, or to one minor mode, will avail for all the rest of the same modes.

1. THE MOST IMPORTANT TRIADS.

Which are in general the most important *tones* in

and of seven tones—chords of the thirteenth:—

More there could not be; since the next third, the eighth tone, was nothing but the second octave of the fundamental *tone*, and therefore not a new *tone*.

But they must themselves confess, that their chords of the eleventh and thirteenth, as they give them, are never employed, nor can be employed (we mean apparently cannot; see the author's Instruction for Composition, Part I), excepting they be essentially altered, by the omission of several of the *tones*. This scheme, therefore, is arbitrary, and contradictory to all the previous notions of harmony, long since acquired by the student. If it were desired to begin by two *tones* (which is quite useless), the first (or rather, indeed, the only one given by nature) would be the fifth and not the third. And in like manner, the first chord of the seventh (the only one produced by nature), is not *c, e, g, b*, but *c, e, g, b♭*. And the first chord of the ninth (as well as the pretended chords of the eleventh and thirteenth), in the same manner, is not to be founded on *c, e, g, b*, but on *c, e, g, b♭*. Moreover it is matter of history, that every development of harmony has been attained by following the path indicated by nature; as every real historical progress must have been conformable to reason. In short, these chords, as the theorists have displayed them, are *merely mechanical contrivances;* methodical indeed, but ill-imagined auxiliaries, in contradiction to the reality of art and to the true system of the connexion of *tones;* and apparently render the study of harmony more difficult and confused, in lieu of offering the facilitations for which they were invented. The chords of two *tones* are also a purely mechanical contrivance. The chord given to us by nature—the first rational true chord—is a triad, the major third. From this the chord of the dominant and of the ninth proceed; and only from this latter *can* the chord of the eleventh come into existence—therefore, from the dominant. In this sense the author was obliged to employ a chord of the eleventh (perhaps the first ever used) in his *Mosè*, (page 163 of the score), impelled by the feeling of the moment. More intimate details in this matter will be found in the Instructions for Composition, and in the Science of Music.

The chords, as well as the intervals, have been divided into *consonant* and *dissonant*. The major and minor triad, with their inversions, are called consonant—all other chords, dissonant. Here as formerly, and on the same grounds, we must banish all ideas of consonant and dissonant, and the distinction altogether, as idle and useless.

each scale? First, the *tonic*, (page 24), then the *dominant* and *subdominant*.

If we construct in a major mode for example in C major, triads upon the tonic, dominant and, subdominant—that is, if we take these degrees as they occur in the scale, as fundamental *tones*, and add thereon the third and fifth from the scale—we shall form three triads—

240.

of similar construction. They have all three
A FUNDAMENTAL TONE,
MAJOR THIRD (*c—e, f—a, g—b*) and
PERFECT FIFTH.

If we construct triads in a minor mode,—for instance, in C minor,—in like manner on the tonic, dominant, and subdominant—

241.

we obtain two kinds of triads. The triads of the tonic and subdominant have a minor third; but the triad of the dominant has a major third, as was the case in the major mode.

We call a triad with a major third and perfect fifth, a

MAJOR TRIAD;†

a triad with a minor third and perfect fifth, a
MINOR TRIAD.

The major triad governs the tonic, dominant, and subdominant in the major mode, and is therefore properly called the major triad. The minor triad governs the tonic and subdominant in the minor, and is therefore properly called the minor triad.

There are two other triads to be noticed, first, the
DIMINISHED TRIAD,‡

whose nature and construction we shall learn in the next section, under No. 2; and secondly, the
EXTREME TRIAD,

which consists of a fundamental tone, major third, and extreme fifth, arising from an intentional raising of the fifth and major triad, thus:—

242.

The admission and justification of this raising is to be found in the Instruction for Composition, and in the Science of Music.

The triad on the tonic, whether in major or minor, is called the
TONIC TRIAD;

the triad on the dominant is called the
TRIAD OF THE DOMINANT.

We see now, that the essential harmonic difference between major and minor modes is, that the tonic triad in the first is major, and in the second minor.

† In old books of instruction this is also called the *perfect* triad, although naturally it is not more perfect than any other chord, and also (as we shall hereafter find) can be *imperfectly* employed; that is, it can be deprived of one of its intervals, without becoming thereby another chord.

‡ This also, in the old language of teaching, was called the *false* triad, from its having a so-called false fifth; although, in its proper place, it is as correct as any other chord in its own place.

2. The Chord of the Dominant Seventh.

If we add a third (the seventh of the fundamental tone) to the triad of the dominant major or minor, as it is found in the scale, we form a chord of the seventh, whose fundamental *tone* is the dominant, and which for shortness we call the

Chord of the Dominant,*

and moreover to distinguish it from other chords of the seventh, which we shall become acquainted with hereafter. This chord has, besides the fundamental tone,

> A Major Third,
> Major Fifth, and
> Minor Seventh,

and is the same in the major or minor modes.

It has another peculiar property. Every chord of the dominant is to be found in its scale only: that is, it can be constructed out of the *tones* of its scale only. The chord of the dominant of C major or minor can be found only in C major or minor; in no other major or minor scale. The triad *c—e—g*, for example, may appear as tonic triad in C major; as dominant triad in F major; as sub-dominant triad in G major; and in other combinations.

How do we show that property of the chord of the dominant? Let us consider any major scale,—for instance, C major. On the one side, the scales with sharps are shut against it,—in the first instance, G major with *f♯* instead of *f*: on the other side, the scales with flats,—first that of F major, with *b♭* in lieu of *b* natural. Now, what constitutes the chord of the dominant of C major? *g—b—d—f*. Can this chord be constructed in G major? No, *f* is wanting—it is changed into *f♯*; therefore the chord, *g—b—d—f* cannot be formed in G major; therefore it cannot in any other scale with sharps, for in them all, *f♯* remains instead of *f* natural. But can it be constructed in F major? Again, no; for in F major we have *b♭* instead of *b* natural; consequently *g—b—d—f* cannot be found in any scale with flats, since they have all *b♭* instead of *b* natural. The same proof might be gone through in the minor modes.

This observation we consider important. Since the chord of the dominant is possible only in one scale, major and minor, it serves us as the most sure

Sign of the Scale.

The signature (as we have seen at page 23) cannot serve us for that purpose, since each signature is employed in common for two scales,—the relative keys. A composition without signature may be either in C major or A minor. Also, the last deepest tone may be some other than the tonic. A two-part passage in C major may close thus:—

243.

and is not always therefore a definite sign (page 23),

---

* It has been called also the chief chord of the seventh, because it certainly is the most important chord of the seventh. We prefer the shortest name Some older theorists have called it the *leading chord*, because it leads to the tonic triad: but the name is inexact, because other chords also do the same, while the chord of the dominant leads not only into the tonic triad, but also into other chords.†

† It may not have been generally observed, that the chord of the dominant seventh is formed essentially of the dominant and subdominant. Hence its strong impulsion to the tonic to which it is thus doubly related.—Translator.

but the chord of the dominant always is so. The moment we hear, *g—b—d—f*, we are quite sure that the scale is C major or minor. So soon as we hear *e—g♯—b—d*, we know that the scale must be A major or minor.

The chord of the dominant shows the scale, but not the mode, whether it be major or minor. What now is the surest

Indication of the Mode?

The tonic triad following the chord of the dominant at the close; for it gives us, besides the tonic, the decisive third. But this rule is not without exception; for sometimes compositions in a minor mode close with a major triad. This conclusion was a special favorite with the old ecclesiastical composers.

Other chords of the seventh are constructed from the chord of the dominant by arbitrary changes of one or other of its *tones*; thus, by raising the seventh or depressing the third, these two chords are formed:—

244.

and others also. Upon what grounds and with what right these changes are made, and how such chords are to be employed, will be shown in the instruction for composition.

3. The Chief Chord of the Ninth.

If we extend the chord of the dominant in major and minor, by the addition of a third (the ninth of the fundamental *tone*) we form chords of the ninth, but differing in mode. In C major, for instance (from the tones of C major), we find *g—b—d—f—a* to be the chord of the ninth—

245.

with a major ninth, and we therefore call it the

Major Chord of the Ninth.

In the minor, on the contrary, we find the chord of ninth to be *g—b—d—f—a♭*

246.

with a minor ninth, and we therefore call it the

Minor Chord of the Ninth.

Out of these chords of the ninth we also form, arbitrarily in the doctrine of composition, other chords of the ninth, by a judicious change of one or other of the *tones*; for instance, out of the major chord of the ninth, *c—e—g—b—d*, we make this—

247.

with a major instead of a minor seventh.

These are the chords most worthy of observation in major and minor. If we seek what other triads, major and minor, can be constructed on any other degrees of the scale, we shall find that in the major mode, in C major for instance,—

248.

there are *minor triads* on the second, third, and sixth degrees; but in the minor mode, in C minor for instance,—

249.

we have again another major triad on the sixth degree. C major therefore has

    Major triads on *C*, *G*, and *F*,
    Minor triads on *A*, *E*, and *D*,

and consequently upon all the tonic chords nearest related to it (page 25)—G major, F major, and the relative keys, A minor, E minor, and D minor. In the irregular minor mode this is exhibited irregularly and incompletely.

Let us turn, in conclusion, again to the chord of the dominant. We know now, at least in part, the peculiar importance of this chord, as the most sure sign of the scale, as the chord in common of major and minor, whereby it is to them as a bond of union, and as the foundation of both the chords of the ninth. For all these reasons it was not to be affected by the minor mode; its third (the seventh of the tonic) was not to become minor, as we have already said. And on these grounds (better than which are still to come) it is already manifest, as we endeavoured to show at page 24, why the fundamental *tone* of this important chord, the fifth of the tonic, has received the pre-eminent name of dominant, the governing or directing power.

REMARK.—An uncommonly ingenious and useful representation of the system of scales (keys) has appeared, by C. V. Decker, Berlin, at Mittler's. It is of great assistance in impressing on the mind the various scales, signatures, chords, modulations, &c.; and we recommend it particularly to teachers of music in schools and seminaries.

SEVENTH SECTION.—THE EMPLOYMENT OF THE CHORDS.

Upon this subject we can only say here, that which is of primary necessity; further information will be found in the Instructions for Composition.

1. DUPLICATION.

Duplication takes place when one, or more, or all the intervals of a chord in different parts, are employed doubly or oftener. Here, for example,—

we see first the triad on *c* alone; then the fundamental *tone* is doubled (in the octave); then the fundamental *tone* and the third are doubled; then the fundamental *tone*, third, and fifth; and lastly, the fundamental *tone* is doubled a second time.

Duplication may be employed in the same manner in any chord.

2. OMISSION.

One or several of the intervals of a chord may be omitted.

This rule, however, cannot certainly apply to those intervals which are the chief signs by which the chords are known. If we left out the third from a triad, we should no longer distinguish whether it were major or minor. If the seventh were omitted in a chord of the seventh, or a ninth in a chord of the ninth, the former would become merely a triad, and the latter a chord of the seventh. Just so in leaving out the highest or fundamental *tone* of a triad, it would become doubtful which of two chords was intended, whether one without a fundamental *tone*, or one without a fifth:—

But in the chord of the dominant and chords of the ninth, the fundamental *tone* may be omitted with a peculiar effect. By this omission, a new triad arises from the chord of the dominant, consisting of minor third and minor fifth (already mentioned at page 67), and is called the diminished triad. Another chord of the seventh, (without any peculiar name), is produced from the major chord of the ninth, with minor third, fifth, and seventh; and from the minor chord of the ninth is produced another chord of the seventh, having a minor third and fifth, and a diminished seventh, which is called the

CHORD OF THE DIMINISHED SEVENTH.

Here we have the three new chords with their root chords:—

252.

We will only observe that they are nothing more than the previous chords without their fundamental *tones*.

3. TRANSPOSITION.

We say a chord is transposed, when its *tones*, as here at (*a*)—

253.

are removed from their position into other octaves; an alteration which (excepting in the following of thirds) makes no essential difference in the chord.

If in the doubling of the fundamental *tone* in a triad, the doubling *tone* or octave lie highest, the arrangement is called the

FIRST POSITION OR OCTAVE POSITION

of the chord; if the third lie highest, it is called the

SECOND POSITION, OR POSITION OF THE THIRD;

if the fifth lie highest, the

THIRD POSITION, OR POSITION OF THE FIFTH

of the chord. Other teachers of music call the position in which the fifth is above, the first,—that where the octave is above, the second,—and where the third is above, the third. These names are of little or no consequence, provided that the expressions be reciprocally understood; but those which we have selected, seemed to us to deserve the preference, since they recognize the most important *tone* in the most important parts of the chord, as highest and lowest.

Changing the form of a chord will appear more striking, when the fundamental *tone* itself leaves its place, and ceases to be the lowest *tone* of the chord. This kind of transposition is called

4. INVERSION OF THE CHORD,

and gives it new names.

Let us examine, therefore, what inversions are possible, and how they are to be called.

When the fundamental *tone* ceases to be the deepest, some other *tone* of the chord must of course become so.

This, in a triad, may be either the third or the fifth. Here—

254.

we see a triad with its two inversions.

How shall we name the latter? We measure from each deepest *tone* to both the most important *tones*, and therefrom we name.

But which are the most important *tones*? First, the *fundamental tone*, upon which the chord is constructed. Secondly, the *third*, which distinguishes the major and minor modes. Therefore the first inversion of a triad is called

THE 6 CHORD;

(we could not count to *e*, but only to *c*), the second,

THE 6/4 CHORD,

for *g—c* is a fourth, and *g—e* is a sixth.

The *chord of the seventh* gives the following three inversions:—

255.

The most important *tones* in the chord of the seventh are, in the first place, the *fundamental tone*, secondly, the *seventh*, for this latter constitutes it a chord of the seventh. If we count, therefore, from the successive deepest *tone* to the fundamental *tone*, and to the seventh (*g* and *f*) the first inversion (*b—f; b—g*) must be called the

6/5 CHORD;

the second (*d—f, d—g*)

THE 4/3 CHORD;

the third (*f—g*)

THE 4/2 CHORD.

That some musicians should call these chords the 6/5 chord, 4/3 chord, and 4/2 chord (quite unnecessarily) can be no matter of difficulty to us.

The chord of the ninth can be inverted also, but not without transposition of the *tones*, because otherwise, these become confusing among each other. Here—

256. (a) (b)

we see, by way of example, the two first inversions of a chord of the ninth; at (*a*), without inversion, and so confused as to be impracticable; at (*b*) separated from each other by virtue of transposition and practicable. The inversions of the chord of the ninth have received no peculiar name, as they are still more rarely employed than this chord itself. What we have here said of the inversion of one triad, chord of the seventh, and chord of the ninth, applies to every kind of triads and chords of the seventh and of the ninth. Every triad has its two inversions, the 6 and 6/4 chords. Every chord of the seventh has its three inversions, its 6/5, 4/3, and 4/2, &c. Now, we can also mark every inverted chord in two ways: first according to its deepest tone; for example—

The 6 . . on *e* (*e—g—c*),
The 6/4 . . on *f* (*f—b—d*),

secondly, according to its root, for example—

The first position of the (major and minor) triad on *c*, &c.

The latter mode of indication is more circuitous, but more instructive to the scholar; for it shows us that an inversion is certainly a material and striking *appearance in a chord*, but that it is in no way a *change of the chord*. The chord

g—b—d—f.

remains a chord of the dominant, *g* continues to be its fundamental *tone*, *f* continues to be its seventh, and everything that has been and will be said of it, will continue to be true, whether *g, b, d,* or *f,* be its deepest *tone*. But it may be confusing to retain all the names. The fundamental *tone*, as the invariable foundation of the chords, might everywhere retain its name. The other intervals we would measure (as is done above) from each lowest *tone* in the inversions; for instance, in the 6/5 chord, *b—d—f—g, d* (the former fifth) shall be called the third; *f* (the former seventh) shall be called the fifth; and we may call *g* (the fundamental *tone*) the sixth, that is, of the 6/5 chord.

How are we to recognize a chord among all these transpositions and inversions? The *tones* must be arranged in higher or lower octaves, until they come to assume the position of thirds. By experiment, therefore, the original position of the chord in thirds is discovered. *Tones* already in the position of thirds, would not, of course, require altering. If we did not know, for example, by the first inversion of the chord of the ninth (Example 256, *b*), what to consider it—what chord it might be, in the first place, *b—d* and *f—a* must by all means remain together, for they are already thirds; but *d—g* and *g—f* are not so; *g* is therefore the questionable *tone*. We therefore place *g* below, and get this form:—

257.

We now see easily, that *f—a* are to be placed lower. Had we not perceived the opposition of *g*, we might perhaps have transposed *f—a*:—

258.

but seeing the fault, immediately corrected it, by transposing *b—d*:—

259.

With a little practice, the eye and ear soon hit upon the *tones* required.

We may use chords untransposed (as fundamental chords) or uninverted; and for this end they can be placed in

5. CLOSE OR DISPERSED POSITION,

as close or dispersed harmony. The harmony is called close, when all, or the greater part of the intervals are as near to each other as they can be; as at (*a*)—

260.

dispersed, when (as at *b*) they are farther from each other, not occupying the degrees next to the fundamental *tone*, nor the highest part.

But the most important use of the chords is naturally in their

6. Combination,

or rather in the motion of the simultaneously entering parts throughout the chords. In this matter, however, we can give only the most essentially necessary information. The rest belongs to the doctrine of composition.

In general the chords should have

(A)   Connexion.

Connexion depends, in the first place, upon chords having *tones* in common. Thus we see here—

261.

connected; the three first chords by *g*, the third and fourth by *c*, the fourth and fifth by *a*, the fifth and sixth by *d*, and the sixth and the last by *g*.

Another kind of connexion arises between chords which as tonic chords are considered to be of the next, or nearly related scales. Here for example—

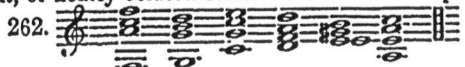
262.

the first and second chords, third and fourth, and fourth and fifth, have no connecting tone; but they represent nearly related scales (F and G major, C major and D minor, D minor and the dominant triad of A minor). The last case indicates further ways of connexion. Usually

(B)   Certain Progressions

are to be avoided. If two parts move together in octaves or fifths—

263.

they produce *in several cases* an unpleasant effect. In other cases it is not so. These progressions are called

False Octaves and Fifths,*

or briefly octaves and fifths. Until we know in what cases such octaves and fifths may be allowed, it is wiser to hold to the prohibition, and to proceed with the chords in other directions; for example, thus:—

264.

Octaves which without any intervening *tones* serve merely to strengthen or enforce a part, are not included in the foregoing rule:—

265.

---

* We prefer, passing over for the present, some other progressions, at times of importance, such as the so-called hidden fifths and octaves, in order not to give the student too much at once of that which is here necessarily imperfect. In like manner, we shall be obliged to omit other matters touching the duplication of those *tones*, which require a determinate resolution.

nor duplications of two and three parts in the higher octaves, for example—

266.

which are immediately understood to be merely corroborative additions. Regularly some chords require a

(C)   Determinate Resolution;

that is to say, motion of some or all the *tones* into the determined *tones* of some other determinate chord.

From the chord of the dominant the seventh goes usually a degree downwards—the third goes usually a degree upwards—the bass *tone* to the tonic:—

267.

The seventh and the third retain this disposition, also in the *inversions*—

268.

and the same is the case with the derived *diminished triad* and its inversions—

269.

Also, all chords of the seventh derived immediately from the dominant, follow the laws by which this latter is regulated.

The chords of the ninth, also, follow the laws of the chord of the dominant, as they originate from it. But the ninth, which in them becomes the seventh, goes also with the seventh; that is, a step downwards:—

270.

The chords of the seventh, derived from the chords of the ninth, are again nothing but chords of the ninth, without a fundamental *tone*; consequently all their *tones* move as they would in the chord of the ninth itself:—

271.

The *inversions* of this chord retain the same motions, viz:—

272.

We have hitherto communincated merely general indications as to the employment of chords; the continuation of this matter belongs to the study of composition. There are, however, two applications of them, which we must explain with more precision.

7. The Close.

It is customary for every work of art, and consequently, for every musical composition, to have a distinct and satisfactory conclusion. How then is it to be effected? *Harmonically*, by the most important distinguishing chords of the scale, through the combination of the

CHORD OF THE DOMINANT, and
TONIC TRIAD;

and in the original position of the fundamental *tone*, without inversion of either one or the other. Melodically, by placing the most important *tone*,

THE TONIC,

in the most important parts,

UPPER AND LOWER.

Rhythmically, by making the closing chord fall on a chief part. Here, therefore—

273.

we have two *perfect closes*, they being satisfactory in every respect. But here—

274.

we see at (*a*) closes imperfect in melody—at (*b*) imperfect in rhythm—at (*c*) imperfect in harmony.

A perfect close is required to the true end of a phrase that is at the end of a subject. How then, should we close the opening phrase of a subject? The whole subject, or the closing phrase, was (as we have said above) to be closed from the dominant on the tonic. As therefore, the opening and closing phrases are opposite phrases, distinguished by the contrary motion of their melody, it is natural that the close of the opening phrase should be in contrariety to the close of the closing phrase, or of the whole subject; consequently the opening phrase will close from the tonic on the dominant—

275.

Sometimes, however, instead of the tonic triad, that of the subdominant (the third chord in importance) is used, and a half-close is thus formed:—

276.

These closes are called

HALF CLOSES.*

Upon this point we remember our appendages (page 61) by which our subjects were lengthened.

* Sometimes the half close assumes the form, in part, of a perfect close. If one were to write, for example, in a composition in C major, thus—

277.

from the second to the third bar, would be in reality a complete close, and indeed in G major: but the repeating form of the half close, in which c—e—g so often appears, makes us feel assured, that really there is no intention to deviate permanently into G major, but on the contrary, to close finally in C major; while the apparent close on G major is merely a more powerful half close on the dominant of C.

An appendage belongs to the subject itself, but it steps in just where the subject should close. How is their union to be preserved?

In the first place, the subject does close perfectly; but a continuation is added immediately to the close:—

278.

This connexion is indeed only external, and is little satisfactory.

In the second place, by changing the close of the subject, for example, of the above close, into an imperfect close:—

279.

In the third place, by giving to the chord of the dominant, which governs the close, a resolution differing from its original direction:—

280.

and thus, instead of going immediately to the closing chord, it deviates into a foreign scale, in order to begin the appendage therein, and thence return into the principal scale, wherein the real close of the phrase will be formed. Such a determination into a new scale, in lieu of the properly indicated and expected close, is called a

FALSE CADENCE.

8. THE PRELUDE.

It is sometimes advisable, for several reasons, to introduce the performance of music by a foretaste of the art, in order to arouse the attention of the audience, to give the singers the key-note of what they are about to sing, &c; such an introduction is called a prelude.

The most proper use of this performance, is to make known thereby the scale of the music about to be produced.

The simplest way of effecting this object, is to play the tonic chords two or three times in different positions or inversions—

281.

with various doublings or repetitions, upwards or downwards, and progressions by gradual ascent or decline, &c.

A more determinate character can be given to a prelude, by the chord of the dominant and tonic triad, as in No. 273. Moreover, either or both of these chords may be interchangeably carried through any of their positions or inversions; for example:—

282.

which already gives a more varied performance.

Greater completeness is given, when the nearest related chords, or even the harmonies of more distant scales, but always in orderly combination, are brought to aid the effect. Thus, for example:—

283.

or thus:—

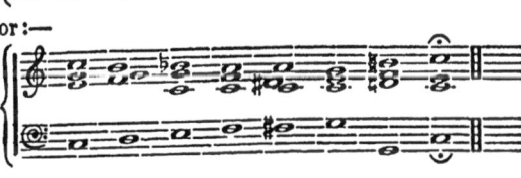

or:—

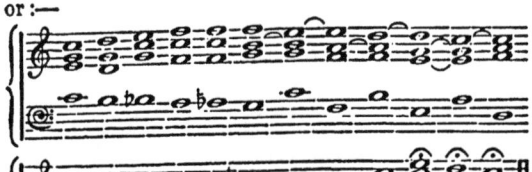

or:—

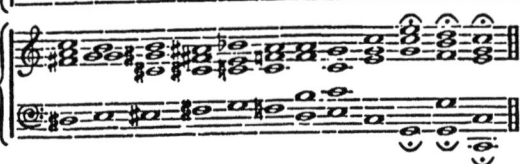

The following section will give elucidations of the chords from foreign scales employed here and in No. 280. We cannot give in this book more than that which is absolutely essential to those who have not hitherto had, nor perhaps ever will have, time for the study of composition. Everything beyond, more elaborated and more beautiful, must be reserved for that study, or left to the good fortune of those who may seek for it. We will not, however, quit the subject, without giving one word of advice to the amateur, which may be sometimes useful to him, and spare him many errors. When he wishes to unite one chord to another, let him endeavour to "hold on" every *tone* which is common to both chords; and to give every new *tone* to that Part, which can most conveniently reach it; that is, to that Part whose present *tone* is nearest to that which is to come. By no means, however, is this hint to be considered as a universally directing rule of art. The accompanying phrases give some examples.

EIGHTH SECTION.—MODULATION.

Large compositions are not generally confined to one scale. They leave that in which they began, and pass into others. After a while they return, in order to close in the original scale—or perhaps to repeat the same process of departure and return.

The scale in which a composition begins and mostly continues, is called the
PRINCIPAL SCALE;
the going from one scale into another is called
THE DEPARTURE;
and if the stay in the foreign scale is to be of long continuance,
THE STAY;
and, the combined action of departure, stay, and return to the principal scale, is called
MODULATION.

We therefore say: This composition is in such and such a scale, passes into this or that scale, returns into the principal scale. This is its modulation.

Moreover, in the widest sense, all harmonical construction is called modulation.

Some knowledge of modulation is useful to every practitioner of music, were it only to keep him aware of what scale he is playing in, and that thereby he may be able to read the notes and chords with greater ease and certainty. Here we can only mention that which is most necessary.

(A) LAW OF MODULATION.

Whither, into what scales can we modulate? In general we may answer to this question—that regularly, the principal tone has the predominant power; that it embraces the whole compass of its dependencies, and must govern their manner of closing.

The nearest related scales of both dominant and subdominant, and the relative keys of the principal *tone*, and of the dominant and subdominant, may be first combined with the principal *tone*; after which only, and in smaller masses, more distant scales may be associated in the modulation. The latter, however, must be touched in passing only; while in the former we may remain some time to perform a considerable part of the whole composition.

The most important scale in composition in the major mode is (next to that of the principal tone) that of the
DOMINANT,
and in compositions in the minor mode, its
RELATIVE MAJOR SCALE.

We cannot here dilate on the numerous exceptions to, and further exemplifications of, this rule.

(B) MEANS OF MODULATION.

How is the passing to be effected? This question is easily answered if we reflect, that passing, means nothing but changing one scale for another; that is, changing the *tones* of one scale for the *tones* of another. We pass from C major to E♭ major, when we no longer use the succession of *tones* (or the scale)

c, d, e, f, g, a, b, c,

but take the succession of *tones* (or scale)—

e♭, f, g, a♭, b♭ c, d, e♭,

as the materials of our composition.

Now, the scales mostly, do not differ in all, but in some only of their *tones*. E♭ major, for example, agrees with C major in the *tones f, g, c, d,* and differs through the tones *e♭, a♭,* and *b♭.* We need not therefore consider all the *tones*, but merely those which differ; that is, for example, for the passage from C major to E♭ major, only the *tones e♭, a♭,* and *b♭.*

But that seems not to be sufficient. The *tones e♭, a♭,* and *b♭,* are not in E♭ major only. They are also in A♭ major, in D♭ major, &c. Their appearance convinces us, probably, that we are not in C major, but not that we are in E♭ major. We seek, therefore, for a surer sign, and find it in the

CHORD OF THE DOMINANT,

for the chord of the dominant of a scale (major and minor) is to be found in no other scale than in that in which its fundamental tone is the dominant; and it is therefore the surest sign of the scale of its tonic. We have seen, for example, page 68, that the chord of the dominant, *g, b, d, f,* is possible only in C major or minor. When this chord appears in a composition written in G, D, F, B♭ major, &c., it indicates to us that we are no longer in the original scale, but in C major or minor. In like manner, if we are in C major, and the chord of the dominant, *e, g♯, b, d,* occurs, it shows us that C major is no longer the position of the music, but A major or minor.

Here are a few examples for verification. We pass from

284. C to D.   C to B♭.   C to D♭.   C to E.

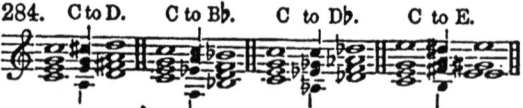

So then the chord of the dominant seems to be the most sure means of passing from one chord to another, and again justifies its name of governor and leader. Our command over this branch will be considerably increased by frequently passing from one chord to another very distantly related to it, through the auxiliary chords; for example, thus:—

285.   C to E.   C to E♭.   C to D♭.

or through enharmonic changing of the names of the chords; for example, from

C♯ (for which D♭) to E♭   G♭ (for which F♯) to G.

286.

The two chords of the ninth participate fully with the chord of the dominant in this power; for they contain, indeed, the whole chord of the dominant, and moreover, they indicate the key; although just as well major chords are allowed to follow the minor, and minor chords to follow the major chord of the ninth, as it were, in momentary transition on departure to another key.

The chord of the seventh, derived from the chord of the ninth and the diminished triad, also share the modulating power of the chord of the dominant, but with less effect.* Even a major or minor triad,—nay, under certain circumstances, a single *tone*,† may become a safe means of modulation. Upon this point, however, the instructions for composition alone can give the competent information. Here we have some neighbouring modulations united to a harmonic passage:—

290.

It begins in C major, goes by (*a*), through the chord of the diminished seventh, to A minor; by (*b*) through the chord of the dominant, or rather through the

---

* Among all chords for modulation, none is more convenient than the diminished seventh. In order to be of some service to amateurs, who are generally fond of preluding and exercising their fancy before they study composition, we will say a few words upon this most serviceable caterer for modulation.

The diminished seventh has this peculiarity, that its inversions continuously reproduce the sound of a diminished seventh: for it consists of nothing but minor thirds. If the fundamental *tone* be placed over the seventh, an extreme second is formed:—

287.   A minor.   F♯ minor.

thus, by the inversion of *c♯—e—g—f*, the extreme second *f, g♯* is formed. But this is enharmonically equal to a minor third, *c♯—f♭*; consequently a new diminished seventh has been produced, *c♯—g♯—b—d*, which leads us into a new scale. We have then in every chord of the diminished seventh, the introduction to four different scales, that is, the scale in which we are, and three others by modulation. This chord in A minor for example (*g♯—b—d—f*), places under our hands, by enharmonic changes, the following modulations besides A minor:—

288.   A   C   E♭

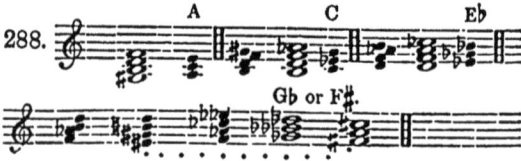

G♭ or F♯.

The same takes place in another form, if we continually depress the lowest tone by a semitone.—

289.   C.   E♭.

F♯.   A.

We pass over many other kinds of changes. More complete directions and explanations are given in the Instructions for Composition.

† From this circumstance the old theory connects the doctrine of modulation with the so-called *leading tones*. The leading *tone* was sometimes the seventh degree of the scale, as for example *b* in the scale of C major, and *e* in F major. Hence its Latin name, *subsemitonium modi*. But if I wish to pass from C to F, is the *tone e* sufficient for me? or generally, is it a sign of the new scale, F major? Again at other times, the leading *tone* was to be considered as the *tone* which distinguished one scale from another. In order, therefore, to pass from C major to F major, *b♭* would be the leading *tone;* but if it were wished to perform this operation, not *b♭* but *e* was to be the leading *tone,* so that the attribute of leading *tone* was constantly wavering and uncertain. We may learn, however, in the Doctrine of Harmony, that single *tones*, without any influence in harmony and modulation, can be introduced,—for example, as *b♭*, in C major,—without passing into F. So then the doctrine of leading *tones* is quite unsatisfactory.

chord of its second to D minor; by (c), through a similar chord, to G major, which is changed at (d) into G minor, &c. By (i) and (h) chords of the ninth are introduced. There is no close; indeed, the whole is superabundant of modulation, the exemplification of that process having been the object of the composition.

NINTH SECTION—OF THE MOVEMENT OF THE PARTS IN CHORDS.

From the beginning we have considered the chords merely as the result of the meeting of different parts.* The parts, the melody of each part, is the vivifying principle; and to this we return.

The parts of a chord have a fourfold movement. We must point out at least the general nature of this motion.

1. MOTION WITHIN A CHORD.

Every part, or several parts jointly, can move in manifold ways within a chord from *tone* to *tone*. This application of the chord to the production of melodic forms, is called

HARMONIC FIGURATION† (*Figurirung*);

and also, more with a view to harmony than to melody,—

ARPEGGIO.

Here are some examples in the chord c—e—g:—

We see now the foundation of melody, which we mentioned at page 58, brought into employment.

It is scarcely necessary to mention that every chord or succession of chords, such as the following, for example,—

may be dispersed or spread in the following or any other manner conformable to rhythm:—

2. EQUAL MOVEMENT IN THE CHORDS.

By this is understood the equal progress of all the parts of a chord from the one to the other, which we have observed in all our harmonic examples, Nos. 250, 292, and others. Since all the parts go step by step with each other, we have every moment a concluded chord before us—for example, in No. 290, first the chord c—e—g, then the chord g—b—d—f, &c.

This method of movement, therefore, requires for itself no further consideration. It furnishes us merely the contrary to the following.

3. UNEQUAL MOVEMENT IN THE CHORDS.

This consists in the passage of one or more parts of a chord, to a second chord, while the others remain in the first. Here we must distinguish the following forms:—

(A) SUSPENSION OR RETARDATION.

A suspension ‡ is a *tone* which moves from one chord into another to which it does not belong, but of which it afterwards forms a part.

Here we see—

at (a) the tone g step out of the first chord into the triad f—a—c, and then only, enter into the tone of the chord f, or (technically speaking) *resolve itself*. At (b) (c) and (d) respectively, e, b, d and b, are cases of suspension. The latter resolve themselves upwards, and come, therefore, from under, and are hence called *suspensions from beneath*; the others, on the contrary, are called *suspensions from above*. At (e) (f) and (g) we see suspensions from above and beneath at the same time: f and a resolve themselves from above, b from beneath, d at (g) once from above and once from beneath.

(B) ANTICIPATION.

We see a *tone* enter into a chord without any kind of introduction (the suspensions were led in, or *prepared*, by having formed a part of a previous chord), and without belonging at all to that chord, but belonging in fact to a chord which appears only some time afterwards, as here the c, enters—

---

* Although nature herself has given us the self-originating *tones*. C—e—g—c—o—g, arising from the vibrations of a string. See page 47, in note, and the author's Composition-lehre, Part I.

† For an explanation of this term, see page 85.

‡ We now refer again to the pretended chords of the eleventh and thirteenth, mentioned at page 67, in note. They are nothing but suspensions, which make their appearance over one or more *tones* of the following chord. The pretended chord of the eleventh shows itself in No. 296, at (f), and the chord of the thirteenth at (g). When we know from the Instructions for Composition (Part I), that, regularly, a suspension *tone* cannot appear simultaneously with the *tone* of the chord, whose place it assumes for a time, we shall understand why these pretended chords cannot have a *third*—instead of this third, the suspension *tones*, (f and d above), present themselves. This circumstance shews precisely the impropriety of representing a form so easily explained as a chord, which ought indeed to be formed by thirds from the fundamental tone, but which, in this case, begins exactly with having no third at all. If, however, it were wished to explain the suspensions at (f) and (g), by admitting those imagined chords, how many more admissions would be still necessary to explain the other suspensions! Otherwise, most inconsequentially, we must allow some suspensions to be chords, while others are to remain considered as suspensions. And how many double, and therefore perplexing rules, would be necessary to explain such groups of notes—for example, in No. 296, at (a) and (c), the groups f—a—c (eb or e nat.)—g, and c—e—(g)—b), which at one time are real chords, at another, merely suspensions, which have the appearance of chords— while according to the pure and clear doctrine of suspension, one single law governs all.

at (*a*,) in the chord *e—g—b*, to which it does not at all belong, but only to the next following ⁶⁄₃ chord: and at (*b*,) in the chord *d—f♯—d* (*a* is wanting and *g* is a suspension), the entirely foreign tone *e♭* comes in, which is connected only with the chord of the ninth of the third crotchet.

(*C*) ORGAN POINT.

By the suspension we have conveyed a *tone* only from one chord to another. But if we "hold on," or sustain a *tone*, until the occurrence of an entire foreign chord, or during several of these latter, as here, for example,—

until a chord appears in which the sustained *tone* is contained, whereby it becomes reconciled and endurable to the ear, such a *tone* is technically called an Organ point.

It forms a strong band of combination to the suite of chords flowing over it, and is employed, occasionally, after an extensive and somewhat violent modulation, to impress and magnify the return of the principal *tone*. In this case the *dominant* in the *bass* is sustained during a more or less extended succession of harmony, to some of whose chords the sustained tone is related, and to others not related. Here is an example of this form of composition :—

The sustained tone *g* is related to the first chord *g—b—d*, not to the following chords, *a—c♯—e** and *d—f—a*. It is again related in *g—b—d—f*, in *c—e—g*, and *g—b—d*. Again, not related in *f♯—a—c*, and so forth. The upper parts in such an Organ point generally make a greater display of melody than is attempted here. This figure is applied also to the closing *tone* of the bass: the tonic is sustained, and the upper parts allowed to wander in manifold harmonical configurations at pleasure. Moreover, in serious and important compositions, the beginning is at times ornamented by this kind of introduction. One of the most dignified examples of this method of beginning is that of the *Matthäischen Passion*, of Seb. Bach.† Sometimes, in lieu of the bass, an upper part or a middle part, or an upper part and the bass, are sustained. This last is most employed for the closing note ; the previous ones, during the course of the composition: the two first (as before said) for the introduction and corroboration of the close.

---

* Or does it form, perhaps, with *a—c♯—e*, a chord of the dominant *a—c♯—e—g*? Such a chord would resolve itself into *d—f♯* (or *f*)—*a* and the *g* as a seventh (page 71), pass to *f♯* or *f*. But, as that does not take place here, we cannot consider *g* as a *tone* of the chord, as seventh of *a—c♯—e*.

† The beginning of most of the French overtures is a caricature of the Organ point. In these compositions from poverty of harmony, the bass is allowed to stand still.

4. MOTION BETWEEN THE CHORDS.

A part may be accompanied by the intervening *tones* between one chord and another. Here—

we see a simple example of such a procedure. The upper part, at (*a*), has *tones* in accordance with it; but at (*b*) *tones* continue and accompany it which by no means belong to it. It then meets a chord of which it is a harmony. From its manner of proceeding it is called a

PASSING OR TRANSIENT *tone*.

We can call the *tone* at (*c*) also a passing *tone*, and through it the ⁶⁄₄ chord becomes a ⁴⁄₃ chord. It is certain, however, that the *tone* at (*d*), namely *e*, does not belong to the chord under it. It begins with the chord, and hinders for a time the right harmonic tone, *d*, from assuming its place in the chord. Such passing *tones* as this latter, at (*d*), are also called

EXCHANGING TONES.

Not only one *tone* alone and not diatonic *tones* alone, but two or more, and also chromatic *tones*, may be used as passing *tones*; as for example, here,—

at (*a*), the *tones e* and *f♯*, at (*b*), the *tones c♯, d, d♯*, and *e*: and thus are constructed, out of passing and accordant *tones*, all kinds of cadences and figures. For example :—

And as we have not always time to go through all the intermediate *tones*, we take, instead of the entire diatonic or chromatic succession, only the passing *tones* (called auxiliary *tones*) next to the *tones* of the chord; thus,—

in order to produce greater motion and variety of melody, together with the predominating firmness and perspicuity of the harmony.

All this can be done, not only in the upper part, as we have shown, but also in the under or middle parts, for example ;—

or, also, in two or more parts together, thus :—*

305.

It frequently happens that chords are formed by simultaneous passing *tones* in several parts; thus, in the third bar above we see *f—a—d, g—b—e, a—c—f, e—a♯—c♯, f—b—d,* which are called

PASSING CHORDS.

In conclusion of this, certainly nothing less than exhausted development, we have yet to exemplify a particularly prominent mode of conducting the parts through modulating chords and foreign passing *tones*, which often appears faulty and repulsive, and is designated by the term

FALSE RELATION.

When in two following harmonies a degree in the higher part in the first harmony becomes flattened in the other part in the second harmony, this occurrence is called a false relation—we say, the parts form a false relation, they are in a repulsive and false relation. Here—

306.

we see at (*a*) the minor triad of *c* following the major; and the minor third, *e♭*, appears in a different part from that which previously had the major third, *e*; the one part performs *e—c*, while the other produces *c—e♭*; therefore the one seems to be in C major and the other in C minor. Herein lies a contradiction, which, however unintelligibly, offends the ear. At (*b*) we have the same case, excepting that the contradictory *tones* are separated by passing *tones*, by means of which, the offence is moderated, if not entirely removed. Very frequently the false relation is occasioned simply by the neglect of the advice we gave at page 73—to let each part proceed by the nearest *tone* of the following chord. The above modulations might, according to the said advice, have been written thus,—

307.

without any false relation.

That other false relations are less repulsive, and that many admitted successions of *tones* have a falsely related appearance, is quite indubitable. Here are a few examples thereof:—

308.

* In this information upon passing *tones*, imperfect though it be, we think we see a sufficient justification of our assertions in the note at page 74, upon the uncertainty of the so-called leading *tones*, as signs of modulation. We see in the phrases above, No. 301 to 305, many foreign *tones* employed as passing *tones*, exchanging *tones*, and auxiliary *tones*, which nevertheless neither perform nor indicate any modulation into a foreign scale.

REFLECTIONS.

We see easily after these short elucidations, how immeasurably rich is the web of harmony, and how impossible it would be to include anything like a complete development of it in *preparatory* lessons, such as we can give in the General Musical Instruction. Such a task can be fulfilled by the Doctrine of Composition only, and is indeed the principal object of that study. In these sections we have pointed out merely so much as will enable the student to acquire a tolerable conception of the different forms he will meet with in composition.

We entertain hopes, however, that this introductory instruction will give him a sure insight into the elements and combination of musical productions, and also greater ease in reading the notation, in comprehension and in performance. But most assuredly a two-fold practice is essential, if this instruction is to produce a fine and abundant harvest.

In the first place, the student must be able to play every scale upon the instrument; then every chord in its positions, transpositions, inversions, and the indicated progressions. Conversely, he must learn to recognise by the ear any given chord, and not only in one, but in all the scales, by gradual and frequent repetition. It is very instructive to the musical perception to practise the *tones* of each chord separately, and the transition to the chord of the dominant, in such forms as these, for example :—

309.

and also vocal exercises on the chord of the ninth and its derivations, with clearness and precision. A man knows only *that* well which he can himself produce, unless hindered by deficiency of physical power: and he who cannot recognise and produce by ear any chord or form of composition, so far as his voice will reach, knows it not at all—or at least, has but a very indistinct and imperfect knowledge of it.

In the second place the student must go through, (and, indeed, with indefatigable repetition), complete compositions with the utmost minuteness. In doing this, he must ask himself point by point—

What scale do the signature and close indicate ?
What are its chords ?
What modulations ?
Then—Part by Part—
Wherefore this, the following or the third *tone* ?
Is it a *tone* of a chord or a passing *tone* ?
In the same manner the rhythm must be examined—
What order or arrangement, kind of bar, value; what passages, phrases, subjects, &c., where they begin and where close. The more deeply and intimately we labour at these examinations and dissections, the more skilled we shall be in performance, and more especially in

SCORE PLAYING

for even to the most practised eye it is impossible

really and faithfully to read all the parts, and in each part all the notes, constantly, simultaneously, and in the right absolute time (*tempo*), at once from the book, in a large score. But he who is perfectly at home in the simple mysteries of chords, and in the construction and movements of the parts, is able from a few notes to seize the harmony, from one or two parts to guess in a measure at the others, and so by a swift glance to become master of the score.

But it is also impossible to play upon one instrument, literally, all the parts of an extensive score: nor, were it possible, would it be an advantage. The *tones* and parts, which in an orchestra flow distinctly and characteristically from the hands of several performers, would form a mass of confused perplexity upon a single instrument. The score player, therefore, must before all things be able to distinguish the essential from the secondary; to grasp and enhance the former, and to subordinate, or if need be, to sacrifice the latter: but even this could not be done with any certainty of success, without a mature inspection into the inward construction of the composition.

Let every one, therefore, examine how far cultivation is necessary, for his inclination or propensity to music. The more grievously he is sensible of his deficiencies, the more noble and real he may consider his disposition for Art; and the more ardently he strives to supply these deficiencies, the more strongly, by consequent advantages, will his talent be confirmed.

TENTH SECTION.—FIGURING OF BASSES.

In order to facilitate the inspection of the harmony for a reader of score, and to give the composer a short-hand for the instant noting down of his work, a system was introduced, composed chiefly of ciphers, by means of which the most important chords and modulations can be indicated with rapidity, and read with equal dispatch. This writing is called

FIGURING THE BASS,

and the same word is applied to the signs themselves. These latter are also sometimes called signatures. The figures are applied to the lowest part of the movement, over or under it, and such a part with the ciphering is called

THOROUGH BASS.

The faculty of playing thorough bass is worth acquiring, because in many compositions, for example, recitatives (chorales also in many elder works) are accompanied by this invention only, without any harmonies in notation.

We will now give the most needful information on this point.

The first question in figuring basses is, what is to be indicated?

If it be merely a succession of intervals, such as octaves, thirds, or sixths, the indications,

all' 8va. or *alla 3za.* or *alla 6ta.*

(as noted already at page 12) must be written as at (*a*); or also a simple 8, or 3, or 6, followed by little oblique lines, as at (*b*) :—

The performance is then, as is seen in the following notation, No. 311, at (*a*) and (*b*) :—

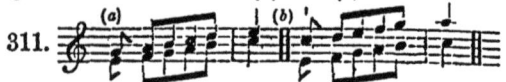

If a *tone* is to be sustained (or be constantly repeated) during a succession of *tones* in the under part, the cipher of the interval must be placed first, and then a long, horizontal line, or several small ones. The phrase (*a*) for example, is to be played as at (*b*) :—

If any *tone* or succession of *tones* of the thorough bass part is to be quite alone, that is, unaccompanied, the single note is marked with a naught, and the succession of notes with

t. s., tasto solo.

This phrase at (*a*) is to be played as at (*b*) :—

If a chord is to be signified, a distinction must be made between triads and all other chords.

Triads, as the most simple chords, are understood when no other indications, no other chord, no *al unisono* (all the parts in unison) no *tasto solo*, *all'* 8, &c. are expressly marked.

This case apart, every chord is signified according to its interval, from which its name is derived. Therefore,

6 signifies a chord of 6 (that is, of the bass tone over or under which the cipher is placed);

$\frac{6}{4}$ or $\frac{4}{6}$ signifies a chord of $\frac{6}{4}$;

7 signifies a chord of the seventh;

$\frac{6}{5}$ or $\frac{5}{6}$ signifies a chord of $\frac{6}{5}$;

$\frac{4}{3}$ or $\frac{3}{4}$ signifies a chord of $\frac{4}{3}$;

2 signifies a chord of the second;

9 signifies a chord of the ninth.

If we wish to indicate a triad, we must employ a

3, or $\frac{5}{3}$, or $\frac{3}{5}$ or $\frac{8}{5}$, or $\frac{3}{8}$, and so forth;

so also with the other chords, more intervals may be signified than are necessary according to the above custom, or all indeed may be given in ciphers; thus the $\frac{3}{4}$ chord, and chord of the second, so :—

$\frac{3}{4}$, $\frac{6}{4}$, and $\frac{6}{4}$, and so forth.
 $\frac{}{6}$ $\frac{}{3}$

All these ciphers point to the indicated degree, *as they stand in the scale according to the signature.*

If the following ciphering, for example, were to occur in G major—

the ¾ chord on *a*, would be *a, c, d, f♯*, and the ⁶⁄₄ chord on *a*, would be *a, d, f♯*. But if it be desired to raise or depress a *tone* of a chord from its state according to the signature, we must use—

[1] *instead of the third*, the needful to cause an elevation or depression; that is, a

♯ or ♭ or ♮.

[2] Before any other cipher in the same manner, the needful

♭ 6, ♯ 5, ♮ 4;

or if it be judged necessary, the 3 may also be added to the sign of depression or elevation.

Instead of using the sharp, it is also customary to cross the cipher; thus—

2, 3, 4, 5, 6, 7.

Also double sharps and double flats may be used before ciphers, as well as before notes.

If the interval in a chord is not contained in the usual ciphering, and is to be taken either depressed or raised, its proper cipher must be employed, and the sign of elevation or depression be placed before it. As an example of all these rules, we present here the bass ciphered of the suite of chords, No. 290:—

from the comparison of which with the harmony in No. 290, all the points will become clear. At (*a*) the fourth was necessarily inserted in the ciphering, in order to show that the fourth was to be raised. The same case happened at (*b*). In like manner the fifths were required in the chords of the seventh at (*c*) and (*d*), and the seventh in the chord of the ninth at (*e*).

It is seen here that the ciphering expresses that which is most essential, namely, the chord itself, but does not direct its position. Sometimes its intended position is sought to be indicated by the arrangement of the ciphers. If, for example, the ciphers ⅗ had been thus placed under the first bass *tone* in No. 290, it might have been guessed (as in general, no ciphering is necessary for a triad) that the ciphers referred to the intended place of each *tone* of the chord. Sometimes for the same object a 10 is ciphered instead of a 3; although in general each cipher points out the interval only, and not the octave where it is to be placed.

For the sake of convenience, when a chord is to be sustained over a bass in motion, it is usual to draw horizontal lines in lieu of many ciphers. This ciphering, for example—

is to be understood so—

But if a chord is to be repeated on many degrees after each other, instead of repeating the ciphers, we place little inclined lines under each note in the bass, as we have already done with repeated intervals at page 78. This bass, therefore,—

with its ciphering, is thus to be understood.

319.

If two or more cipherings should be found under one bass note, the chords indicated should be played one after the other during the value of the bass note. These cipherings, for instance,—

320.

show that the triad of *C*, and the ⁶⁄₄ chord, and chord of the dominant of *F*, are to be played with *C*; the triad of *F*, &c. are to be played with it. But how are those chords to be distributed in the bar?

In the first place, to the chief part and ex-chief part; that is, in ¼ measure, the 1st and 3rd crotchets; then, to every part of a bar, its harmony. The above phrase might be played thus:—

If a bass note has more cipherings under it than parts of a bar, the *members* of the bar receive separate harmonies; and first, those of the secondary parts, and last those of the chief parts, in order that the predominance of the latter be not lessened by too rapid a mutation of harmony. Hence, the following ciphering—

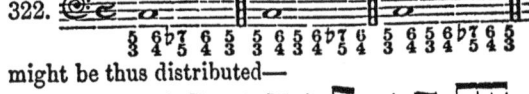

might be thus distributed—

323.

So now *retardations* also are indicated by the ciphers of their intervals, and by those of their resolution. This ciphering, for example,—

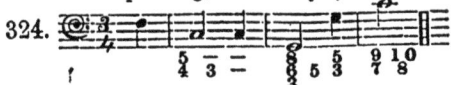

denotes the following phrase:—

It is manifest, that with the retardation so much ciphering of the chord is always added, that no misunderstanding with regard to the former can occur. Since a ninth appears over the last *tone* as a retardation, and was to be resolved into the tenth, it was natural to cipher the resolving *tone* with a 10, and not with a 3.

The harmonies are also indicated in like manner on a sustained bass, in an organ point, with all the ciphers belonging to the harmonies of that *tone*. So the harmonies, for instance, in No. 299, might be thus indicated:—

The system of ciphering is certainly not calculated to replace the system of notation. Many essential particulars it cannot communicate at all, and others it indicates but very imperfectly; and further, the more we require of it, the more confused and illegible it becomes. But that is not its proper function—its object is to serve as a momentary record of the ideas of a composer, until he can find time and space to expand and determine his conceptions by notation. It is useful, also, as a facilitation to the inspection of score, until we have learned to read it with more completeness and certainty from the notes themselves; and helps us also to unravel those entangled phrases, for which the composers (of the elder school more particularly) did not think notation necessary. For these objects we trust the foregoing explanations will be considered sufficient, although they do not embrace all the forms which the ciphering system brought (many most unaptly) into existence.

In elder works, such, for instance, as the Recitatives of Seb. Bach, we find at times, basses even without ciphering (called unciphered basses), which nevertheless were to have a harmonic accompaniment. Here it was necessary to guess at the harmony from the course of the singing part, and what appeared to be needful or fitting,—or from the usual progressions of composition. We do not think it necessary to enter into the particulars of this very problematical and little important art of conjecture.

FIFTH DIVISION.

Of Artistic Forms of Composition.

FIRST SECTION.—GENERAL CONSIDERATIONS ON ARTISTIC FORMS OF COMPOSITION.

We have become acquainted with the elementary forms in which music appears to us. If we collect together what we have hitherto learned, we shall find the following:—

1. All music may consist either of a simple succession of sounds, or of two or more such simultaneous successions. The first we call *in one part*, the second in many parts.

2. Every musical composition may be adapted to one or to several musical apparatus. In this respect we have learned to distinguish *pure vocal music*, *accompanied vocal music*, and *instrumental music*, and so forth.

3. Every musical thought may exhibit itself in three forms: passage, phrase, and subject.

If we dwell on this list of distinctions, we shall observe that a subject, or even a phrase, has an independent coherence,—that it can by itself alone express some determined idea; whereas a passage having no appreciable close, cannot be considered as a concluded totality, nor available as a work of art, since it enounces itself, its own incompleteness.

In like manner we can already anticipate that all works of art cannot by any means be constructed with the form of one single subject, or phrase, or passage; but that they all require the combination of several phrases, subjects, and passages. Everyone who has heard any considerable composition, must be aware of this.

This review enables us to form a conception of the particulars, wherein essentiality and difference in artistic forms consist, out of which forms all compositions are constructed. We may enumerate herein—

1. The number and management of the parts.
2. The manner of representing and employing phrases and subjects.
3. The manner of combining phrases and subjects, so as to form an entire composition.
4. The musical apparatus for which a composition is destined.
5. The combinations which music may form with other arts, and its employment in the celebration of public worship.

A general knowledge, at least, of the forms of art, is desirable to every musical amateur. It is not merely because such knowledge is within the scope of what is considered essential to musical reputation, but on account of the positive advantage it affords. He who has been in the habit of discriminating the varied forms of a composition, will penetrate deeper into the objects of the composer in the structure of his work, and in every part of the work. He will comprehend more easily what the composer intended to express, and will be so far better able to express the same himself. Upon this ground, we offer our explanations of the artistic forms.

But on this matter, we can still less than in the preceding sections, avoid many omissions, and for the following reasons:—

The artistic forms are not indeed so very numerous. But each of them, however essentially it may differ from all others, can assume so many kinds of deviating, though unessential configurations, that occasionally it requires a very experienced eye to detect the conformity in essentials, through the mazes of varied employment in different works. It is also allowed, as in the free exercise of any art, to invent new forms. But these can be scarcely anything else than middle forms between one and another, mixtures of two different forms. Herein, therefore, lies the difficulty of giving this classification a determinate or established and permanent character.

The General Musical Instruction has not space, nor is it intended, for teaching all these varieties. They would require more examples and a deeper insight into melody, harmony, the conducting of parts, &c., than can be here given, and than the student at this grade could be expected to possess. We must therefore refer this matter to the Instructions for Composition, and content ourselves with a mere introduction into a subject, which on deeper penetration becomes highly interesting. The examples even will be but sparingly given, since it is impossible to impart them with completeness. He, however, who shall observe constantly the brief hints we have been able to give, will not require much time for the attainment of tolerable certainty in this province of composition.

SECOND SECTION.—DIFFERENCES OF FORMS IN THE CONSTRUCTION OF THE PARTS.

Every composition, as we know, may be in one or more parts. Under the latter, we understand every musical construction of more than one part; therefore, also, two-part compositions.

Compositions of several parts may be of two intentions, as to the reciprocal action of the parts in respect of each other.

In the first place, out of several parts, one may be the principal or chief, while the others may serve merely as its support and accompaniment.

This kind of composition we call
HOMOPHONIC.

In homophonic compositions, therefore, two kinds of parts are to be distinguished:
THE PRINCIPAL PART,
which has to produce the essential ideas, and must fulfil the requirements of artistic melody; and the
SECONDARY PARTS,
which exist only on account of the principal, and have no proper contents of their own, but such only as strengthen or produce a desirable effect on the principal part. Here—

327. *Andante.*

we see a homophonic phrase. The upper part has a melodic passage, which may of itself be satisfying. The four other successions of sounds are evidently intended merely to support the principal part with harmony and rhythm. Not one of these secondary successions of *tones* could exist alone as a melody, or could dispute with the upper part for pre-eminence.

Usually the upper part is made the principal part. It is also the most appropriate for that function, from its position, its easy mobility, and the more penetrating nature of its *tones*. But all the other parts are capable of assuming it. The bass, for example—

328.

or the tenor—

329.

or, we might add, the alto. Or, again, one part may appear after the other as principal part. For example, the phrase No. 327 might be played first as it is written, that is, with the upper part as principal part; then the bass or the tenor might repeat the principal melody, and the upper part take the accompaniment as it is begun in No. 328 and 329; or the parts might all be united in one phrase; thus, for instance—

330.

If we compare, now, No. 330, and particularly Nos. 328 and 329, with No. 327, we see that the secondary parts also become more varied and interesting; that each of them (as in No. 329) goes its own way, or (as the upper part in No. 329) that it can make itself conspicuous. Nevertheless, there could be no doubt of which was the chief part in the foregoing cases. But it can be easily conjectured, that a second part may be so far elaborated, that it may seem questionable whether it be not a second principal part. This brings us back to our two intentions.

In the second place, then, a phrase or a whole composition may be so constructed, not that one part shall be principal and the other only secondary, but that all the parts shall have important melodic contents, and an equal share in the whole. This is *properly a many-parted composition.* A phrase so formed, and the manner of writing it, are said to be

POLYPHONIC.

Here is a small example of this description—

331.

This phrase is so constructed, that neither part can be considered as satisfactory without the other; and neither, also, can claim a superiority.* Each of the parts strives for perfection in reference to melody; each supports and completes the other, and is reciprocally served in like manner. Let him who is not satisfied with this little example look over any good fugues—for instance, Seb. Bach's—and compare their manner as to the under or accompanying parts in any dance or march; such a comparison will show the difference at once.

Otherwise, polyphonic and homophonic are not so absolutely distinct, that in certain cases it could not become doubtful whether a part were only an interesting accompaniment, or a part (at times, even a little more important) of a polyphonic phrase. The polyphonic parts are sometimes called *real parts*,† in contradistinction to mere accompaniment. No composition, indeed, is perhaps entirely throughout either homophonically or polyphonically composed. Most compositions consist, usually, of an alternation of polyphonic and homophonic passages, or some parts are *real*, and others accompaniment.

The composition or construction of polyphonic phrases,—sometimes also the construction of many-part phrases, whether polyphonic or homophonic,—is called

COUNTERPOINT,

of which we must distinguish many kinds: namely, the single, double, triple, quadruple, in several parts and inverted.

SINGLE COUNTERPOINT

is concerned only in the invention of two or more real parts, and consequently with polyphonic phrases, as we have described them.

DOUBLE COUNTERPOINT

is the combination of two real parts in such a manner that they are capable of exchanging positions relatively to each other—the upper becoming the lower part, and the under the upper part. The transposition of the parts is called

INVERSION.

Here we see a two-part phrase—‡

332.

which we at once recognize to be polyphonic. It is, however, so arranged, that the upper part may be placed under the lower, or this latter over the upper part:—

333.

This is, therefore, a phrase constructed according to double counterpoint; and we perceive immediately the power of this form, which enables it, without any change in its arrangement, to produce by the mere inversion of the parts, a new configuration, which has its own peculiar significance.

How is this inversion effected? Either by placing the upper part lower, or the under part higher. This transposition may be made at the distances of eight, nine, ten, eleven, twelve, thirteen, and fourteen degrees. There are, therefore, seven kinds of double counterpoint: That in the

OCTAVE, NINTH, TENTH, ELEVENTH, TWELFTH, THIRTEENTH, and FOURTEENTH,

of which the first is the most easy, and also the most serviceable.§ The above phrase, No. 332, as may be observed, is in the octave.

THE THREE, FOUR, AND MANIFOLD COUNTERPOINT

is concerned, as might be conjectured, with the construction of a three, four, and manifold part phrase, whose collective parts may be inverted. Here is an example of three-part counterpoint:—

334.

---

* This is more especially the case in the following phrases, Nos. 332 and 334.

† Every part which has in general its own separate motion, is sometimes called *real*—not so, a part which moves with another in unisons or octaves.

‡ The above upper part is indeed the beginning of the *Chorale Vom Himmel hoch da komm ich her*. It was necessary, therefore, to invent only the second part thereto.

§ We may at once declare the other positions in counterpoint to be useless—at least, with the exception of the 10th and 12th—their construction being restricted with so many conditions and calculations. There is a facilitation for the counterpoint of the 10th and 12th, but here also at the cost of artistic freedom—that is, of the most essentially necessary condition for the existence of true works of art. But anyhow, the advantage from them would be most insignificant.

The three parts of the phrase (*a*) allow of six positions (five inversions), as is shown at (*b*) (*c*) (*d*) (*e*) (*f*). All the six may not perhaps be used; but the number of varieties possible is seen, and any or all may be employed or neglected at pleasure. Four-fold counterpoint would yield 24 variations, and Five-fold would admit of 120 different positions. By

INVERTED,

or doubly inverted counterpoint, the parts are not only reversed towards each other, but are also conducted, step by step, in a contrary direction. Every step, every third, fourth, &c. which goes upwards, is moved an equal step downwards and reversed.

So much on these different productive kinds of writing, in order that their nature in general may be clearly understood. Further particulars, and more especially the examination of the question, which of them have *practical value to the musician*, must be left for the Instructions for Composition. Parts for simple accompaniment may be employed also in conjunction with parts capable of inversion. In speaking, therefore, of double, triple, or manifold counterpoint, we must reckon those parts only which can be inverted in respect of each other; not those which are added, but do not possess that faculty.

We may now calculate, in some degree, in how many ways a phrase may be exhibited. We can present it in a single part or in many. In the latter case it may be either homophonic or polyphonic. Again, if it be arranged polyphonically, it may be formed in single, double, and manifold counterpoint.

All artistic forms are constructed, then, either in the homophonic or polyphonic method of writing, or of homophonic and polyphonic phrases alternating and intermingled. We will avail ourselves of this distinction, and consider, first, the pure or preferably polyphonic forms, and then proceed to the homophonic. At a later period only, when we shall have unravelled the forms from their manner of writing, the application to the various musical apparatus will follow.

THIRD SECTION.—THE POLYPHONIC FORMS.

There are three separate and principal kinds of polyphonic forms; namely, figuration, fugue, and canon; of which we must observe the most important properties.

1. FIGURATION.

Figuration we call, first, the accompaniment of any unchangeable melody; for example, a psalm tune, with one or more molodically constructed parts. The principal melody chosen for this purpose (generally a psalm tune), is then called

CANTUS FIRMUS,

or plain song. The added parts we will call

FIGURATED PARTS;

and the operation itself,

TO FIGURATE.

How is accompaniment by figurated parts distinguished from mere homophonic accompaniment? By the circumstance, that figurated parts have an independent melody of their own, whereas homophonic accompaniments have no such melody. Here—

we see the psalm tune employed already in No. 332, with homophonic accompaniment; at (*a*) in close, at (*b*) in dispersed harmonic position. No one of the accompanying parts has any peculiar contents, nor lays claim to particular interest. This is clear at once, from no one of them having a rhythm of its own. They appear there simply on account of the principal part, to support it with harmony. If even they had here and there a little lively movement, such as this, for example,—

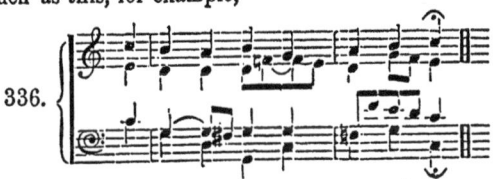

still it would be recognised that, taken in its totality, each of these parts was but secondary; a mere accompaniment to the *principal part*. If, on the other hand, we examine the part added in No. 332 to the same *Cantus firmus* (plain chant), or this phrase—

it is visible, that the lower parts do indeed accompany the *Cantus firmus*, but that each of them differs materially from it, and strives to complete itself as an individual melody.

Such figurations assume the most variegated shapes. At one time the *Cantus firmus* is in the upper part; at another in the under; and then in the middle part—now alternating from the one to the other; and presently accompanied by one, two, three, or more of them, all together. Out of many figurated parts, at one time, each will go its own way—then they will try to make a little motive together; either after each other, or simultaneously, keeping close together (as above, in the motive marked *a*)—again, they will seek each other in larger phrases, as for instance, in this small example, in the little phrase marked *b*:—

338.

At one time they begin and close with every strophe of the *Cantus firmus*: then they form introductions, intervening and after-phrases, or as they are called in respect of the psalm,—

PRELUDE, INTERLUDE, AND AFTER-PLAY.

In all these configurations the greatest variety of intention can be expressed.

In fine, figurations occur in which the *Cantus firmus* is not strictly observed; but on the contrary, is brought into another scale, and appears more or less changed by various additions, transformations, and augmentations in its original manner. Thus Seb. Bach* has changed the melody of the chorale, *Wer nur den lieben Gott lässt walten*,—

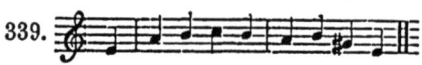

339.

into this figuration.—

340.

Another form of figuration was very much used by the old composers, especially by Handel and Seb. Bach. The bass begins with a short phrase of four, six, or eight bars alone, and then continues to repeat it, while the upper parts at every repetition perform a constantly richer and more powerfully devoloped figuration. The unity maintained by the continuous fundamental theme and the diversified song of universally polyphonic upper parts, produces a correspondingly varied effect upon the feelings. Here we give as an example, the beginning of such a figuration on a bass:—

341. Grave.

A B

* See an Introduction to the works of the great masters at *Challier's, Berlin—Selections from Seb. Bach's Compositions.*

Here, the theme at A is repeated at B, and at this moment the three upper parts begin to intermingle: at C, the theme is renewed, and the song of the upper parts seems intended to become more flowing and variegated. A masterly application of this form is to be found in Handel's *Alexander's Feast*, in the chorus *Weck' ihn auf aus seinem Schlummer*.

This *obstinately* repeating basso is called

(*Basso ostinato*), GROUND BASS,

and this name characterises the whole form. The richest, from which we have taken our example, will be found in Seb. Bach's *Passecaglie*.

In conclusion, we will mention another employment of figuration, without either *Cantus firmus* or *ground bass*. The parts pursue their course, and move as it were alone, through a succession of chords or modulations, and so close without any manifest distinction as to principal or secondary parts; when, at about the close, one part, generally the first, assumes the ascendancy, and leads off the melody. This form is chiefly used in preludes or introductions to larger compositions, and in studies or exercises for the piano or organ.

2. THE FUGUE.

The fugue is a composition in two or more parts, in which a phrase of one part, and called the

SUBJECT,

appears first in one part and then proceeds to another part, and forms the chief substance of the composition.

While a second part takes up the subject, the part which first had it, pursues its song, which being continued along with the subject, is called the

COUNTER-SUBJECT.

After the second part has taken up the subject, a third, fourth, or more parts do the same. They then take up the counter-subject, and form altogether the

GENERAL HARMONY.

But it would be too uniform if the subject were constantly produced by each part on the same degrees. Changes are therefore made in various ways. The most regular method is for the second part to reproduce in the scale of the dominant, what the first part has performed in the tonic. This is called the

ANSWER

to the subject.

In general, the answer is formed exactly, note for note, like the subject. Particular circumstances, however, admit of slight deviations in this respect, provided always that the subject be not so altered as to be difficult of recognition. Let us observe, first, a little fugue phrase, in which shortness and simplicity are more aimed at, than artistic effect:—

342.

Here we see at (*a*) the subject of the fugue which we have already often used. It begins alone in the alto. The treble takes up the answer at (*b*), in which no doubt the subject will be recognised, although in another scale (viz. that of the dominant), and a few intervals be altered. While the treble is playing the answer, the alto proceeds in its song. What it produces at (*c*) is the

COUNTER-SUBJECT.

We should now expect to hear the subject immediately in the third bar, in a new part. But we have preferred to delay the entrance of the third part with the subject. An

EPISODE

interrupts the repetitions, leads us back conveniently to C major, where the subject is to begin, and diminishes the wearying effect of constant repetition. In the fourth and fifth bars, the bass and tenor are introduced with the subject and answer; and in the last bar, the sixth, we have again an episode.

Here we might bring our fugue to a close, since we had returned to C major from the last bar above, and had ended. It may, however, proceed further (and generally does so), and after the episode the theme may be repeated in any other part, and be answered by other parts.

Each passage of the subject through the parts is considered perfect, when it has appeared in all the parts, as in No. 342; imperfect, when it has not appeared in all; and more than perfect if it have appeared in one or some of the parts more than once. We recognise, therefore, that a fugue may consist of one or more repetitions, and at the same time we perceive the advantage of the episodes, which serve to separate the single passings of the subject, and thereby produce facility of inspection and variety into the whole composition.

But how do we recognise the subject of a fugue? We see indeed, its beginning in the first part; but where is its end and its point of separation from the counter-subject? In the first place, by seeking for the satisfactory end of the subject upon the general principles of melody. Secondly, by comparing together the two beginning parts: so far as they correspond with each other, so long usually is the subject. In this comparison, however, trifling deviations, which are sometimes necessary in the course of the answer, need not be regarded.

Some peculiar changes of form in themes of fugues are worthy of remark. They are sometimes written

IN AUGMENTATION,

that is to say, in notes of double value; as for example, in crotchets instead of quavers. Sometimes

IN DIMINUTION,

that is, in notes of half their original value; for example, in semiquavers in lieu of quavers. Sometimes

IN INVERSION,

that is, in such a manner that where a note should ascend, it is made, on the contrary, to descend; and *vice versâ*. Here,—

343.

we see the subject of our preceding fugues in notes of two values, next to each other. We may either call the first part an augmentation of the second, or this latter a diminution of the first, Here,—

344.

we see at (*a*) the theme in direct motion (in its original values); at (*b*), in augmentation; and at (*c*), in diminution: therefore, in notes of three different values. Here,—

345.

we see the theme at (*a*) and (*b*) in the under part in direct motion, in the upper part inverted; at (*c*) in the under part in its proper motion and values, in the upper part inverted and at the same time diminished. It will be easily understood that these variations of form will produce a much greater effect in a real composition than here, where we give the smallest and most simple examples.

If any part should begin, while another part is proceeding in the subject, such a construction is called a

STRETTO,

Nos. 343, 344 and 345, (*b*) and (*c*), are therefore strettos of two and three parts.

Of the many kinds of fugues, we mention those most in esteem only.

Fugues are named from the number of parts of which they consist.

Besides the parts properly constituting the fugue, other parts may be introduced merely as accompaniment, and they may proceed interweaving their course among the configurations of the fugue. The accompanying parts, which act merely as a support to the fugal combinations (for example, the instrumental accompaniment to a vocal fugue, in unisons and octaves only), do not alter the character of the form. But if the accompaniment should have a course of its own, with separate or different melodies, passages, and confiurations, the fugue is then called an

ACCOMPANIED FUGUE.

An example of this description is the fugal beginning of *Quam olim Abrahæ*, in Mozart's *Requiem*—

346.

in which the wind instruments play the parts of and with the voices, while the bowed instruments perform the quartet accompaniment.

Sometimes a figurated upper part is added in a fugue to the merely accompanying parts, and this additional part is called in preference the

COUNTERPOINT

to the subject of the fugue. Sometimes a similar counterpoint to the fugue is written in the bass, which is then called a

CONTINUED BASS,

particularly if it proceed in notes of uniform value.

Among other compositions, the *Kyrie*, in Seb. Bach's Mass in G major, and the *Credo* in his High Mass, are accompanied by a continued bass. Figurated upper parts are often found in the Masses of Haydn, Hummel, and others.

3. DOUBLE AND MANIFOLD FUGUE.

Instead of one simple theme only, two, three, or more may enter into, and be elaborated together in a fugue. Here—

347.

we have the almost shortest possible beginning of a double fugue. The tenor introduces the first subject at (*a*). The bass begins the second subject at (*b*). At (*c*) the alto answers the first, and at (*d*) the treble answers the second subject. If this is to be thoroughly carried out, the bass must produce the first, the tenor must take up the second; moreover, the treble must perform the first, and the alto the second subject; so that each subject may have appeared in every part. That from (*e*) and (*f*) the two under parts form a counter-subject, is visible from page 84. It will be clearly understood also, that in

TRIPLE FUGUES,

and others of more parts, all the subjects must be carried through with each other in all the parts, as is done in double fugues with the two subjects. It is, however, seldom or never judged expedient to construct fugues upon more than three themes.

The double or triple fugues are governed, excepting in what results from the plurality of their subjects, exactly by the same rules as the single fugue. The two or more subjects must, according to custom, be carried through at least once together. They may, however, be taken through separately and singly. Often, indeed, double fugues begin with one subject only, and carry it through alone; then enters the second (so that the beginning resembles two different but combined fugues) in a separate course of passing through; after which only, both subjects proceed together, so that properly, the double fugue begins with this last procedure only. Of this construction is the *Confiteor unum baptisma*, in Seb. Bach's High Mass in B minor. Or, the first subject begins alone in one part, and when the second part answers in the same theme, the preceding part takes the second subject, as if it were a counter-subject; and so the first theme and the counter-subject (the second subject) run through all the parts. The fugue in G minor in Seb. Bach's *Wohltemperirtem Klavier*, Part 1, is an example of this construction. It is also customary in triple fugues, not to introduce the three subjects all at once, but two only at first, in order that they may be understood, and then to admit the third. The *Kyrie*, in Seb Bach's Mass in G major, is an instance of this observance. Another way is, as in the 1st Psalm of the author, to begin with one subject, and afterwards admit the two others.

A fugue with only one subject is called, in contradistinction to a double or triple fugue,

A SINGLE FUGUE.

A composition approaching to the fugal form is called

A FREE FUGUE,

in contradistinction to

A STRICT FUGUE,

in which the form and its laws are rigidly observed.

A short phrase, worked as a kind of fugue: in an

extensive composition (as a sonata, symphony, &c.), is said to be

FUGATO.

So much—it is indeed but the essentially necessary, and the most general information—on the most superabundantly rich and important form of fugue. Of the many combinations of this with other forms, two must especially be mentioned.

THE FUGUE TO A CORALE

is the accompaniment of a corale melody by a fugue, as we have formerly seen a similar melody accompanied by a simple figuration;

THE FUGAL CORALE

is a fugal construction of a whole corale, in which *one strophe after the other* is taken separately as the subject of the fugue, and is carried through.

Both forms are found abundantly in Seb. Bach's ecclesiastical music and compositions for the organ. The latter form is admirably employed in the composition *Ein 'feste Burg ist unser Gott*, and in the management of the corale, *Aus tiefer Noth schrei ich zu dir.**

4. THE CANON.

In the fugue the subject was taken up by one part after the other, but in the counter-subject and intervening phrases each part had more or less its own melody, and the subject, even, did not continue entirely unchanged. If, now, we introduce two or more parts, the one after the other, which proceed together in equal time, and imitate, note by note, the succession of each other, so that each part have precisely the same melody as the other from beginning to end, we shall produce a canon.

A canon is therefore a composition in which one part performs not merely a particular phrase, or theme of another part, but performs the melody of the other part entirely, note for note, throughout. In this performance, the first part or sole melody may be followed by one single other part, or by two, three, or more parts; wherefore a canon is said to be in

TWO, THREE, FOUR, OR MORE PARTS.

Moreover, the following parts may begin the melody on the same degree, and in the same octave. This is a

CANON IN UNISON,

or in a higher or lower octave, and would then be called a

CANON IN THE OCTAVE,

or in any other interval from the second to the seventh, when it is called a

CANON IN THE SECOND, &c.,

up to the seventh; or, again, in a canon of many parts, the parts may begin at different intervals. These latter are called

MIXED CANONS.

All these canons are considered regular, if they can be arranged, and their parts be transposed (the upper serving as the under) according to the laws of double or manifold counterpoint.

If they are not susceptible of this arrangement, they are considered to be apparent canons or mere imitations.

We give here, as passing examples, some beginnings of canons, which may be imagined to be extended to any length *ad libitum*:—

At (A) we see, if we consider the first and second parts only, a canon in unison. The third part imitates in the octave. At (B) we find the beginning of a two-part canon, a fourth below. If we transpose the parts, we produce a canon a fifth above:—

349.

At (C) we find a mixed canon, whose parts follow a fourth below, and ninth below (or under second in the lower octave). If we place the second part as the upper one (*a*), or the first as the undermost, and the third as the uppermost (*b*)—

we shall produce imitations of canon in the fifth above and ninth below, or in the fifth above and seventh above; other inversions may be sought at pleasure.

If in the construction of a canon, all the laws of this form be observed,—that is, if the first part be exactly re-echoed by the following, it is then called a

STRICT CANON.

But if the canon be not in perfect accordance with the rules, the melody of the first part not being followed throughout,† the canon is then called a

FREE CANON.

If we consider the plan of a canon, we shall perceive that, properly speaking, no close can take place of all the parts together; but that as they began, so must they cease, one after the other. But as this is essentially contrary to the nature of a work of art, which of necessity requires a marked and determined end, it is usual to choose arbitrarily any moment for the end of a canon, when all the parts

---

* See Appendix B.

† One kind of deviation from rule takes place of necessity in all canons excepting those in the unison or in the octave. They must all answer in the same scale or key, and consequently small intervals must at times become great, and great small. In No. 348, (C) for example, the first part, in the beginning, makes steps of a semitone, semitone, tone; the second, of three *tones*: the third, of twice a whole tone and then a semitone.

are in progress; or a free close is added to it, in which the form of a canon is no longer preserved. So, we might have added this close to the canon, No. 348, (C):—

351.

In this manner, however, the form of the canon would be maintained only as far as (*a*) in the second part, and that of the third only to (*b*) in the first part.

Since, as we have seen, every part in a canon has the same melody, although on different degrees, it is customary occasionally to write only one part, giving notice in how many parts it is to be repeated, and at what intervals. The point where each part is introduced is marked also over the notes. We might therefore have written the canon, No. 348, (C,) in this manner:—

352.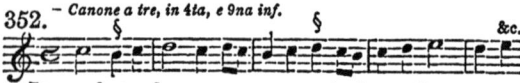

It used to be an amusement formerly among students, to write canons in this manner, *without* any indication of the number of parts, intervals, or points of introduction,—or indeed, with false directions,—under the name of

RIDDLE CANONS,

which, served to excite the ingenuity of those of their companions who had nothing better to do.

In conclusion, we must mention a particular kind of canon, called the

CIRCLE CANON.

This is a canon whose first part closes in a different scale from that in which it began; generally in its dominant; thus, for example, beginning in C, it will close in G. Now, since each part imitates exactly, the second part must close in D, the third in A, and so forth. Thus this canon would gradually pass through all the scales, if an arbitrary end were not somewhere introduced. Here is a small example of this species of canon:—

353.

The first part goes to G major; the second begins therefore in G major (in the fifth), and goes to D major. Here the third begins in the under fourth, and goes to A major. In the mean time, the first part has closed, and would begin again in the next bar in A major, in order to go to E; and so forth.

This form is most beautifully applied in the *Christe eleison* of Bach's Mass in A major.

FOURTH SECTION.—OF HOMOPHONIC AND MIXED FORMS.

The first class of the forms we are about to bring forward, is usually included in the laws of polyphonic phrases. We might, therefore, have begun by the consideration of the pure homophonic form. But on the one hand, this class will not detain us long; and on the other, it is also capable of assuming and containing polyphonic phrases. We will therefore consider it, unseparated from the mixed forms.

Here we meet with the following classes:—

1. THE SONG-FORM.

Under this form we comprehend all compositions, which consist of one principal phrase only, constructed either as an extended phrase, or as a subject (with opening and closing phrases), or as an interrupted subject, with first and second part, or with a first, second, and third part—in which latter case, the third part is generally a repetition of the first. Two or three of these constructions may be combined in a composition in the song-form; but then they have no closer connexion nor intermixture than the mere following of each other,—as twice two, or three times two parts. The second couple of parts is called the

TRIO;

and the third couple is called the second trio, and is considered merely as an appendix. Such trios are usually written in another scale for the sake of variety, or in another mode, major or minor, as the case may require. After them, however, the principal part in its original scale is repeated, and thus a superficial unity is sought to be established in the whole composition.

In the song-form, songs (properly so called), dances, marches, and many studies and introductions, are written. Of all the species which belong to this form, there is only one of sufficient importance to be especially mentioned;* that is, the

VARIATIONS,

or more correctly, the theme and variations. A variation is the change of figure of a phrase by means of melody, harmony, counterpoint, and rhythm. The phrase used as a foundation is called the

THEME.

This is generally varied in different ways several times, and then the theme and variations are considered as a whole, which is closed either by returning to the theme by a more richly ornate and extended variation, or by an appendix. At times, the separate variations hang together by slight transitions, but more frequently each marks its own termination; and the adhesion of the whole rests upon the unity of the theme, which is lying under all, and on the pervading intention of the composer, if, indeed, any such should be manifested.

In variations, the theme is diversified, not only by particular successions of *tones*, but also by the assumption of especial varieties of form, such as those of marches, dances, fugues, rondos, and others. It is a very profitable exercise for every one to go through many books of variations, and to endeavour to see and feel as clearly as possible, how and by what means each variation is constructed.

* Together with the modern dances, the old must be included, of which many are still used in our ballet music (for example, that of Glück), and those found in the works of Handel and Bach; the Gavot, Passacaglio, Corante, Saraband, Bourrée, Jig, Musette, Passepied, and also the Fandango, employed by Mozart in *Figaro*.

2. THE RONDO-FORM.

The distinctive characteristics of this form are a principal phrase, which is extended or carried out in combination with other phrases, and then is heard again alone. The principal phrase may either have a single subject, or *two* parts; and in the latter case it is customary to repeat the first part (either altogether or partially) after the second part. The phrase may, indeed, also have three parts. Rondos are distinguishable into five forms.

The first is constructed in such a manner, that, after the principal phrase, a longer passage or a long succession of short phrases follows, which passes through many scales, but returns finally to the principal scale, where the principal phrase or an appendix (perhaps taken from it or from the passages) immediately closes. It sometimes happens that this form greatly resembles an extensive song-form in three parts—mostly, however, the principal phrase of a rondo is distinguished by too important and determined a close, to be mistaken for the first part of a song.

The second rondo-form has, besides the principal phrase, a *second theme*, a *secondary phrase*, likewise unseparated; or two or three parts which are in the scale either of the dominant or of the subdominant; or in the *relative key;* or in the principal scale in minor, if the principal phrase be in the major; or in the major, if the principal phrase be in the minor. But the difference from the song-form with a trio consists in this, that the second theme does not appear detached, by itself, but is mostly combined with the first. A passage or a chain of phrases leads* from the first to the second, and from this again a passage or a chain of phrases leads back to the first, where, with this, or with an appendix out of the first or second phrase, or out of the passages, the rondo comes to a close.

The *third rondo-form* has, besides the principal phrase, two secondary phrases—the one, in the mode of the principal phrase, and then generally in the sub-dominant; the other, usually in the relative scale. A passage or a chain of phrases leads commonly to the first secondary phrase; from this a return is effected to the principal phrase, which is then repeated. A passage is then made to the second secondary phrase, and from this again back to the principal phrase, with which, or with an appendix, a close is made.

The fourth rondo-form joins the principal and first secondary phrases together in a firmly conbined mass, as belonging to each other. After the first secondary phrase, it returns to the principal phrase (like the preceding forms), and thence proceeds to the second secondary phrase. After this, however, it does not merely repeat the principal phrase alone, but with it and at the same time, the first secondary phrase. This latter, which at first appeared in the scale of the dominant (or in minor phrases, in the *relative key*) comes forth now with the principal phrase in the principal scale. The first secondary phrase enjoys less consideration in this form (since it appears merely as a closing addition to the principal phrase), but the second subsidiary phrase is constructed with all the more expression and emphatic completeness, inasmuch as it must sustain its importance against the combined two first phrases.

The *fifth rondo-form* rejects the middle return of the principal phrase, and closes the mass of the principal and first secondary phrases with a more extended form of conclusion and of greater decision, so that three well rounded and distinct masses are exhibited—viz., the principal phrase with the first secondary phrase; the closing phrase and the second secondary phrase; the principal phrase with the first secondary phrase and the closing phrase.

So much for the comprehension of the rondo-form. It will not be difficult of recognition with a little observation, although here and there deviations may occur, particularly with regard to change of scales, repetitions &c., upon which we cannot here further dilate.†

3. THE SONATA-FORM.

It is well known that certain instrumental compositions for one or for two or three instruments are called sonatas. On these we shall make some observations in the next section. Not these compositions, but only one determined form shall be explained under the above name, other than which we know not what to adopt.

The sonata-form is distinguished from the higher and particularly from the fifth rondo-form, essentially by its rejection of the second subsidiary phrase, and consequently by its retention of only the first mass of the principal phrase, first subsidiary phrase, and closing phrase, together with the repetition thereof in the principal scale as its last mass. In this limitation, the composition as a

SONATINA-FORM

becomes distinguished from the proper sonata-form. Here, according to custom, the single parts of the composition are of slight construction; otherwise, sonatina-forms as well as sonata-forms employ figurated phrases and fugal successions, instead of the song-formed phrases, or the subjects (or the simple phrases) which serve in the rondo-form, as principal and subsidiary phrases. They receive, also, two or even more different phrases or subjects as so many themes which are held together merely by the scale in common (sometimes not even by that, but solely by a related scale), and can be considered collectively merely as the principal and subsidiary phrases; whence it would be more appropriate to call them a

PRINCIPAL AND SUBSIDIARY PART.

The sonata-form agrees in this with the sonatina-form; it constructs its two masses essentially in the same manner; but it is distinguished by having a third mass between each, and so forms three parts. It moreover resembles the fifth rondo-form, in having the middle part only of different contents.

The first part begins immediately with the principal phrase, or with an appropriate introduction to, or pre-representation thereof; then follows, immediately, the subsidiary phrase in the scale of the dominant, if the principal be in major; or in the

---

* The leading from the principal to the first secondary phrase is mostly unnecessary, and the leading back again is rare.
More complete information upon this matter, and upon the forms of sonatas, with reference to numerous works of the composers, will be found in the third part of the Instructions for Composition.

† See Appendix C.

relative key, if the principal be in minor; or the principal, if in major, modulates by a transition passage into the scale of the dominant; or if in minor, into the relative scale; and in one scale or the other leads to the subsidiary phrase. With this latter, the first part immediately closes; or a passage follows with a special closing phrase; or perhaps, again, instead of the latter, or after it, a repetition will be seen out of the principal phrase. Thus the first part has shown both the phrases. The first in the principal key, the second in the nearest related key. The close is effected in the last; and here it depends entirely on the intention and determination of the composer, whether the whole first part shall be repeated or not.

The *second part* is joined immediately to the first, or leads on again. It begins with a leading passage or an indication of the principal phrase, or with a quite new and short *secondary* phrase. From this it leads to the subsidiary or to the principal phrase; then by a second passage to the phrase which has not yet appeared, or at once to the dominant of the principal *key*. The phrases themselves appear in this part in new and generally nearly related scales; the passages go through these and still more distantly related keys; and the whole second part becomes replete with the most brilliant modulation. Without repetition, and usually without any determined close, it passes over into the *third part*. This latter gives again the principal phrase in the principal *key*; leads, this time, the subsidiary phrase in like manner into the principal key, either immediately or by means of a passage; and, with this, with the passage and closing phrase belonging to it (sometimes also with a special appendix out of the principal phrase, perhaps), brings the conclusion of the whole in the principal key. The end of the first part is usually marked by the sign of repetition or closing cross bars. The two following parts are generally written without any such sign of separation. They are generally considered as a whole; and, in common parlance, are called briefly the *second part*. Sometimes, also, this second part (that is the second and third together) is repeated, and then an appendix as a final close is always added.

Many deviations, especially in the choice and arrangement of the scales, may be left to the discretion of individuals, or be referred to the study of composition for those who wish to penetrate further into this matter.*

These are the most important forms of art: all others that we may meet with in vocal and instrumental music, are either a selection from these or a combination of them.†

FIFTH SECTION.—THE PECULIAR FORMS OF INSTRUMENTAL MUSIC.

Instrumental compositions are distinguished in the first place by the instruments for which they are destined. There are compositions for single instruments—for example, for the organ, pianoforte, violin, &c.; or for two or more instruments, as duetts, terzetts, quartetts, quintetts sestetts, septetts, &c.; or, again, for masses of instruments, such as an orchestra, as we have already said cursorily at page 45.

All compositions for these single or combined instruments assume determined forms of art, of which we shall give a short elucidation, if not already described in this book

1. THE SONATA.‡

The Sonata is a composition for a solo instrument (or very properly with accompaniment of one or two others), which, according to custom, consists of three or four separate compositions, which are called

MOVEMENTS.

The first movement, which is sometimes preceded by an introduction, has generally the sonata-form, and fixes the principal scale of the whole work. Generally its motion is quick (Allegro, &c.)

After the first, a slower and shorter movement (Adagio, Andante, or perhaps Allegretto, &c.) follows; mostly in a small rondo-form, or abbreviated sonata-form, or *cantabile* with some variations. This movement is in another scale, perhaps of the dominant, subdominant, or relative key. The conclusion makes a third movement, sometimes, expressly called a *finale*, in which the sonata-form appears again, or great rondo-form mixed with fugue and variations. The motion is here more lively (Allegro, Presto, &c.). It is in the principal key, which, if minor, is occasionally changed to major.

After or before the second movement, an intervening movement occurs in extensive compositions called a

MINUET OR SCHERZO,

mostly in the song-form, and in four or six parts (that is, with the trio and repetition of the principal movement), or also in the rondo and other forms. At times, also, there are more parts—for example, in the well known Septett of Beethoven, Op. 20 —Minuet and Scherzo, Andante and variations. Sometimes the sonata has only two movements, as in Beethoven's Op. 111; or only Adagio, Minuet, and Finale, and other smaller deviations.

This form is predominant in all duos, trios, quartetts &c., and in them the construction is generally richer and more polyphonic (or at least ought to be), because the powers of several instruments can be employed and must be kept in action. A smaller, more simply constructed sonata of less complicated ideas and development, consisting only of two or at the utmost of three movements, is called a

SONATINA;

while, on the other hand, the name of

GRAND SONATA

is applied to very massive and extended compositions of this description, consisting generally of four movements. To this class belongs also the

NOTTURNO,

a composition for different instruments in the sonata-form, and characterized by the soft repose in accordance with the calmness of evening.

---

* See Appendix D.
† A particular mixture of the rondo and sonata-forms is exhibited in the Appendix D.

‡ We omit the old form of "*suite*," still living amongst us in Bach's and Handel's works, as also the modern *Divertimento*, which are nothing but a combination of phrases at the free discretion of the composer. We pass by also the *Pot-pourri*, in which all kinds of phrases are mixed together in any kind of arrangement.

2. THE OVERTURE,*

called by the Italians *Sinfonia,* is an orchestral composition in one movement, always prepared by an introduction, or interrupted by an intervening movement, mostly in sonatina, sonata, but sometimes also in fugue-form; rarely, however, in rondo-form, and still more rarely with variations. The overture is properly employed for the opening or beginning of any great artistic work—for example, a play, an opera, an oratorio, or a concert; hence its name.

3. THE SYMPHONY,

is an orchestral composition in the sonata-form, but, in accordance with the great powers of an orchestra, it is usually constructed upon large, massive, and well-defined proportions. It mostly consists of an introduction, allegro, andante, scherzo, and finale; all of which movements are more fully developed and more powerfully marked than is thought necessary in a sonata.

On this ground, the student may be advised to seek for sonata-forms first in symphonies (and overtures); and, in this pursuit, those unacquainted with scores will derive much assistance from the numerous "arrangements" for the pianoforte. Here they will find the fundamental forms more simple and distinguishable; while, in the sonata itself, phrases and themes are often crowded in a fine and as it were miniature construction, whereby the identification of the parts is rendered difficult to the unaccustomed eye. This is the case, also, in J. Haydn's symphonies.

4. THE CONCERTO.

Under this name, in more recent times, has been understood a composition in several parts, in which

THE PRINCIPAL INSTRUMENT

(or the principal part) or also several

CONCERTING INSTRUMENTS

undertake the chief parts, and thereby exhibit the superior powers or artistic skill of the performer. For this end, the orchestra performs a subordinate accompaniment, which occasionally, however, is raised to greater importance. Here, also, the sonata-form is the groundwork, but is limited to three movements; the scherzo is generally omitted. How far the concerto may deviate from the sonata-form, must be learned from the Instructions for Composition. A small concerto limited to two movements is called a *concertino.*

5. THE FANTASIA.

Such is the name of a combination of the most diversified forms, constituting a determined whole, for a *solo* instrument with accompaniment, or even with an orchestra.† Number, selection, arrangement of the forms, modulations, &c., are most freely left to the apparently objectless flights of the imagination of the composer, in "a fine frenzy rolling." It begins perhaps with a *cantabile* introduction; passes into an adagio or allegro; thence into a rondo-form, fugue, variation, &c.; closes with an extensive phrase, or with a repetition of the first; chooses its scales from the impression of the moment, and scarcely considers itself bound to close in the principal *tone* Everything, in a word, is surrendered to the peculiar feelings and ideas of the composer, and, therefore, a distinctive identifying rule for this kind of composition is impossible.

6. CAPRICCJ, TOCCATE, AND STUDJ

must be named last. They are compositions, sometimes in sonata or rondo-form, and sometimes, again, they assume the unbridled licence of the fantasia. They endeavour at times to illustrate and shadow forth a peculiar thought or passion; and, at others, their object is merely the attainment of rapid performance, or the command on the instrument of certain configurations of notation or modes of playing.

SIXTH SECTION.—THE PECULIAR FORMS OF VOCAL MUSIC.

Vocal music in the first place is exhibited in two ways alone; as,

PURE VOCAL MUSIC,

or as

ACCOMPANIED

by one or few instruments, or by an orchestra. It is, moreover, divided into

SOLO SINGING,

in which only one voice or single voices sing; and

CHORAL SINGING,

in which several parts are performed by several combined voices.

Passing over what we have already learned, we will proceed to that which requires elucidation.

1. OF RECITATIVE.

Recitative is a song of a single voice, or sometimes of several voices, which does not take the invariable form of a melody, nor determined artistic form; neither does it conform to the strict value of notation, nor to fixed musical rhythm—on the contrary, it strives in its successions of sounds and in its rhythm to assimilate itself as much as possible to the declamatory accents of speech. Hence, recitative has no determined measure or bars, although it is commonly written in $\frac{4}{4}$ bars for the assistance of the eye.

In its progress, or at its close, recitative may assume a more determined form, such as a short song-shaped phrase, which is then called

ARIOSO,

and consists of sustained melody in fixed measure.

If it be accompanied by simple chords, it is called *recitativo secco* or *parlante*; but if the accompaniment have its own melody, it is called *obligato*, or also *accompagnato stromentato*. If it should move for any time in regular measure, it is called *Rec.? a tempo.*

2. THE AIR, OR SONG *(Aria).*

The aria is an accompanied song of a solo voice, in which a determined state of the mind, a progression of the feelings, and the inward emotion of the singer are exhibited. Its form is either that of the small rondo or the sonata-form, but with abbreviation or omission of the second part.

Great arias are constructed by the combination of more forms. They begin, for example, with a song-like introduction, pass over into the rondo-form, and then, instead of repeating the chief phrase, they

---

* Overtures to fill up the space between the acts or for the introduction of other acts, are called interludes. Beethoven's overture and interlude to Goethe's *Egmont,* are especially celebrated, and with justice.

† Thus Beethoven has written a Fantasia for the pianoforte, accompanied by an orchestra, solo singing, and chorus.

proceed in a new phrase, perhaps in sonata-form. If, in fine, recitative and aria be combined, and thus form a larger whole, this latter is called a

SCENA OR SCENE.

Among these forms, we shall find the attendant ballad, duett, terzetto, &c., and the cantata for one voice. This last is nothing but an extensive scena, or a succession of contending or varying emotions.

On the other hand, the

ARIETTA OR CAVATINA

is a song or aria consisting of one phrase only; it is concerned with gentler, more calm, and less important sensations, and is also less developed.

3. THE CHORUS

takes the most diversified configurations: song-form, sonata or rondo-form (both closely held together), fugue-form, or a combination of several forms. It is mixed with solo phrases for one voice or for several single voices: it proceeds with them, at the same time, into phrases of many parts (chorus with song, solo), or forms the counter-phrase and background for a solo song (aria and chorus, &c.), all of which according to its form, requires no further elucidation. Only one form remains now to be explained:—

THE MOTETT,

of which there are two kinds. In the first form it is an ecclesiastical cantata, consisting of several *separate* movements, &c., of different forms, such as solo, trio, corale, fugue, &c. In the second it is a choral composition (mostly of devotional contents), in which, after a cantabile or figurated introduction (or without it), a fugal theme is carried through once; then a second, and then a third time; and finally with this, or with the introductory movement, or with a separate closing phrase, it ends. This form is distinguished from the fugue of two or more subjects, not so much by the freely-written phrases added to the beginning and end (for these might occur in the fugue and be omitted in the motett), as by the circumstance, that the different subjects are carried through by themselves, without ever passing through simultaneously or in conjunction with each other.

The fugal corale, mentioned at page 90, is a particular species of motett.

By a combination of recitatives, airs, choruses, &c., is formed the

4. CANTATA,

an extensive composition, in which different feelings and circumstances of lyrical or dramatic interest (but not intended for theatrical performance) are represented in a combined form.

We must now especially notice the

FINALE,

a great vocal composition, used for the close of an act of an opera, which is constructed of all kinds of vocal and instrumental movements, solo and choral parts, at the absolute control of the composer. For the totality of such a combination no determined rules can be given; but the laws relating individually to the various forms employed, may be observed with greater or less exactness, and the capabilities of each species may be drawn out with more or less fullness and effect.

For the sake of completeness, we must not omit to mention, in concluding, the

SOLFEGGI,*

which are merely exercises for the voice, and are therefore composed without any text.

SEVENTH SECTION.—MUSIC IN COMBINATION WITH OTHER OBJECTS.

He who has formed a just appreciation of our statements relative to forms of art, will be able to perceive, without difficulty, in what manner music is connected with other objects, and what peculiar configurations it assumes in such combination.

We are here to mention briefly only the most important of these associations.

In the *first place*, it is united with the divine service. Herein, as is well known, it is employed as song in the corale (song-form), in the administration of the liturgy (mostly a kind of recitative); and instrumentally in the introduction of the service, &c.

The more considerable forms are—

THE HYMN,

consisting usually of one choral phrase only, though sometimes mixed with solo phrases. Then we have

THE SPIRITUAL CANTATA,

called peculiarly ecclesiastical music, and consisting of several solo and choral movements. In the Catholic service there is

THE MASS,

and—although in our times no longer forming a part of the divine service, still mostly dedicated to the expression of religious feelings and sentiments—

THE ORATORIO,

a spiritual drama for musical performance only, not for representation by person and action, as a theatrical drama. In all these creations, all kinds and species of solo and choral phrases are combined according to the requirements of the text, and to the intention and imagination of the composer.

In the *second place*, music is combined in a much greater variety of ways in the drama. Here we find

1. THE BALLET,

in which pantomime and dancing are united. The music, chiefly instrumental, must be suitable to all kinds of action, and employs, for that object, sometimes real dance forms, and at others various arbitrary successions of forms, both for the imaginative matter and for the finale. Whole ranges of such forms occupy great scenes or entire acts together, held in connexion merely by modulation, ingenious repetition of previous phrases, and the internal sense of the action and music.

2. THE MELODRAMA.

shows us instrumental music as an accompaniment to, or as phrases intervening with, discourse, whereby the latter becomes deeper in its meaning, and more powerful in its impressiveness: the action is illustrated and rendered intelligible in its preconcerted situations, and the melodramatic intentions, in general, are accomplished. Here, the music has

---

* They are so named from the syllables which were formerly given to the *tones* (page 7, in note), and with which, up to the present moment, exercises for singing have been written. The pronunciation and the voice are thus both cultivated at once.

only to give gentle, passing indications, and is heard, occasionally only, with marked expression. It is to be considered, throughout, as secondary and subordinate to the speech and action.

Melodramatic music, therefore, is employed during the action, principally in easily interspersed passages, harmonic successions, occasionally returning phrases (or otherwise), &c., and introduces now and then only a march or a dance, when the action of the drama requires it.

With the melodrama,

3. THE PLAY WITH MUSIC

is connected. Here we find much employment for music in the poetical objects of the drama. In these compositions, the poet requires music conformable to the circumstances of his plot—for example, marches, convivial music, songs (pastoral or warlike), solemn church music, and so forth, just as the like might occur in real life.

THE BALLAD OPERA,

and the French *Vaudeville*, are, to a certain extent, imitations of this occasional form, but more laboured and with a more strongly marked intention. These are constructed with slight dramatic involution; with songs, replies, and so forth, out of popular life; or composed on, or abundantly interwoven with, popular airs. In this production, also, the songs, for the most part at least, should be introduced exactly as they may be imagined to be sung and heard in daily life.

From this point music is elevated into real artistic value in the drama.

4. THE OPERA

is a drama in which, in lieu of ordinary speech, an elevated utterance, the language of music and song, is introduced, with the same artistic rights and truth as in the higher drama poetry supersedes the prose of common life.

An opera is either composed throughout or consists of spoken dialogue, interspersed with vocal compositions for one or several voices. In either case, we distinguish

THE GREAT OPERA,

which is tragic, and almost constantly composed throughout from

THE ROMANTIC OPERA,

which, like the romantic plays in Germany and England, is serious or gay, elevated or common, in alternating moments or situations, and is generally interwoven with dialogue.

THE OPERETTA

is distinguished by the lightness and gaiety of its subject and treatment. We have, further,

THE COMIC OPERA

(opera buffa), and many intermediate or mixed species. Into all of the foregoing, all forms of singing music—recitative and aria, part-music and chorus—and various kinds of instrumental music, are freely admitted, at the entire discretion of the poet and the composer.

A derivative from the opera, is the

PLAY WITH CHORUS,

in which choruses are sung between the dialogue of the actors in ordinary discourse,—a combination which appears out of character inasmuch as the chief personages remain in the lower sphere of common speech, while secondary performers (the chorus) are raised to the higher attribute of song.

The more intimate explanation of all these forms must be reserved for another place (the Instructions for Composition, the Philosophy of Art, and the Science of Music). Here we can merely point out in a general sketch, the contents and objects of each of these constructions.

And so, in conclusion, we shall briefly state, that the doctrine of art generally separates all forms of music into the following classes:—

It divides (I.) *The forms of vocal music* into—
1. ECCLESIASTICAL MUSIC.
2. DRAMATIC MUSIC.
3. CHAMBER MUSIC.
4. POPULAR MUSIC, or NATURAL SONG.

Under ecclesiastical music, the

ORATORIO

is usually comprised, although it is no longer any part of the divine service, and is generally performed in concert rooms, not in churches. The corale, also, must be considered as ecclesiastical music, although it is become really popular song.

Chamber music embraces all music not included in the other classes; more particularly that which is more suitable for performance in a small circle, or in domestic and social assemblies.

(II.) Instrumental music is divided into—
1. CONCERT MUSIC.
2. CHAMBER MUSIC.
3. MILITARY MUSIC.

To the first, belong symphonies, overtures, and concertos; to the second, solos, duos, quartett compositions, and similar productions, for domestic and small assemblies.

In conclusion, according to the different objects to which the art is applied,

THREE DIFFERENT STYLES

are distinguished—as church, opera, and chamber styles; and also

FREE AND STRICT STYLES,

which latter is peculiarly dedicated to church music, in which it is expected that all the rules of art be followed in the most rigid manner, and all the forms be carried out with unwearying diligence to the fullest completeness. It is desirable, moreover, in this style, that polyphonic forms, and more especially fugal, should be employed rather than homophonic forms.

In an earnest and deep investigation into the nature and objects of art, the foregoing appears partly one-sided and false, partly an idle and profitless fiction of the imagination.

As to the distinction between *free* and *strict styles*, it is manifest that a rule of art must have a rational ground or not; and that, in the affirmative case, the rule ought to be observed throughout; or, in the negative, not at all. If, for example, it be true, that following fifths and octaves (page 71) have sometimes,—or, according to the over-hasty belief of the old masters,—have always a repugnant effect; that certain chords (page 71) generally or always advance in a determined progression; moreover, that retardations or suspensions must often or always be prepared and resolved, if they were not to have a repulsive effect; then, according to right reason, these principles should be of universal application, or it must be maintained that in non-ecclesiastical compositions, it is of no consequence to the composer or to the hearer, whether the effect be repulsive or not; or again, it would be necessary to imagine that something repugnant in itself, in one place, would not be so in another;—that for example, this succession of fifths and octaves, or progression of chords—

354.

is indeed repulsive in itself, and would sound ill in church music, but would sound differently, and be proper in an opera, or in chamber music.

This distinction is contrary to the old theory, for that holds as the foundation of its rules, the principle, the superficial principle, that that is good which sounds well, and *vice versâ*. But he who has penetrated deeper into art, and become familiar with it, knows from his own experience, and from the innumerable testimonies of all artists and enlightened men, that the object of art is not to tickle the senses of the multitude with pleasant sounds or pretty combinations, but that its function is to convey the spiritual emotions, the inward feelings of the musician-poet, to the minds of his audience. From this high position it is no longer the question, whether anything (a movement of chords for instance) sounds pleasantly or otherwise; but what mental emotion is manifested by it, and is thereby created in the hearer. This brings us to the second point of the preceding question.

If the distinction between church, opera, and chamber styles should not be entirely vain and frivolous, with no more meaning than that such things are, as church, opera, and chamber music, it must be maintained that in the one species of music, representations and sensations occur, which have no existence in the other; and that accordingly also, a suite of musical expressions and forms are compatible with the one species and not with the other.

This is in part true. We can scarcely imagine the admission of dances into the divine service, or of fugues into a ball room. But is so trivial an observation worth utterance; or further, of being considered the foundation of the high-flown distinction of artistic styles? Or can the distinction be carried out? Cannot pious and even religious feelings occur in the opera, and in instrumental music? Cannot even ecclesiastical representations take place; have they not, hundreds of times? Or, do not religious impressions produce joy and suffering? Are they not elevated to zeal, and still more passionate emotion? Is this not seen both in the Old and New Testament, nay, prefigured in the discourse of Our Lord himself? and has it not been employed by Bach and Handel, and all genuine artists? And with regard to technicalities, have not fugues, &c.

been used times out of number in secular music; homophonic phrases in spiritual; and even march and dance forms in the oratorios of Handel, and those more recent of F. Schneider; and with apparent indispensable necessity? And, in fine, have either the elder or the modern masters, Seb. Bach and Handel, Haydn, Mozart, and Beethoven, used any other principles of harmony, of arrangement of parts, &c., in their ecclesiastical compositions, than those which they have employed in their secular productions? They have everywhere let their large hearts speak faithfully from the full inspiration of their subject, without prudery or reservation. There, no idle differences of styles were required, or rather to the true artist they are impossible.

It is only in quite another sense that the idea of

STYLE

has a true meaning. Every real artist has a peculiar manner of viewing the universe and its combined attributes, and so forms his own method of expressing and representing its impressions on himself, which method may be observed in all his works, and may be called the type of his artistic creations; or, in short, his style. Thus it is, that artists of a school, or of a country, or of a particular period, agree more or less in their manner of representation; and in this sense we may talk of the style of *Palestrina*, of Saxony, of the Italian Opera writers, &c.

But all these conceptions can be fully investigated only in the philosophy of art.

SIXTH DIVISION.

ON ARTISTIC PERFORMANCE.

FIRST SECTION.—GENERAL IDEAS OF PERFORMANCE.

What we have hitherto considered, is that general information or knowledge which is necessary for every person who is engaged or interested any way in music.

From this point, two paths of practical application branch out, besides the scientific study and art of teaching music. One path is that of the *composer* which leads to the invention and production of musical works of art; the other is that of the performer—artist or amateur, whose function is the instrumental performance of music.

The performance of music seems to require two capabilities. *First*, the perfect understanding of the notation, and, in vocal music, of the text; and *secondly*, the technical and mechanical skill to execute what is written. Both of these are indispensable. The preceding divisions of this book are an introduction to the first requisite; the second must be obtained by professional instruction and diligent practice.

But we soon become aware of a *third* qualification, which is also essentially necessary. It has long been an honoured saying, that *the letter killeth, but the spirit giveth life*; and for this reason, that it is impossible to confine the spirit in the letter. This is the fact, in the greatest force of the words, in our musical notation; and would perhaps be equally the case in any other system that might be invented;

for it does not seem to proceed merely from the imperfection of the notation, but from the nature of things.

We have signs for all the *tones* of our system; that is, for all the gradations of sound which we consider as essential, and which we consequently must be capable of producing. But we know that a whole tone is divisible into nine perceptible and distinguishable gradations, the nine commas; and that countless gradations are perceptible, although not generally and determinately distinguishable. It is true that we make no express use of these gradations; but an approximative advantage to be derived from them is quite imaginable, as we shall comprehend further on, and under certain circumstances, is allowable and serviceable. We shall be taught by experience that it may be expedient to raise or depress a given *tone* in a small degree, from its pitch, according to our temperament. We shall have to observe, moreover, that in the closest *legato* passage from one tone to another, intervening sounds* are perceptible, for which sounds we have neither notes nor names.

We must also have observed, in the articles on rhythm or measure (page 26), that the length or shortness of each single *tone* is not absolute, but only relative, in respect of other *tones*; and that, also, the usual indications of quickness or slowness of motion, by the words *allegro*, &c.,† are quite indefinite and uncertain. The metronome gives us, it is true, the means of measuring and marking absolute time. Everyone, however, can easily convince himself of the impossibility of using this measure in works on a large scale, or of observing it in any compositions with uniform exactness. For all the finer gradations of *ritardando, accelerando*, &c., of course any measure is not to be thought of.

In like manner, we have no determined measure for force. We know that *piano* is weaker than *forte*, but neither how strong the latter, nor how much weaker the former. In this matter, also, we can give only general ideas, unless the page is to be so overcrowded with signs and letters, that no eye can unravel the entanglement.

In No. 128, we have an instance of such an excess of directions. In fine, we are taught by particular instructions for performance, that the same indications to the performer (*f, p*, and so forth) under different circumstances and in different places, require different expression.

Thus, no written language has sufficient letters to express all the shades of sound; all the intervening gradations from *a* to *o*, or from *b* to *p*. In short, everywhere, whether in notes or in letters, we find writing incapable of expressing the finer distinctions of our organs of sense, or of the understanding.

But it is just in these finest, constantly varying and interchanging gradations, that the gentle and delicate, but mighty wave of inmost feeling resides, immeasurable and unutterable; and he who cannot seize and exhibit it in his musical performance, and make his listeners participate in the emotion, must not hope to render the full scope and meaning of a work of art, intelligible, either to himself or to his audience.

In the previous portion of this work we have spoken of the elements only of a work of art, not of their meaning and object as a whole. A work of art, as we all know, contains, or ought to contain, more or less abundantly, matter for our senses, for our feelings, and for our judgment. These contents, however, are manifested to us only by writing and signs, but feebly capable, though the best imaginable, of the full accomplishment of their functions; and yet from these only must we grasp the dimly shadowed spirit, and convey it to our hearers.

What writing has done in this respect, is the following: in the *first* place, it has endeavoured to point out by artistic expressions (taken from the Italian) the intention of the whole or of particular parts of the composition. Here we give the most usual:—

Con abbandono—despondingly, with submission.
Accarezzevole—caressingly, coaxingly.
Adirato—angrily.
Affabile—in a friendly manner, familiarly.
Affettuoso—affectionately.
Con afflizione—afflictedly, with grief.
Con agilità—rapidly.
Agitato—with agitation or emotion.
Con allegrezza—cheerfully.
Amabile, Con amabilità—lovingly.
Amarevole, Con amarezza—bitterly.
Amoroso, Amorevole—tenderly, lovingly.
Angosciamente—with anguish.
Animato, Con anima, Animoso—with animation, boldly.
Appassionato—passionately, with tenderness.
Appenato—with concern or grief.
Ardito—boldly, spiritedly.
Audace—audaciously, boldly.
Brillante—shewily, with splendour or display
Brioso, Con brio—with animation or courage.
Bruscamente—bluntly, snappishly, rudely.
Calando—decreasing, abating.
Calmato, Con calma—calmly.
Cantabile—song-like, tenderly.
Capriccioso—capricious.
Commodo, Commodamente—comfortably, with ease.
Compiacevole—kindly, pleasingly.
Delicatamente, Con delicatezza—delicately, tenderly, gently.
Determinato—firmly, with resolution.
Divoto, Divotamente—devoutly, religiously.
Dolce, Con dolcezza—softly, gently.
Dolente, Doloroso, Con duolo—with grief or pain.
Elegante—with elegance.
Con elevazione—with dignity.
Energico—with energy, forcefully.
Eroico—with heroism.
Espressivo, Con espressione, c. espr.—with particular expression or feeling.
Fastoso—magnificently, pompously, vaingloriously, haughtily.
Feroce—ferociously.
Fiero, Con fierezza—haughtily.
Flebile—dolefully, mournfully.
Fresco, Frescamente—with liveliness, gaily.
Funebre—funereal, dismal.
Fuocoso, Con fuoco—ardently, with fire.
Furioso, Con rabbia—furiously, raging,

---

* Every one must have heard these, unpleasantly enough, in the tuning of a piano, when a sounding string is drawn up or let down.

† To this must be added, that these indications, at different periods, and by different composers, vary considerably in their force or meaning, and therefore require a different interpretation.

Gaio—with gaiety.
Generoso—magnanimously, with dignity.
Giocoso—playfully, merrily.
Grandioso—ostentatious, proud.
Grave—serious.
Grazioso, Con grazia—with benignity and loveliness or kindness.
Impetuoso—impetuous, hasty, violent.
Innocente—simply, innocently.
Irresoluto—irresolute, undetermined, hesitatingly.
Lagrimoso—tearful, deplorable.
Lamentoso, Lamentabile—lamenting.
Languente, Languido—fainting, languishing.
Leggiero, Con leggierezza—lightly, softly.
Lugubre—mournfully, dismally.
Lusingando—flatteringly, soothingly, coaxingly.
Maëstoso—majestically, pompously.
Malinconico—sorrowfully, heavily.
Mancando—faintingly, with diminishing power.
Marcato—well defined and made emphatic.
Alla Marcia—as a march, with measure strongly marked.
Martellato—struck with violence, hammered.
Marziale—martial.
Mesto—doleful, grievous, sad.
Minacciando—threatening.
Morendo, Smorzando—dying, decreasing.
Mormorando—murmuring.
Con moto—quickly, with animation.
Nobile, Con nobilità—nobly, with dignity.
Con osservanza—with great exactness.
Parlando—speaking.
Patetico—pathetically.
Pesante—impressively.
Piacevole, Placido—pleasantly, composedly.
Pomposo—pompously.
Rapido—rapidly.
Religioso—devoutly.
Risoluto—courageously, boldly.
Risvegliato—awakened, with increased energy.
Scherzando—playfully, jocosely.
Sciolto—freely, without restraint.
Semplice—simply, inartificially.
Con sentimento, Con molto sentimento—with feeling, with deep feeling.
Smanioso, Con smania—distractedly, infuriated with passion.
Smorzando—waning, falling off in force.
Soave—gently, sweetly.
Spiritoso, Con spirito—animated, with spirit, briskly.
Strascinato—dragging, decreasing in velocity.
Strepitoso—noisy, clamorous.
Tenero, Con tenerezza—tenderly.
Tempestoso—tempestuous, boisterous.
Tranquillo, Tranquillamente—quiet, tranquil.
Veloce—rapid.
Vigoroso—with energy, fire.
Vivace, Con vivacità—with gaiety, briskness.

In the *second* place, individual composers have endeavoured to ascribe and fix a character to their different works by a name. To this class belong the well-known titles of

PASTORALE,—a pastoral composition,
SONATE MELANCOLIQUE—a melancholy composition,
SONATE PATHETIQUE—a pathetic composition.

Moreover, there are the titles of *Eclogues, Elegies, Funereal* and *Triumphant Marches*, and many others which indicate the particular intention and significance of the composition.

Thirdly, composers have sometimes endeavoured to represent determined imaginings, whose course is depicted by the character of the music. Thus have been produced Haydn's immortal overture (called "Chaos") to the *Creation;* Beethoven's admirable sonata, *Les adieux, l'absence,* and *le retour;* and many other compositions.

But here, also, it is easy to perceive, that with all these artistic directions and indications, merely a most general significance is imparted; while the different forms and gradations of feeling—the whole range of ideas, the circumstances of the soul and of the outward world,—cannot absolutely be given in words, are not susceptible of adequate expression by signs and epithets.

Fourthly and lastly, an appropriate system must be devised, by means of which the higher and more important passages in a composition may be distinguished from those of less consequence. This is the choice among differently named, but equally significant kinds of bars.

Essentially, every bar of two parts, of three parts, or of four parts, &c., is equal to every other bar of two, three, or four parts, &c. The chief and secondary parts, the great and smaller accents, remain the same. Here, for example, in a four part bar,—

the parts may be minims, crotchets, or quavers; and in like manner, the division into members is the same, whether the members be crotchets, quavers, or semiquavers. Also, the size of the parts of a bar has no influence on the quickness or slowness of the measure: an *Allegro* in 4/2 measure, and an *Adagio* or *Andante sostenuto* in 4/4, or a *Presto* in 4/4, and an *Allegretto* in 4/8, may have equal velocity of motion.

Nevertheless, a very general feeling has attached a distinction between these characters. An impression seems to have been largely assented to, whereby the larger notes are considered to indicate more important matters, while the smaller characters have been assumed to represent ideas of a light and transient description. Therefore we should write serious and important phrases preferably in 4/2, 3/2, 2/2, measure, light and frivolous phrases in 4/8, 3/8, 2/8,* and fix the quickness or slowness according to the kind of notes. Herein, also, we have a hint as to the character of the composition. But apart from the consideration that as such it is very imperfect and general, we must add, that this fact is subject to very numerous exceptions, particularly among the elder composers. Many deeply serious phrases and movements of Seb. Bach are written in 3/8 measure;

---

* However strange it may appear to a non-composer, the mere technical business of writing exerts a certain influence (as every composer has experienced) on the construction of his works. Large notes, such as semibreves and minims, are written wider, and more slowly, and are less combined, and therefore invite to a larger or broader, and less light and evanescent, or fugitive arrangement of our thoughts. Fugues, or even corales in 2/2 or 2/2 measure, are more easily drawn into a broader and more serious progression, than in 2/4, 4/4, or 2/3 measure. The mind will not, indeed, allow itself to be governed by the pen, but nevertheless we choose the most appropriate form of writing.

while lighter and less important subjects are composed in ¾, or even ⅜.* We must therefore, in this instance also, recognize the insufficiency of all prescription, and in this respect there is no remedy, since various other circumstances may influence the choice of the composer.

We therefore feel convinced, that after technical skill (of which we shall say no more) a perfect knowledge and observance of the notation, &c., is indispensable to correct performance. But for this object we hold susceptibility and perception of that which no writing can completely express, to be also necessary. The power, in short, is required, of exhibiting the full meaning, scope, and tendency of the whole work of art, and of all its parts, be they written down and determined, or must they derive their manifestation from our own sensations. We must not omit to mention, that all the separate features can have received their form and destination from the idea and object of the whole work only; and that we also, in the comprehension, study, and performance of a work, must therefore proceed from its fundamental idea.

The perfect comprehension and exhibition of a work from this fundamental idea in all its parts, is the object of

ARTISTIC PERFORMANCE.

Up to this acme of musical executive perfection, there are several grades.

He who contents himself with making the notes and signs of a composition perceptible, without further notice of its contents, *performs mechanically.* His highest pretension is to produce distinctly that which is distinctly marked; that is, everywhere the right *tones*, everywhere correct measure, everywhere the exact interchanges of *piano* and *forte*, of *legato* and *staccato*, &c. What is praiseworthy and positive in this kind of production we may call the

CORRECT PERFORMANCE.

He who, in addition to the foregoing, affords an insight into the construction of the composition, not apparent from the mere notation, may be said to have exhibited an

INTELLIGENT PERFORMANCE.

This latter brings into action the perceptions of rhythm. Here the performer knows that the sections, phrases, passages, and parts, form small connected portions of the whole composition, and endeavours to make the combination of some parts, and the separation of others, clearly perceptible, by binds and similar playing on the one hand, or on the other, by varying force in playing, contrast, &c. So also, he seeks to give greater importance to the larger rhythmic constructions, and to allow to each its due influence, without disturbing the flow and entireness of the whole. In movements in many parts and polyphonic phrases, he endeavours to make each part distinguishable from the others by different playing; for instance, by playing one *forte*, and the other *piano;* or the one *legato*, and the other *staccato*.

The *correct* and the *intelligent* modes of performance may be taught and learned according to capacity.

He who has received from nature, and preserved, a sensitive feeling for equipoise in *tone*, motion, and all the properties of sound, will perceive at once, without any reference to art or works of art, where the *charm* lies which affects the *senses*, in the separate parts of an artistic work. He will obtain from the instrument, or select from the parts, the most pleasing effects and passages; he will constantly vary, by agreeable changes, the gradations of *piano* and *forte*, laying peculiar accentuation in one place, combining the melody in all varieties of ways, enhancing occasionally the rapid passages by a successful *staccato*, avoiding always the precipitate, rough, or shrill counter-phrases, and procuring by the interchange and blending of all these and similar means, the satisfaction of the senses, and a participation in the charming though superficial excitement. This exhibition we will call the

GRACEFUL PERFORMANCE;

and wish it may constantly be united to the intellectually comprehensive. For this performance, after the natural disposition, nothing is more desirable and more improving than frequent and attentive listening to similar performances of others. Appropriate materials will be found, also, in the sweet coquetries of a Rossini, sung by superior artists; in the beautiful playing of some of our pianists; and, in a higher sense, from many of the works of Haydn and Beethoven, in whom, however, grace and beauty are merely the outward garb of deep and important matters.

But the playing of superior violinists is peculiarly instructive. They produce from their obedient, subtle, and plastic instrument, more kinds of playing, combinations, contrasts, &c., and finer shades and transitions, than any other instrumental performers.

If the execution of a composition should produce in us an unknown emotion, we may attribute to it the praise of a

FEELING PERFORMANCE;

but feeling, as such, gives no account of its perception, or of its action,—not even when it is derived from intelligent comprehension. It lives and works in the moment, from moment to moment, perhaps in all the single moments, but not in the whole as such. It may move and excite us in each single moment; but it remains doubtful whether, in this succession of excitements, we have received the full idea and sentiment of the work,—whether the intentions of the composer have been produced in us,—whether it were *the composition* that we felt, or merely *its performance;* whether we appreciated the work itself, or the undetermined representation of the performer.

This power, of such high value in itself, and quite indispensable to the artist and amateur, exists and operates as it is and as it chooses to manifest itself; it cannot be taught nor formed, but it may be *nourished* and *enhanced;* indeed, it shrinks in its

---

* A misunderstanding on this point has caused in many places the erroneous performance of the music of the school of Palestrina; indeed, of all compositions anterior to the period of Bach. When the uninitiated see the works of Palestrina, Orlando Lasso, Gabrieli, Joaquin de Pres, and others, chiefly composed in semibreves and minims, they are easily induced to perform them too slowly. But these elder musicians only used larger notes than we do. In general, their minims should be considered in this regard as crotchets.

nature, from an intimate inspection, since its being and beautiful existence would be thereby disturbed without any adequate compensation.

If all these powers and acquired faculties be left to themselves, they may produce *much, but not all,* and *fundamentally, not the right object;* for a work of art contains more than all of these: it has a quality in a degree indescribable and ineffable; it has, in conjunction with that which charms the senses, a spiritual power; it has, beyond the dark perceptions of individualities, *the idea* which originated its development, and gave it force and significance. Its exhibition in this sense, is what we have called above the *artistic performance.*

For this we need
ARTISTIC EDUCATION,
in whatever form it be attainable. Rare indeed is the existence, from the beginning, of so strong, safe, and pure a feeling, and at the same time, such self-sufficing activity, however obscure in its operation,* as to lead its possessor always in the right path, and preserve his footsteps from all deviations and errors.

This, in a word, is the gift of the highest genius. But we employ in our choirs and chapels, in our schools and public amusements, thousands and thousands of musicians against one artist elevated by his genius. And besides professional musicians, many thousands of amateurs wish to take an active part in music, who still less can all of them hope for that high distinction of musical pre-eminence. It cannot, therefore, be recommended to any one to trust to his feelings only; since, to the greater number, help and instruction are absolutely indispensable.

Now, there are two ways of acquiring this instruction. The one is the immediate dedication of oneself to the *practical participation in the business and work of music. It is absolutely indispensable to everyone intending to be educated and actively engaged in music. The hearing of much good music,* well performed indeed, and *practising oneself* with choice and zeal, awakens, animates, purifies, and corrects the feeling; it even produces a kind of instinctive perception, whereby in the performance of similar compositions, of which we have heard no pattern or model to direct us, we often accomplish them with tolerable success. But feeling, that most obscure and least manageable activity of the soul, is formed, as we must have been obliged to confess, but very tardily, and with the greatest uncertainty. Therefore our inward consciousness urges us constantly outwards, to seek for higher security.

As we become improved by good music and good performance, so by bad we are led into error, and our feeling looses its liveliness and its accuracy. However sincerely, indeed, we may wish to select the good out of the music offered to us, we must always be apprehensive of taking the false, through our dark and undisciplined feelings.

Our self-knowledge, therefore, urges us beyond the circumference of our feelings to *the other way,* which has no other object than *to form a safe criterion of judgment upon the proper consti-tution of art,* whereby to estimate the contents and tendency of each work of art and every part thereof. Here again, direction and instruction can lend assistance, while mere feeling and its experiences must be set aside. This, then, is the proper object of the doctrine of performance: to awaken the consciousness of the spiritual contents of art and artistic works, or to direct its path aright.

If this consciousness is to be fruitful, it must be true and living. The acceptance as truth, of the explanations or calculations of any teacher or book of teaching whatsoever,—the carrying about and referring constantly to works of art, are fruitless and dead observances. To cling literally to the words of any teacher, would lead to most fatal one-sidedness. and perversion; for most assuredly, the nature of musical configurations is not such as to be comprehended in a word. The *word,* therefore, must be considered merely as an indication of these transient æriform appearances; and he who has not felt the indicated forms as *living in his own soul,* will find all elucidation and comment dead and profitless. We must give especial warning against those playful pseudo-poetical descriptions, in which æsthetical poets and poetastering æsthetical philosophers so much delight, and by which they pretend to give a satisfactory description, all in a mass,† of a whole musical subject or instrument, &c., by an imaginary representation or fancied axiom; such as, for example, "The clarinet is the instrument of love;" "A wind instrument and a bowed instrument form a musical marriage;" "The $\frac{2}{4}$ measure is peculiarly adapted to the expression of love."

These expressions, even if there were a particle of truth in them, would of course be considered by the serious student as idle dreams. But the thoughtless scholar who should be seduced by them, would snatch at a phantom, while the rich reality of art would escape him.

On the other hand, we will not abandon ourselves to the cold and dead abstractions of those who assure us that music has no spiritual existence appreciable by our consciousness—simply because it cannot be demonstrated to the understanding, or because it cannot be satisfactorily expressed in one word, or because the supporters of spirituality have so often erred and contradicted each other.‡ We will not allow ourselves to be led astray by this idea, but rather endeavour to penetrate deeper and deeper into the nature of art, its forms and works, that we may thereby render our consciousness more and more enlightened. Herein we may profit by the experiences of those who have gone before us, but they must serve us only as hints and encouragements. It is from our own observation, and from the sensations and feelings of which we are conscious, that further progress must arise.

Therefore, let everyone be governed in our future remarks by his own impressions and observations.

---

* For example, in Mozart.—See the author's biographical remarks on him in the *Universal-Lexikon der Tonkunst.*

† Many similar expressions, taken from other writers, may be found in the *Charinomos von Seidel,* in *Wagner's Ideen über Music* (Leipz. Mus. Ztg. vs. 1823), and others, old and modern.

‡ The most respectable and the most learned author in favour of this opinion is *Nägeli,* in his lectures on music. See, as to both opinions, *Ueber Malerei in der Tonkunst, ein Maigruss an die Kunstphilosophen,* by the author.

We wish our word to be taken only so far as our assertions may find living confirmation in each person's own bosom. The deeper explanation, the scientific and complete knowledge of the nature of art, does not belong to this preparatory instruction, but to the science of music. The introduction to the character of different periods of art, artists, and different kinds of art, must be referred to the history of art. Neither studies should be entered into before we are deep in art, and in playing and singing; in order that we may not form exaggerated conceptions in lieu of our own observations, and empty formula in lieu of living inspections. The whole of the instruction for performance, indeed, even in the slight sketch we have given of it, *is certainly not for beginners.* To such it is empty sound; and must be merely confusing and misleading to any one who has not been long intimate with art and its external materials, and who has not often experienced its influence, and been filled with its emotions.

SECOND SECTION.—THE MEANING OF ARTISTIC CONFIGURATIONS.

We have become acquainted with rhythm—*tone* and character of sound as the fundamental materials of music. The mind of the artist employs them all for its objects, and therefore for mental and indeed artistic objects. This could not be done if those fundamental materials were incapable of accomplishing the objects of the artist's thoughts and feelings. And if they had not, moreover, *a peculiar and sure significance,* they could not produce *a peculiar and sure effect* upon other persons. The artist might otherwise produce he knew not what. He might feel and intend to announce joy, perhaps, while the hearers, or even each individual hearer, might experience quite a different sensation; one perhaps grief, another anger, &c. Such art would not be art, but a meaningless, if not a senseless jest.

Our consciousness and daily experience teach us something better. We are conscious of certain emotions and feelings produced in us by music, and recognise very clearly that those effects are not accidental—caused, for example, by the disposition we carried with us; otherwise the same composition would affect us differently at different times, sometimes affecting us with joy, at others with sorrow, &c. We see, also, that the effects of music are not singular, as affecting an individual only; for so far as men in general resemble each other, the same composition in general produces the same effect upon each. That would be a bad march which were not stimulating to all, and a wretched funeral song which caused some to mourn and others to dance. Only such compositions as have no decided contents (and there are, no doubt, plenty such), can produce such contrary effects.

It may be a question *how far* determined musical contents may be considered as operative? But this question we now put aside, it being our present business to point out and introduce, but not to carry through to the end. The Science of Music must answer this question.

If a composition has any determined contents, they must exist in its constituent parts, or in their combination. We must therefore observe both. We here give some most general indications touching the first.

(A)   RHYTHM.

In rhythm we distinguish between *motion* and *accent.*

1. MOTION.

As to the meaning of motion—swift, slow, interrupted, equable, unequal, &c.—it were idle to speak. We are all aware of these attributes, not only in music, but in speech, in action, in demeanour, &c. We therefore withhold any observations upon slowness or quickness of time in musical measure; it must be in correspondence with the more or less lively emotions, which the composition is intended to excite.*

If we wish to interpret the meaning of motion, we must distinguish the *motion in itself,* the quicker or slower passage of a succession of *tones,* the *motion from a fixed point;* thus for example:—

355.

to which point the fleeing *tones* seem to hold, and the *motion towards a fixed point,* as to an object thus:—

356.

where the succession seems to be drawn, as it were, into the fixed point. The meaning of these forms of motion depends upon the force with which they are detained or drawn by the fixed point; by the power which we display over, or in the motion; by the action of the will, with which we strive for the point, either uninterruptedly or through delays and varying retardations. Hence we perceive in an objectless flight of *tones,* as for example in this—

357.

that no single *tone* is a principal object, but that the *hastening through all* is the meaning of the phrase, or at least of its rhythmic form. Again, in another quick motion towards a fixed goal, as here—

358.

we see the *power of the object*—TONE, which draws with such violence so many *tones* in uninterrupted

---

* As the emotions of the mind have in their nature no determined measure, and do not depend solely upon their cause, but also upon the disposition of the party suffering, and upon numberless external and inappreciable circumstances, we see how natural it is that our indications of time should not be an exact absolute measure: and moreover, that the determinations of the *Metronome* (page 33,) cannot be used as an absolute law, but only as a *more exact indication* for performance.

succession towards itself; while the same succession of *tones* in *interrupted rhythm*, thus—

359.

exemplifies its meaning by its name.

We must here bring forward again the method of performing the *legato* and *staccato*, as mentioned in our remarks on rhythm at page 30. We there considered them as acting on single *tones* only, which become longer in *legato*, and shorter in *staccato*.

Here we perceive in the *legato* a more flowing and gentle manner of producing successions of *tones*; in the *staccato* a more detached and unrestrained manner, and therefore sometimes more *piquant*. A combination, indeed, of the two manners is attempted, which is indicated by the signs of both, thus:—

360.

Here it is true that the *tones* must be *held on* until the beginning of the succeeding *tone*; but each is to have a separate expression, about so,—

361.

in such a manner, that notwithstanding the *holding on*, each *tone* is separated by accentuation.

2. Accent

This is produced in two ways, but with one object only. What we accentuate, we indicate as the more important. We effect this either by dwelling longer on it, or by giving it a greater volume of sound, expression, or loudness. The tones *e*, *g*, and *c*, in the preceding example, No. 359, are already distinguished from the others by greater length. By loudness, not only can the accent of greater length be supported (as we have pointed out by the *fz.* in No. 358), but an entirely different meaning may be given to one and the same succession of *tones*. Such would be the case if we performed the example, No. 357, according to the upper or under accentuation, marked in the following copy thereof:—

362.

or accented in any other manner, at pleasure.

Hence, we comprehend the distinctions of different kinds of bars. The less accented notes a bar contains, the more easily it moves and flows. Consequently, the three-part bar is easier and more flowing than the two-part; and again, the combined or compound bars, than the single, &c. It is therefore by no means indifferent whether a phrase be written in $\frac{3}{8}$. or $\frac{6}{8}$, or $1\frac{2}{8}$. In the first case, at (A)—

363.

we have four accented notes; whereas in the second (B) we have only two; and in the third (C) only one. The last will therefore be the most flowing, and the first have the most members and be the most expressive. That possibly, however, by the division of a bar into members, the rhythm may be more exactly determined, and an excessively difficult bar be rendered easier, and an easy phrase be rendered more difficult, is clear; for example, this phrase in $\frac{3}{8}$—

364.

appears more flowing and lighter than this phrase in $1\frac{2}{8}$, which is so strongly accented, and violently driven along by the sharply articulated members of its rhythm, viz.:—

365.

which does not require any further explanation.

3. Larger Rhythmic Members.

We have spoken already (page 61), of the greater rhythmic masses into which the single bars of a composition are combined. We know, also, that these sections may follow each other symmetrically or not.

What is the meaning of these configurations? The same as that of the bars, but of more free and extensive application.

Each section is a whole by itself, and as such is a moment in the whole composition. The shorter this moment, the lighter is the progress of the whole, and the more lightly and flowingly we hasten from the one to the other; as here, for example,—

366.

in a little phrase whose members consist of one bar only. The more extended and comprehensive we make these moments, the more connected and satisfying will the whole become. The following phrase constructed on the preceding, but in two-bar rhythm, will make this immediately perceptible:—

367.

Here we must advert to a considerable distinguishing influence of the numbers two and three.

The two-bar rhythm, like the number two in division, is the simplest and easiest or most flowing. The four-bar rhythms seem more ample and dignified, but they also are intelligible and flowing, because the number two (or half) is perceptible in them. The three-bar rhythms, on the contrary, seem to step forward unwillingly, and with a kind of violence. Their character is so decidedly different, that Beethoven, for instance, thinks it necessary in one of his greatest works, expressly to call attention to it. In the *Scherzo* of his ninth symphony, there are four-bar rhythms, thus:—

368.

and they change, further on, into three-bar rhythms,—

369.

which Beethoven marks with *Ritmo a tre battute*— that is, rhythm in three beats (bars). Rhythms of five bars, in fine, are long and burthensome, if not dragging, &c.

We will repeat, that symmetrical or equipoised sections give to the whole a more equable, intelligible, and quiet character. Varying or irregular sections produce disturbance, or even unsteadiness, and at last disconnection of the whole; which, indeed, might either be a fault or occasionally a very proper mode of expressing a passionate hesitating state of mind. Here, also, it becomes the question what sort of sections, symmetrical or unsymmetrical, follow each other. So many combinations are possible, that to think of showing them all would be to misapprehend the object of instruction. Let each one accustom himself to recognise the rhythmic order and its meaning in real compositions, and to feel and understand their influence on the whole.*

---

* It is not in general considered difficult to persons somewhat gifted with musical talent to distinguish the rhythmical sections; and it has

(B) On Tones.

In tonic matters, also, several different meanings may be distinguished. Here, however, we enter upon a more foreign and delicate subject, and we must consider how far our readers can and will accompany us in the discussion thereof.

In general, the higher a *tone* is, the more it becomes strained and shrill: the deeper it be, so it grows lax and hollow. Rising successions of *tones* increase in vehemence, and *vice versâ*. But here several other relationships come into joint operation, all of which we cannot now contemplate; for example, that at a certain point the height is too strained to operate with force, and now, on the contrary, breaks down in the finest and most charming tones—which certainly, to a reflective mind, points significantly enough to the original sense.

1. The Kinds of Tonic Movement.

The motion *by jumps* (over-intervening degrees), is uneasy and violent; that *by steps*, from one degree to the next adjoining is more quiet and gentle. The *diatonic scale* is on that account more quiet, softer, and more tuneful than any kinds of jumping motion; and still more so, because its succession of *tones* (the major scale) contains the nearest related and next necessary *tones*, in the most convenient and equable order. The *chromatic scale* moves in still smaller and more equable steps, being half tones only; but just for that reason it is trivial and distressing.

If we turn from the scales to the motion in jumps, we have before us the successions of *tones* arising from the chords. Every succession of *tones* formed out of a chord, appears to us in its unity as an assemblage of parts belonging to each other, and flowing readily together; and so, we have two originally separated elements now in conjunction, the distance of the steps between the *tones* (exteriorly uncombined), and the internal harmonic connexion. Thus these successions of *tones* are sometimes light and flowing, while at others they are unsteady and tottering:—

370.

Sometimes they make a bold dash, somewhat thus:—

371.

and are applied according to rhythm, accent, &c.

been suggested, that, in doubtful cases, a thin transverse line should be inserted thus, for instance,—

369A. Andante.

as a sign of the division of rhythmical sections or members. This proposition, however, has not met with success: and, indeed, it does not seem necessary, and is therefore not advisable. Our notation is already overcrowded with signs.

2. THE INTERVALS.

We have hitherto considered the steps of the *tones* merely in a superficial view with regard to their distance. We become soon aware, however, that each of them has its own proper meaning: that the different steps do not differ in quantity only. Some, at least, of the observations belonging to this place, will be confirmed by every zealous and attentive student of music.

In order to proceed with the greater security, let us take the major scale, since it contains greater intervals only; and let us separate one octave from the upper higher one. We know that in the higher octave, the same succession of *tones* and the same *tones* reappear, only in a higher and more attenuated sphere; first the octave of the tonic, then the ninth or second in a higher octave, and so forth.

Hence it is clear why all intervals beyond the octave, compared with intervals within the octave, are of an overstrained nature. The ninth is a step into the second, but in a higher region; and the octave is the overstrained return of the tonic. Hence the force of soaring into the octave, the violence, excess, and exaggeration in the ninth and tenth, until at last, in much more extended strainings, the relation ceases to be perceptible, and the interval falls off into two incongruous *tones*.

Within the octave, the *fifth* has an undefinable hovering excursive tendency; the *fourth* is firmly and strongly appropriate (therefore the kettle-drums are mostly tuned in fourths); the *second* is for quiet, measured continuance; the *third* is decided and calculating; the *sixth* tends to gentle union; the *seventh* is full of solicitude. To this we will add, that all *minor intervals* produce diminution or alleviation; all diminished intervals produce uneasiness; all extreme intervals produce passionate emotion, and even distorted exaggeration of the sense of the major intervals. Let each one make these facts perceptible to himself, by trial with the major and minor third and seventh, the diminished and extreme fifths, the major and exteme fourths, and with that striking extreme second in the minor scale (page 19).

Here we must revert to that extraordinary departure from the rule of our whole system, which we mentioned at page 95, namely, the *pitching the tone too high* in strong and vehement emotion, and *too low* in depressed sensations; and also, that violent and passionate conjunction by transition from one tone into another. They are extreme measures whose meaning speaks for itself, and ought to be employed only with the greatest caution.

Lively sensibility will recognize immediately what we have here so cursorily pointed out; but one misunderstanding must be avoided: it must by no means be supposed, that the significance of the intervals is universally exhibited. We have ourselves, seen already (page 99) that it is often intentional, that the single *tone*, or its relation, should not have its own proper effect, but that it should be an indistinguishable part of a greater whole, or be very little perceptible. It is also conceivable, that, often, intervals without meaning, and even against their proper meaning, should be used by the composer, as all means whatsoever are sometimes used by painters, poets, and so forth; and occasionally, indeed, in error. Such a mistake does not always show itself by the manifest failure of the work, as it may have been palliated or concealed by other means. Who would wish to measure the nature of intervals in all possible cases of art; or to make an important matter of their having been now and then misunderstood? All that we wish, is to make use of the sense or meaning of an interval, when it is properly and intentionally indicated. When they appear in the right sense, they are a means of comprehension, and performance; when they are intentionally used, but erroneously, we can explain the error to ourselves, and perceive the right course, but we cannot ground upon it our comprehension of the work, nor our performance of it.

3. THE CHORDS

come to our assistance, in order to give us a clear and sure understanding of the character of the relationship of *tones*.

If we begin with the *fifth*,* forming an incomplete triad, we feel the character we have pointed out proceed from the combined sound of two French horns or clarionets, or even a simple pianoforte—

372.

or two voices.

If we add the *major third*, the *major triad* resounds forth, pure, bright, and satisfactory, the *fundamental chord*; if we lower the third, we perceive the sorrowful *minor triad*; if we also lower the fifth, the distressed *diminished triad* appears.

The sense or character of these chords becomes more apparent when they are repeated in succession. The major triad—

373.

steps forward resplendent and vigorous: it can be pure and delicate, but also piercingly strong. The minor triad—

374.

in successions becomes more and more dolorous and hollow; or, also, strange and desolate, and does not admit of being continued long. The diminished triad—

375.

drags itself painfully along. If, now, we return to the major triad and raise the fifth, the shrill and grating *extreme triad* is heard. A succession of these chords has not hitherto been hazarded; and we know not, indeed, how to set it in motion.

* Why with the fifth? Because it is produced immediately after the fundamental *tone* and its octave. The further particulars must be sought in the Science of Music.

Perhaps it might be attempted in this irritated, snarling form:—

a succession which we would not admit without further consideration; but which, if allowed to subsist, will correspond exactly with its character, as we have pointed it out.

The minor seventh being added to the major triad of the dominant, we produce the chord of the dominant—a soft harmony solicitous for resolution. If we add further the greater ninth, the chord of the major ninth is produced; or with the minor ninth, the chord of the minor ninth, which resolves into the upper octave. In both, the character of the chord of the dominant, and its seventh, predominates. In the chord of the greater ninth, the feeling of solicitude may be considered as exaggerated; in that of the lesser ninth, however, it is much diminished.

But we have already overstepped our object, which was merely to point out the internal sense of the *tones*. It is, however, difficult to stop at the proper moment, for when we are absorbed in so dark a subject as the nature of our inward sensations of music, we are almost irresistibly drawn deeper and deeper into the exciting mystery. Here, however, we must restrain ourselves, as it is not even the proper place to give further explanations, upon part, even, of what we have said. Outward example, and more complete development, are still required for those who now for the first time enter upon this path. The object here is to awaken and excite the sensations; and that only will nourish and avail which they recognize and are able to retain.

It is now easy to understand the characters of

4. THE MAJOR AND MINOR MODES.

The *major* proceeds with firmness, certainty, and clearness, in greater intervals, only, from the fundamental *tone*,—

and in a well ordered succession of tones and semitone,* according to the scale. The *minor* has a mournful third and sixth from the fundamental *tone*:—

378.

and according to the scale, the snarling extreme second (between the sixth and seventh degrees), and thereby, also, a disturbed equipoise. It sounds therefore to us more dull and sorrowful. As, however, it is often obliged to change that strange step, by altering the sixth and seventh, it assumes a greater variety, but also a changeable and uncertain meaning.

After the two modes, major and minor (not to mention the Ecclesiastical modes treated of in the Instruction for Composition), the

5. VARIOUS SCALES

present themselves; and in the first place, those in the major mode.

Among them appears the normal scale of C major, as the clear and calm central point; on the one side of which are ranged the sharpened scales in lighter— and on the other side, the flattened scales in more shadowed character; until the opposite ranks meet enharmonically at the remarkable point where they mutually become involved in each other (in F♯ and G♭): much too deep a subject to be discussed with any advantage in a work of introduction.

OBSERVATIONS.

We think it proper here to pause in our remarks. It would be very seriously desirable to discuss the character and inward tendencies of the scales, of the various organs of sound (instruments and voices), of the vowel sounds, &c. But the beginning of it, even, would carry us beyond the intention of a preparatory work; and moreover, the nature of the object would scarcely allow us to break off suddenly. He whose sensations have been moved or excited by what we have so far written, or by any part of it, may be assured that the same spirit which has manifested itself to him in any part, may pervade the whole organism of art. His own mind will lead him further, or prepare him for higher instruction. To him, however, who is not yet perceptive of this inward feeling, or whose natural susceptibility has been deranged or seared by over-hasty conclusions or determined opinions,—to him we say, any further development would be nothing but an increased burthen.

But we would wish to express one desire—that compositions should not be changed from one scale into another, with such thoughtlessness as unfortunately often occurs. Many circumstances may indeed render such transpositions necessary; but without such necessity, without irremediable urgency, it ought never to be done. If we ourselves have no conviction of the significance or aptitude of each scale, we might at least have sufficient respect for the imaginator and constructor of a work of art, to presume that he did not select without motive, this and no other scale for his work. His determination ought to be honoured, simply because it is his. He who has not a proper respect for artists and works of art, has not a true love for art itself; for which he justly suffers in the loss, also, of its pleasures.

THIRD SECTION,—OF THE MEANING OF ARTISTIC FORMS.

Easier or more generally intelligible is the meaning of artistic forms; for they are not creations of nature which we are to unriddle, but inventions of the human mind, whose object in their formation is sufficiently obvious. He, therefore, who can see distinctly the single forms, and perceive their combinations, can rarely fall into error.

So it is clear, that one part or voice alone is

---

* The scale would be more even from the seventh, thus: *b—c—d—e f—g—a* (½.1.1.½.1.1); a form which becomes important in the science of music.

simpler and more comprehensible, in general, than compositions in many parts or voices; but it is also less effective. Homophonic formations show us one part acting as principal part, the accompanying parts as subordinate accessories. These latter may combine into an indiscriminate mass, as in No. 327; or they may annex themselves in the shape of successions of octaves, thirds, or sixths, in the submissive *suite* of the principal part; or they may occasionally, as in No. 329, seek to emancipate themselves for a moment from servitude.

The powers of the mind are more abundantly displayed in polyphonic phrases, where each part strives for distinction; where each part speaks for itself, and answers the other; where at one time, some combine against others; and one mass challenges the other—and finally, one part obtains the victory and becomes the principal. Here the object is to do justice to each part: to make it distinguished where it is to be predominant: to subdue it when another is to have the pre-eminence: to give it distinctive characteristics, when others of equal importance are to tread the stage with it. All methods of constructing a phrase,—combination and contrast, accentuation, polishing, *forte* and *piano*,— must contribute to enhance the richness, and elevate the sense of polyphonic phrases.

If we particularise the forms, we should say, that the passages are the most susceptible of motion; the phrases are determined and complete; the subject requires the most equipoised roundness and division; the appendix must appear as an addition, but be in character as a part of the whole.

The *song-forms*, or *small rondo-forms*, are easy to comprehend as a whole. In the song form, so soon as two different phrases (for example, the *principal phrase* and the *trio*) are joined together,—or in the *greater rondo-form*, when one or two secondary phrases are added to the principal phrase, the different phrases appear as principal moments of the whole. These phrases must be kept distinct by the performance also, each being comprehended in its own peculiar manner; and moreover, they must be distinguished in the stream of the whole composition, without any disturbance of their mutual connexion. The return of similar phrases—for example, of the principal phrases—requires, of course, the return of the same exhibition. As, however, between the intention and relationship of the work, and of the performer and hearers, differences occur, so the performance will assume differences of colour; it will be strengthened, quickened, retarded, &c. The passages in the meanwhile will form at one time softer, and at others bolder interventions and transitions from one principal moment to the others.

These forms are the most easy and most transient, for they demand only one principal part, or join together several principal moments with but slight adhesion. The sonata-form is not so compliant. In this, *two principal moments* assume distinction above all—and probably in each there are several phrases. These principal moments enter the first part against each other; they drive through and compress each other contentiously in the second; wrestle through several scales; change their mode, and occasionally their whole manner; and combine together at last in the third. With them, come closing phrases, appendixes, introductions, passages, &c.; and all these must be distinctly separate, and yet must be comprehended and performed as a whole. How shall he who knows not how to separate the members and parts of such a whole— how to recognise and exhibit each by itself, and yet to combine the whole again—how to make the reappearing phrase again cognisable by similar performance, although varied from its previous exhibition, and according to its present circumstances—how shall such a one, we say, be able to impart with certainty the idea of the composer?

In all these forms, the separation into determined parts comes very opportunely. If we can keep the great masses together, and perform them correctly in themselves, we shall have accomplished a great deal. But in fugues and great figuration, this assistance fails us. These compositions have indeed their parts, but they are not generally so distinct nor formally separated as phrases; they move like great waves—distinguishably, but flowing into each other; but the performer must be able to mark both with precision.

Finally, in the combined forms, for example, of sonatas, symphonies, &c., the single movements are generally separated from each other by formal sections, and intervals of time. But an inward tendency reigns throughout them. An internal unity of idea or intention must essentially combine them together in one true and consistent whole, and be perceptibly manifested in their performance. And so, in conclusion, let it it not be doubted, that in the most extensive works, such as operas and oratorios, every part must be formed and comprehended and carried through, as a portion of the universal unity.

FOURTH SECTION —OF THE COMPREHENSION AND PERFORMANCE OF PARTICULAR WORKS.

All our observations hitherto have been general only. They were directed to the explanation of the sense or meaning of the different musical configurations or forms in general. Our present object is how, in the individual works which we are to understand and to exhibit, all these means and forms show themselves—what the composer in each particular case has intended, and the performer is expected to realize.

We know already, that the notation is not adequate to our object, and that words and various signs and indications have been resorted to for relief. These expressions, of course, we must understand and strive to put in practice. But we have been long aware that a general word can only give a very general hint; and that a hundred such words are not sufficient to point out the proper performance of a single phrase.

To the knowledge and beneficial employment of all that is contained in notation, artistic signs and expression, and in the attainment of the deeper meaning of the elements and forms of art, so far can general instruction offer assistance.

But living instruction can lead farther, if we have the good fortune to find a teacher, himself possessed of the deeper sensibilities of the art, and capable of manifesting them in performance. This, unfortunately, is not easy of accomplishment. In all cases, however, the chief matter depends upon the zealous and well conducted will of the pupil; for all knowledge and teaching is useless, is dead and fruitless, where there is no susceptibility and *reproductiveness*,—the power of returning a living sensation for a living sensation received. All instruction can only awaken, excite, nourish, and conduct this power, but can neither create it, nor supply its place.

Here we will add our last advice. An experience not very limited, in practical education in music, persuades us that our counsel will neither be superfluous, nor will it induce to error.

When, all presuppositions and judgments being made, it comes to the point of grasping a determined composition in the most impressive and complete manner possible (taking into consideration, however, the proper time and company), let the performer give himself up boldly, without diffidence or reservation, to the new work; let him, indeed, throw himself into the work, and plunge into the most important parts of it, whatever little fractional bits may escape him. For a work of art is a whole, a living thing, which must be embraced in its life and entireness. No work of art is made up of independent unities, and none such can be grasped. Let him who is accustomed to construct an imaginary combination of notation without the help of an instrument, seek in a sudden glance to form at least a general representation of it, and start at once to its first performance, immediately the preceding momentary inspection of the notes has given him a little hold of it. In this first performance, the fortune and zeal of the moment must be relied on implicitly for the presence in himself of a correct apprehension of the composition in question. In this first seizure, difficulty may be heaped on difficulty,—faults and omissions may abound; nevertheless it must be persisted in, in the time first chosen as the correct time, until the end of the whole composition; and if it have many movements, all of them must flow uninterruptedly after each other.

Whatever small errors may have been committed, one thing has been gained, which would hardly have been attainable in any other way; that is, the *general comprehension* of the whole without prejudice or disturbance by the idea of technical difficulty, and moreover, with the first fervour. In vocal compositions we consider it very advisable not to add the text to this first performance; for as every text may be treated in various ways, and as it is rare that a text be done justice to in all its parts, so a previous reading of the text induces prejudgments, which may place us in contradiction with the intentions of the composer.

It is only now, when by a single or repeated performance we have obtained a lively apprehension of the whole of its contents and tendency, that the time is come to give ourselves a more particular account of the two latter objects. Herein the knowledge of forms is of great assistance to us, inasmuch as it enables us to find at once the mode of formation of the whole; the division, the principal phrases and their return, the changes, the combinations, &c. Now we examine everything in portions; we separate the first part, the second, the principal theme, the accessory or secondary themes, and strive to form an inward feeling of their significance.

If a theme be repeated and altered, for instance, in a sonata-form, we compare together all its fundamental configurations and the turnings of its fundamental thought, in order to arrive at their meaning and proper performance; and thus only, when we know what becomes of a theme, we acquire the power of managing it with assurance; we recognize its original position, how it is to be corroborated, or to be softened, and how it is to be carried forward in its different parts.

When we have pondered over the principal and its combinations singly, we return to the whole. Every composition has one, or perhaps several *chief points*, which serve alike as objects and as characteristics of the whole musical construction. Everything is grouped around these chief points; is urged constantly or at intervals to the same end, and is led back to it, for the conclusion, or for further progress. So, in every musical creation, small or large, one great or many small waves (and if there be more than one, there will still be one of them more powerful than the rest, were it only because it is the last) move swelling forward until the ebb, and then subside. He who does not imitate this progress of the waves,—who knows not how and when to rise, and then in proper time to fall, may do much in individualities; but the prize of a perfect composition, fully worked out as a whole, will not be his. Therefore, again and again we must learn from a whole to produce a whole,—but now we shall labour with a more enlightened comprehension of its parts and combination.

Now only can we feel assured that we have a perfect understanding of what is essential, and we may therefore pursue at discretion our *study of particulars*. Now we must recall and study all that in a technical point of view was imperfect. In vocal pieces, the text and the whole rhythmic construction must be nicely weighed. And here our intimate knowledge of the elements and forms of art will show its full value; for by their means only, can we become certain of what the composer intended to express; what interval, what rhythmic or melodic motive is considered important; in fine, what we are to elevate, and what to leave in shadow. In this scrupulous examination we find fundamentally; whether our first performance was correct or not. In compositions to be performed by several singers and instrumentalists, it is clear that this examination cannot rest with our part only, but must comprehend the whole orchestra. How could a singer perform his part with freedom and effect, if he had not knowledge of how he was to be accompanied,—what instruments would associate with, and what be concurrent or contrasted with him? So, therefore, we shall have penetrated at last to the smallest individualities; but we did not conceive of them as unities alone, but as parts of the whole, and with a firm impression of the whole.*

It is true that this method is not so easy and short as the impetuous desires of many persons anxious for musical power would wish it to be; but it would be difficult to attain certainty and completeness at a less cost. To the zealous and enduring, the path becomes soon easier and more pleasant, and the goal appears nearer than we dared to hope. For he who has laboured through a few compositions seriously, proceeds afterwards with such a sharpened sight and increased velocity, that with comparatively trifling labour, he reaps redoubled satisfaction.

We would, however, advise any person desirous of perfecting his higher education in this manner, not to pass suddenly from one species of composition to another, nor from one composer to another; but to allow himself sufficient time to become familiar with each. If he have been busy with a fugue or sonata, for instance, let him go through a few more fugues or sonatas, in order to acquire a complete and satisfying knowledge of the form and general manner of handling such compositions. But let him then, also, compare the different works of like form, and seek in their contents the characteristic differences which determine their manner of performance, in order that he may not get into a *mannered performance*, and exhibit in a like manner all compositions of a like name.

So it is also advisable, after having gone through a work of any composer, to proceed immediately to the study of others by the same author, in order to form a complete image of the manner of the artist, and fix it in the mind. Every artist, every nation, and every age, has had a peculiar manner in music, as in every other art, and in the conduct of life itself. This must have been always evident to every one at all acquainted with history and mankind, and may be readily perceived by a musician, if he will compare the works of artists of different nations,—of Rossini with those of Mozart; of Auber with those of Gluck. The deeper we penetrate into the national circumstances of the times, and into the life, qualities, and habits of an artist, the more clearly can we comprehend him in his works, and arrive at their scope and tendency. Little as our fellow artists seem disposed to admit it, a right and full understanding of art is not to be obtained without the revelations of the history of art. All the pretty figures of speech,—that art belongs to human nature universally, that it belongs to no age, that it is everywhere the same, that it requires merely a susceptible heart—are just merely figures of speech, which conceal an atom of truth under a mountain of error and falsehood; and whose most zealous propagators usually have the narrowest visual horizon. As they maintain that art is of no time or place, they have certainly reserved the most considerable portion for themselves,—that is, the art of all past ages. Of contemporaneous art, all that is not their own is a closed book, and all art to them is limited to one or two artists, whom for that very reason they do not understand. All others have been false, or labouring in vain, or have grown old. But how can an artist be grown old, or be modern, if time has no concern with art? They don't like to hear this question.

Here it might be our duty to insist on the importance of historical instruction, but to impart it is not the object of preparatory teaching.† But this history, when written, should not be of dates and facts only, but of the mind of the artistic periods and of artists. We must, however, here repeat what we have more than once said before,—that the words of history will be an empty sound, and all the thoughts of others a useless possession, unless we employ them for self-improvement, for the formation of our inward mind—unless we really see and feel what history and instruction endeavour to announce to us.

FIFTH SECTION.—OF CONCERTED, OR ORCHESTRAL PERFORMANCE.

The manner of conducting the performance of several persons together, requires our especial consideration. This can take place in two ways. Either one person serves merely to accompany a song at the pianoforte, for instance; or several persons asso-

---

* Little as it may consist with the province of this work to enter more deeply into the minutiæ of performance, which indeed are better taught by private instruction and study, the Author is anxious not to part without leaving a few remarks, which long experience has taught him to consider as useful.

In the first place, let no one employ all his means upon every composition—let him not in all cases, for example, use the utmost *forte* or *piano*, nor all his singing and playing ornaments. Nothing gives performance less truth nor more sameness than this erroneous practice, which proceeds either from prejudice in favour of a particular manner, or from a vain fondness for display. A pretty song or rondo, a delicate sonata or a touching adagio, cannot require the massive power of a great scene or of a passionate sonata or symphony, and cannot endure it without exaggeration of its true value. A significant or even a polyphonic phrase, in which one might wish to make every turn and the course of each part perceptible, would be destroyed by so quick a time as might be perfectly appropriate to a shewy bravura composition. The Author must here take the opportunity of protesting against many of the indications of time, which occur in the otherwise most excellent and praiseworthy edition of Bach's works (at Peters, in Leipzig), by Mr. C. Czerny—with an appeal, indeed, to Beethoven—but probably, indeed, rather under the influence of his own highly distinguished powers of performance.

Also with regard to the *capacity of the instrument* or of the *voice and space*, a performer of judgment will be attentive so to arrange the measure of his *fortes* and *pianos*, as not to exceed the powers of the one nor of the other (therefore, with weak organs to begin with moderation), to delay the motion in greater ranges, in order that the *tones* may have time to spread without mixing, &c.

Secondly, let it be considered, that equal or very similar results may often be produced by different causes, and consequently that sometimes different means may be employed to supply the place or remedy the deficiencies of others. Thus, a quicker motion can increase the power of a whole movement, and an imperceptible retardation give enhanced expression to a note or passage, if the voice or instrument should fail, or other motives should suggest delay. In this manner, in song, the charm, expression, and energy of delivery, can compensate for many defects of the voice.

Thirdly, it must be remembered, that hastening or delaying ought not to be resorted to so frequently, nor be extended so long, as to endanger the feeling of the time—unless as a preparation for a new time. That also in changing time it has a good effect to let the new time be in a relation of even proportion to the old (so that the new be half, twice, or four times quicker or slower than the preceding), excepting in cases where a particularly passionate subject requires different treatment.

Fourthly, we should keep in mind that the signs used by the composer, as indications for performance, have not always and everywhere the same force. That, for instance, in a movement whose general character is gentleness, and which should be played quietly, in reference to its total significance, *sf.* or *f* ought not to be produced with the same force as in a movement, which in its totality demands a more powerful performance.

We may, in fine, adopt the general rule, that the meaning of the whole artistic work is to be kept constantly before our eyes in the performance of every individuality in it, as sole law and object.

† Many notices relative to the above matter may be found in the Author's *Kunst des Gesanges*, in his *Ueber Malerei in der Kunst*, and in the already mentioned *Mus. Lexikon* upon Seb. Bach, Handel, Gluck, Haydn, Mozart, Beethoven, and other artists; also from many excellent articles in the said *Lexikon* by other authors, and in Nägeli's lectures.

ciate in an equal participation in the performance; as in quartetts, orchestras with or without a vocal choir.

Accompaniment requires quite a peculiar talent; and it is easy to find good, nay, excellent players, who are bad accompanyers. The accompanyer does not require merely, like every performer, the complete insight and practical skill to comprehend and perform the work to be exhibited: he must moreover possess the *self-denial* to subordinate his playing entirely to the chief part,—that is, to the song. He must be ready and able to follow in all respects the idea of the chief person; to guess beforehand, indeed, his weak points; to cover his faults, and enhance his good qualities: and all this art, this self sacrifice, will have merited most, if it has been able to conceal itself from the hearer. To this latter, no difference or disagreement between the performers should be visible; no concealment of defect be appreciable—the performance must seem to have issued from one mind.

But on the other hand, the accompaniment must not sink into passive, lifeless submission. Nothing would be more enfeebling for the work, nor more dispiriting to the principal part; especially in song. In every singer (and also in every principal player) there is much rather a want of, or a desire for, powerful concurrent striving,—not in contradiction, but in reciprocity and emulation with the accompaniment. An energetic and strongly accented expression of the accompaniment at a proper moment, with the recognition of the singer, is peculiarly refreshing and exhilarating to the voice, naturally so prone to undulating deviations; while a timorous, dissolving accompaniment, robs even robust male singers of certainty and power. That, therefore, to female singers (and of high order, too,) a manly and spirited accompaniment, at a proper moment and in a cordial manner, must be encouraging and acceptable, will be acknowledged by every one. We have spoken before, of the duties of an accompanyer at the moment of performance. That by previous agreement and practice, the parties concerned should come to a perfect understanding as to the meaning of the work and manner of its performance, is a matter of course.

The accompanyer to song in many parts has other duties to perform. It is usually his business to be director, or conductor, also. Time, *ensemble*, production, the whole performance, in fine, is under his guidance. This conducts us to the second point of our considerations.

CONCERTED OR ORCHESTRAL PERFORMANCE, presupposes (if the result is intended to be sure and satisfactory) agreement and rehearsal in common; and, particularly in large orchestral or choral assemblies, a director or conductor.

After the choice of the composition, it is incumbent on the conductor to secure its best possible performance. Distribution of the parts, position of the performers, time, production, everything is in the last instance determined by him. He must therefore know everything in all directions, have everything prepared and ready, and be capable of carrying it through. He that does not know the necessary means in all relations,—who is not penetrated with the work to be performed, and does not carry in his soul a perfect image of the manner in which it ought to be produced; he who cannot communicate intelligibly by word and action his conceptions and views to the performers, and perceive their errors and correct them, or even possibly foresee and prevent them; who cannot keep all the performers together by power of nerve, and will, and an all-present eye; he who is not, in fine, vested with absolute authority, and placed in an appropriate personal locality, cannot flatter himself with the hope of being a good conductor.

The mere procedure of beating time is soon learned. *Two-part* bars are struck downwards and upwards—the principal part with the down beat, and the secondary with the up beat:—*

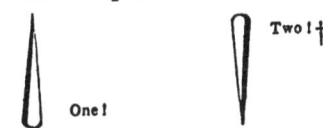

In *three-part* bars, the principal part with the down beat, and the two secondary obliquely upwards, thus:—

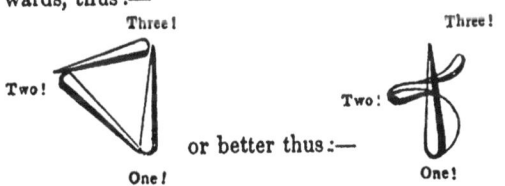

or better thus:—

In *four-part* bars, the principal downwards, the second crotchet to the left, the third to the right, and the fourth upwards:—

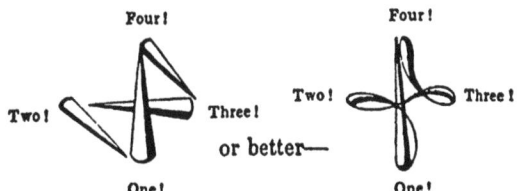

or better—

In *six-part* bars, the same procedure is adopted, excepting that the two first parts (one! and two!) are counted with the down beat, the third to the left, the fourth and fifth (four! five!) to the right, and the sixth with the up beat. In quick motion, halves or thirds only of bars are beat. For example, in quick 4/4 bars, the first and third parts; in quick 3/4 or 3/8, the principal and second part with the down, and the third with the up beat:—

---

* In Italy and France, beating time is often performed reversely to the above (and as it seems to us, against the feeling and nature of the matter), that is, the principal part is signified by raising the hand, or the baton, in order to make this more visible.

† It will be easily observed here, that each line represents a beat in a bar produced in the direction of the expansion of the line.

The quick $\frac{6}{8}$ is marked by two beats, the $\frac{9}{8}$ by three, similarly to the $\frac{2}{4}$ and $\frac{3}{4}$, whose parts are solved into triplets.

If it be necessary to beat all the parts or even members of the bar repeatedly, as in slow six-part motion, it is done about in this way:—

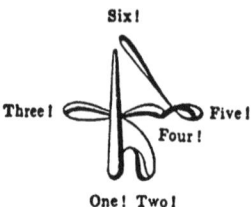

Many other arrangements are made which require no special mention here, since they easily come to mind when necessary, or the conductor expressly orders them.

The performers ought not only to be perfectly submissive to the will of the conductor, but they must have the capability of being so in reality. The proper and effective submission, or rather resignation, is not dead or torpid, nor (worse still) an exterior compliance united to an interior resistance; it is a lively and cheerful acceptance and cordial performance of the ideas and directions of the conductor, be they conformable or not to the sentiments of the performer,—and an indefatigable watching of, and correspondence with, his indications. This latter duty presupposes a more extended capability and promptitude than solo playing or singing. He must be perfect master of his own part, to be able to perform it correctly, and at the same time to be all eye and ear for every nod of the conductor; herein is shown the perfectly educated artist for concerted performance.

How much this task is facilitated and enlivened by a deeper insight into the nature of art and of the particular work which is to be performed, does not require any comment. But here,* where, after unavoidable pupilage and education, the leading of the conductor awaits the performer, the simple General Musical Instruction, which has introduced the scholar and has hitherto guided his steps during his first studies—now to be extended and completed—must restrain itself within its proper limits.

APPENDIX.—SCORE PLAYING.

Our disquisitions on concerted performance have brought us back to a subject which is not indeed very interesting to every musical amateur, but to all who aim at high distinction, and to all fully grounded musicians, is of the utmost importance; we allude to the performance of score. Its immediate advantage and its principal external characteristics have been pointed out in the tenth section of the third division. How much the knowledge of harmony, acquaintance with and skill in cyphering (thorough-bass), insight into the forms of art, but especially the practical composition of music, must facilitate and expand our understanding of score, will be obvious from our preceding observations. Practice in graduated order, and then acquaintance with the manner of writing and style of the composers whose scores we wish to study, are the last requisites for an easy and sure comprehension.

The understanding of score being presumed, we shall now make a few observations upon its manner of performance. It is so natural that we should wish ourselves and others to hear that which we have read with interest, and it must be so often desirable to parties unprofessional to perform or lead from scores, that these few hints, if not of general interest, may still hope to merit the attention of the emulous and aspiring lesser number. We take the pianoforte for our instrument, as the only one adapted to score playing, which is everywhere at hand.

After the already-mentioned requisites for score playing, one more is necessary.—a sufficient, that is, *considerable skill in pianoforte playing* in general. In this, however, we do not understand any distinguished ability in bravura passages (although these may also be most favorably employed), but much rather the dexterity to lead two, three, or more varying or diverging parts, clearly and expressively together,—to bring distinctly and faithfully to the ear many-grouped phrases and octave passages, with energy or with softness,—to seize distant intervals with either hand, and generally to perform melodies and passages in every mode of playing. Very often, almost at every moment, the score player will have to perform passages quite unadapted for the pianoforte (having been written for other musical organs), which force him to deviate from ordinary rules. He must have the ability, therefore, besides his scholastic attainments, to invent at every moment new applications and modes of playing, adapted to his peculiar circumstances, in order to free himself from the inconvenience and entanglement in which the score player often quite unexpectedly finds himself.

Persons in the habit of improvising at the instrument, will find advantage from it in score playing. It will have been observed, however, that the regular art of playing may be somewhat endangered by it; we recommend therefore, seriously, that score playing be not resorted to until a considerable degree of certainty and habit have been acquired in the ordinary mode of using the instrument.

So much touching the preparatory conditions.

All that we have further to say regarding score playing is in reference to the question

What is the score playing to exhibit?

Whoever clearly answers this question to himself upon each occasion of performance, and for every part of it, will find therein the right introduction to advantageous employment.

Score playing should produce the contents of the score as fully and completely as possible; and this either alone or associated with some of the parts—for instance, voices—of the score. In this latter case, the parts sung might be omitted in the playing.

It might be imagined from this, that it was necessary to produce from the instrument only those parts which were not performed by some other

---

* The publication of Dr. Grassner's "*Dirigent and Ripienist*" at Groos's in Carlsruhe, is very full and instructive on this subject.

organ. But this is not so. In the first place, the notes collectively of a score would not have the same effect on a pianoforte which they produce in an orchestra. What power is there not in a single chord from bowed instruments! What fulness in a brass band!—

and how little would the same *tones* transferred to the pianoforte produce the original effect! All means of strength, the most comprehensive grasp, a full resounding bass, must be resorted to; and one might employ (but no general rule can be given) a lower octave for the upper parts, which in the wind instruments are strong, while they are the weakest on the pianoforte. The sound of the horn may be perhaps represented by the insertion of fifths;—*

Secondly. The collective notes of the score often cannot be played: and often can be played only in a confused manner. Already in the preceding instances, the wind instruments cannot be given by two hands on the pianoforte. Still less could many figurated parts be adequately given, as the first glance at a score would show. If completeness were possible, it would in many cases only confuse the course of the parts. Here is a very simple example; the beginning of Mozart's vehement symphony in G minor:—

It cannot be played completely. The contra-basso must be omitted. In the third bar the bass must be transposed, and the intermixture of the hands in such quick time must be extremely difficult, if not impossible. But if it were accomplished with mechanical perfection, the melody and the accompaniment would be entangled in each other, and the

* With what right fifths and octaves are taken here (see page 71) must be sought for in Instructions for Composition, and the Science of Music.

light and airy passages of the violins completely overwhelmed by the deeper octaves. The second violin, therefore, must at all events be omitted, if the sense of the original were at all to be preserved. In more numerous or more diverging parts, still more must be sacrificed to obtain fluency and clearness of playing. When, for example, in the same symphony, the same phrase returns, but with the addition of the oboi from the third bar, they must be omitted, how beautiful soever their effect is in the orchestra, in order not to disturb the effect of the melody.

If part of the score must be omitted, the question arises, which part? we answer, that only whose non-execution seems to interfere least with the intention of the composition. Then again, among many parts, the least important. Thus we omitted above, the merely covering and accompanying hautboys, in favour of the principal melody; and at No. 381, the merely corroborating second violin, in favour of the first. The same phrase appears again, but is introduced by an intervening phrase of flute, hautboy, and bassoons, so that the violins come in with their melody between the wind instruments. Here the latter can by no means be omitted, not even in order to make the principal melody more perceptible.

We should play it thus:—

382.

and omit only the last *tone* of the flute and hautboy (.*f♯*), in order to favour the expressive sixth of the principal melody; but it is the will of the composer that this principal melody should be introduced, covered and veiled by the wind instruments.

But we are not always obliged to omit that which according to the score is impracticable, or which seems unfavourable It is sometimes sufficient to transpose a part by an octave. To this we cannot here add any further directions. It must be considered in each individual case, whether the transposition effects its object, viz., to make the score practicable and intelligible—whether it occasions any errors or unfavourable positions, or any diverging sense in the composition. Then again, it is necessary to return into the order of parts in the score, skilfully and without any disturbance.

Thirdly. There are many passages and configurations of *tones* of other instruments, which are either impossible on the pianoforte, or so difficult as to become inefficient on it; or again, which require other treatment. The viola or tenor accompaniment, in No. 381, may serve as an example: still more strikingly, however, such repetitions as the following on bowed instruments, viz.:—

383. *Allegro.*

which produce them easily in the most rapid succession, and with every gradation of *piano* or *forte*; whereas, upon the pianofore (particularly in third, sixth, and octave duplications) they are either impracticable or excessively difficult, and the *piano* of the original instrument is perfectly unattainable. In this case we must imagine other forms, capable of producing upon the pianoforte the same effect, or nearly so, as that produced by the other instruments through the original forms of the score.

If we have to *accompany* from the score, another system must be adopted. In most cases of this description, it is choral, or compositions in many parts, which are to be accompanied, and it now becomes the duty of the accompanyer to assume also the direction, or at least the leading of the song, and of assuring and aiding it in difficult passages, in the event of hesitation, &c. Here it can no longer be necessary, and would often be very injurious, to think of exhibiting all the parts of the score on the instrument. If the voices are sure, and not too weakly set, their parts can be passed over, in order to allow the player to make the performance more full from the diverging accompaniment.

With regard to sufficient strength, it is necessary in the first place to think of the bass voices; and we would willingly omit wide harmonies, and a complete exhibition of the middle voices—particularly in strong, serious, and otherwise elevated compositions,—in order to leave the left hand free to play the bass exclusively in octaves, and thereby increase its strength. In like manner, for the characteristic forms of the higher voices, which ought to be distinctly produced, we would devote the right hand exclusively, in order to make them effective or to play them in octaves. We would even occasionally omit such secondary parts as the hand might reach (page 109), only in order to leave the principal part quite free, and that it might be the more effectively heard. It may indeed easily happen that the accompaniment of a passage in many parts, should be limited to two forcible and elevated parts, or even to one only; and in that manner the composer's own precise object has been probably hit upon, namely, the performance with a pianoforte and not with an orchestra.

If any error or wavering should be perceptible in a single voice or in the whole mass, it is the immediate duty of the accompanyer to give assistance. During the performance of a perhaps richly-played accompaniment, this is scarcely to be expected. It would be better, instead of simplifying it, to have recourse to strong thorough-bass chords, as they are called; or to play the faltering voices particularly loud, or, if necessary, quite alone. But this should not be done without urgent necessity, and then it requires judgment and skill to return from such deviations to the richer accompaniment from the score.

So much we offer, as a few directions in one of the most interesting exercises in the practice of music. Diligent application, proceeding always from the more simple to the more elaborate and complex—personal reflection—and, if possible, the leading and supervision of an enlightened teacher skilful in score (of whom, indeed, there is no excess), will now conduct us to the goal. With regard to the order of study (apart from the rule that we are to go from compositions in few parts to those in many), the most easy will be generally the Italian ecclesiastical music; then Handel's and Gluck's scores; Haydn and Mozart's symphonies and quartets; then Mozart's operas; after which Haydn's oratorios; and lastly, Beethoven's and Seb Bach's works; not to mention many other masters—would form a reasonably progressive plan of instruction. It must be understood as a matter of course, that this can be only an approximative indication; and that many of Beethoven's and Haydn's movements are easier to perform than many Italian or some of Handel or of Haydn; Haydn particularly, is rich in peculiar combinations, and often surprises the performer with passages difficult of execution, but precious as artistic ideas.

It might here be asked, whether an arrangement for the pianoforte carefully constructed, might not perform the office of score-playing much more surely and better?

The first *it certainly might;* for the constructor of an arrangement has time at will to consider everything, and to choose the most favorable out of all possibilities. The last, *certainly not.* Arrangements for the pianoforte* are generally made for sale, and therefore in a manner suitable to the greater number of less advanced and educated players; and hence, moreover, they are far from containing all that a good player would derive from the same source. But were that not the case, an arrangement can contain only one exemplification of the score; but it is evident that even the most full performance of a score can only imperfectly unfold the riches of the composition. The player who has a deep insight into the score, will not, however, play at one time in the same manner as at others; he will introduce various parts on various occasions, and omit them as it may suit the different turns he may give to his always imperfect production; and so by degrees, at least, he will produce more from the score than the best arrangement can represent.

Not without weight, also, are the higher enjoyment and deeper inspiration which flow from the contemplation of the score, to him who is master of its performance. We often find that such a one plays preferably and better, and even with greater ease from the score than from the arrangement.

SEVENTH DIVISION.

MUSICAL EDUCATION AND INSTRUCTION.

FIRST SECTION.—REMARKS ON THE PRESENT STATE OF MUSIC.

The consideration of what is the true end and aim of musical instruction, and the surest path to its attainment, must be very interesting to an author, anxious to be serviceable to those whose early steps

---

* A celebrated exception from this accusation is the arrangement for four hands, by F. Liszt, of Beethoven's symphony in C minor (at Breitkopf and Härtel's), in which the magnificent orchestral constructions are rendered with completeness, dignity, and power; and moreover, with a deep and accurate insight into the nature of the Pianoforte. The Pastoral Symphony however, elaborated with equal care, could not be equally successful. In this composition, the orchestral effects are as unattainable as they are indispensable.

he guided, and desirous, also, of imparting a few hints and remembrances to his more advanced scholars, now perhaps teachers and guides themselves. For these objects no place is perhaps better suited than the present.

We therefore add these remarks, which partly belong immediately to our subject, and are at all events nearly related to it, *on the object and method of musical education for the people, and for the profession.*

Such observations, however, can be founded only on a clear view of the nature and tendency of music, and on a free and unprejudiced inspection into its present condition; and in the first place, in our own country, if indeed any one can flatter himself with the hope of possessing sufficient knowledge and freedom of opinion. Each individual commands only a limited circle of vision; and he who has looked around with lively interest, and has perceived the necessity of seeing with his own eyes and from his own point of view, knows how insufficient and uncertain are the communications of others in comparison with his own experience. Every individual must further confess, that he himself is influenced more or less by the circumstances of the moment, and that posterity alone can pronounce judgment upon all.

But if we are obliged to leave the decision to our successors, it is also our duty to consider what we are, and what they may become. We are bound, therefore, to examine and weigh our times, and we are content that our judgment on them be converted into evidence on ourselves before a higher tribunal.

If we cast a glance at the present state of music amongst us, we behold an all-pervading musical activity, unexampled in any former period; unless, perhaps, in the golden days of Italy and Spain. Then from vast cathedrals, and from hills crowned with pilgrims, streamed the wave of sacred song; then the festive trumpets clanged from glittering balconies, at rejoicings of princes and nobles; then the balmy nights were musical with harp and guitar in lovely hands. Then, also, our own country reechoed in Luther's great days with his mighty melodies, which rolling from the holy choir, awakening, confirming, and inspiring, swept through the crowded market, and busy streets, into the domestic circle and private chamber.

What in those days gushed from excited nature and internal emotion, has been transmitted to us, closely allied as it is, to the deep poetical nature of our countrymen, and now seems to exercise an unlimited dominion over us.

So our public gardens, our domestic circles, our festivals teem with music;· numerous and continually increasing bands march with our armies; and our tremulous ball-rooms are sinking under the oppression of pleasure.* What town is there so small, as not to have at least winter concerts? What numberless amateurs, what quartet associations, what concerts of all descriptions crowd our larger cities! What period has ever seen in all places, and the whole year throughout, so many operas performed? and can anything at any period be compared to our immense gatherings of cities with cities in our musical festivals? In fine, what period has ever acknowledged, as ours has done, by word and deed, and with such sacrifices of time and gold, the indispensable and salutary effect of music in human education?

This spread of music, this universal sympathy in the concourse of sweet sounds, corresponds with the means which have been applied to it. However expensive instruction, instruments, and musical matters may be, all families of the middle classes, as well as of the higher, seek to procure them. Nowhere is there a deficiency of masters. In all schools singing is practised,—seminaries, universities, and especial music schools continue the instruction to a higher grade. Everywhere singing academies, instrumental classes, and musical societies for private and public performance are established. City and state officials provide means, and assist in the performances in chapels and choirs, and in public instruction. Our book trade supplies works of art of all times, more numerously, commodiously, and cheaply than ever; and the construction of musical instruments is improved with the advance of the mechanical arts.

Such is the wonderful power of music to open all hearts, to gain sympathy and support from those even, who, by deficient education or organization, are unable to participate in its joys,—who bring their offerings to her fane, and then pleased, but unendowed, retire.

How has music acquired this influence, and how does she requite our love and devotion?

She has the power, she is all-powerful in man, because she grasps him in all his fibres and nerves, corporeally and spiritually, the whole body and soul, sensibilities and thoughts. The roughest natures tremble at her dread clangour, while none resist her soft and captivating *tones*. Her corporeal effect is irresistible, magical—for the simply corporeal sensation suggests already that these tremblings of the nerves reach the inmost depths of the soul; that this corporeal charm is rendered holy and consecrated by its connexion with the foundation of our existence. He who has drawn from his soul its most delicate, most powerful, most secret feelings,—who has commanded them at will,—who has cast a light into the unknown depths of the mind, and there passed a dreamy consciousness; he who has seen in this undulating play of the soul, aspirations, visions, and the deepest ideas, erect as the commanding spirits,— who knows that our existence would be incomplete without the world of sounds, such a one comprehends that the spiritually sensitive pleasure in music leads us on only to make our sensibilities more delicate and more excitable, to civilize and fructify the inmost foundations of the mind, and to manifest to our souls the highest expectations, a new invisible world of ideas, a new aspect of existence.

But its nature is two-fold, like that of man—it is corporeal from matter, and spiritual from the mind. Its influence may elevate us from a rough, hard, and

---

* Let any one witness the insatiable spell-like influence of our waltzing, accompanied by the resounding swell of the trombone in Strauss's dances.

useless condition, to humanity, sentiment, and action—it can soften and correct our sensibilities, awaken our expectations, enable us to soar above the purest humanity into the region of the god-like; and, in this inward elevation, fill us with the real working power of goodness. But this same influence of sounds may bury us in the seductive waves of corporeal sensation, always existing, though concealed; it may efface all noble feelings and sustaining power from the soul, and abandon us to thoughtlessness, infirmity of purpose, and the ever-destroying attractions of the senses, in whose train follow the strange twins—satiety and insatiability; and, lastly, the fearful loss of interest in everything.

How does the dangerous and well-loved art repay our love and gifts?

Everything in art is pure, and noble, and good. Our weakness is to blame if her gifts turn to poison; if we, being arrived at the threshold of her temple, lie sinking there; if we hear her voice in our souls, but forsake her consecrated halls, and lose ourselves in the outer courts, destined only for the offal of the beasts of sacrifice.

Much has happened which is calculated to disturb and distress, in our time, the pure enjoyment and the legitimate progress of art. The waves of political events beat awfully in the minds of men, and into all forms of social and inward life; but still there is wanting in the masses a uniting, elevating, and spiritually exciting idea. Overwhelming circumstances and recollections have called forth on the one side, vehemence of desires, and the habit of impetuously-changing impressions; and, on the other, their opposite conditions—relaxation and a deep want of quietude of mind, and of a cessation of mental struggle. In both relations, materiality—as the element of more powerful excitations and effects, or as the soft tranquilizer of mind by lulling the senses—has obtained a height of command unknown to art; and the spectacle more than once witnessed before is now repeated—that in such moments, when the tension of the German mind and character of their own peculiar feelings become relaxed, and collapse in the masses of the people, a foreign hand, especially the frivolity and fluttering prosaicalness of France, or the enervating sensuality of Italy, assumes the sceptre. Then it is, so far as regards music, at the opera, that the foreign productions gain an easy and sure victory by display and exaggeration. How many wiles are employed to charm the senses in those exhibitions, to distract and intoxicate the mind of the spectator, and to cloud his judgment as to the real matter before him; and how can all the other branches and departments of art remain uninfected by such an influence, when they proceed from the theatre—the highest and most commanding position of the arts.

If, on the one hand, we must confess the degrading direction to materialities of the foreign operas, a direction which in these times derives so much influence from our being accustomed and, indeed, forced, as it were, by the public and political circumstances of the west, to keep our eyes on that quarter, as to the dial-plate of disturbance in Europe; so, on the other hand, we will recognise the positive advantages we have received from them (which have been but too much neglected by our musicians and poets) in the more urgent endeavour to produce dramatic, or, at least, scenic animation and effect from combined personal situations in more common relations, and in the public and ordinary events of life. Only when, through the real poverty, degradation, and error of the foreign opera, our musicians shall have recognized this element, and have adopted it with dignity and truth in the German opera, will our art herein also celebrate its inevitable triumph.

Until that period the foreign style will be predominant,—will be loved; it will draw after it the artistic requirements of the multitude, and will satisfy them. The inevitable consequences of this dominion are,—outward attractions and excitements of the senses—external magnificence with internal poverty—superficial contentment in lieu of soundness and depth—a yielding to unworthiness, and a base condescension of dignity and position to mere parade of effect. Degraded music, a mere matter of amusement, is dragged everywhere; it pursues us into our gardens and at our meals; and, in endeavouring to fill up the void in desolated social intercourse, it alike deafens our ears to all rational converse, and deadens our feelings to the true powers of art. Loss of character and significance pervades all its branches, and is followed by increasing loss of interest. The more we depart from the idea of the whole, from the meaning, from the conception of art and the unity of artistic works, the more decided is the progress of that disorder,—that inward death of art occasioned by considering the means as the principal, and neglecting the end. Thus, those foreign seductive operas have been able to attain their influence over us. We have been blinded by the authority of their origin, and by the fame of their highly-gifted singers; by the extraordinary means employed to produce effect; by the very ridiculousness of some of these incidents, such as a sale by auction, a tender, sentimental post-boy, not to mention more recent instances, which, from their utter novelty on the opera boards, are absolutely startling. On the other hand, we are ourselves reproached, and not without some reason, with not being sufficiently attentive to our means—a bad habit of which we trust bitter experience will correct us.

Hence, music assumes to us at present an aspect which is by no means satisfactory.

We have abundance of music, but little pleasure from it. We obtain from it distraction and amusement, where we might derive thought and elevation. Thus is is with our fashionable opera, where its frequenters are swooning with giddiness for a moment, and then are left empty, and in another moment forget it. So in our concerts, whose utmost effort is to display an extraordinary artist, creating astonishment, the most fruitless of all states of the mind. So in our public music, which, without moving our sympathy, destroys our conversation. So it is, in fine, in our social parties, where confined to heartless school exercises, or ill-judged repetitions of fashionable airs, instead of producing the enjoyments of art, it causes more embarrassment, envy, and tediousness than we are willing to confess to each other, or even to ourselves.

We willingly avert our eyes from the unpleasant spectacle. It is not, however, here the place, nor our object, to pronounce a judgment; but we should certainly wish to call the attention of those to the subject, who feel an interest in art, and in popular education. And indeed, notwithstanding the corruptions and weaknesses which we have lamented, we must be total strangers to the feelings of our kind, not to acknowledge and honor the most earnest and promising exertions and struggles, the strong adhesion to the works of the elder masters, from Beethoven back to Gluck and Seb. Bach, the most extraordinary, although perhaps technical industry of executants, the zealous competition of youth for scholastic and universal cultivation, so indispensable to artists, all of which has never been so conspicuous as in our times. There is to be observed, however, in all this very praiseworthy labour and exertion, a considerable degree of unconsciousness or indifference as to matter and object, which must be overcome before the proper fruits can be expected; and which presents to our view, occasionally, depth and superficialness, genuine and spurious art, in equal estimation; while the undistinguishing pursuit of good and bad is honored by the name of impartiality, and discrimination is denounced as illiberality.

A widely-spread activity, of great promise if well conducted, prevails in the track and propagation both of the good and of the spurious, but the individualizing, animating idea, the leading consciousness, the highest power of art, have still to be drawn out from their deep recesses.

Many noble-minded and earnestly-thinking people have viewed in this confused whirlpool of struggling powers, the death of that art which has been the bright sunny ray of their lives, in Bach, or Gluck, or Mozart, or Beethoven; but we will hold fast to the conviction that art is a necessity of human nature, and is therefore equally imperishable. On the same ground, we conclude that, in any particular nation, music cannot be destroyed and lost but with the nation itself; although both together may undergo moments of error, delusion, or failure. A well-pondered review of the history of music teaches us this; and an elevated contemplation of what our nation is, and of what music requires and can expect from it, upholds, in times of undeniable retrogression, those hearts which beat for something beyond the fleeting moment.

SECOND SECTION.—THE RIGHT OBJECT AND THE RIGHT MEANS.

What is really the proper object of all musical education and employment?

Joy in the art—we declare as the first object. A joyless occupation in it—and how frequently do we meet it! how common is the observation, unfortunately, that in the learning and practising of music, the original delight is quickly extinguished, never to be felt again in its pristine vigour and productiveness—is fatal to the artistic sense, and is, indeed, more injurious than total disoccupation, since it not only misapplies the time which might have been otherwise profitably employed, but also destroys our capacity of receiving satisfaction from art.

But the joy must be really *artistic*—not foreign; and still less must it be opposed to art. We would hereby deprecate the *tickling vanity* which loves to make a display of extraordinary technical facility, and plumes itself on difficulties overcome. Nothing is more foreign nor further than this littleness from true art, whose high calling it is to raise us from the narrow limits of personal feelings, into the region in common, of universal joy, love, and inspiration; nothing is more inimical and destructive to the true sense and enjoyment of art, than this poisonous mildew, which overlays artistic activity and its productions. Nothing more surely draws the mind from the purifying atmosphere of art, into the petty, narrow strivings and contentions of self-seeking vanity, than this eager ostentation of personal skill; and, in fine, nothing manifests more clearly to an intelligent mind, the wide gulf which separates vain from true art, than this exchange of its outward means, for its inward soul and object. How general, however, is this striving in our parties and concerts! How rarely is the joy of the listeners the object of our concert players and amateurs! How much nearer have they not at heart, to astonish the less proficient, and to startle the unartistic crowd with newly-invented contrivances, with a technical composition of a Chopin, or a study of a Thalberg, or whatever the latest finger-artist may be called. And how often is it not the teachers who urge their pupils to this pernicious competition, simply in order to obtain more scholars! The lowest, most unreflecting, merely corporeal pleasure of music, the most superficial enjoyment of a skipping dance, is more artistic, more productive and nobler, than this monstrosity, which is so widely diffused amongst us. The feeling performance of the most trivial song or the most simple waltz, is a stronger proof of the ability of the scholar and of the teacher, than those precocious and forced, though in reality cheap productions of vanity.

The corporeal pleasure caused by art, awakens by itself a spiritual participation; and this *spiritual participation in art*, we regard as the highest object to which our employment therein is to be directed. If we do not close our heart and sensibilities, by caprice and ill-directed exertion,—if we do not ourselves destroy our feelings, and the natural operation of our minds, emotion will spring of itself from the corporeal apprehension of the artistic work; a more elevated life will flow through our nerves, and joy through our mind, such as the pure enjoyment of art alone can produce; the assurance of community, of well-being, will loosen the hard crust of egotism from our hearts, and bind us the more closely in sympathy and affection with the friends who participate in our pleasures. The heart opens itself willingly to new sensations and an altered state of mind occasioned by works of art, and receives them

H

devotedly, pure, and free from all the dross and sharp asperities of real personality; it is a communion of one soul with others, full of the internal feelings of humanity, and yet exempt from all oppressive materiality, or other disturbing objects. And thus this shadowy being, invoked by the musician's art, waves its life of high significence before us; we live in it, in pleasure or in pain, as the spirit of the artist wills; with him, faultless and untouched, our personality becomes involved in a manifold spiritual existence, and we experience in ourselves the countless riches of this spiritual life, together with our narrowly-limited corporeal reality. Herein we behold long departed beings and circumstances—those pure forms which *Gluck* evoked from Greece and the enchanted East: the patriarchal simplicity and dignity of that people, out of whose darkness the light of the world was to come, in *Handel's* songs: the mad confusion of the Pharisees and their party, before the holiness of the new covenant, in Bach's immortal works. All these pass before us; ages long in oblivion, seem sensibly present.

Whatever can move the human heart in innocence, joy, delicacy, and childish humour, the most lovely play of the imagination, and the most mysterious sensations of our spiritual essence,—all that Haydn, Mozart, and Beethoven could feel or imagine, is laid open to us, and becomes our own.

The real indwelling in art, and sincere devotion to it, are essential conditions in artistic education; without them we cannot participate in its inestimable gifts; *they are absolutely indispensable.*

It is not the possession of great artists, nor of great works of art, which insures to a nation or to its gifted individuals, a genuine artistic education, and thereby the full enjoyment, the highest pleasures of art. If such were the case, no nation could be more assured than ours of the highest musical education; since, during the last century, at least, our musicians have produced the most lofty and most pregnant ideas that have ever been embodied in sound. We have, on the other hand, experienced within a single century, after three noble exaltations, in the days of Bach and Handel, of Gluck,—Haydn, and Mozart, —and of Beethoven; also three several depressions from our upward flight; nay, if we will believe the loudest and most numerous voices of the day, it would seem that in many minds *even the remembrance* were lost of what in former days were universally acknowledged to be our brightest landmarks to excellence.

Playing and hearing only, cannot be relied on as a sufficient means of education, although they must be the foundation and companions of all musical cultivation; for we hear bad music as well as good; and we know that the weak and spurious produces its effect (often quicker and to a greater extent) as well as the elevated and genuine. We must herein the more readily acknowledge the power of sound, that even in its perverted employment it still exerts a vast influence over the mind and senses,—apart, moreover, from the effect of secondary objects, of prejudice, and of fashion. Indeed, it is not to be denied, that the corporeal effect of sound acting in large masses, in conjunction with considerable talent, magnified, perhaps, by partiality into great superiority, in the performers, is capable of producing from very moderate or indifferent works an effect which may surprise artists of judgment; but the cause of that effect is not in the composition—it is the attribute of the large body or volume of sound, and of the influential partiality for the performers. Hence we may perceive how small the claims may be of many a vaunted work of art, whose pretensions have been estimated by its immediate consequences. Those persons, however, are acting very injudiciously, who, desirous of no further struggle, seem contented and satisfied with the good that exists. It will indeed endure without further exertion. It will be conveyed from artist to artist, and the magnificent structure of art will be completed, so far as may be permitted to humanity. But the communication, the participation *of artistic, and therewith civilized elevation to our contemporaries*, cannot be allowed to remain stationary. The history of the world is reckoned by centuries, and at wide intervals. The moments of improvement progress like stars in the heavens, and with them as they roll; but the limited space of human life cannot dispense with its portion of their beneficent illumination.

In fine, the mere external, technical, mechanical, formal education, does not reach to the deep spring, where the lifestream of art is generated and preserved. It is but too often observable, unfortunately, how empty and unproductive this false external cultivation leaves the mind; how, in its pursuit, year after year, full of the noblest germs of life, and capable of the highest joys of art, are allowed to fade and wither away. It has been remarked but too frequently, that these disciples of technicality, these virtuosi, these amateur dilettanti, these thorough bass cognoscenti, and æsthetical critics, have the most unsatisfactory conception of art, that they have little sympathy with it, and are utter strangers to its nature and operation.

True artistic education, like true art, is not concerned merely with the technicalities, which make only a handicraftsman, nor with mere outward considerations, which, instead of living art, produce nothing but dead abstractions. It is governed by the essential nature of its duties, and assumes for its object the bringing into life and action the highest and fullest conception of art in each individual, and in the greatest number of individuals in the whole nation. In the pupil, it searches for the germ of artistic susceptibility and capacity. This spark it cherishes and frees from obstructions, and nourishes and strengthens into the power of life. It then contemplates the regions of art, and examines what has hitherto been produced. Of all this, and of that which is most worthy, it endeavours to convey as much as possible to the scholar, according to the power of each individual. This education does not move the hand and fill the ear alone, but penetrates by the senses into the soul; through the deeply moved sensibilities it awakens the inward consciousness. And now the waves of sound may surge and roll—what the inward consciousness has apprehended, that which has become a sentiment and property of the mind, can be safely preserved and extended.

This, in brief, is *the object of true artistic education,—to elevate the capabilities, mental and corporeal, to the highest point.* This is the indispensable process, without which, high attainment in art is not possible. This is more or less the enlightened struggle of all who either wholly or in part devote their life and powers to artistic employment; this, whether it be acknowledged or not, is the absolutely undeniable and indispensable obligation of all teachers to produce.

Shall it be considered an empty dream to desire for our country, so deeply gifted in the art of sound, a general *popular education* in music, in that high and only true sense? Does not this want and right proclaim itself from the deep inborn feelings of the people, from the overflowing abundance of their conceptions, from our countless artists, from our display of the richest productions of art in advance of nations? Shall our festivals be never more joyous with our *national songs*, which are more abundant, more varied, more melodious, and more deeply touching than those of any people on earth? Shall the evangelical church be perpetually deprived of her own appropriate music, which centuries ago was created for her? Shall the catholic church, in whose sacred service music assumes so important a function, suffer in our country so deep a degradation as it has endured in Italy, where movements from Rossini's and Bellini's operas, and Auber's overtures, disgrace the most holy moments of the service? Or in Spain, where in recent times, church music is dumb, even to the psalmody of the priesthood? We fear it not, and those who with us have a higher trust, will labour incessantly with all their strength, and on all occasions, to attain the highest object. We, a laborious people, strong in body and mind, must strive for a higher elevation than tender nature has conferred on her southern children, to amuse their happy hours.

In so important a matter, however, the word or deed of individuals can do but little. The State only can produce the accomplishment of our aspirations. From this source much may be expected, if to good will, be added the power of finding fit agents,—not handicraftsmen who would propagate their own peculiarities, but men who would add the spirit of art to its form, mind to technicality; in short, men who have made true art the object of their lives.

We must, at the same time, acknowledge that the condition and progress of art are entirely dependant upon the state of the political and moral relations and movements of the people. This has been already observed by many in the direction of art during the last ten years. But the history of art proves that her destiny in this regard has been governed by the highest wisdom and goodness. Let, therefore, each individual in joyful confidence do all he ought, and may, and can; and tranquilly await the result of doing his duty.

THIRD SECTION.—OF THE DISPOSITION OR VOCATION FOR MUSIC.

Considering the importance which we attribute to musical education, and the large demands on time and powers which application to it requires, the question becomes serious; what result can be reasonably expected by each individual from his exertions in this pursuit?

This education, in order to be profitable, assumes certain predispositions in the pupil; and many a person may be drawn into a chain of labours and sacrifices, which, from want of natural appliances, may remain unrewarded. Many indeed, not ungifted individuals, capable of participating to a certain extent in art, being seduced by its charms, devote their whole lives to it and discover too late that their musical power is not sufficient for the profession, although it enables them to increase their enjoyment of art, and to have a deeper inward perception of its richness and beauty. The danger of a grave error, perhaps of a life thrown away, is more considerable to a gifted individual, than to one not so endowed; and even in the minor case of a mere amateur, the question is so important, that we cannot pass it over in a serious view of musical education, although we cannot hope to give a general and particular answer, which shall be, in all cases satisfactory.

All men, with extremely few exceptions, *have a disposition for music.* They have even *more disposition* than is generally attributed to them; more than they themselves are accustomed to think. But nothing is more common than that this disposition, unrecognized by hesitating prejudice, neglected through idleness and indifference, or led astray by erroneous treatment, should become suppressed. The extremely rare exceptions are manifested by a perfect indifference to music, even to its corporeal effect, or indeed, in some cases, by a physically perceptible repugnance to it. In this case, pleasurable sensations can be derived from the measure, or from the rhythm only.

It is much more difficult to decide, *how far the disposition* of any determined individual extends; what may be expected from its cultivation; and whether it be such as to justify the adoption of music as the special vocation of life.

It may be asserted in general, *from hundreds of experiments and instances,* and from the contemplation of the subject, that

The disposition of each individual is equivalent, and is worth cultivation, in proportion, to the pleasure felt by the individual in the art itself.

The pleasure in the art itself, not in the many subsidiary gratifications it may produce, and which may accompany an artistic life—not, therefore, the *caprice of fashion,* to learn music because others do —not the *vanity* of being better educated, nor of gaining the highest prize by redoubled exertion; all these pleasures abandon us, either before or soon after we have accomplished our object; they have been our reward, such as it was, but they were not the true pleasures of art, which in the real artist grow with his growth, and are immortal as the soul that feels them. Hence, we see so many scholars, discontinuing, as soon as the days of instruction are past, all connexion with art; and hence, also, many a master, when his daily task is done, drags on the burthen of a weary life in an unloved profession, in useless sighs or resigned indifference.

But that the disposition exists in the proportion of our love of art, will be confessed by every keen observer of experience; and even without experience, we might infer that such would be the fact, since it would be purposeless to have a faculty implanted in us, which we have no power of calling into action.

He who takes pleasure in music, will soon try to imitate it; as we may remark in the youngest children, who generally sing, after their fashion, before they speak. *It is chiefly in the means* of musical employment, from ignorance of technicalities, that errors occur. A person may be seized with a desire to sing, but have only an indifferent voice, or rather, more probably, whose voice has been injured; or he may devote himself to an instrument, for the performance on which he is deficient in power or in corporal structure. But even in this latter case, nature will often maintain her rights, if the musical desire be original (not instilled or caught from example), and the insufficient organ will at last be developed, or it will be sustained by other powers, and completed or replaced. In all such cases, however, it is advisable to seek counsel from the skilled in the matter.

If, apparently contrary to our views, the disposition for and pleasure in music be so often concealed, or, indeed, seemingly absent,—or, if the advance or delay of the learner vary from our expectations, we shall be led to acknowledge the probability of our departure from *the system required by nature* for education in music, in addition to our doubtful judgment, as to the musical disposition. This disposition is composed of several powers, which are sometimes found singly, and sometimes in combination, but each of which must be separately sought and nourished, long before musical instruction, commonly so called, begins. We must come to a clear understanding upon these points. They are decisive as to the question, whether music ought to be comprehended within the course of our occupations, and very important in the consequences of its admission.

Every participation in music presupposes that it makes some pleasurable impression either corporeal or mental. The most immediate is that which is produced by the mass of sound, or any particularly agreeable character of sound, the crash of a brass band, or the silvery tone of a little bell, &c. It is simply of an elementary and material nature, and warrants no mental participation, and therefore no mental disposition. It is only in the higher region that the spiritual effect of sound is perceived, and the corporeal sensations then show themselves to be a distinct portion of the disposition for art.

Our attention is next called to motion, measure, and rhythm. A deep meaning may be in rhythm: and the forms of bars are susceptible of endless variety, whereby significance is endeavoured to be shown. The groundwork of all this is the placing or distribution of more or less emphatic moments in equal measures of time. Rhythm and measure depend upon the fixing or estimating one *tone* to be twice, four times, or half, one fourth part, &c., as long as another. The process is facilitated by placing together parcels of moments collectively equal (though unequal among themselves) into equal divisions of time, which time within the divisions is divided in the simplest manner possible, by two or three, forming the bars of two or three parts, or of more parts in the same ratio. This is a matter merely of the understanding, of measuring and reckoning. The distinguishing of the chief and secondary parts of the bar, by accentuating the first, is also purely mechanical. We may therefore consider the rhythmic disposition to be within the capacity of any rational being. We may conclude further, from the multitudes of raw recruits who march in exact time, and of threshers, who wield the flail in perfect three or four-part order, that the idea that men in general are defective in the perception of measure in time, is a mere prejudice.

A higher qualification, quite distinct from the preceding, is the *perception of tone;* the capability of distinguishing different *tones*, and of forming a determined and more or less durable conception of their relation to each other.

The pitch, or height or depth of a *tone*, is represented scientifically by the number of vibrations of the sounding body which produces it. Leibnitz has even described Music (mathematically considered) as a concealed mental arithmetic, making unconscious calculations. But it seems more probable that the immediate apprehension of *tones* depends on a sympathy between the nerves of the hearer and the vibrations of the sounding body. The vibrations, however, of even inanimate bodies, produce sounds in other bodies similarly tuned, and moreover, call forth different but related sounds: and we find also, that trained or imitating birds; and the youngest infants, when they begin to learn singing or whistling from us, become imbued with, and can reproduce *tones* and successions of tones simply from hearing them.

Hence we may presume that also the faculty of a musical ear is common to most, if not to all men, so far as they can hear at all. But in this particular quality, the degrees of endowment are widely different, according to inward disposition or foreign assistance. The Author has never met with an instance of any person incapable of perceiving the difference between low and high; but it is common to find persons unable to distinguish with certainty a tone from half a tone, a third from a fourth, or a fourth from a fifth, until after some instruction and practice. Smaller intervals, as for example, a comma, or even what is called a quarter-tone, are often unappreciable to otherwise gifted musicians, especially pianists; while on the other hand, the finest gradations are usually perceptible to persons not possessed of any considerable musical qualifications, such as experimenters in acoustics, and pianoforte-tuners, who have educated the ear to such minute discrimination.

It is very common to confound this fine appreciation of sounds, with talent for music; or at least, to consider it as an indication of that talent. This, however, must not be assumed without many allowances. If this faculty be deficient or manifestly feeble, we may certainly suppose that the original powers of the mind have not been applied to the living sounds of music; nevertheless, more than one example can be named of very small or very imperfectly-developed appreciation of *tone*, accompanied by very considerable susceptibility for music.* On the other hand, the keenest perception of *tonic* differences is by no means a sign of, nay,—it is not essentially necessary for musical talent. Still less are certain external capabilities of this faculty, which are not uncommon, to be considered of any importance. Thus, there are persons not at all remarkable for musical talent, who can carry home with them from the orchestra the pitch of any piece of music, and reproduce it at pleasure. This is certainly not a useless faculty of memory, but it has no connection with deeper powers, and may indeed rather indicate a diminished activity of the imagination, unless it have been acquired by long habituation to the orchestra. On the other hand, it occasionally happens that highly-gifted singers and violinists permit themselves certain deviations from abstract purity of intonation, not from any want of perception, but from an impulse of the original and natural relations of sound, as distinguished from our artificial temperaments, or possibly from exaggerated expression.

If to these fundamental qualifications we add memory for musical compositions, a moderate activity of intellectual comprehension, and a certain degree of courage or confidence, with the necessary dexterity of limb, member, voice and speech,—we shall have assembled all the qualifications necessary for the cultivation of music. We should, however, never delay encouraging the growth of the higher faculties —the sensibility of the mind, and feelings for the significance of compositions, and of the forms of composition, and that direction of the mind which tends to give musical form and embodiment to sensations and ideas—the so potent spell and mystery of the poet-musician.

We have thus endeavoured to give a determined idea of disposition for music. It is, as we have seen, a combination of properties, and is therefore found in different states of completeness. It is rarely denied altogether to any individual, but seems to exist in the most diversified gradation and variety.

* This seems to be particularly the case among the mass of the people of France. In that country, singing is perpetual, and yet it is, in an incredible proportion, false and unsteady in *tone*. The small development of the musical faculties, in this instance, seems to arise from the manner of life, more external than intellectual, of the nation. It is indicated by the circumstance, that, notwithstanding general education and a great susceptibility for music, so few great composers have been produced in France, and that the most remarkable advances in art in that country have been occasioned by foreigners, namely, Lully, Gluck, and Spontini. We Germans, however, remember with gratitude that our Gluck acquired his perfection and recognition in the bosom of the refinement and intellectual activity of that highly distinguished nation in his days, and that the susceptibility of that nation has shown an equally noble appreciation of Haydn and Beethoven.

But as this aptitude, like every other human faculty, is capable of indefinite extension and improvement, it is never possible, at least in the beginning or before some cultivation, to predict how far we may expect any specified individual to advance. We must return to our original assumption—

Every one will advance or be led so far as his *sincere* but *unalloyed pleasure in music* calls him.

He, therefore, who has a susceptibility for music, and feels pleasure in it, may with confidence devote so much time and labour to it as his peculiar calling and circumstances may allow. So long as it is a labour of love with him, it will be a labour of profit also; and thus, to such a one, instruction will be no unnecessary nor useless burthen, until the limits of his faculties be attained. And let every one remember, that the chief end of all artistic education is no other than the exaltation of our susceptibility of, and participation in art, for our greater happiness and improvement. In this view, neither will a heated imagination drag us into a professional life against nature and intention; nor will the poor ambition of showy attainments, quite foreign to the true idea of art, rob us of the genuine reward of our exertions.

He, however, who thinks he feels an impulse to devote his entire life to music, should examine seriously whether this impulse be not imaginary; whether it be not rather a feeling of occasional and momentary enthusiasm, than a permanent and steady love for art. Whether the chief inducement be not, perhaps, the apparently unrestrained and joyous tenour of artistic life, or ambition excited by the brilliant career of others. These outward seductive allurements are, for the most part, bitterly repented of when too late. There are, indeed, examples of success attained under such insufficient motives, but rarely accompanied by inward satisfaction, and generally embittered by the loss of the real pleasure of art, and of bodily health.

Those, finally, who consider themselves called upon to adopt composition as a profession for life, should undergo a most rigid self-examination. Their calling is the highest, but it is also the most exacting and uncertain; and no one can counsel them with well-grounded decision. *No person ought to dedicate himself to this branch of the profession, unless constrained by every impulse of his soul;* no one who can endure with patience any other occupation—who is not willing to sacrifice, for the satisfaction of that vehement and resistless vocation, all the security and comfort of his existence, and who cannot look with firmness on the chance of missing the chief aim of all his exertions. Such a vocation is generally, if not always, indicated in early years, by fanciful preluding, and attempts at composition. He who waits to compose, until he has learned the rules of composition, will rarely, if ever, be a composer. It is also to be considered, that a disposition thus early manifested, and in some degree fostered and nourished, has had time for development before the application of scientific rules,—that it is therefore in a more expanded and invigorated state, and gives the scholar the inestimable advantage of many imaginings and experiences, whereby confidence has been acquired, equally remote from timidity and from presumption This advantage, however, is not indispensable. True love and perseverance, although later in the field—but not too late—may still gain the victory.

A composer by profession will, however, soon discover that his occupation cannot be the exclusive business of life, for the simple reason, that no one can compose always. Poetry, whether in *tones*, or words, or colours, demands the most vivid moments only of our existence; and with all the requirements for its production and exhibition, must still leave much of our lives in vacancy: the brightest and richest genius has no other destiny, neither would any other be endurable. Further still from the student, must be the vain and unhallowed hope of obtaining a competence by his productions. The greatest artists, Bach, Haydn, Mozart, and Beethoven, were not able to accomplish that object. Such, indeed, has been sometimes effected by fashionable composers of the Italian Opera, patronized by the caprice of *prime donne*, but then only in advanced age. A subsidiary occupation has always been found necessary to a composer, such as singing, playing, conducting, or teaching; and notwithstanding the hindrance and burthen this occupation may perhaps now and then seem, it will be found a salutary and invigorating companion. Each of these occupations has a favorable and important aspect to the composer—one or more of them he must embrace, and this circumstance should have due weight in the choice of the profession.

FOURTH SECTION.—THE DEVELOPMENT OF THE MUSICAL FACULTIES.

We must have recognized that nature has given musical capabilities to most individuals; but that these powers and susceptibilities exist in the most manifold variety of gradations. The germ of these faculties, like that of all our other powers, is strengthened and unfolded by all the appearances and impressions of the outer world on us, from the moment of our birth; and when placed at the disposal of the instructor, it has already undergone a certain degree of expansion from the unconscious tuition of daily experience.

The development of the musical faculties, however, as far as regards the meaning of sounds, labours under disadvantages, particularly in northern climates, from which our other faculties are comparatively free. The most pressing wants and constantly urging requirements of life, call chiefly into action that other spiritual sense, the eye, in combination with the understanding. The child learns to distinguish earlier by the eye than the ear; while its understanding is almost incessantly employed in seizing the significance of sounds, as indicative of the objects of sense by which it is surrounded, rather than the meaning of sound in any musical relationship; a kind of affinity, which to the uneducated ear remains, perhaps, through life unknown. The musical element has less occasion to be exhibited by us more silent Germans, than among our southern and western neighbours. It is, nevertheless, as deeply significant, well defined, and powerful in our language, even as in the Italian, which, indeed, can claim superiority only in some degree of clearness, and an old prejudice in its favour.

Long continued neglect and suppression, indeed, of musical qualifications, are much to be lamented; more particularly during musical education itself, when such neglect operates most severely. Parents and teachers are more apt to complain of the want of disposition in their pupils, than to seek in themselves the cause of that deficiency. Only when the delays and the misapprehensions shall be attacked on all sides, and overcome, will our conviction be complete, that the musical qualifications given to most men are much more considerable than is generally believed.

OF THE TIME PREVIOUS TO LEARNING.

This period requires domestic care and solicitude, as a preparation for the directing hand of the master; and here it is, that the mother, as monitor of the awakening senses of her child, is called upon to exercise the budding susceptibilities on salutary objects, and shield their tender impressiveness from violent and distracting sensations. Certain determined sounds have an incalculable and lasting effect on the infant mind and senses, when presented to them without constraint or obvious intention. The pure sound of a little bell, the combined sounds of two or three glasses, producing, for example, $c—g$, and then $g—d—b$, the contrast of high clear sounds and low murmurings (in a decided rhythm, such, for example, as the following—

which appears sufficiently conformable to nature) are best calculated to affect the infant perceptions. It can easily be imagined, how at a later period, listening to the rolling thunder, to the whispering and rustling of the evening breeze, to the murmuring brook, to the moan of the impending storm, to the warbling of the nightingale, may penetrate into, and influence the yearnings and aspirations of fresh youthful existence, wherein are imbedded those bright germs of thought, whose future expansion and manifestation are exhibited in the high productions of genius, at once the glory and the despair of each succeeding age! But how many circumstances conspire to disturb, counteract, and disenchant these beautiful and fructifying moments of early youth, particularly in large cities! How necessary is help, where nature cannot be left alone! How harrassing and destructive, while the precious moments of culture are so few, that the delicate and tender perceptions should be jarred by the harsh rolling of the streets, the deafening crash of brazen bands, and the rough growl of drums; that their fine organizations should be either rent or palsied by coarseness or force, while yet scarcely awake to their legitimate functions! Let, therefore, every mother who has a perception of the charms of music, and of its civilizing influence, weigh well the importance of the early education of the senses. Her simple song,* in which perhaps the infant voice is blended, is the most natural, and often the most fruitful lesson. A march of the most simple melody, and merely drum rhythm, which the boy and his father perform together, round about in their apartment, inspires more delight and feeling of measure, than many a half-year's instruction. If by great good fortune the tender ear of childhood should be indulged with the delicious enchantment of an opera, the few enraptured hours thus spent may cast a broad and glowing beam of sunshine to the latest days of life. For such an initiation we could wish every child to enjoy the dear old, but ever fresh and young *Zauberflöte*, that child's fairy-play, which Mozart has immortalized with the power of prolonging and reproducing during all our lives the earliest and most innocent blossoms of youthful delight. In this play, congenial childhood enters with the sweetest self devotion into the wondrous and inconceivable passions of maturer age, and is carried away at last to the perception of the truth, to the dreaded dagger; but with such guileless purity, such forgetfulness of self, that the star-flaming queen can scarcely be reproached when she rises delicately, and without effort, in melting harmonies, from the midst of her sufferings. On the other hand, we would withhold from the young sensations, the old and revived operas of mere show and exaggerated effect; and more especially those prosaic representations of ordinary life, in which the music sinks with its subject into mere triviality and nothingness. In like manner we would spare our young pupils the infliction of chamber or social music, which in general they do not understand; and lastly, we recommend moderation in quantity. The first opera once,—the full organ in the church, when empty,—seldom warlike music, and still more rarely, a concert. These are important moments in the young and impressible existence, and must be of extraordinary occurrence. Moreover, we would petition for the liberty for all children to play freely after their own fashion, on the pianoforte; to invent, and search, and lose themselves as they please, so long as they do not injure the instrument. This *ad libitum* playing is mostly prohibited, particularly if the days of instruction have begun. The child is told to employ itself more usefully, in finger exercises or written compositions. But how shall the individual musical feelings, or the yet feeble inventive imaginings, be fostered and educated to self-power and trustfulness, if the only, and at this age indispensable means of cultivation be withheld? We are delighted to hear of the infant Mozart, who, in the third year of his short life, sought to arrange sounds in musical combination; and at the same time, we forbid the like practice to our own children, or disturb their often burning dreams of harmony with our shortsighted and self-sufficient worldly prudence.

We wish to say another word in these nursery details, concerning speech. It might almost be maintained, that we, in Germany, have more men who write, than speak well; so hollow and uncertain, so feeble and oppressively restrained does our magnificent, copious, and universally appropriate language appear in speech, while its perfections have only obtained for it the calumnies of undistinguishing foreigners, and the neglect of our own countrymen, who have mistaken, disfigured, and corrupted it. How seldom do we hear any one among us speak openly and freely from the chest! How rare is the pure, full sound of the vowels, or the clear distinctness of the manifold characteristic varieties of the consonants! When do we hear modulation of the voice in speaking? and rarer still, any attempt of raising or depressing the intonation, without the most abrupt helplessness? Much of this defective condition of our speech is probably owing to the rarity with us, of public speaking, and other restricting circumstances; but we doubt not that early education, and want of attention in after life, are, at least, equally culpable, in not removing these disadvantages, whose baneful influence indeed does not affect music alone.

Thus much we have thought it necessary to say, touching the fostering and development of the musical faculties before and with the commencement of musical instruction. More definite and minute particulars must be had from the teacher.

Of Instruction.

How often—we ask again—do we hear teachers complain of the want of disposition in their pupils, and how rarely is any serious exertion made *to develope and strengthen this disposition?* How seldom are the means anxiously and assiduously sought for, to strengthen the weak, and supply the deficient! Is, then, the object of musical instruction merely to enable the pupil to play a certain number of compositions,—to acquire an amount of mechanical cleverness, and a quick perception of visible signs? All this can be mastered by the understanding and corporeal aptitude alone, without any deeper participation in the soul; but it is also fruitless in the mind and disposition, and without life in artistic feeling. He, however, who is not satisfied with that empty and ineffective advantage, but thirsts for the really operative benefit of artistic cultivation, must seek it nowhere but in the fountain and domain of all art—in the artistic feeling,—and in the natural disposition from or to which everything is developed or tends.

Here a fundamental principle presses forward, which might seem too evidently correct to require mentioning, if it were not so often violated in practice. *We ought never to place anything before the scholar—no composition whatsoever, which he is not capable of completely understanding.* Works of deep meaning, much combination, or even merely great extent, require a certain maturity and settled formation of the mind for their performance, if they are to be presented with feeling and judgment, and not simply with mechanical dexterity. It would be thought ridiculous to give the works of Dante or Shakspeare to children, or even the easy extravagant fictions of Ariosto, and yet we require them to play

---

* We take this opportunity of recommending, for the above object, the collection of German Popular Songs, by Erk and Irmer, which we have already mentioned at page 34, in note. It contains a rich treasure of natural, refreshing, and joyous song.

Bach's fugues, and Beethoven's deepest works, or richly figurated concerted compositions; and we give grand opera scenes to beginners, who might delight both themselves and us in a simple natural song. Unfortunately, this process, with a little cleverness and mechanical diligence, cannot easily fail of producing an ostensible effect; and thus parents and scholars are deluded with the outward appearance of having made some progress—of a great step forward having been achieved; whereas, in reality, only one thing has been done, that is, nature has been paralysed and placed out of the reach of sympathy.

Of the Development of the Feeling of Measure.

It is in this matter that the complaints of want of perception chiefly originate. This defect is, indeed, often formally instilled into the scholar. The feeling of measure and sensation of rhythm—we repeat it,—are innate in every human being gifted with understanding, but, like every other faculty, in different gradations; and they are certainly not so far elaborated by nature, as to enable their possessors to distinguish and perform the manifold and artistically combined rhythms of our compositions. Let us examine one of the easiest sonatas of Mozart, Haydn, or Beethoven, or one of the airs of Spontini, Weber, or Rossini: what a number of digressing and artistically entangled rhythms! How the parts of bars are divided into quavers,—sometimes into semiquavers or triplets, with dots,—or joined together by binds and syncopations; what a variety of accentuations must occur in such a composition! Everyone who has but a proximate idea of this rhythmic multiplicity, must perceive at once, that without much care and education, the natural feeling of measure could not suffice for the performance of such productions. But this is just what the generality of teachers concern themselves the least about. If they pursue any regular plan in the instruction of the scholar, the compositions follow each other, almost exclusively, in the ratio of the dexterity they require in their execution. The entangled rhythm remains uncomprehended; and it is considered sufficient, if the measure, that is, the equableness of motion, be forcibly preserved by the perpetual counting of the master, accompanied by the pupil, and by incessant beating time in extraordinary and ridiculous attitudes. By these means, however, the feeling of measure, the finer rhythmic sense, and the insight into the nature of rhythm, cannot assuredly be inspired and developed. With every new composition, this misery of counting, beating, and stamping begins afresh, until a *mechanical habit of equality* is formed, instead of a *living feeling* for equal and uniform measure and its expression. It is unfortunately too true, that most musicians are content with the sense and capacity for mechanical equality of measure,—for the cold inanimate beat; and consider the rich and living rhythmical feeling as superfluous.

How easy is it, on the other hand, to an enlightened teacher, particularly in the beginning, to elucidate the various forms of rhythm by a methodical arrangement in respect of simplicity and increasing complicity or mixture! Marches for the boys, dances for the girls—four-hand playing upon the pianoforte, or playing with other instruments, making the accentuation perceptible from the beginning—repetition of purposely accented playing—in case of necessity, marching or exercising arranged motions by the pupil, to the playing of the master, or of another pupil under the eye of the master; all these expedients,—preceded, of course, by a perfectly clear explanation and analysis of the rhythm, and many small helps and incidents arising from the instruction itself, and which cannot now be named,—are the most appropriate means of cultivating the feeling of measure.*

Development of the Feeling of *Tone*.

Students of the pianoforte are in a still worse position with regard to the development of the sense of *tone*. Here elementary teachers imagine they have accomplished everything, if the scholar can play correctly the note before him. Whether he have a living perception of what he plays, or whether this excite any emotion or consciousness in him, is not thought worthy of consideration.

With better intentions, however, many teachers fail in their means. We will not again mention, that in respect of this faculty also, the choice of a profession must depend upon the capacity of the scholar; but proceed at once to the first means of awakening the perception of *tone;* to those means indeed, which, on false fundamental principles, are generally avoided or thrown aside.

The first practice is the exertion of our own faculties diligently, in seeking and inventing successions of *tones*.

In beginning the pianoforte (or any other instruments admitting similar exercises), the first lessons generally consist of a string of finger exercises, which are repeated in all the scales. On this occasion, we advise that no exercise be written for some time, but that the scholar imitate them from the teacher, and thus immediately imprint them on his

---

* It is only against excess in counting—against incessant and deafening counting aloud, and that insufferable beating time—that we wish to inveigh. These cannot be altogether dispensed with, particularly in the beginning. When their employment becomes necessary, the word used must be uttered sharply, whereby the feeling of measure is kept lively and attentive. A drawling utterance occasions indecision and uncertainty; impatient loudness deafens; and stamping the time disturbs the holding-on. A short loudly whispered "One! two!" of the teacher at the proper time, a gentle and punctual tap with the finger on the reading desk or on the arm of the pupil, governs the measure more surely, and excites the feeling of measure more intimately, than the unseemly grimaces by which many a leader endeavours to display his zeal. In distributions or divisions not easy to apprehend, and two-part order (for example, in the solution of crotchets into quavers, semiquavers, &c.), instead of "One!" two! we may count "Firstly! second!" in which the word may indicate the part of a bar, and each syllable a member thereof. If the phrase should change at once into three-part distribution, the Firstly! second! must be changed again into One! two! three! &c. In quick movements, half or even whole bars only are counted. The playing of difficult passages an octave higher by the master with the pupil, is very inspiring; and also counting parts only of bars in quick passages, and smaller members in slow passages. When the scholar has acquired some certainty, it is particularly desirable that he be led to omit the counting in easy passages, and resume it on the recurrence of passages of importance. In general, the scholar should be induced to relinquish external aid so soon as his apprehension and practice will allow it.

Mälzel's Metronome is a useful assistant to enable the pianoforte student to preserve equable measure in his exercises. It ought not, however, to be placed upon the instrument on which he is playing, because its regularity might be disturbed by the devious energy of his execution, as differently going clocks will assimilate in their movements if placed upon the same board.

memory. Only when the exercises become so numerous, that we might apprehend they would be forgotten, would we allow them to be written, and then in brief, the major in the scale of C major, and the minor in the scale of A minor. Then the scholar must seek out the same exercises in all the other scales by the aid of his ear alone. In like manner, when an exercise has been given to the pupil in chords, he must seek it out also on every degree and semitone; during which performance, the utmost assistance we could allow from the teacher, would be, the exclamation of "False!" whenever an error were committed. Only when the scholar has attained a certain proficiency, may he be told how the scales and tones are to be named, and he may then be allowed to write them out. It is very desirable, also, to induce the pupil to perform the scales and chords with his voice.

A second means of producing a lively impression of *tone*, is to *play and sing from memory*. The dread expressed by most parents and teachers, of playing by heart or from ear, must appear ridiculous to all persons who are well informed in matters of teaching and education in general; since, in all other objects of mental cultivation, the employment and strengthening of the memory is so seriously and authoritatively insisted on. The only ground of objection is, that the beginner, not looking at the notes, is liable to play incorrectly, that he will gradually forget his exercises, and never be able to play with certainty from notes. Against these evils, there are very sure remedies close at hand. Shou d this incorrectness be apprehended, only give the scholar such long and so many compositions at once, that it will be impossible for him to learn them by rote. Occupy him early with four-hand or accompanied compositions, which are difficult to learn by heart, since no single part contains them entirely. In fine, do not allow everything to be so learned; and in what is permitted, insist upon the most rigid fidelity to the notes, and on the slightest deviation in this respect, let the notes be resumed. In an extreme case, an unfinished composition can be given to a scholar who seizes by heart with extraordinary rapidity; and different parts of the composition can be filled up, altered, and corrected continually, so that the attention of the scholar must be constantly engaged in detecting the changes. There is no doubt, indeed, that an intelligent and attentive teacher will always find means to prevent the abuse of a faculty so agreeable and pregnant with such innumerable advantages to the player, and so manifestly precious to a composer. The highest freedom, power, and feeling in performance, or in conducting, are not to be attained while we are chained to the notes; and how composition and improvisation are to be carried to any perfection without a sure memory, is not easy to be imagined.

Learning to play and sing by heart, not only strengthens the feeling of *tone*, inasmuch as it necessitates the imprinting of single relations of *tones*, and the recalling of them according to such impression,—but it enables us, also, to imagine whole compositions, with all their combinations present to our minds. Here we may add a third means, which is peculiarly adapted to quicken the attention, to excite the watchfulness of the scholar, to accustom him every moment to instant and enlarged apprehension and decision, without which no deep penetration can be effected in art or in artistic works. This means is, *frequent playing and singing at sight*, especially four-handed or with accompaniment, and, indeed at once, in the absolute time (tempo), or nearly so, required in the composition. The teacher in this case must make the pupil understand, that it is absolutely necessary for the success of this procedure, that the composition should be played throughout without omission, interruption, or remission in time, to the end; that no reflection, no repetition, no looking back for errors, is permitted; but on the contrary, that the eye must constantly press forwards, and the performance must instantly and inevitably follow the eye. This alone must be required of the scholar, and must unrelentingly be insisted on by the teacher, and be more particularly and unfailingly observed in practice, if the latter should play with his scholar. On the other hand, the scholar must be comforted with the reflection that under such circumstances, he is not answerable for single failures, omissions, &c. The first attempts at this practice are often, indeed, wretched performances—quite laughable even, to those who do not consider how many qualifications must work herein together for the best possible effect to be produced. Usually, however, a vast improvement is manifested with unexpected rapidity, if the teacher begins and proceeds with judgment.

Of course, together with the above exercises, other compositions are most carefully studied, and are considered the chief materials of instruction. For the playing at sight, easier compositions are selected; and when they have been used for this object, they may be carefully studied. Then the disadvantages arising possibly from sight playing, that is, over-rapidity and inexactness, &c., may be corrected.

In fine, may we never, indeed, willingly suppress that most fruitful means of animating and exalting the musical sense, *invention;* but with joy and hope, on all occasions, most tenderly foster and encourage it, whether it be exerted in writing or at the instrument. How often is the young pupil reproved by teachers and parents, if he allows himself to try and try, and seek out his fancies on the piano! How often—we have already deplored it—is he told that that is useless dreaming, and that a finger exercise is much more improving! How often are his first attempts at writing thrown away with contempt, and his want of talent, or the widely different profession for which he is destined, urged upon him, in order to withdraw him from such nonsensical fancies and vain exertions. To a highly-gifted individual, such insults are simply discouraging. To a less gifted person, they are too often destructive. Let no man be enticed into the profession of a composer. He who does not feel interiorly an irresistible calling to that course of life, has no security for its success. But let not the highest and most prolific form in which musical sense and power can be worked out and perfected, be disturbed. We are all exercised from childhood upwards, in classical employment, even in versification. Are we, therefore, all educated to be authors or, perhaps, poets? By no means. But there is no more powerful means of developing the mind, and making it master of its organ—speech, than the elaboration of its own thoughts and imaginings. How much more important, then, must such a means be in music, for which we have no such enormous preparatory formation, than in thinking and writing, for which our whole life has been a school, by our incessant thought and speech, from the earliest age.

FIFTH SECTION.—OBJECTS OF MUSICAL EDUCATION AND THEIR TIME.

What is to be learned, and which is the proper time for each kind of instruction? These questions, of the utmost importance in their minutest particulars, demand the gravest and most searching consideration from parents and teachers when they have determined to dedicate a child to musical education. To professors of music, these questions must always be of the highest interest. In order to point out, at least, the most important periods, we will take a cursory view of all the relationships and circumstances of musical employment, whether as a profession or otherwise.

We must, in the first place, clear away a deep and widely diffused prejudice. On the question being asked, What ought to be learned in music? it is usual, particularly among teachers, to make a distinction between those persons who make music a profession, and those who cultivate it merely for pleasure and general humanizing education; between future professional men and mere amateurs. The former, according to the judgment of the teachers, ought to be *fundamentally*—the latter, however, only *superficially*, or less fundamentally instructed. This distinction is one of the most erroneous and destructive that ever crept into discipline. That education alone is beneficially fruitful which is most perfectly grounded; and, what is more, it is the easiest, and consumes the least time. In order to be convinced of the truth of these assertions, it is only necessary to have a right understanding of the nature of this fundamental knowledge; not of the false pedantry which assumes its name (and is as useless to the professional man as to the amateur), but of the study absolutely necessary for the comprehension of the real nature of the science, of the close connection of all that is essential, and of the constant and rational development of one form or figure from another, so that the preceding form necessarily leads on the succeeding, and the succeeding form is always prepared and facilitated by the preceding.

Between the instruction of the artist and of the amateur there is only this difference—that the latter may discontinue his pursuit of the science earlier than the former, at any point or position of artistic power he may choose to fix; whereas the artist is necessarily obliged to dedicate himself entirely, once and for ever, to the art of his election.

Now to return to our own proper question—What is to be learned, and which is the right time for each study?

SONG.

We have already said that if possible every one should learn music: we now pronounce our opinion more specially, that *every one, if possible, should learn singing*. Song is man's own true peculiar music. The voice is our own peculiar connate instrument—it is much more—it is *the living sympathetic organ of our souls*. Whatever moves within us, whatever sensation or emotion we feel, becomes immediately embodied and perceptible in our voice; and so, indeed, the voice and song, as we may observe in the earliest infancy, are our first poetry and the most faithful companions of our feelings, until the "shrill pipe of tremulous age." If, as in song, properly so called, music and speech be lovingly united, and the words be those of a true poet, then is consummated the most intimate union of mind and soul, of understanding and feeling—that combined unity, in which the whole power of the human being is exhibited, and exerts upon the singer and the hearer that wonderful might of song, which by infant nations was considered, not quite untruly, as supernatural; and whose softened, and therefore, perhaps, more beneficent influence, now contributes to social elevation and moral improvement.

Song is the most appropriate treasure of the solitary, and it is at the same time the most stringent and forcible bond of companionship, even from the jovial or the sentimental popular catch of the booth, to the sublime creations of genius resounding from congregated artistic thousands assembled by one common impulse in the solemn cathedral. Devotion in our churches becomes more edifying; our popular festivals and days of enjoyment become more mannerly and animated; our social meetings more lively and intellectually joyful; our whole life, in short, becomes more elevated and cheerful by the spread of the love of song and of the power of singing among the greatest possible number of individuals. And these individuals will feel themselves more intimately connected with society, more largely participating in its benefits, of more worth in it and gaining more by it, when they unite their voices in the social harmony of their friends.

To the musician, but more especially to the composer, song is an almost irreplaceable and indispensable means of calling forth and seizing the most delicate, tender, and deepest strains of feeling from our inmost sensations. No instrument can be a substitute for song, the immediate creation of our own soul in our own breast; we can have no deeper impression of the relations of sound, of the power of melody; we cannot work more effectively upon our own souls and upon those of our hearers than by heartfelt song.

Every friend of music, therefore, should sing; and every musician, who has a tolerable voice, should be a master of song in every branch. Song should, also, in the order of time, be our first musical exercise. This should begin in the earliest childhood, in the third to the fifth year, if it be not possible earlier, but not in the form of instruction. The song of the mother which allures imitation, the joyful circle of children playing together, is the first natural singing school, where, without notes or masters, simply according to hearing and fancy, the fibres of the soul are first freely excited and set in vibration. Instruction in music, properly so called, should not in general begin until the second step of life's ladder, between the seventh and fourteenth years.

By far the greatest number of individuals have sufficient qualifications of voice for singing, and to justify their pursuit of the art with reasonable hope of success. Indeed, very considerable and valuable vocal faculties are much more common than is generally imagined. There is certainly less deficiency of natural gifts than of persons observant and talented enough to discover, to foster, and to cultivate them. In the meantime, if indeed every one have not disposition and means (and good fortune) to become of some consequence as a singer, let us consider that even with an inconsiderable voice, much of the most touching and joy-inspiring capabilities may be attained, if feeling, artistic cultivation, and a vivid conception speak through a medium but slenderly endowed. Why should any one be dissatisfied if small means and trouble have made him capable of touching our hearts with a joyful or tender song; or have enabled him to participate skilfully in the choral assemblies of his fellow citizens. Whether it may be advisable to proceed farther in singing and the cultivation of the voice, must be decided by the circumstances and inclinations of each individual. From composers, conductors, and higher masters, a complete knowledge of everything belonging to singing is to be absolutely demanded, and also practical execution thereof; unless, indeed, organic defect should render it to them impossible. A composer who does not expressly study singing, and practise it as far as possible, will scarcely be able to write for the voice; he will with difficulty acquire the more delicate musical declamation; he will never become entire master of the life-like conducting of the voice, which is something far different from mere correctness.

Playing on the Piano.

After singing, the command of the pianoforte is our most essential qualification, and among us is so considered. The piano is the only instrument, excepting the scarcely accessible organ, on which melody and harmony, and the rich web of combined and simultaneous voices or parts, can be produced with accuracy and almost unlimited magnificence of effect. It is also highly adapted to accompanying song, and to conducting. From these advantages it has happened, that for this single instrument more masterpieces have been written, since the time of Seb. Bach up to Beethoven, than for all other instruments put together. Most songs have been composed with accompaniment for that instrument—organ parts can be transferred without any change—and whatever quartet and orchestral music found favour with the public, was immediately presented to pianoforte players in the form of arrangements, &c. Therefore, no branch of practice can promise so rich a harvest as piano playing; and it must be acknowledged, that, without so abundant a field, any extended acquaintance with our musical literature would be scarcely possible to the world in general. To the composer this instrument is nearly indispensable, partly on the foregoing grounds, and partly because no other is so appropriate, both for exercising and exciting his own imagination and for proving the effect of many-part compositions. It is equally important to the conductor and to the singing master. Even its defects are advantages to musical education, and particularly to the composer. The pianoforte is greatly inferior to bowed and wind instruments in inward feeling and power of *tone* or quality of sound, in the power of sustaining a *tone* in equality of force, in crescendo or in diminuendo, in melting two or more *tones* into each other, and in gliding imperceptibly from the one to the other, all which so admirably succeeds on bowed instruments. The piano does not fully satisfy the ear: its performance, compared to that of bowed and wind instruments, is in a manner colourless, and its effect, in comparison with the resplendence of an orchestra, is as a drawing to a painting. But exactly on this account the piano moves more powerfully the creative faculty of both player and hearer; for it requires their assistance to complete and colour, to give full significance to that which is but spiritually indicated. Thus imagination fosters the new idea, and penetrates therewith to our hearts; while other instruments immediately seize, and move, and satisfy the senses, and by their means attack the feelings more powerfully, perhaps, in a sensuous direction, but not so fruitfully in the soul. This is probably the chief reason why the piano has become the especial instrument for spiritually musical education, and particularly for composition; since other instruments easily overcome their votaries, whom they seduce into their own instrumental peculiarities, and create a one-sided mannerism in their productions.

For the earliest instruction, also, the piano has the advantage (good tuning being supposed) of presenting to the pupil correct *tones*, and a clear insight into the tonic system by the key-board.

But just from this point arises the important quality of the instrument, which may be perilous to all the real advantages derived from it, unless it be sedulously counteracted; and this, we must confess, is at present but little thought of—nay, indeed, that dangerous quality is speculated on, and an entirely false system of education is built on it for outward show, through whose apparent advantages even the true artistic education is represented in a false light, as ignorant and baneful. Since the pianoforte has its fixed *tones* provided, it is easier to play upon this instrument than upon any other, without any internal feeling of correctness of *tone*, or even without hearing, and to arrive at a certain degree of mechanical dexterity. How often do we meet ready piano players, who, from want of a cultivated feeling of *tone*, are incapable of singing a correct succession of *tones*, or of imagining it, who have no clear notion of what they are playing—nay, who in reality hear nothing correctly! How many bravura players might one name, to whom the artistic meaning of a simple movement remains a sealed book, and who therefore perform the greatest and the least compositions, with assumption and vanity indeed, but without inward participation—without awakening joy in themselves or in their audience, but merely a fruitless astonishment at their technical cleverness! And how deep has this perversion of art into dead mechanism penetrated into artistic life! Whoever has an opportunity of observing many students of music and their teachers, cannot conceal from himself that at present, particularly in large towns devoted to vanity and fashion, the greater part of the pianoforte students are in this manner led astray; and that a great part of the teachers are themselves ignorant of the right path, or otherwise have not the courage to oppose the stream of fashion, or the allurements of example and personal advantage.

If, however, satisfactory instruction is not to be expected from all masters, nor every student is to hope for the choice of a good master, there remains still a tolerably sure method of guarding against this wide-spread evil. It consists in rigidly examining the work, which is exacted from the pupil, in the pupil himself, and his parents or preceptor insisting absolutely that the teacher shall furnish really profitable work; or, if that cannot be secured with certainty, in seeking immediately another teacher more trustworthy to his art.

We have already said that the pianoforte possesses an extremely voluminous literature, partly written expressly for it, and partly adaptations from other works foreign to it. What can be more natural or more enlightening than to make these works the chief means of instruction, their complete possession being one of the objects of pursuit. For this end, technical readiness, finger exercises, and studies are required. But these are manifestly only means to an end; and as certainly as their use ought not to be delayed, so certainly also they ought to be set aside when the required dexterity has been gained, and the principal difficulties overcome; or else, from a want of methodical arrangement, exercises may be prolonged without end. We cannot conceal from ourselves that in these latter times this error has been stretched to excess, and has overwhelmed us with countless studies, &c. Every respectable teacher, every distinguished amateur, considers himself bound to present the world with some dozens of studies, from which a few particular artistic forms of fingering are to be acquired. And since the composition of a well-sounding study exacts nothing but the occurrence of an idea to be worked in the ordinary routine of composition; since, moreover, a little burst of enthusiasm is highly thought of in these matters; and, further, since the brilliant playing of the author, or the reputation of his master, renders him tolerably sure of his public, we can never tell when this composition and spread of studies will come to an end: neither, indeed, can we imagine how the pupil shall find time to labour through the most respectable of them only; to say nothing of the real works of art themselves, for whose sake alone the whole drudgery has been endured.

Let the non-musical inquirer consider the foregoing as a token of good and bad instruction in the question before us.

Sebastian Bach and Handel, Joseph Haydn, Mozart and Beethoven—these are the artists to whom we owe the greatest and the most numerous works of art for the pianoforte. Among these, Bach and Beethoven stand forward, the one in elder, the other in our own times, as those who have reached the highest eminence. After them, Emanuel Bach, Clementi, Dussek, Karl Maria von Weber, Hummel, and many more may be named. We abstain from giving a more numerous list, particularly of those still living, as it is not the province of this work to pass judgment upon individuals. Upon the highest, the vast preponderance in estimation of the five first-named artists, there is not the slightest question among those who have the least tincture of art. The one may indeed be compared with the other, but the high preeminence of all is unquestioned.

We can therefore declare as a condition for good pianoforte teaching, that the works of those five eminent men[*] shall be considered as the distinguished and governing lessons in the instruction. Whatever finger exercises, hand lessons, or secondary work, a teacher may find necessary for his pupil, must be left to his decision, as it cannot be estimated. But the teacher who does not conduct his pupil into the study of the five great masters, as soon as it can be done with any precision, and the time of the lesson permits it, and does not make them the chief object and goal of the instruction, such a teacher, we say it without hesitation, is not able to give a true artistic education, however clever and careful he may be in other parts of his duty. Teachers who keep their pupils to fashionable dances and such trifles, to arrangements from ·favorite operas, &c., are altogether unworthy of the confidence of those who seek for genuine education in art. Therefore, no teacher ought to be chosen without the previous knowledge of his method of instruction.

---

[*] We have to give an urgent warning with respect to Seb. Bach's work, the "Wohltemperirte Klavier," that the younger scholars be not set too early to the study of it; and that neither they nor others should be persuaded that everything that that great man has composed—often composed for momentary objects of instruction, &c.—was of equal value. Bach's manner is so different from the modern style, that we cannot without reflection employ his works. This, and the usual beginning with pianos of the most accustomed temperament, have driven more friends of art from this master than the pleasure of his music has created him admirers; and, therefore, with the greatest veneration in his regard, we will not refuse to acknowledge that another portion of his works, namely his dances, have outlived their time and become antiquated. But the enlightened teacher will find in the six preludes pour les commençans, in the inventions and single fantasias, namely in the English and other suites among the preludes, sarabands, jigs, &c., a rich choice of the most charming and imperishable compositions, most intimately adapted to our tastes and feelings, and highly calculated to produce both pleasure and improvement in his scholars. We would here wish to recommend the new collective edition of Bach's works, at Peter's, in Leipsig. As an Introductory School for conducting from our own time and manner into those of Bach, which are so importantly different, and for primary instruction in polyphonic playing, the Author has published a selection from Seb. Bach's compositions, at Challier's, in Berlin, at 20 Sgr.

The above warning may also apply to Handel, whose works, however, for the piano, are not numerous. We can recommend his Six Fugues and a Capriccio, at Frautwein's, in Berlin, for more advanced students.

Pianoforte learning may begin very early—in the seventh or eighth year, or even earlier, even before the hand can span the octave. There is, moreover, a sufficiency of excellent works of Haydn and Mozart, well adapted to the sensibilities of that tender age, if the teacher be but capable of choosing them.

COMPOSITION.

We name the study of composition as the third object of general musical education. Deep penetration into art and its productions, a rich development of musical talent, cannot be attained without this study. If it be undertaken in the right sense, it rewards every step forwards with clearer insight and increased pleasure; and, indeed, those also who are not destined by peculiar talents to the profession of composers.

This circumstance demands the more deliberate consideration, the more imperfect and erroneous the representations are which have been attached to it.

Music consists, as can be seen from this book, in an inward comprehension of innumerable most diversified forms, constantly approaching and separating, perpetually combining and dissolving in each other. Their operation can be perceived, more or less, without previous cultivation, and can be understood and represented by a superficial instruction; but to comprehend them entirely, to penetrate into their whole nature and attributions, is to know the meaning and force of each form by itself, and also when in combination with every other. Now, let us imagine a great composition before us, in which different parts are united in the most varied manner, in all sorts of artistic forms, each part having its cantilena, its rhythm, its succession of *tones*, while each *tone* has a determined relation to the *tones* of the other parts, and with all this are combined different degrees and kinds of motion, of *forte* or *piano*, and of manner of performance. Now, we say, with such a composition before us, we presume it will be admitted that without study such a composition could not be understood, and that the study for that object must be thorough, systematic, and methodical.

Let us suppose for a moment that any one unaccustomed to composition undertook the dissection of the above imagined work. Then would he be overwhelmed with an intolerable burden of unities. The completion of his task would be impossible, were it only from the creation of new forms and applications of them which daily takes place in art.

The only ready, practicable, and fruitful procedure is, therefore, to set one's own hand to work, to learn oneself how to bring the forms from out the world of sound, to "call the spirits from the vasty deep;" to learn to feel the rhythm of the forms, so that all present and future forms shall be within our scope and comprehension, because we have grasped the root of their existence—because we know how they have come into existence, and why. This the doctrine of composition teaches us. This science alone gives us, not abstract ideas upon art—not merely superficial notions upon the operations of art—not a few cut out dead parts, but the whole entire, with all its individualities, and in its unity, matter, and spirit, form and meaning, in that single entirety which is the material of true art.

We may add, from a large experience of every age and of both sexes, that the study of composition, without any proportionate loss of time, even for amateurs, most surely rewards every step, even when but small disposition exists in the student, or circumstances should prevent a lengthened pursuit of the subject. The first few lessons in one-part[*] compositions will at once awaken the sense for melody, and give a significant idea of its fundamental forms, of the efficacy of rhythm, and of the origin and accumulation of passages and phrases. Already the doctrine so comprehensive and so easily comprehended of the two and two composition in two parts, built upon the natural harmony, makes the foundation of all harmony and tonic progression perfectly obvious, and furnishes to moderately endowed students, pleasurable and exciting lessons. So much can be acquired in two or three weeks, with a couple of lessons a week and but little exertion; and, moreover, we might abandon our studies at this point, without having lost our labour. Then the gradual development of harmony and the richer progression of parts, will have, in the mere inspection, the charm of a perfectly rational and highly copious display, from the most simple fundamental forms and the most obvious laws. But to any one who enters upon this pursuit with inbred activity, to such a one the regions of sound are illumined and extended with every effort,—the sense of music is vivified, excited, and strengthened by every fresh manifestation of the internal art. Now, with the knowledge of the limitation of chords, freedom in the unfolding of art returns, and her play becomes continually richer and more variegated. Then all artistic forms are imagined and explained, the one from the other—the order of the succession being pre-supposed—the one quite as easy as the other, until finally, their realization on determined instruments or in song, in ecclesiastical, dramatic, and other objects of our art, completes the whole study. At any point the study may be relinquished with profit, in proportion to the labor bestowed, if circumstances should so command, or the zeal of the student should not urge him to further investigation.

The study of composition may begin early, particularly with talented and lively children, but not before they have made some progress upon a musical instrument,—if possible the pianoforte, and have

---

[*] The author has conformed himself here to the tenour and tendency of his Doctrine of Musical Composition (Lehre von der Musikalischen Komposition), at Breitkoff and Härtel. How little can the above assurance be given by the old thorough-bass and doctrine of harmony: how unartistic is it in foundation and method, how extremely incomplete and unsatisfactory. This the author has exemplified from time to time in the Instruction for Composition, but more demonstratively in the work "Die alte Musiklehre im Streit mit unsrer Zeit" (the old Doctrine of Music in contention with our times), at Breitkoff and Härtel, 1841,—as had been acknowledged and declared long enough before him by Reicher and every thinking professor of composition. The indolence of so many old masters, or the ignorance of masters absolutely unacquainted with the real nature of composition, is still answerable for the painful and useless labour of many young persons. Many such, indeed, are still enduring in the continually disappointed hope that they will at last, some day, arrive at composition, or at least at a clearer insight into the nature of art; they endure until the time has passed, and with it all pleasure and natural feeling, which either dies away or becomes corrupted.

thereby gained some participation in and capacity for art, and also more penetration and habit of reflection. They ought at least to have got beyond the elementary exercises, and be able to play with feeling and technical correctness larger works, such as, for example, the sonatas of Haydn and Mozart. Instruction in composition at an earlier period than this would be mere empty playing; or, what is much worse, would disturb, in the still unself-supporting scholar, the free and immediate enjoyment of the compositions lying before him; and thrust, in the place of lively, soul-inspiring, artistic employment, cold and profitless mechanisms of the understanding. This is one of the greatest errors of a system pursued in many shapes, of instruction in the piano and harmony combined, which apparently advances the students through an intricate mechanism with great rapidity, but at the cost of the feeling of music itself, which remains undeveloped, and becomes, indeed, oppressed and stifled by the disturbance of the understanding, and the mechanism which that system brings into action. The true joy of art and artistic accomplishment becomes the more surely destroyed thereby,—the more deceptive to the observer is the joy of the scholar at his mechanical success,—and the more his sudden progress in certain parts of music is in the beginning inexplicable to the uninstructed.

We consider thus much to be necessary upon general education. The choice of other instruments may be left to each individual, under the advice of the better-informed. The science and history of music must in like manner be left to the disposition and leisure of every friend of art. The composer, and particularly the well-educated musician, will scarcely be able to restrain himself from the history of his art, not merely from books, but from the works of art themselves.

SIXTH SECTION.—TEACHERS AND METHODS OF TEACHING.

It is manifest that, in order to attain the object of musical education, the choice of a teacher is highly important to the student, while the choice of the most sure method of teaching is equally so to the master. So many parents know not how to help themselves in this regard—so many respectable well-intentioned teachers are anxious to ascertain and rectify, if needful, their methods of proceeding—so many scholars have already been led astray or ruined, in a musical sense, either by a mistaken choice or an erroneous system, that we have considered it to be our duty to suggest a few hints on this subject. We give only a few hints on the principal points applicable to the matter in general. A fundamental improvement cannot be arrived at by a book; it must be the result of a more elevated education of the teachers, by institutions of the state, and through a real enlightenment of all educated persons on the nature and necessity of music.

The profession of music is highly important, from the powerful influence this science exercises on our senses and on our spiritual and civil life. Parents should weigh well, in the choice of a teacher, what power is given him through his art over the mind of their child; that he may elevate the youthful mind to the most noble sentiments, or defile and lower it to the most grovelling: how prejudicial it is merely to leave the mind vacant, while music is acting irresistibly upon the senses and the mind. Listlessness, thoughtlessness, sensuality, vanity, unbridled passion, may be implanted and fostered by the teacher of music; but we may also be indebted to him for awakening and cherishing the noblest powers and sentiments of the soul.

From the foregoing, it would appear that the weightiest point to be considered, in the choice of a music master, is, what influence may be expected from him on the mind of his scholar. His good manners, however necessary, are no sufficient guarantee for suitability. But, indeed, the high and pure sense in which he has formed his conception of art, and the degree of his general capability and education, which enables him to transfer his conception to his pupil,—all this must be maturely pondered. But the choice made, boldly and with full confidence give free hand to the teacher. Half confidence, interference in the instruction, would only disturb the efficiency of the master.

We must, therefore, with regard to music, consider, in the first place, what view the teacher takes of it, and what motive urges him in its employment. The mere technical man, who uses art simply as handicraft, will produce nothing but a handicraftsman. The player, from understanding, will give cold lessons and perceptions; he can give technicality with ease and certainty, but he will never warm the heart with inward fire: he will rather rob it of its natural warmth. The mere man of feeling will perhaps allow the scholar to sympathise in company with him, but never insist upon sure instruction. Art is not mere technicality, nor mere understanding, nor mere feeling. It is the expression of the whole man; and only he who embraces it in its entireness can ingraft and rear its true nature and power. Talent and knowledge, a feeling heart, and a rational consciousness of the reality of the nature and operations of art—these are the indispensable qualities of a teacher of music. One of the signs of his artistic standing—we must repeat a former observation—is the works at which he and his scholar are employed. A teacher who occupies himself with small worthless compositions, in lieu of the abundant masterpieces of our art, shows the inferiority of his position, and a poor estimate of art. There are, indeed, masters who limit themselves to approved works, on the sole authority of the name, without taking any lively interest in them; in this case, certainly, their instruction can be but of small benefit. The next general qualification which a teacher indispensably requires, is the faculty of working with decision and effect on the mind and disposition of his pupil. The mere capability of playing himself a piece of music with propriety and effect, does not here suffice. It may delight the scholar, it may move or excite him, it may induce him to a successful imitation, and even, perhaps, finally to a more or less noble and happy manner;

but will not create in himself a free independent feeling, and conscious certainty in art. It is not necessary only that the teacher should enable the scholar to play whole compositions as he does himself, but that he lead him into the composition itself—that he enable him to see and comprehend thoroughly each unity therein, their combination and mutual dependence, and their constitution as a whole. A bright consciousness only of the nature of art, and of the contents of each work of art, advances the pupil to a free comprehension and performance peculiar to himself, and conducts him by his own productions to the summit where individuality of the artist and nature of the art join in conscious union, and give style to his creations. Only such a method of instruction works beyond the circle of lessons which he has run through. If the scholar has seized the essence of the matter, he will not hold it fast in studies and forms only, which the teacher has worked out with him; he will seek and seize it everywhere equally when the master is absent. This is the true life in art; this alone guarantees that the exercise of art will not cease with instruction, but will adorn the whole of life. For this object there is required, on the part of the teacher, deep insight, extensive knowledge, and in both such ability and certainty that he can comprehend and explain his subjects under all their aspects. A teacher must know more, much more than he is required to teach; he must be everywhere at-home, and perfectly master of his subject, in order to be able to answer every question, and supply every unnoticed deficiency.

After the elementary and technical instruction, we require absolutely from a good singing and piano master the study of composition, as the most sure, if not the only means of penetrating with full consciousness into the recesses of art. We require of him an extensive and well-grounded knowledge of the masterpieces of art of the elder and modern times; and strongly recommend a continually observant and sympathizing eye on new productions, in order to acquire every movement in artistic life, even although masses of unsuccessful or retrograde composition should make the duty burthensome. The higher teacher, especially one who is concerned in the education of composers and teachers or conductors, ought not to delay his acquaintance with the history of art and the science of music, besides his study of fundamental composition; since everything, and therefore music, can be perfectly known and fully understood only by the help of its history.

To the properly artistic capacity and education must be added the knowledge of mankind, and the talent of working upon the mind of others; but then, also, love of the business of instruction, and a heartfelt interest in the advancement of the scholar. An able master studies the disposition and inclination of his pupil. He judges from them, how he may be won, how convinced, upon what qualities he may rely, where he wants assistance, and by what other powers his deficiencies may be compensated. He does not consider himself as another being, foreign to his pupil; he neither presumes on his own superiority, nor lowers himself to his pupil (both false methods of teaching), but penetrates with his higher ideas and education into the mental condition of his pupil; comprehends, as it were, from the soul of the young disciple the conceptions he has acquired of art and its forms; he here separates, by his superior knowledge, the true and healthy from the false and insufficient; he encourages, expands, and exalts the former, and corrects and amplifies the latter. In short, he endeavours to originate or unravel every desirable faculty in the pupil himself, because only that which is engendered in and grows out from ourselves, not that which is brought to us from without, is vital, and works with the energy of life.

Such a teacher will lose courage only in the case of total indifference or absolute incapacity; or much rather, with our feelings, he would decline the scholar. But each single deficiency, every erroneous or one-sided conception, he knows how to meet. If the feeling of measure cannot be trusted, or is perhaps confused by earlier teachers, the master will prescribe very simple lessons of determined rhythm, and then make rhythmic—melodic variations on them, so that the pupil will proceed on the same simple lesson from simple rhythm to more rich, placed together and increasing in difficulty. If the sense of *tone* be undeveloped, the teacher will apply the earlier to the practice of chords; first the major triad, then the chord of the dominant, lastly the major and minor chords of the ninth (major chords always before minor) by ear on the piano, and then have them sung by the pupil. For since those chords are the first indications given by nature herself, one of her *tones* helps the imperfect feeling of *tone* in the student, to the other; and the most important intervals, such as the octave, fifth, fourth, major and minor third, minor seventh, whole tone and semitone, will be gained from the laws of nature. If the scholar has a strong partiality for brilliant and off-hand playing, the teacher will fall in with this inclination (since to oppose it abruptly would rather alarm than overcome), and by gradually shading the passages, separating and binding, changing the *forte* and *piano*, &c., in a manner comprehensible and agreeable to the scholar, he will make the latter perceive how one and the same passage may, by different playing, become newer, more attractive, now more neat and delicate, and then more forcible, &c. It will now be easy to take a more noble direction from this point, and to awaken the deep sense of melody. Should the intelligent element assume a pre-eminence, let us profit by it to comprehend and seize with more intimate feeling, accentuation, which is the nearest associate to rhythm, in relation to the understanding. Let us penetrate, as at page 43, into the innumerable degrees of accentuation, and awaken thereby the conviction that musical matters are not exclusively the business of the understanding, but that it is often necessary to trust to feeling only. Hence it is easy to see that feeling must have free operation, and participates of right in musical composition and performance. If, on the other hand, the scholar should be inclined, perhaps from enthusiasm, to devote himself to the unknown feeling, let that noble power of the soul be respected and upheld which lies at the foundation of this one-sidedness. Let us apply to heartfelt compositions, and with preference to those whose effect has been already experienced, and point out the chief traits which have caused our emotion; illustrate occasionally such passages, by comparison with similar or dissimilar instances, or by changes which would rob us of our power or tenderness. Should our sensibilities be excited, as is generally the case with superabundant feeling, by melody, chiefly or exclusively, we will apply gradually to movements in which a captivating chief melody is met by a leading passage full of character, or where two or more highly interesting melodies combine and proceed together. In so far as the pupil, either by himself,—or induced by the teacher, can be brought to notice in each of the significant parts that which has hitherto exclusively occupied him, he is on the way to elevate himself above the one-sided, obscure, and overworked feeling, to a higher consciousness, to a more comprehensive and fruitful spiritual sympathy.

It is impossible here to accumulate all the counsels and advantages arising from a perfect intimacy of the master with the mind of the pupil. It is enough, if, from a few examples, we have made ourselves clearly understood.

That there are now but few teachers, such as we require for so many scholars, is true. But this is, however, no refutation of the justice of our demands; it is only a sign of the insufficiency of our supplies for the requirements of our consciences; and proves a concurrent striving for a recognized good, according to our power. It cannot also be denied, that often persons, clear-sighted enough in general, instead of selecting the obtainable good masters, procure others far from proficiency, out of thoughtlessness, want of knowledge of the parties, or other secondary considerations. Here, however, the reproach falls on the musicians and teachers themselves, who have given themselves but little trouble in enlightening the public in general on the true nature of their art and the means of acquiring it— a conviction which has had great part in the production of this book.

We must also notice another erroneous idea concerning instruction. It is the deceptive notion, often repeated, that for the beginning an inferior teacher is sufficient. This persuasion often arises from the wish to save for some time the cost of a good master. But we must consider this opinion as an erroneous delusion. The unskilled master lays a bad foundation. He delays the fundamental elements and exercises upon which all future progress must be founded. He neglects the awakening and expansion of the natural dispositions, gives a false direction to all artistic procedure, and misuses or destroys the pleasure and activity of the scholar. The succeeding better master finds a scholar half tired out with wandering hither and thither without profit or reward. He meets everywhere with only imperfect or false preparation, and he finds difficulty enough in exciting attention and activity in the scholar for the attainment of an object of which this latter imagines himself to be already possessed. What teacher, under these circumstances (and they are of frequent occurrence), does not wish that no instruction had been given—that he might freely and with good heart build upon fresh and unencumbered ground; and how many a gifted scholar has abandoned art in disgust, when he has discovered, after years of labour, that in order to succeed, he must begin again from the beginning.

In conclusion, it is the method itself of teaching which claims our consideration. In this matter, after every necessary qualification as to ability, we will limit ourselves to one fundamental requisition, which seems to us important and comprehensive, and which to the reflective teacher will develope itself so advantageously in every direction, however simply it may be expressed. The teacher must constantly bear in mind that he teaches an art. Consequently he must treat his scholar and the subject of his teaching in the sense of an artist and of art, and prove himself to be an artist.

He must also constantly show to his scholar that love and respect which are due to his fellow artist and to everyone engaged in higher and intellectual occupations.

He will foster and elevate the disposition of the pupil for art. Artistic activity must flow spontaneously from the heart, if it is to fructify into life: we cannot force even ourselves into its possession, much less others. The pleasure we derive from it is therefore the first and indispensable condition of all success in this region; and the teacher who knows not how to preserve and increase it will certainly miss his aim. He must, however, awaken true pleasure in the art itself; not false pleasure—vanity, desire for reward or profit; and, in order, indeed, that the student may become constantly more susceptible of her pleasures and more capable of producing them, he must moreover excite his pupil to a worthy use of his powers by an en-encouraging word, by a well-timed performance of the works of art, &c.

The following point is most worthy of consideration. Art is not abstract thinking,—it is not feeling without thought nor unconscious activity; neither should the teaching be an abstract combination. Every lesson, every rule, must be derived from nature herself before the eyes of the pupil, and immediately, if by any means possible, reduced to practice. That this is practicable in teaching composition, we think we have shown from the fact in our Doctrine of Composition. It was one of the most unartistic aspects of the earlier art of teaching, when all possible intervals and all possible chords were thrown before the pupil in a heap together, and then all the forms of counterpoint in small unartistic passages, before the application of any of them was sought for. Most, indeed, of the books of instruction give no application at all. Nature and the history of art point out another way. Wherever a free course has been open to reason, she has immediately proceeded to the absolutely necessary, and in art to the actual practice, without delay. She has followed reflection by holding fast that which the moment required, and so in every instance she has elevated her mode of action into consciousness, her thoughts into living incarnated operation. Such also has been the development of art—entirely according to reason, proceeding by facts, by real operation, as her history, properly understood, demonstrates.

Also, in the practice of music, this fundamental proposition is thoroughly practicable. The tonal system, the system of notation, the arrangements of rhythm, are so entirely according to reason, that every scholar, under the gentlest guidance of the teacher, can unfold them further from their first intimations, and can again discover them for himself. It appears to us one of the crudities of the usual mode of teaching, to burden the scholar with the whole tonal system at once, then (or even before, as some books of instruction do*), with the whole system of notation (and perhaps in several clefs at the same time), then with the whole system of bars, while for the moment he wants only the smallest part of them; such as a few notes in one clef, leaving the remainder to be acquired on further advancement. By this misapplication, the scholar is withdrawn from immediate living and improving comprehension to an unartistic work of memory.

It follows, therefore, that the order of these books of instruction, which merely present the materials of instruction to the memory, should also illustrate and complete their work; and not doing so, can have no claim to be considered an order or plan of really practical instruction.

Even the exercises, whose immediate object is to produce readiness of hand and voice, must not only be brought into the service of the hand and the observant understanding, but also be used for the pleasurable feelings of the scholar, whenever practicable, so that what he has learned may as soon as possible be applied in artistic form. From these considerations we cannot look without hesitation upon an invention lately introduced, to make beginners practice upon finger-boards made of paper. However convenient and cheap this may appear, it is evident that artistic participation must be injured, or, to say the least, not excited or vivified.†

This is the true doctrine, which, in the smallest and the greatest, holds fast and advances the reality of art, and upholds the student from the lowest up to the pinnacle—however high he may be able and willing to climb—in perfect artistic sympathy and activity. But this is possible only to a teacher, who, himself an artist, is replete with the spirit of art.

APPENDIX.

We take advantage of the form of an appendix, in order to give a more detailed explanation of some particularities of certain works of art, for which we did not wish to interrupt the direct line of our instructions, seeing that the object of the book would allow us only the most necessary elucidations in the most compressed arrangement.

With the same view, we refer only to such works as we must suppose every educated artist or zealous student must have within reach. In fine, we can only point out, not thoroughly explain.

A.
RHYTHMIC DIVISIONS.
Page 64.

For the first example, let us take Beethoven's sonata for the pianoforte in E♭ major, Op. 7, the first phrase.

Bars 1 and 2, 3 and 4, are two members of a phrase, which end on the entrance of the 13th bar. With this bar a repetition begins (the melody lies in the under part) which is intended to close at the 17th, but continues in the same motion to the 21st, and then to the 25th bar. Independently of the falling together of each closing and beginning bar, the following members in reality step forward—
2—2—8 (4 times 2 bound together)—4—4 bars.
More clearly now follow four members of 2 bars each, which, from the similarity of their contents, blend together into two sections of 4 bars each; the close is made by a phrase of 8 bars, again in members of every 2 bars.

On going over the next phrase, we would call attention to the following in dotted crotchets. It becomes more comprehensible in 4 times 2 bars, and is repeated after a firm close in the dominant. But thereby it is prolonged from its third member.

The Largo of the same sonata shall be our second example. Its first phrase, consisting of 8 bars, shows members of

1—1—1—1—and 4 bars.

Now, a phrase of 2 bars is three times repeated, changed; after which, the first phrase (extended by 10 bars in the middle) returns. In the following bar, a new phrase begins of 4 and again 4 bars, whose first half, altered, is repeated and closes in the 5th bar, with which a member of 2 bars begins,

---

* They therefore teach the sign before the thing signified, so that their notation is objectless, and must remain incomplete until we become acquainted with *tones*.

† This manner of teaching was adopted in Berlin by the late Mrs. Schindelmeisser and Dr. Lange, so far as the author knows, with good results for the quick attainment of technical readiness. The scholars perform the exercises on paper or real keys (without strings), while another person produces the sound on a real instrument. The progress of the pupils, at all events, gives evidence of the talents of the otherwise already advantageously-known teachers, and if youth is to be taught in large masses where an instrument is not to be had, or if the unpleasant sound of technical passages is to be avoided, this plan furnishes, perhaps, the best remedy. But it must be allowed that a method of practice so abstract that the scholar [does not hear himself—in which he himself produces no sound—that music, which he is to learn and bring forth, he is only to hear by the operation of another: such a musical exercise cannot be so animated and animating as the living sound which the scholar himself produces, and therefore feels with greater vivacity and judges of by his own feelings. But then, must all the world learn the piano? must it be taught in masses? and is not technical skill in inseparable union with true musical practice, and therefore to be acquired before everything audible? The author hopes to publish soon, in another place, and after a future more minute investigation, a more extended disquisition on this subject, and he will freely and joyfully retract his objections if any good grounds should appear sufficient to destroy their validity.

repeats itself, and with another repetition of its last bar, leads back to the first but altered theme.

Let us take the scherzo or allegro phrase for our last example. The first part is a subject in a more extended form. A phrase of 4 bars, and a following one of members of 1, 4, and 2 bars, compose the opening phrase. The closing phrase consists of the repetition of the first phrase (altered) of 4 bars, a member of 2 bars taken from the latter, and a closing phrase of twice 4 bars, the latter of which is extended by a ninth bar.

So much for the rhythmic construction of this composition, which by no means belongs to those of simple construction. The tonic contents, the return of the themes, &c., will facilitate the comprehension of the rhythm of this and other works, even to the uninformed. After a moderate number of these investigations, the feeling thereof will awaken, and be gradually so strengthened, as to require no more such minute dissections; so that we shall proceed at once to comprehension and performance.

B.
THE FUGUE FORM.
Page 87.

For the first example, we will take the simple fugue in E♭ major, in the first part of the *Wohltemperirten Klavier*, of Seb. Bach.

If we compare the two first entering parts (bass and tenor) with each other, we find, that setting aside a change of the first interval, seven bars proceed with each.

The seven first bars of the bass* show us, therefore, the theme of the fugue, which enters as subject; thereupon, the tenor enters with the answer; then enter, without episode, the alto with the subject, and the treble with the answer. This is, therefore, the first passing through. An episode of two bars leads to a close in the third bar in B♭ major. The counter subject, which the bass placed against the answer of the tenor, is used in part only by the tenor and alto; every participating part in the counter-subject in the counter-harmony, moves in the whole *ad libitum*.

This was then the order of the first passing through, from below to above:—

BASS, TENOR, ALTO, TREBLE,

and the theme changed regularly as subject and answer on the tonic and dominant.

At the close, B♭ major, the second passing through begins. The tenor joins in with the answer—the bass follows before the tenor has got to the end of the theme; indeed, in the next bar,† and therefore in the stretto, with the subject in the eighth and ninth bars of the passing through, the alto enters with the answer, and the treble with the subject, in likewise the closest passing, so that the following order of the parts takes place:—

TENOR, BASS, ALTO, TREBLE,

and the theme appears in regular but reversed order, as answer and subject. The passing has again been chiefly in E♭ major, and in it has ended. Or more likely (for the close does not follow), it goes into an episode of eight bars, after the tenor in the following ninth bar has led the subject (as answer) into A♭ major;‡ and now, in both the following bars, treble and bass bring again the stretto, which was previously here (as the tenor and bass had done before), which therefore this time appears in the two outward parts; and then a few free bars close the fugue.

The fugue in C minor in the same work, Part I., shall be our second example.

This is so carefully elaborated, that we must go through it by bars.

The theme closes with the first crotchet of the second bar. The alto has begun, the treble follows the second bar with the answer; then after an episode at the fourth bar, the tenor with the subject, and after a longer episode at the seventh bar, the bass with the (somewhat altered) answer. Here the passing through might close; it becomes, however, super-complete, inasmuch as in the following bar the treble again appears; at bar 10 the alto, and at the 11th bar the bass enters again with the theme, whereon at the 14th bar the fugue closes in G minor.

In the same bar the treble enters in the closest stretto, passing with the theme in the regular size, and the alto with the same in augmentation; at bar 15, the tenor joins the theme inverted; at bar 16, the alto and treble; and at bar 17, the tenor and treble take the theme in orderly size and motion, but in the stretto (the treble has the theme twice without interruption), upon which, at bar 18, the alto has it again in regular size (and stretto towards the treble), and at bar 19, the bass has it in augmentation, as also without interference afterwards at bar 21 in reversed order, and at bar 22 in the regular size and motion. So, in this manner, in an undivided passing through, the theme has passed eleven times, and that in stretto, inversion, and augmentation. The further investigation we leave to the inquisitive reader.

We will take a third example from the E major fugue itself. We mention only out of it, that from bar 26 the theme is carried through all the parts, from above to below in diminution. At bar 30, the diminution passes (for the fifth time in the bass) in close passages towards the theme in the proper size in the alto.

C.
THE RONDO FORM.
Page 89.

The rondo forms are in modern music so abundant and so easily distinguished, that the most hasty allusion to a few examples of them will be sufficient. For greater convenience, we take them out of a single collection; namely, the three sonatas of Beethoven, Op. 2.§

First Example.—The Adagio of the first Sonata.

The chief subject is a two-part song; the first division of it of 8 bars (4 bars opening, and 4 closing phrases) closes in the chief *tone*. The second division begins with two slighter or weaker members of

---

* We add, for the professional eye, that in rigour, the entrance of the seventh bar is the close of the theme.

† The first tone is shortened in order to separate it better from the tenor.

‡ The first tone shortened in consideration of the bass.

§ More intimate and numerous investigations of the Rondo and Sonata forms are given in the 3rd Part of the Instruction for Composition.

every two bars, upon which the chief subject, otherwise directed, closes with 4 bars. Here begins the secondary subject, which, in the manner of a passage, proceeds forward, and with a motive taken from the chief subject, closes in C major. Now the chief subject steps again forward, complete (but altered) and an extensive coda closes the whole.

Second Example.—The Largo in the second Sonata.

The chief subject (in D major) formed as the preceding, closes at bar 19. Here the first secondary subject (in the relative key) proceeds freely forward, and at bar 31 leads into (the second time altered) the chief subject, which continues from bar 32 to 50. Here the second secondary subject enters, and also in the principal *tone* (D major) leads to the chief subject, at first in D minor (because D major had been already used), then into D major and to the close. In this last arrangement the first division only of the chief subject is repeated.

Third Example.—The Finale of the same Sonata

The chief subject (A major) closes at bar 16. It is of similar construction to the forementioned. A passage-like phrase conducts bar 26 to the first secondary subject (E major), after which the chief subject, somewhat altered, returns. The second secondary subject follows in A minor, in extended order, whereon the chief subject and the first secondary subject (this latter in the principal key) are repeated. A lengthened coda, whose contents are taken from the chief and second secondary subjects, closes the whole.

We consider the last rondo-form as more effective after the sonata-form.

D.
THE SONATA FORM.
Page 90.

We will take, for the first example, the first subject of Beethoven's Sonata, Op. 2, F minor.

The chief subject is contained in the first eight bars: its repetition is begun in the dominant, not pursued, but turned to the dominant of the relative key (E♭ major), upon which, at bar 20, the secondary subject enters in the relative itself (A♭ major). It proceeds in the manner of a passage, and at bar 40 a closing subject begins, with which the first division ends.

The second division begins with the chief subject (A♭ major), leaves the secondary subject (in the sub-dominant of the principal key, B♭ minor) to follow, and goes with it, after a passage-like procedure (at bar 33 of the second division), into an organ-point.

The third division brings now all the first—chief subject, secondary, and closing subjects, both the last, in the chief key again. We take a second example from the third Sonata (F major) of Mozart; Part No. 1 of Breitkopf's edition, from the first subject. The chief subject consists of two themes: the first closes at bar 12. The second, quite different, and altogether separated from the first, closes at bar 22. Both make their perfect close in F major. Now begins a third passage-like subject in D minor, which leads to G minor; but this close changes to a half-close in C minor in the manner explained at page 72. Now a first theme of 16 bars follows the secondary subject in C major; then, after a passage, a second theme (at least indicated by, if not borrowed from, the foregoing); and after some passages comes the closing subject.

Further elucidation remains for individual research.

Here we come to the mixed Rondo-sonata form, mentioned at page 89, and consider them as exhibited in the finale of Beethoven's Sonata, in G major, Op. 31.

The chief subject appears in a two-part song form, page 88. An opening phrase of 4 bars, closing in the key of the dominant, which is repeated with a close in the principal key, forms the first division: another phrase of 4 bars, likewise repeated but closing imperfectly, constitutes the second. This chief phrase, with transposition of the melody to the bass, is repeated and proceeds through E minor and D major to A major. Here, at the closing *tone*, is introduced the secondary phrase in D major, a phrase of 4 bars, very free and easy (suitable to the character of the whole), consisting of three repetitions of a member of two half-bars and a usual closing form. It leads to a closing phrase intimately combined with it, which, with the help of the sub-dominant (G major, for we are now in D major), assumes an appearance of closing in the key of the dominant. In this event, the first division would be constructed in perfect sonata-form.

But the close does not follow. In lieu of it, the sub-dominant of D major (G major), which was in reality a mere note of transition, becomes, without more ado, held fast as principal *tone*, and the whole chief phrase (with some alteration) is repeated. So far, in order to have recognized the third or fourth rondo-form, page 89, we should have strengthened the first division by a closing phrase.

In the meanwhile this form also is given up. The first division of the chief subject is again brought into G minor, carried forward, a quite new phrase is brought for assistance (it has only 4 bars and will not become a secondary subject), and exchanging with the first division of the chief subject, it is carried forward, exactly as in the second division of the sonata-form, to the dominant and organ point. Now follows the third division again in regular sonata form.

THE END.

GENERAL INDEX.

A.

Entry	Page
A, the *tone*,	7
A flat, the *tone*,	14
A double flat, the *tone*,	15
A sharp, the *tone*,	14
A double sharp, the *tone*,	15
A major, scale of,	19
A due, a tre, &c.,	50
A tempo,	31, 32
Absolute time,	31
Accacciatura,	64
Accarezzevole,	95
Accelerando,	32, 95
Accent,	100, 101
Accents,	42
Accentuation,	42
Accentuato,	44
Accompagnato,	91
Accompaniment,	80, 107
Accompaniment, conjectural,	80
Accompanied fugue,	86
Accompanied vocal music,	7, 91
Acoustics,	7, 49
Adagio,	31
Adagio, a movement,	90
Adagiosissimo,	31
Adirato,	95
Advice to Performers,	73, 74, 106, 108
Ad libitum,	30
Affabile,	95
Affettuoso,	95
After-play,	84
Æolian Harp,	48
Æolian mode,	25
Æsthetical poets,	98
Agitato,	95
Air,	58, 91
Al fine,	64
Al rigore del tempo,	31
Al unisono,	78
Alla Marcia,	96
Alla breve bar,	35
Allegramente,	31
Allegretto,	31
Allegro,	31, 32, 43
Allegro agitato,	31
Allegro assai,	31
Allegro con brio,	31
Allegro ma non troppo,	31
Allegro moderato,	31
Allegro appassionato,	31
Allegro con fuoco,	31
Allegro con moto,	31
Allegro vivace,	31
Alpine regions,	48
Alto Cleff,	10
Alto (middle part),	66
Alto voice,	46
Altus, alta vox,	46
Alexander's Feast,	57, 84
Amabile—Con amabilita,	95
Amarevole—Con amarezza,	95
Amateur,	94
Amoroso, Amorevole,	95
Andante,	31, 33, 43
Andantino,	31
Angosciamente,	95
Animato—Con anima, Animoso,	95
Answer in a fugue,	84
Anticipation,	75
Apparatus, Musical,	7, 44
Appassionato,	95
Appenato,	95
Appendage,	61, 72
Appendix,	104, 108
Appendix, explanatory,	120
Appoggiatura,	64
Aretino, Guido,	11
Ardito,	95
Aria,	91
Arietta,	92
Arioso,	91
Ariosto,	119
Arpeggio,	39, 75
Arrangements,	55, 56, 91, 113
Arrangements, Orchestral,	56, 57
Arrezzo, Guido d',	8
Art, Artists, and History of Art,	99, 106
Articulation,	47
Artist,	94
Artistic configurations, meaning of,	99, 100, 103
Artistic performance,	97
Artistic education,	98, 110
Atmosphere of sound,	53
Attacca Subito,	35
Auber,	106
Audace,	95
Augmentation, in	85
Aus tiefer Noth schrei ich zu dir,	87
Auxilliary *tone*,	76, 77

B.

Entry	Page
B, the *tone*,	7
B flat, the *tone*,	14
B double flat, the *tone*,	15
B sharp, the *tone*,	14
B double sharp, the *tone*,	15
B Quadratum,	8
B Rotundum,	8
Bach, Em.,	124
Bach, S.,	49, 51, 56, 76, 82, 84, 86, 87, 88, 90, 94, 96, 97, 106, 110, 113, 114, 118, 120, 124
Ballad Opera,	93
Ballet,	92
Ballet music,	7
Band, Military,	51, 52, 54
Bar, dividing the,	38
Bar-lines,	35
Bar, initial imperfect,	40, 60
Bar, initial perfect,	40
Bars,	33, 35
Bar rest,	36
Bars, 2 crotchet, 4 crotchet, allabreve, 3 crotchet, &c., &c., &c.	35
Bars, division of,	36
Bars, half,	36
Bars, irregular,	40
Bars, kinds of,	34
Bars, parts of,	37, 39, 40, 42
Bars, 5 and 7-part,	34
Bars, Rhythm of,	62
Baritone voice,	46
Bass,	8, 46
Bass Cleff,	9
Bass, continued,	86
Bass, Ground,	84
Bass Horn,	51
Bass (lowest part),	66
Basso ostinato,	84
Bass-tenor (instrument),	53
Bass-tube (instrument),	53
Bass voice,	46
Bass voice, extraordinary,	47
Basses, unciphered,	80
Bassatel,	49
Basset Horn,	50
Bassoon,	50
Bassoon, Double,	51
Bassoon (Fagotto),	51
Bassoon, Organ stop,	54
Bassoon, quart,	51
Beat,	65
Beating time,	38, 107, 120
Beethoven,	10, 36, 41, 52, 90, 91, 94, 96, 101, 106, 110, 113, 117, 120, 124
Bells,	6, 45
Bell of the Horn,	51
Ben pronunziato,	44
Berlin Singer of 12 years of age,	47
Bind,	27, 30
Bourrée,	88
Bowed instruments,	48
Boy's voice,	46
Brace,	39
Brass Instruments,	45, 51, 53
Bravura passage,	60
Brevis,	27
Brillante,	95
Brioso,	31, 95
Bruscamente,	95
Byron,	47

C.

Entry	Page
C, the *tone*,	7
C flat, the *tone*,	14
C double flat, the *tone*,	15
C sharp, the *tone*,	14

GENERAL INDEX.

	Page
C double sharp, the *tone*,	15
Cadence,	76
Cadence, false,	72
Calando,	32, 95
Calmato—Con calma,	95
Canon,	87
Canon, circle,	88
Canon, free,	87
Canon, in 2nd, 3rd, 8vc., &c.	87
Canon, riddle,	88
Canon, strict,	87
Cantabile,	95
Cantabile, a, movement,	90
Cantata,	92
Cantilena,	58
Cantus firmus,	46, 83, 84
Cantus planus,	27
Capella, a, vocal music	45
Capriccj,	91
Capriccioso,	95
Castagnets	54
Catalani	46
Cavatina,	92
C Cleff,	9
Chain of shakes,	65
Chamber music,	38, 93
Changes of measure,	36, 37, 40
Changing Cleffs	10
Chants, church	26
Chaos	96
Character of sound,	5, 46
Charinomos von Seidel,	98
Chief note,	65
Chief part,	34, 43
Chief parts, in composition,	81, 89
Chief points in the scale,	24
China,	48
Chirping,	6
Chladny,	53
Choir,	45
Chopin,	113
Choral singing,	91
Chord, chief of the ninth,	68
Chord, close or dispersed,	70
Chord, inversion of,	69
Chord, major of the ninth,	68
Chord, minor of the ninth,	68, 103
Chord, motion in a,	75
Chord of the diminished seventh	69
Chord of the dominant,	68, 72, 74, 103
Chord of the seventh,	66, 74
Chord of the ninth,	66
Chord of the ninth, major,	103
Chord of the eleventh,	66
Chord of the thirteenth,	67
Chord of two *tones*,	66
Chord, the 6, 6/4, 6/5, 4/3, &c.	70
Chords,	66, 102
Chords, combination of,	71
Chords, connection of,	71
Chords, employment of,	69
Chords, equal motion in,	75
Chords, motion between the,	76
Chords, passing,	77
Chords, unequal motion in,	75
Chorus,	92
Chorus of tubular instruments,	56
Chorus, play with,	93
Chorus, vocal,	57
Christe eleison, S. Bach,	88
Chromatic scale,	14, 18
Chromatic signs,	42
Chronometer,	32
Church chants,	26
Cinelli,	54
Ciphering,	78, 79, 80

	Page
Cipher system of notation,	11
Circle canon,	88
Circle of fifths,	21
Cithern,	48
Clarinet,	50, 58
Clarinet, the A,	50, 58
Clarinet, the Alt. (tenor),	51
Clarinet, the B♭,	50, 58
Clarinet, the bass,	51
Clarinet, the C,	50
Clarino,	52
Classes of intervals,	16
Clashing,	6
Clattering,	6
Clavicylinder,	55
Claviature,	53
Cleff,	9
Cleff, alto,	10
Cleff, bass,	9
Cleff, C,	9
Cleff, F,	9, 10
Cleff, G,	9
Cleffs, changing,	10
Cleff, French violin,	9
Cleff, soprano,	9
Cleff, tenor,	10
Cleff, violin,	9
Clementi,	124
Close, a,	31, 35
Close (conclusion)	71, 72, 88
Close, half,	72
Close, imperfect,	72
Closing phrase,	61, 72
Coi flauti,	55
Col arco,	49
Colla parte,	31
Col secondo,	56
Colour of the *tone*,	6
Combined order,	34
Come sopra,	55
Come stain your cheeks with nut or berry (Oh, who has seen the miller's wife!)	34, 35
Comic opera,	93
Commodo,	31
Common times,	34
Composer,	94
Composition,	6, 7, 77, 80, 125
Composition, forms of,	6
Composition, parts in,	81, 89
Con abandono,	95
Con afflizione,	95
Con agilita,	95
Con elevazione,	95
Concertino,	91
Concerto,	91
Concert music	93
Configurations, artistic meaning of,	99, 100, 103
Conjectural accompaniment,	80
Con allegrezza,	95
Conductor or Director	107
Confiteor unum baptisma,	86
Commodo, Commodamente	95
Con moto,	96
Con osservanza,	96
Con sentimento—Con molto sentimento,	96
Consonants,	47
Consonances,	17
Consonances, imperfect,	17
Consonances, perfect,	17
Contralto voice,	46, 47
Con sordino,	49
Contano,	55
Con tutta la forza,	44

	Page
Counter-phrase,	61
Counterpoint,	82, 86
Counterpoint, double,	82
Counterpoint, single,	82
Counterpoint, 3, 4, and manifold,	82
Counter-subject,	84, 85
Counter-tenor voice,	46
Counter-*tone*,	8
Corale-fugal,	87
Corale, fugue to,	87
Corales,	96
Corante,	88
Cordæ vocales,	46
Cornet, the high B♭,	52
Corno,	51
Corno cromatico di tenore,	53
Corno Inglese,	51
Correct performance,	97
Creation,	96
Crescendo,	44
Cresc: al forte,	44
Cresc: al fortissimo,	44
Crescent, Turkish,	54
Crook,	52
Crotchet,	26
Crotchet, triplet,	28
Cymbals,	54
Czerny, C.	106
D.	
D, the *tone*,	7
D flat, the *tone*,	14
D double flat, the *tone*,	15
D♭♭♭,	18
D sharp, the *tone*,	14
D double sharp, the *tone*,	15
Dampers,	48
Dance,	88
Dance music,	7
Dante,	119
Decker, C. V., Berlin,	69
Decrescendo,	44
Decuplet,	29
Degree,	7, 15, 18, 58
Degrees of relationship,	24
Delicatamente—Con delicatezza,	95
Demisemiquaver,	26
Demisemidemisemiquaver,	26
Departure,	73
Depression, threefold,	18
Determinato,	95
Development of the musical faculties	118
Diatonic scale,	14, 18
Diluendo,	44
Diminished interval,	17
Diminished triad,	102
Diminuendo,	44
Diminution, in,	85
Direct, a,	14
Dispersed position,	83
Dissonances,	17
Divertimento,	90
Divisi,	50
Division of bars,	36
Divisions, rhythmic,	129
Divine service,	92
Divoto—Divotamente,	95
Dolce—Con dolcezza,	95
Dolente—Doloroso—Con duolo,	95
Dominant,	24, 60, 67, 72
Dominant, chord of,	103
Dominant, scale of,	89
Don Giovanni,	32, 41
Doric mode,	25
Dots,	28
Dots, double,	28

GENERAL INDEX.

	Page
Dots, treble,	28
Double bass	49, 56
Double bass, organ stop,	54
Double shake,	65
Dramatic music,	7, 93
Drums,	6, 54
Drum, great,	54
Drum, Moorish,	54
Duet,	90
Duos,	49
Duplication,	69
Duration, lines of,	27, 38
Duration, signs of indefinite,	30
Dussek,	124

E.

	Page
E, the *tone*,	7
E flat, the *tone*,	14
E double flat, the *tone*,	15
E sharp, the *tone*,	14
E double sharp, the *tone*,	15
Ecclesiastical modes,	24
Ecclesiastical music,	7, 93
Ecclesiastical scores, Italian,	110
Eclogues,	96
Education, artistic,	98, 110
Egmont, overture to,	91
Eight-part order,	34
Ein 'feste Burg ist unser Gott, S. Bach,	87
Elegante,	95
Elegies,	96
Elementary forms,	58
Embouchure,	51
Energico,	95
English,	47
Enharmonic,	15, 18
Enharmonic intervals,	18
Enharmonic scales,	21
Episode,	85
Equal rhythm,	62
Erk and Irmer,	62
Eroico,	95
Espressivo—Con espressione,	95
Exchanging *tone*,	76, 77
Ex-chief part,	34, 43
Exercises,	84
Extreme interval,	17
Extreme triad,	102

F.

	Page
F, the *tone*,	7
F flat, the *tone*,	14
F double flat, the *tone*,	15
F sharp, the *tone*,	14
F double sharp, the *tone*,	15
F cleff,	9, 10
Fa,	7
Fagottino,	51
False cadence,	72
False fifth,	17
False relation,	77
False tones,	7
Falsetto,	46
Fandango,	88
Fantasia,	91
Fastoso,	95
Feeling performance,	97
Feroce,	95
Fiero—Con fierezza,	95
Fifth, quinta,	15, 66
Fifth, perfect,	67
Figurated parts,	83, 86
Figurated phrases,	89
Figuration, Harmonic,	75, 83, 84, 104
Figuring Basses,	78, 79

	Page
Finale,	92
First performance,	105
Fischer, the bass singer,	47
Five crotchet bar,	35
Five and seven part bars,	34
Flat,	14
Flat, double,	15
Flauto piccolo,	50
Flebile,	95
Flute, the,	50
Flute, octave,	50
Flute, organ stop,	54
Form, great rondo,	104
Form, small rondo,	104
Form, song,	104
Forms, elementary,	58
Forms, exceptional,	40
Forms, fundamental,	60
Forms, homophonic and mixed,	88
Forms of composition,	6, 80
Forms of vocal music,	91
Forte,	44
Forte, possibile,	44
Fortissimo,	44
Foundation of melody,	58
Four crotchet bar,	35, 37
Four minim bar,	35
Fourth, quarta,	15
Four-part order,	34, 35
Four quaver bar,	35
Franklin, Benj.	54
Free canon,	87
Free fugue,	86
Free and strict styles,	93
French,	47
Frenchmen,	117
French overtures,	76
French violin cleff,	9
Fresco, Frescamente,	95
Fugato,	87
Fugue,	84, 85, 86
Fugue, accompanied	86
Fugal corale,	87
Fugue to a corale,	87
Fugue, double and manifold,	86
Fugue form, dissection of, in Appendix.	130
Fugue, free,	86
Fugue, single,	86
Fugue, strict,	86
Fugue for violin,	49
Fugal successions,	89
Full orchestra,	45
Fundamental *tone*,	66
Funebre,	95
Funereal marches,	96
Fuocoso—Con fuoco,	95
Furioso—Con rabbia,	95

G.

	Page
G, the *tone*,	7
G flat, the *tone*,	14
G double flat, the *tone*,	15
G sharp, the *tone*,	14
G double sharp, the *tone*,	15
G cleff,	9
Gaio,	96
Gavot,	88
Generoso,	96
German popular songs, at Erk and Irmer,	119
German,	47
Giocoso,	96
Gluck,	47, 88, 106, 110, 113, 114, 117
Gong, Chinese,	54
Graces, melodic,	64

	Page
Graceful performance,	97
Grandioso	96
Gran tamburo,	54
Grassner's, Dr., Dirigent and Ripienist at Carlsruhe,	108
Grave,	31, 96
Graun's "Tod Jesu,"	41
Grazioso—Con grazia,	96
Greater and lesser intervals,	17
Great opera,	93
Great orchestra,	45
Great rondo form,	104
Greece,	48
Greek,	47
Groups,	39, 40, 42, 59, 60
Guitar,	47

H.

	Page
H, the *tone*, B English,	8
Half bars,	36
Hammer of Pianoforte,	48
Handel,	57, 84, 88, 90, 94, 106, 110, 114, 124
Harmonica,	54
Harmonic figuration,	75
Harmonics,	49
Harmony,	6, 66
Harp,	47, 48
Harp, hook,	48
Harp, pedal,	48
Hautboy, (Oboe),	51
Hautboy, organ stop,	54
Haydn,	29, 52, 56, 86, 91, 94, 96, 97, 106, 110, 114, 117, 118, 124, 125
Hebrew,	47
Hollow floors,	48
Homophonic and mixed forms,	88
Homophonic phrase,	81, 104
Homophonic phrase, principal part in,	80, 81
Homophonic phrase, secondary part in,	81
Hook harp,	48
Horns,	37, 51, 56
Horn, English, (corno Inglese)	51
Horn, the A,	52
Horn, deep B flat,	52, 58
Horn, high B flat,	52, 58
Horn, the C,	52
Horn, the D,	52, 58
Horn, the E flat,	52
Horn, the E,	52
Horn, the F,	52
Horn, the G,	52
Horn, Kent,	53
Horn, notation for the	52
Horn, post,	53
Horn, with valve,	52
Hummel,	124
Hummel, Mass,	86
Hymn,	92
Hypoionic mode,	26
Hypodoric mode,	26

I.

	Page
Imperfect close,	72
Imperfect consonances,	17
Impetuoso,	96
Impressions from notation,	96
Indefinite signs of duration,	30
India,	48
Influence of numbers 2 and 3,	101
Innocente,	96
Instruction or Teaching,	119
Instruments,	44
Instruments of brass,	45, 51, 53

GENERAL INDEX.

Instruments by friction, - 45
Instruments, bowed, - 48, 57
Instruments, percussive, - 45
Instruments, reed or tubular, 45
Instruments, stringed, - 45, 47
Instruments, wind, - - 45
Instrumental music, - 7, 45
Intelligent performance, - 97
Intellectual performance, - 48
Interlude, - - - 84
Intersections, - - - 63
Interval, - - - 16, 102
Intervals, classes of, - 16
Interval, diminished, - 17
Intervals, enharmonic, - 18
Interval, extreme, - - 17
Intervals, greater and lesser, 17
Interval, major, - - 17
Intervals, measurement of, - 16
Interval, minor, - - 17
Intervals, mode of learning, 18
Intervals, paper, - - 18
Introductions, 84, 88, 89, 104
Inversion, in, - - 85
Inversion in counterpoint, 82, 83
Inverted 2nd, 3rd, &c. - 16
Ionic mode, . - - 25
Irregular rhythms, - - 63
Irresoluto, - - - 96
Italian, - - - 47
Italian opera, writers of, - 94
Italian opera, French, - 52
Italy, - - - 48

J.
Jig, - - - 88

K.
Kent horn (instrument), - 53
Kettle-drum, - - 54, 56
Key-board, - - - 53
Key, relative, - - 90
Keys of the finger-board, 6, 14
Key-note, - - - 73
Kinds of bars, - - 34
Kinds of motion, - - 101
Klappen horn, - - 53
Kyrie eleison, - - 56

L.
La, - - - 7
Lamentoso—Lamentabile, - 96
Languente—Languido, - 96
Lasso, Orlando, - - 97
Lagrimoso, - - - 96
Larghissimo, - - 31
Largo assai, - - 31
Larghetto, - - - 31
Largo, - - - 31
Larynx, - - - 46
Latin, - - - 47
Ledger line, - - 9
Legatissimo, - - - 30
Legato, - - 30, 49
Leggiero—Con leggierezza, 96
Leibnitz, - - - 116
Lentando, - - - 32
Lento, - - - 31
Les adieux, l'absence, and le retour 96
Light, - - - 53
Lind, Jenny, - - 46
Lines of duration, - 27, 38
L'istesso tempo, - - 37
Liszt, F. - - - 110
Little alla breve bar - 35
Logier, J. B. - - 11, 21

Longa, - - - 27
Longs, - - - 47
Lugubre, - - - 96
Lully, - - - 117
Lusingando, - - 96
Lute, notation for, - 11, 48
Lydian mode, - - 25

M.
Maestoso, - - - 96
Major interval, - - 17
Major 2nd, 3rd, 4th, &c. - 17
Major mode, - - - 103
Major scales, - 18, 20, 22
Major triad, - - - 102
Malinconico, - - 96
Mälzel, - - - 32
Mancando, - - 44, 96
Mandolin, - - - 48
Manuale, - - - 54
Manuals of organ, &c. - 53
Marcato, - - 44, 96
Marches, - - - 88
Martellato, - - - 44
Marziale, - - - 96
Mass, - - - 10, 92
Mass, Bach in G major, - }
 ,,   ,, B minor, -   } 86
Mass, Hummel, - - 86
Matthäischen Passionsmusik, 49
Maxima, or duplex longa, - 27
Measure, changes of, 36, 37, 40
Measures, mixed, - - 41
Measurable music, - - 27
Measurement of intervals, 16
Medesimo tempo, - - 37
Mediant, the, . - - 24
Melodic graces, - - 64
Melodrama, - - - 92
Melody, - - 6, 58
Melody, foundation of, - 58
Members of a bar, - 35, 38, 40, 43
Member, chief, - - 43
Member, ex-chief, - - 43
Members, rhythmic, - 61, 100
Members, secondary, - 43
Meno, - - - 31
Meno allegro, - - 31
Meno forte, - - - 44
Meno piano, - - - 44
Mesto, - - - 96
Metronome, - 32, 99, 120
Metronome and Chronometer, tables of, - - - 33
Meyerbeer, - - - 51
Mezzo forte, - - - 44
Mezzo soprano, voice, - 46
Mezza voce, - - - 46
Mi, - - - 7
Military band, - 51, 52, 54
Military music, - - 93
Military scores, - - 57
Minacciando, - - 96
Minim, - - - 26
Minim, triplet, - - 28
Minima, - - - 27
Minor 2nd, 3rd, 4th, &c. 17, 18
Minor interval, - - 17
Minor mode, - - - 103
Minor scales, - 18, 20, 22
A minor, scale of, - - 20
Minor triad, - - - 102
Minuet, - - - 90
Mixed value, - - - 28
Mixolydian mode, - - 25
Mixtures, of an organ, - 53

Mode, Æolian, - - 25
Mode, Doric, - - - 25
Mode, Ionic, - - 25
Modes, ecclesiastical, - 24
Mode, hypodoric, - - 26
Mode, hypoionic, - - 26
Mode, Lydian, - - 25
Mode, major, - - - 103
Mode, minor, - - - 103
Mode, Mixolydian, - 25
Mode, Phrygian, - - 25
Modes, scales or keys, - 18, 19
Mode, sign of, - - 68
Moderato, - - - 31
Moderately quick motion, 31
Moderately slow motion, - 31
Modulation, - - 62, 73
Modulation, law of, - - 73
Moments, in composition, - 104
Morendo, - - - 44
Morendo—Smorzando, - 96
Mormorando, - - - 96
Mosé, oratorio, - 35, 67
Motett, - - - 92
Motion, - - - 99
Motion between the chords, - 76
Motion, quick, - - 31
Motion, equal, in a chord, - 75
Motion, kinds of, - - 101
Motion in a chord, - - 75
Motion, moderately slow, - 31
Motion, moderately quick, - 31
Motion, quickest, - - 31
Motion, unequal, in a chord, 75
Motions, slowest, - - 31
Motives of successions of *tones*, 59, 60
Motives, rhythmic, - - 59
Movement, - - - 62
Movement in a composition, - 90
Mouth-piece, - - 51
Mozart, 37, 41, 47, 49, 50, 86, 88, 94, 98, 106, 109, 110, 113, 118, 119, 124, 125
Muller, Ivan, - - 51
Music, ballet, - - 7
Music, chamber, - 38, 93
Music, concert, - - 93
Music, dance, - - 7
Music, dramatic, - 7, 93
Music, ecclesiastical, - 7, 93
Music, instrumental, - 6
Musica mensurabilis, or mensurata, 27
Music, military, - - 93
Musica plana, - - 27
Music, popular, or natural song, 93
Music, science of, - - 7
Music, vocal, - - 6
Music, vocal, accompanied, 7
Music, vocation for, - 115
Musical faculties, development of, 118
Musette, - - - 88
Musical theme, - - 62
Mute, - - - 49

N.
Nageli's lectures on music, 98, 106
Natural, - - - 14
Natural, double, - - 15
Neumen, Greek notation, - 11
Nine crotchet bar, - - 35
Nine part order, - - 34
Nine quaver bar, - - 35
Nine semiquaver bar, - 35
Ninth—Nona, - - 15
Ninth, - - - 66
Ninth, major chord of, - 103

GENERAL INDEX.

	Page
Ninth, Minor, chord of,	103
Nobile—Con nobilità,	96
Noise,	6
Nonuplet,	29
Notation,	7, 8
Notation, auxiliary forms,	12
Notation, cypher system of,	11
Notation for the horn,	52
Notation, Greek,	11, 18
Notation, impressions from,	96
Notation, learning to read,	11
Notation for the Lute,	11
Notation in Mass of Beethoven	10
Notation of Songs,	47
Note, chief,	65
Note table,	11
Notes, tails of,	56
Notes, tailed,	64
Notturno,	90
Numbers 2 and 3, influence of,	101
Numeration by two,	63
Numeration by three,	63

O.

	Page
Obligato,	91
Obligato accompaniment,	48
Oboe,	51
Octave,	2
Octave, 1, 2, 3-lined, &c.,	8
Octave, great,	8
Octave, small,	8
Omission,	69
Opening phrase,	61, 72
Opera,	93
Opera, comic,	93
Opera, great,	93
Opera, romantic,	93
Operetta,	93
Ophicleide	51
Oratorio,	92, 93
Orchestra,	49
Orchestra,	52, 53
Orchestral arrangements,	56, 57
Orchestra, full,	45
Orchestra, great,	45
Orchestral performance,	106, 107
Orchestra, stringed,	45
Orchestras, three,	41
Orchestra, wind,	45
Order, combined,	34
Order, two-part,	34, 35
Order, three-part,	34, 35
Order, four-part,	34, 35
Order, six-part,	34, 35
Order, eight-part,	34
Order, nine-part,	34
Order, twelve-part,	34
Organ, the,	45, 53
Organ, imitative, stops in	54
Organ, key-board of,	53
Organ, manuals of,	53, 54
Organ, mixtures in,	53
Organ, pedals of,	53, 54
Organ point,	76, 80
Organ, registers of,	53
Organ, stops of,	53
Overture,	76, 91
Overtures, French,	76

P.

	Page
Palestrina	94, 97
Paper intervals,	18
Parlando,	96
Part,	6
Part, chief,	34, 43
Part, secondary,	34, 43
Part, ex-chief,	34, 43
Parts, in composition,	81, 89
Parts, chief, in composition,	81, 89
Parts, secondary in composition,	81, 89
Parts, figurated,	83, 86
Parts of bars,	37, 39, 40, 42
Part, of a score,	49
Part, principal in Homophonic phrase,	81, 83
Part, secondary, in Homophonic phrase,	81
Part, real,	82
Passage,	60, 80, 104
Passage, a bravura,	60
Passage of transition,	90
Passecaglie of S. Bach,	84, 88
Passepied,	88
Passing chords,	77
Passing or transient *tone*,	76, 77
Pastorale,	96
Pastoral symphony,	36, 110
Patetico,	96
Pedale,	54
Pedal Harp,	48
Pedals of Organ, &c.,	53
Percussive instruments,	45
Perdendosi,	44
Perfect consonances,	17
Perfect fifth,	17, 67
Performance,	94
Performance, artistic,	97, 104
Performance, correct,	97
Performance, feeling,	97
Performance, first,	105
Performance, graceful,	97
Performance, intellectual,	97
Performance, intelligent,	97
Performance, orchestral,	106, 107
Performer,	94
Performers, advice to,	73, 74, 106
Pesante,	44, 96
Phrase,	60, 61, 80, 104
Phrase, closing,	61, 72
Phrases, figurated,	89
Phrase, homophonic,	81
Phrase, opening	61, 72
Phrase, polyphonic,	82, 83
Phrygian mode,	25
Piacere a,	30
Piacevole, Placido	96
Pianissimo,	44
Piano,	44
Piano assai,	44
Pianoforte,	48
Piatti,	54
Più,	31
Più allegro,	31
Più forte,	44
Più moto,	31
Più stretto,	32
Più vivo,	31
Pizzicato,	49
Play with chorus,	93
Play with music,	93
Poco a poco	32
Poco a poco crescendo,	54
Poco a poco più moto	32
Poco forte,	44
Poco più forte,	44
Polyphonic phrase,	82, 83, 104
Pomposo,	96
Popular music, or natural song,	93
Position, dispersed,	83
Post Horn,	53
Pot pourri	90
Practice,	77

	Page
Practice, vowel,	47
Precipitando,	32
Prelude,	72, 84
Preparation,	75
Pres, Joaquin de,	97
Prestissimo,	31
Presto,	31, 32
Presto assai,	31
Prince Eugen (song)	34
Principal, organ stop,	54
Progressions to be avoided,	71
Psalm-tune,	71
Public Worship,	80
Pure vocal music,	91

Q.

	Page
Quartett,	90
Quatuors,	49
Quaver,	26
Quaver, triplet,	28, 37
Quick motion,	31
Quickest motion,	31
Quintett,	90
Quintett, Beethoven in C major,	41
Quintuplet,	29

R.

	Page
Raising and Depressing	14
Raising and Depressing, double,	15
Rallentando,	32
Rapido,	96
Re,	7
Reading score	58
Real part,	82
Recitatives,	80, 91
Recitativo secco, or parlante,	91
Reed, strip of,	50, 51
Reed or tubular-instruments,	49, 50
Register of Organ,	53
Reicher,	125
Relation, false,	77
Relationship, degrees of,	24
Relationship of the scales,	24
Relative scales	23, 90
Relative major scales,	73
Religioso,	96
Remarks on present state of music,	110
Remarks on the scales,	103
Repetition, signs of,	13
Requiem of Mozart,	50, 86
Resolution, determinate,	71, 72, 75, 79, 80
Rests,	29
Rhythm,	6, 26, 44, 53, 59, 60, 61, 99
Rhythm of bars,	62
Rhythm, equal,	62
Rhythm, irregular,	63
Rhythm, symmetrical,	63
Rhythmic divisions,	129
Rhythmic members,	61, 100
Rhythmic sections,	61
Riddle canon,	88
Rilasciando,	32
Rima glottidis,	46
Rinforzato,	43
Risoluto,	96
Risvegliato,	96
Ritardando,	31, 32, 95
Ritenuto,	31
Ritmo a tre battute,	101
Roaring,	6
Romantic opera,	93
Rondo-form,	89, 131
Rondo-form, dissection of, in Appendix,	130
Rossini,	97, 106

GENERAL INDEX.

Entry	Page
Rubbing instruments,	45
Run,	60

S.

Entry	Page
Saddles of paper,	48
Saraband,	88
Saxony,	94
Scale,	8, 19
Scale of A major,	19
Scale of A minor	20
Scale, chief points of,	24
Scale, chromatic,	14, 18, 59
Scale, diatonic,	14, 18, 58
Scale, enharmonic,	21
Scale, Greek,	8, 25
Scales, major and minor,	18, 19
Scales, major,	18, 20, 22
Scales, minor,	18, 19, 22
Scales, minor, signature of,	23
Scale of the dominant,	89
Scale, principal,	73
Scales, remarks on,	103
Scales, relationship of,	24
Scales, relative,	23
Scales, relative major,	73
Scales, relative minor,	73
Scale, sign of the,	23, 68
Scale of five *tones*,	8
Scena, or scene,	92
Schneider, F.	94
Scherzo,	90
Scherzando,	96
Sciolto,	96
Science of Music,	7
Score,	45, 55
Scores, Italian ecclesiastical,	110
Scores, military,	57
Score, part in a,	49
Score, playing,	77, 108
Score, reading,	58
Score, vocal,	56
Second, seconda,	15
Secondary parts	34, 43
Secondary parts in composition,	81, 89
Sections, rhythmic,	61
Segue,	36
Self-sufficing,	48
Semibreve,	20
Semibrevis,	27
Semiquaver,	26
Semidemisemiquaver,	26
Semitones,	8, 26
Semplice,	96
Senza pedale,	54
Senza ritmo,	31
Senza sordino,	49
Senza tempo,	31
Septett,	90
Septuplet,	29
Serpent,	51
Serpente,	51
Sestett,	90
Seventh,	66
Seventh Settima,	15
Sextriplet,	28
Sextulet,	28, 29, 40, 43
Sforzato, Sforzando,	43
Sforzato assai,	44
Shake,	65
Shake, double,	65
Shakes, chain of,	65
Shakspeare,	47, 119
Sharp,	14
Sharp, double,	15
Shorts,	47
Si,	7

Entry	Page
Sign of the scale or key,	23, 68
Signature,	22
Signature, time,	34
Signature of minor scales,	23
Signs, chromatic,	42
Simile,	36
Single fugue,	56
Singing, choral,	91
Singing, solo,	91
Six crotchet bar,	35
Six-part order,	34, 35
Six, sesta,	15
Six-quaver bar,	35, 37
Six-semiquaver bar	35
Slowest motion,	31
Small rondo form,	104
Smanioso,	96
Smorzando,	44, 96
Soave,	96
Sol,	7
Solfaing,	8
Solfeggi,	92
Solo singing,	91
Sonata,	90
Sonata-form,	89, 131
Sonata-form, dissection of, in Appendix,	131
Sonata, grand,	90
Sonate melancolique,	96
Sonate pathetique,	96
Sonatina,	90
Sonatina-form,	89
Song,	7, 44, 122
Songs,	88
Song-form,	88, 104
Songs, notation of,	47
Songs, popular German,	62
Sontag,	46
Soprano cleff,	9
Soprano (highest part),	66
Soprano-voice,	46, 47
Sostenuto,	31
Sound,	5
Sound, atmosphere of,	53
Sounds, vowel,	47
Sounding-board,	47
Spanish,	47
Speech,	44, 47
Spiritoso—Con spirito,	96
Spontini,	51, 117, 120
Staff,	9, 39
Staff, five line system,	9
Staves, two or more,	39
Staccato,	30, 49
Staccatissimo,	30
Stamp of the *tone*,	6
Stay,	73
Stop, labial,	54
Stop, open flute,	45
Stop of Organ,	53
Stop, reed,	54
Stops of the organ imitative,	54
Stopped pipes of organ,	54
Strascinato,	96
Strepitoso,	96
Stretta,	32
Stretto, in fugue,	85
Strict canon,	87
Strict fugue,	86
Stringendo,	32
Stringed instruments,	45
Stringed orchestra,	45
String pendulum,	33
String, vibration of,	49
Stromentato,	91
Studies (studj),	84, 88, 91, 124

Entry	Page
Style,	93, 94
Style, free and strict,	98
Subject,	60, 61, 72, 80, 84, 85, 104
Subdominant, the,	24, 67
Submediant, the,	24
Subsemitonium modi,	74
Successions, fugal,	89
Succession of *tones*,	58, 59, 60
Succession of *tones*, direction of,	59
Successions of *tones*, motives of,	59, 60
Suite,	90
Superdominant, the,	24
Supermediant, the,	24
Suspension, or retardation,	75
Suspension from above,	75, 79
Suspension from beneath,	75
Symmetrical rhythms,	63
Symphony,	91, 109
Symphony, Mozart, in C major,	37
Syncopation,	40

T.

Entry	Page
Tablatures,	11
Table of metronome and chronometer,	33
Tailed notes,	64
Tails of notes,	56
Tamburo rulante,	54
Tasto solo,	78
Teacher,	94
Teachers, and methods of teaching,	126
Temperament,	7, 26
Tempestoso,	96
Tempo assimilando al movimento seguente,	32
Tempo giusto,	32
Tempo primo,	32
Tempo rubato,	30
Tenor bass,	53
Tenor cleff,	10
Tenor (middle part),	66
Tenor (viola),	49
Tenor voice	46, 47
Tenero—Con tenerezza,	96
Tenuto—Ben tenuto,	30
Terzetts,	90
Thalberg,	113
The right object and the right means,	113
Themes,	88, 89
Theme, musical,	62
Theorbo,	48
Third,	66
Third major,	67
Third, terza,	15
Thorough-bass,	48, 78
Three-crotchet bar,	35
Three-minim bar,	35
Three-part order,	34, 35
Three-quaver bar,	35
Thunder,	53
Timbre,	5, 6, 46
Time, absolute,	31, 37
Time, approximate,	33
Time, astronomical,	32
Time, beating,	38, 107, 120
Time, signature,	34
Times, common,	34
Times, triple,	34
Timpano,	54
Timpani, coperti,	54
Tito, Clemenza di,	50
Tod Jesu, Graun's,	41
Tonal system,	7, 15
Tone,	5, 7, 60
Tone, of one and two feet,	53
Tone, of four feet,	45, 50, 53

GENERAL INDEX.

	Page
Tone, of eight feet,	45, 50, 53
Tone, of sixteen feet,	45, 47, 48, 49
Tone, of thirty-two feet,	45, 53
Tone, colour of,	6
Tone, counter,	8
Tone, exchanging,	76, 77
Tone, fundamental,	66, 67
Tone, measurement,	16
Tone, passing or transient,	76, 77
Tone and semitone,	16
Tone, stamp of,	6
Tones, auxiliary,	76, 77
Tones, false,	7
Tones, leading,	74, 77
Tones, scale of five,	8
Tones, succession of,	58, 59, 60
Tonic the,	24, 60, 67, 72
Trachea,	46
Tranquillo, Tranquillamente,	96
Transition passage,	90
Transition, phrases or passages of,	63
Transposition,	69, 103
Treble,	8, 46
Treble dots,	28
Treble voice,	46, 47
Tremando—Tremolo,	36
Triangle,	54
Triangulo,	54
Trill,	65
Trio,	88
Trios,	49
Triple times,	34
Triplet,	28, 41
Triplet quaver,	28, 37
Triplet crotchet,	28
Triplet, minim,	28
Triad,	66, 72
Triad, diminished,	67, 74, 102
Triad, extreme,	67, 102
Triad, major,	67, 102
Triad, minor,	67, 102
Triad of the Dominant,	67
Triad of Subdominant,	72
Triad, tonic,	67, 72
Triumphant marches,	96
Tromba,	52
Trombone,	52
Trombone, alto,	52
Trombone, bass,	52
Trombone, tenor,	52
Trumpets,	56
Trumpet, the B♭,	52, 58
Trumpet, the C,	52
Trumpet, the D,	52, 58
Trumpet, the E♭,	52
Trumpet, the E,	52
Trumpet, the F,	52
Trumpet, organ stop,	54
Trumpets, valve,	52
Tube, bass, the,	53
Tubes,	52, 53
Tubular instruments,	50
Tubular instruments, chorus of,	56
Tune,	58
Tuning,	7, 26, 54
Turn,	64, 65
Twelve-part order,	34, 35
Twelve quaver bar,	35
Twelve semiquaver bar,	35
Two crotchet bar,	35
Two quaver bar,	35
Two-part order,	34, 35

V.

	Page
Valve horn,	52
Valve trumpets,	52
Value,	6, 26, 28, 37
Value, mixed,	28
Values, mixed,	41
Variations,	88
Vaudeville,	93
Vaulted roofs,	48
Veloce,	31, 96
Vibration of a string,	7, 17, 48, 49
Vigoroso,	96
Viola di braccio,	49
Viol di gamba,	49
Violin,	49
Violin Cleff,	9
Violoncello,	49, 50, 56
Violone,	49
Vivace,	31
Vivace—Con vivacita,	96
Vivacissimo,	31
Vocal music,	7, 45, 46
Vocal music, a capella,	45
Vocal music, accompanied,	91
Vocal chorus,	57
Vocal music, forms of,	91
Vocal music, pure,	91
Vocal score,	56
Vocal sounds,	5, 46, 47
Vocation for music,	115
Voice, alto,	46
Voice, barytone,	46
Voice, bass,	46
Voice, boys',	46
Voice, contralto,	46, 47
Voice, counter tenor,	46
Voice, female,	46
Voice, head,	46
Voice, human,	46
Voice, male,	46
Voice, mezzo soprano,	46
Voice, soprano,	46, 47
Voice, tenor,	45, 46, 47
Volti subito,	35
Von Himmel hoch da komm ich her,	82
Vowel practice,	47
Voxhumana, organ stop,	54

U.

	Page
Ut,	7
Uncyphered basses,	80

W.

	Page
Wagner's Ideen über Musik,	98
Warbling,	6
Weber, C. M.,	120, 124
Weber, Gottf.,	6, 33, 53, 66
Wer nur den lieben Gott lässt walten,	84
Whistling,	6
Wilke, music director,	53
Wind instruments,	45
Wind Orchestra,	45
Wohltemperirte, Klavier,	86
Writers of Italian opera,	94

Z.

	Page
Zauberflöte,	119

ABBREVIATIONS AND SIGNS.

	Page
𝄞 or 𝄞	9
♮ or ♯ or 𝄪 or ♯	9
𝄴 or 𝄴 ‖ :	10
8, or 8va, 8~~~~, or 8va~~~~	12
1, or loco	12
8va~~~~loco	12
all' 8va, or all' ottava	12
~~	12

	Page
alla 3za (terza), alla 6ta (sesta)	12
col B, or col Basso	13
col 1mo. (violino)	13
(repeat signs) or (repeat sign)	13
1ma (prima volta), 2da (seconda)	13
(1ma. 2da. repeat)	13
D. C., or D. c., or d. c. (Da capo)	13
F. or Fine, ⌢, D. C. al fine	13

ABBREVIATIONS AND SIGNS.

Sign	Page
(tremolo/trill marks)	13
d. s. (dal segno)	13
⌢ ≈ ♯ ♭ ♮	14
× or ⊗ ♭♭ ♮♮ ♭♭♭	15
(beams, whole note, grace note, slur)	27
′ ′ ′ ′ . . . . - - - -	30
Ten. (tenuto)	30
c. p. (colla parte)	31
Rit., riten., (ritenuto)	31
Rit., ritard., (ritardando)	31
All⁰. (allegro)	31
And^te. (andante)	31
Rall., rallent. (rallentando)	32
Allentand.	32
t. p. (tempo primo)	32
M.M. (Mälzel's Met.) ♩=60; M.M. ♩=120	32
M.M. ♪=60	32
M.M. ♩=90, or rather M.M. ♩=60.	33
♩=55" Rh. (56⅔ English); ♩=5" Rh. (5⅛ English)	33
M.M. ♩=60; Weber Chron. ♩=38" Rh. (39¼ English)	33
M.M. ♩=50; ♩=60, &c.	33
M.M. ♩=90 about	
M.M. ♩=120 to 130	33
M.M. ♩=140 to 160	
v. s. (volti subito)	35
𝄵, 𝄴, ²⁄₁, ²⁄₄, ⁴⁄₄, ⁴⁄₈, ³⁄₄, &c.,	35
Trem. (tremando, tremolo)	36
Sim. (simile)	36
{ {	39
tr	41

Sign	Page
> ∧	43
sf. (sforzando)	43
rinf. (rinforzato, or rinforzando)	43
sfz >	44
sff	44
. . . . . ▬ 𝆹 𝆹	44
p, pp. ppp.	44
pf. (poco forte)	44
f, ff, fff	44
< Cr., cresc. (crescendo)	44
> Decr., decresc. (decrescendo)	44
Dim. (diminuendo)	44
C. S. (con sordino)	49
S. S. (senza sordino)	49
Pizz. (pizzicato)	49
C. A. (col arco)	49
1mo, 2do.	50
VC.	50
CB.	50
Div. (divise)	50
S (tube for the bassoon)	51
Ped. (pedale)	54
Man. (manuale)	54
S.P. (senza pedale)	54
Timp. (timpani)	54
Cont. (contano)	55
~	64
tr or tr~~~~	65
♦|♦ or ♦♦ or ∿	65
/ / / / /	78
─── ─ ─	78
t. s. (tasto solo)	78
6 ⁶⁄₄ ⁴⁄₆ 7 &c.	78
In 4ta e 9na	88
c. espr. (con espressione)	95

THE END.